U0126352

台灣紀事六十年

馬全忠 編

臺灣 學生書局 印行

集歷史名言為序

漢代的史聖司馬遷，在〈報任少卿書〉中說，他著《史記》百三十篇，「亦欲以究天地之際，通古今之變，成一家之言。」

晉代的書聖王羲之，在〈蘭亭集序〉中說：「後之視今，亦猶今之視昔。」

唐代的詩人杜牧，在〈阿房宮賦〉中說：「滅六國者，六國也，非秦也。族秦者，秦也，非天下也。秦人不暇自哀，而後人哀之，後人哀之而不鑑之，亦使後人而復哀後人也。」

唐代的詩人韋莊，在〈金陵圖〉中說：「江雨霏霏江草齊，六朝如夢鳥空啼，無情最是臺城柳，依舊煙籠十里堤。」

宋代的詩人林升，在〈題臨安邸〉中說：「山外青山樓外樓，西湖歌舞幾時休，暖風熏得遊人醉，直把杭州作汴州。」

元代的詩人薩都拉，在《滿江紅·金陵懷古》中說：「到如今，惟有蔣山青，秦淮碧。」

清代的戲曲家孔尚任，在《桃花扇》的〈哀江南〉中說：「將五十年興亡看飽。殘山夢最真，舊境丟難掉，不信這輿圖換稿。謅一套哀江南，放悲聲唱到老。」

中華民國的詩人于右任，在〈憶首都〉中說：「破碎山河期再造，顛連師友念同遊，中山陵樹年年綠，種樹于郎今白頭。」

"Hegel was right when he said that we learn from history that men never learn anything from history." —— G. B. Shaw

（英國大文豪蕭伯納說：「德國哲學家黑格爾的話很對：我們研習歷史獲知，人類研習歷史從來毫無所得。」）

"It has been said that though God cannot alter the past, historians can." —— Samuel Butler

（英國作家巴特爾說：語云，雖然上帝不能改變過去，但歷史家能夠。）

"No great man lives in vain. The history of the world is but the biography of great men." —— Thomas Carlyle

（蘇格蘭社會史學者卡萊爾說：「大人物從未白活。世界歷史只不過是大人物的傳記而已。」）

中華民國歷史學家吳相湘晚年，不只一次的說：「一九四九年以來的台灣時代，顯然演變成三個階段：備戰、偏安、割據。至於，這六十年來的歷史如何寫，那要看是什麼人寫，更要看是在什麼情勢下寫的。」

台灣紀事六十年

目　次

英文部分

台灣紀事六十年

一九四九年以前的重大事件

一九三一年

九月十八日　日本軍隊侵佔瀋陽（九一八事變）

一九三七年

七月七日　日本軍隊攻擊宛平城（蘆溝橋事變）

一九四一年

十二月九日　中國國民政府對日本宣戰，鄭重聲明中日間「所有一切條約、協定、合同等一律廢止。」

一九四三年

十一月廿三日至廿六日　蔣介石委員長與美國總統羅斯福及英國首相邱吉爾，在埃及開羅舉行會議並發表公報。（公報全文見下）

一九四五年

八月十四日　日本向中、美、英等同盟國無條件投降。

八月廿八日　毛澤東抵達重慶與蔣介石主席會談。

九月三日　何應欽將軍代表政府在南京接受日軍司令岡村寧次降書。

十月廿五日　台灣省光復，全國各地熱烈慶祝，國民政府宣布定為「光復節」。

一九四七年

二月廿八日　台北市警察取締違反香菸專賣的女販，引起警民衝突，事件逐漸擴大。

開羅會議公報

中美英三國領袖開羅會議公報 （中華民國三十二年十一月二十六日發表）

羅斯福總統、蔣委員長、邱吉爾首相，偕同各該國軍事與外交顧問人員，在北非舉行會議，業已完畢：茲發表概括之聲明如下：

三國軍事方面人員，關於今後對日作戰計畫已獲得一致意見，我三大盟國決心以不懈地壓力從海陸空軍方面，加諸殘暴之敵，此項壓力已經在增長之中。

我三大盟國此次進行戰爭之目的，在於制止及懲罰日本之侵略，三國決不為自己圖利，亦無擴長領土之意思。三國之宗旨，在剝奪日本自從一九一四年第一次世界大戰開始後，在太平洋上所奪得或佔領之一切島嶼，在使日本所竊取於中國之領土，例如東北四省、台灣、澎湖群島等，歸還中華民國。其他日本以武力或貪慾所攫取之土地，亦務將日本驅逐出境。我三大盟國稔知朝鮮人民所受之奴隸待遇，決定在相當時期，使朝鮮自由獨立。

根據以上所認定之各項目標，並與其他對日作戰之聯合國目標相一致，我三大盟國將堅忍進行其重大而長期之戰爭，以發得日本之無條件投降。

中華民國三十八年（一九四九）

一月一日　蔣介石總統發表民國三十
　　　　八年元旦文告，闡明政府和戰
　　　　方針，並表示不計個人進退，
　　　　促成國內和平。文告中說：
　　　　「只要和議無害於國家的獨立
　　　　完整，而有助於人民的休養生
　　　　息，……中華民國的國體能夠
　　　　確保、中華民國的法統不致中
　　　　斷，軍隊有確切的保障、人民
　　　　能夠維持其自由生活方式與目
　　　　前最低生活水準，則我個人更
　　　　無他求。只望和平果能實現，
　　　　則個人進退出處，絕不繫懷，
　　　　而一惟國民的公意是從。」
　　　　外交部照會美、英、法、蘇四
　　　　國駐華大使，徵詢對於我國和
　　　　平意見及是否準備予以協助。
　　　　旋四國答覆我國照會皆云：
　　　　「在目前情況下，礙難出任和
　　　　平媒介」。

一月一日　「中國人民解放軍」北平
　　　　區軍事管制委員會成立，葉劍
　　　　英任主任。同時，北平市「人
　　　　民政府」成立，葉劍英任市
　　　　長，徐冰任副市長。

一月十日　蔣介石總統派蔣經國到上
　　　　海，命令將中央銀行黃金運台
　　　　灣。

一月十四日　中共主席毛澤東發表關
　　　　於時局的聲明，提出共產黨願
　　　　與南京國民黨政府在八項條件
　　　　的基礎上進行和平談判。其中
　　　　包括：懲辦戰爭罪犯、廢除偽
　　　　憲法、改編一切反動軍隊、成
　　　　立民主聯合政府、接收南京國
　　　　民黨反動政府及其所屬各級政
　　　　府的一切權力等。

一月十五日　中共軍隊攻陷天津市，
　　　　聲稱全殲守軍十三萬人，俘虜
　　　　警備司令陳長捷等。同時，天
　　　　津市人民政府成立，黃敬任市
　　　　長，張友漁為副市長。

一月十六日　蔣介石總統展謁國父中
　　　　山先生陵寢，低徊禱祝者久
　　　　之，謂「此為離京別陵之紀念
　　　　也」。

一月十八日　國防部發表人事命令：
　　　　湯恩伯專任京滬杭警備總司
　　　　令，宋子文專任廣東省政府主
　　　　席，台灣省政府主席陳誠兼任
　　　　台灣警備總司令。

一月十九日　國民政府外交部通知各
　　　　國駐華使館遷至廣州。

一月十九日　蔣介石總統下最後之決
　　　　心。接見副總統李宗仁，表示
　　　　引退之意，當囑吳忠信及張群
　　　　與李宗仁洽商接代手續。

一月廿一日　蔣介石總統召開中國國民黨中央常務委員會臨時會議，宣布其引退決定，並發表引退謀和文告，其中說：「中正在元旦發表文告，倡導和平以來，全國同聲響應，乃時逾兼旬，戰事仍然未止，和平之目的不能達到，人民之塗炭曷其有極。因此決定身先引退，以冀弭戰銷兵，解人民倒懸於萬一。爰特依據中華民國憲法第四十九條「總統因故不能視事時，由副總統代行其職權」之規定，於本月廿一日起由李副總統代行總統職權。

於是，蔣介石乘飛機赴杭州，由長公子經國隨行，台灣省政府主席陳誠自台北飛抵杭州迎接。

一月廿二日　蔣介石返抵故鄉溪口。

一月廿二日　李宗仁以副總統代理總統職務，聲明願就毛澤東所提八項條件即行開始商談和平，並下令撤銷總動員令，停止戒嚴法之實施，將各剿匪總部改為長官公署，並釋放政治犯。

一月廿三日　華北剿匪總司令傅作義投降中共，揚言「北平局部和平」，中共軍隊入據北平。

美國駐華軍事顧問團撤離中國。

一月廿五日　國民政府海軍最大的巡洋艦重慶號官兵五百七十四名在船長鄧兆祥率領下，在吳淞口宣布投降中共。（重慶號於三月四日在駛往葫蘆島途中，被國軍飛機炸沉。）

一月廿八日　國民政府立法院在南京舉行第一屆第三期院會，白崇禧、何應欽、吳鐵城等出席。

二月一日　國民政府及中國國民黨中央黨部先後遷移到廣州辦公。台灣省政府宣布實行「三七五減租」政策。

二月十二日　國民黨元老、國史館館長戴傳賢在廣州逝世。

三月一日　國民政府代總統李宗仁提名何應欽繼孫科為行政院長，經立法院投票同意。

三月十五日　中共中央黨報「人民日報」遷到北平出版，原人民日報北平版改名「北平解放日報」。

三月廿五日　中國共產黨中央委員會、中國人民解放軍總部，自延安西柏坡遷移到北平，毛澤東、朱德、劉少奇及周恩來等到達北平。

三月廿九日　代總統李宗仁派邵力子、黃紹雄、張治中、章士釗及李蒸為和談代表，與中共代表周恩來、葉劍英、林彪等舉行和平談判。

閻錫山由太原抵達南京。

三月三十日　國民黨中央執行委員會常務委員、中央監察委員會常務委員、中央政治委員會委員，在廣州舉行聯席會議，決定和談五項原則：㈠停戰須在和談以前實現；㈡國體不容變更；㈢修改憲法須依法定手續；㈣人民之自由生活方式必須保障；㈤土地改革首先實行，但反對以暴力實行土地改革。

四月一日　國民政府和談代表張治中、邵力子、章士釗、黃紹雄、李蒸及劉斐抵達北平。

四月五日　中共代表團與國民政府代表開始交換意見。

四月十二日　國民政府和談代表團，與中共代表團雙方擬定「國內和平協定」草案，共八條二十四款，仍以毛澤東所提之條件為內容，並限期於四月二十日以前簽字。

四月十五日　四月十五日為蔣經國四十歲生日，蔣介石親題「寓理帥氣」以勉之。

四月十五日　代總統李宗仁以黨政民意各方面皆反對和談條件，上電聲言請蔣介石復職，並以即日返桂林為口號，其意一在迫使蔣必須曲聽其和談；一在脅蔣出國。

四月十六日　國民政府代表黃紹雄、屈武攜「國內和平協定」回南京，請示簽字問題。

四月十八日　中國國民黨中央執行委員會發表聲明，重申和平談判，應以五項原則為基礎。

國民政府決定拒絕中共「國內和平協定」無理要求。

四月二十日　中國國民黨中央常務委員會發表聲明，指斥中共「國內和平協定」歪曲事實，超出和議原則，失去和平條款之性質，並盼中共懸崖勒馬，立即停戰。和平談判宣告破裂。

四月廿一日　中共主席毛澤東、朱德總司令，向中國人民解放軍發佈「奮勇前進，解放全中國」的命令。

中共軍隊於廿一日凌晨發起長江戰役。劉伯承、鄧小平、張際春等指揮的第二野戰軍，在

西起九江東北的湖口，東至江陰，長達五百公里的戰線上，分三路強渡長江，中路解放軍突破安慶、蕪湖的國軍防線，在二十四小時內渡過三十萬人，並且佔據繁昌、銅陵兩縣城，及青陽、荻港等廣大地區。西路解放軍佔據彭澤東北的馬當要塞。東路解放軍渡江佔據浦縣城。江陰要塞司令戴戎光叛變降共。

四月廿二日　蔣介石以大局嚴重，不得已飛臨杭州，與李宗仁、何應欽、張群、王世杰、吳忠信等會商，決定於國民黨中央常務委員會之下，設非常委員會，先在黨中獲致協議，再由政府依法定程序實施，對當前時局及政府今後政策，鄭重商討，並一致決議，關於共黨問題，政府今後惟有堅決作戰，為人民自由與國家獨立奮鬥到底。國民政府各院、部會皆遷往廣州，總統府遷往上海。淞滬警備總司令宣布上海市進入戰時狀態。

四月廿三日　代總統李宗仁棄職飛往桂林。

國民政府首都南京撤守。

中共人民解放軍進入南京。（廿八日成立南京軍事管制委員會，劉伯承任主任，宋任窮任副主任。）

山西省會太原被中共軍攻陷，代主席梁敦厚等五百人壯烈殉職。

四月廿五日　蔣介石乘軍艦到上海，親自督導上海市保衛戰。

國民政府海軍第二艦隊司令林遵率領艦艇共二十五艘，在南京東北的笆斗山江面宣布投降中共。同時，鎮江江面的國民政府海軍艦艇二十三艘亦投降中共。

蔣介石的座艦太康號停泊於黃埔江復興島，顧祝同、徐永昌、湯恩伯、周至柔、桂永清等來謁。蔣介石於聽取報告後，指示保衛上海戰鬥部署。蔣介石自太康號軍艦移往上海市金神父路的勵志社，淞滬人心士氣為之一振。

蔣介石以國民黨總裁身分，發表告全國同胞書，重申戡亂決心，並呼籲全國同胞一致支持反侵略、反共產、保障民主的神聖戰爭。

四月廿七日　中共軍隊攻佔蘇州。

中國國民黨常務委員會發表告全體黨員書，響應蔣總裁的反共號召，要求全體同志精誠團結，救黨護國。

五月一日　國民政府行政院命令，任陳良為上海市長，取代吳國禎市長職務。

五月三日　中共第三野戰軍部隊攻陷浙江省會杭州市。國民政府派居正、閻錫山、李文範等赴桂林促代總統李宗仁至廣州主持政府，李宗仁遲遲其行，並致函行政院長何應欽，對軍權及人事等提出多項要求。

五月七日　蔣介石乘江靜號輪船自上海復興島啟椗赴舟山群島。蔣經國在五月七日的日記中寫道：「早晨六時，江靜輪由上海復興島啟椗，船出吳淞口外，我才起身。太陽高照大海，顯見著美麗而雄偉的晨景。國事不堪設想，祇有向天禱告，保我父的安全和健康。」

五月十二日　蔣介石總裁抵達舟山。

五月十三日　國民政府立法院在廣州舉行會議，通過「為中共破壞和平支持政府對中共繼續作戰之決議」。

五月十七日　中共林彪、羅榮垣、鄧子恢指揮的第四野戰軍，在武漢以東的地區渡過長江，於五月十六日攻佔漢口，十七日攻佔武昌及漢陽。

五月十七日　蔣介石自舟山乘飛機至澎湖群島的馬公。

五月十八日　國民政府華中軍政長官白崇禧在長沙召開軍事會議，商討華中作戰部署。
中國國民黨中央執行委員會上電蔣介石總裁，以時局嚴重，請其打消高隱之意，積極領導同志，削平匪亂。

五月二十日　中共彭德懷、張宗遜指揮的第一野戰軍攻佔陝西省會西安市。

五月廿一日　國民政府代總統李宗仁發表告全國國民書，承認形勢「相當嚴重」，並表示抵抗到底的決心。

五月廿四日　中共軍隊攻佔浙江奉化縣城及蔣介石的故鄉溪口鎮。

五月廿五日　蔣介石自馬公飛抵台灣南部的高雄市。

五月廿五日　中共第三野戰軍部隊攻陷上海市，並聲稱全戰役共殲國軍十五萬三千餘人。

六月三日　代總統李宗仁提名閻錫山

為行政院長，接替何應欽的職務。

六月十五日　台灣省政府宣布改革幣制，發行新台幣，新台幣對美金的比率為五比一。

六月十六日　蔣介石以黃埔軍校校長身分，在高雄鳳山陸軍訓練司令部（司令官為孫立人將軍）主持軍校第二十五週年校慶，首次在公開場合出現。

六月廿四日　蔣介石自高雄壽山移居台北草山（易名陽明山），主持東南區軍事會議。

六月三十日　中共主席毛澤東，在中國共產黨創立廿八週年紀念日，發表〈論人民民主專政〉一文，揚言向蘇聯「一面倒」的政策。

七月二日　菲律賓總統季里諾來電，邀請蔣介石赴菲訪問，面商遠東局勢。

蔣介石以國民黨總裁身分主持整理黨務會議，討論國民黨改造方案，並決定成立「總裁辦公室組織」。

七月四日　國民政府開始發行銀元券。

七月十日　蔣介石以中國國民黨總裁身分，應菲律賓總統季里諾的邀請飛往馬尼拉訪問，會商有關組織反共聯盟問題，並發表聯合聲明。

七月十四日　蔣介石自台北飛抵廣州，發表對時局談話說：「中正仍當一本總理大無畏之革命精神，團結全黨，擁護政府，為國家獨立，人民自由而奮鬥。」

國民黨中央在廣州成立非常委員會，蔣介石任主席，李宗仁任副主席。

七月十五日　中共上海市軍事管制委員會，命令上海的美國大使館新聞處及英國大使館新聞處自即日起停止一切活動。

七月十八日　國民政府命令成立東南軍政長官公署，管轄江蘇、浙江、福建、台灣及海南島五地區，並任命陳誠為軍政長官，長官公署設於台北。

七月廿三日　中共北平市軍事管制委員會宣布，解散中國國民黨、三民主義青年團、中國青年黨、民主社會黨及其他反動黨派。

七月廿六日　國民政府代總統李宗仁自廣州搭機飛往福州，廿七日由福州轉往台北。

八月一日　中國國民黨中央設置總裁
　　　　辦公室，在台北市草山（易名
　　　　陽明山）成立。
　　　　蔣介石自台北飛往浙江定海視
　　　　察。

八月五日　美國國務院發表〈中美關
　　　　係白皮書〉，內容主旨在為美
　　　　國對華政策作辯護。

八月六日　蔣介石以國民黨總裁身
　　　　分，應大韓民國總統李承晚邀
　　　　請，自定海飛往南韓鎮海訪
　　　　問。

八月八日　蔣介石與李承晚總統舉行
　　　　會談後發表聯合聲明，表示：
　　　　「吾人均承認與人類自由、國
　　　　家獨立不相容之國際共產主義
　　　　必須消滅；並對碧瑤（蔣介
　　　　石、季里諾）聯合聲明中所提
　　　　聯盟之主張完全同意。」蔣介
　　　　石自南韓鎮海飛返台北。

八月十日　美國駐華大使司徒雷登離
　　　　南京返美。

八月十三日　國民黨中央非常委員會
　　　　第二分會（台北）召開第一次
　　　　會議，蔣介石總裁致辭，要求
　　　　重建革命信心，痛下決心，自
　　　　力更生，為革命事業與光榮歷
　　　　史而奮鬥。
　　　　國民政府外交部發表鄭重聲

明，斥責美國對華政策白皮書
的說法。

八月十七日　中共第三野戰軍部隊攻
　　　　陷福建省會福州，聲稱殲國軍
　　　　五萬多人。

八月廿三日　台灣高雄港軍火船發生
　　　　爆炸事件，損失在調查中。
　　　　蔣介石自台北飛抵廣州，與代
　　　　總統李宗仁、閻錫山、顧祝
　　　　國、薛岳、余漢謀、劉安祺等
　　　　會商保衛作戰計劃。

八月廿四日　蔣介石自廣州飛抵重
　　　　慶。

八月廿五日　蔣介石召見四川省政府
　　　　主席王陵基，廿七日召見宋希
　　　　濂，並派李彌赴雲南佈防。

八月廿九日　蔣介石在重慶召開西南
　　　　軍政人員會議，川、黔、康各
　　　　省政府主席，及陝、甘、鄂、
　　　　湘邊區軍事將領皆至，惟雲南
　　　　省主席盧漢未到，因盧漢已受
　　　　到中共誘惑。

八月廿六日　中共第一野戰軍部隊攻
　　　　陷甘肅省會蘭州，國軍馬鴻
　　　　逵、馬步芳主力部隊四萬餘人
　　　　覆沒。

八月廿八日　宋慶齡女士自上海抵達
　　　　北平。

九月一日　蔣介石為安定西南各省局

勢，建議國民政府安定雲南，改革四川、西康人事，並加強漢中的胡宗南部隊，強化陝西防務。

九月二日　重慶市區發生大火事件，災民多達四、五萬人之眾，死亡千餘人。此意外事件顯然與中共潛伏分子活動有關。

九月六日　雲南省政府主席盧漢自昆明飛抵重慶，會見蔣介石後八日飛返昆明，將省議會解散，查封國民黨營報社以外的一切親共報刊。

九月七日　國民政府自廣州遷往抗戰時期的首都重慶市辦公。

九月十日　蔣介石飛抵成都，在完成部署後即返重慶。

九月十七日　由中共主持的「中國人民政治協商會議」第二次全體會議在北平舉行，通過「中華人民共和國中央人民政府組織法草案」等提案。

九月十七日　西安事變的主角之一楊虎城及其妻子等在重慶被國民政府處死。

九月十九日　綏遠省政府主席董其武等宣布投降中共，中共宣稱綏遠「和平解放」。

九月廿一日　中共主持的「中國人民政治協商會議」第一屆會議在北平舉行，參加的各黨派代表共六百三十五人。中共主席毛澤東在開幕式中致詞。

九月廿二日　蔣介石命長公子經國先行飛往昆明，以手書示雲南省政府主席盧漢。蔣氏隨後即至，並在盧宅接見駐軍將領，會商西南局勢後飛離昆明，經廣州返回台北。

九月廿二日　中共主席毛澤東在北平設宴招待國民政府投降中共的文武官員，有張治中、傅作義、鄧寶珊、黃紹雄、劉斐、陳明仁、孫蘭峰、吳奇偉、高樹勛、張軫、曾澤生、李明揚、黃琪翔、鄧兆祥等二十六人。

九月廿五日　國民政府新疆省政府主席鮑爾漢及警備總司令陶峙岳，宣布投降中共。

九月廿七日　國民政府駐聯合國代表團，向聯合國大會提出「控告蘇聯違反中蘇條約侵華案」，指控蘇聯違反中蘇友好同盟條約及聯合國憲章，並掠奪我國東北財產及以武器供給中共。此案經聯大政治委員會通過，列入聯大會議議程。

九月廿七日　中共主持的「中國人民政治協商會議」通過多項議案：㈠中國人民政治協商會議組織法；㈡中華人民共和國中央人民政府組織法；㈢中華人民共和國的國都定於北平，自即日起改名北平為北京；㈣中華人民共和國的國歌未正式制定前，以「義勇軍進行曲」為國歌；㈤中華人民共和國的國旗為五星紅旗，象徵中國革命人民大團結。

九月三十日　中國人民政治協商會議第一屆全體會議閉幕。毛澤東當選為中華人民共和國中央人民政府委員會主席，朱德、劉少奇、宋慶齡、李濟深、張瀾及高崗為副主席。會議並選出中央人民政府委員五十六人，及中國人民政治協商會議全國委員會委員一百八十人。

十月一日　「中華人民共和國」中央人民政府在北京（北平）成立，三十萬人在天安門廣場集會慶祝。毛澤東主席在廣場升起第一面五星紅旗，並宣讀中央人民政府公告，向全世界宣告中華人民共和國的成立及中央人民政府的成立，同時向各國政府公布：「本政府為代表中華人民共和國全國人民的唯一合法政府」。

中央人民政府主席、副主席及委員宣布就職。中央人民政府委員會選林伯渠為秘書長，任命周恩來為政務院總理兼外交部長，任命毛澤東為人民革命軍事委員會主席。

十月二日　蘇聯承認中共政權。

中華民國政府宣布與蘇聯斷絕外交關係。

美國國務院宣布，美國繼續承認中華民國政府為中國唯一合法政府。

十月五日　蔣介石抵廈門召開軍事會議，部署閩廈防務。

十月十日　蔣介石發表中華民國雙十國慶告全國同胞書，指出全國同胞救國自救之道，唯有徹底反共抗俄，光復國土。

舟山群島的六橫、蝦岐及金塘被中共軍隊攻陷，蔣介石飛往定海視察。

十月十二日　國民政府已經自廣州遷往重慶辦公。

十月十三日　國民政府代總統李宗仁自廣州前往廣西桂林，中共軍隊進入廣州。

十月十六日　國民黨的革命實踐研究院在台北市郊的陽明山舉行開學典禮，蔣總裁致辭說明成立研究院的意義，在使受訓幹部恢復革命精神、堅定革命建國信心，厚植實踐篤行之志節。

十月廿五日　蔣介石於台灣光復四周年紀念日，發表告台灣省同胞書，勗勉保持革命抗戰成果，使台灣同胞永為自由的國民。

十月廿六日　中共解放軍第三野戰軍第十兵團約七千餘人，廿五日在金門島的潮尾、古寧頭等灘頭登陸，受到防守金門的六萬餘國民政府軍隊的堅強抵抗，雙方激戰到廿六日，中共的兩批登陸部隊共計一萬餘人全部損失。國軍獲得金門大捷。在此次戰役中，孫立人將軍訓練的新軍作戰尤其英勇，獲得各方人士的稱讚。

十月卅一日　十月卅一日是蔣介石的六十三歲生日，他在台灣宜蘭縣的風景區礁溪慶祝誕辰，特作六三自箴一文說：「虛度六三，受恥招敗，毋惱毋怒，莫矜莫慢。不愧不怍，自足自反。」

十一月三日　國民政府代總統李宗仁，自重慶飛往昆明，特別批准雲南省政府主席盧漢釋放中共分子，盧漢因此復萌異志。

十一月七日　中共軍隊進攻福建沿海的登步島，被國民政府守軍擊敗。

十一月十四日　蔣介石自台北飛抵重慶，因貴陽情勢危急，中共軍隊攻陷秀山，重慶已經受威脅。代總統李宗仁自昆明飛返故鄉桂林。蔣介石迭接行政院長閻錫山函電，懇請蔣介石蒞重慶坐鎮。

蔣介石去電促李宗仁返重慶共商大局，而李宗仁反而自桂林轉往南寧，稍後託病就醫，自南寧轉往香港。

十一月廿五日　中共軍隊已進至重慶市郊的風景區南溫泉及長江南岸的海棠溪地區。蔣介石偕蔣經國巡視重慶市區情勢。

十一月廿九日　重慶市郊發生激戰，市內已聞槍聲，蔣介石於中午召開軍事會議，決定作戰計劃，對胡宗南第一軍部隊撤退亦有詳細指示。此際，中共軍隊已在江津上游約二十里處渡過長江，重慶市已處於包圍中。當夜十時，林園行邸已聞

槍聲，兵工廠亦發生爆炸事件。長公子蔣經國請行，蔣介石說：「我現在不能走，必待羅廣文軍長歸來，處理妥後再定。」

未久，羅廣文來謁蔣，報告其部隊已損失殆盡。於是，蔣介石不得已愴然離邸，途中車輛行人擁擠不堪，汽車難行，蔣介石見此情形，先下車徒步行，稍後改搭吉甫車，抵達市郊白市驛軍用機場，飛往成都，此際共軍相距僅僅二十里。

十一月三十日　蔣介石抵達四川省會成都。

中共軍隊進入重慶市。

十二月二日　國民黨中央常委朱家驊、洪蘭友自香港飛至成都，帶回李宗仁信函稱，以美國務院已允其入境，故仍欲以代總統名義赴美國。

十二月三日　中國國民黨中央常務委員會在成都舉行臨時會議，決定依照十一月二十日臨時會議的決議，懇請蔣介石總裁復行總統職權。

在台灣的立法委員、監察委員

及國民大會代表等，一致電請蔣介石復行總統職權，以挽危局。四川的國大代表亦相率來謁，懇請蔣介石復行總統職權。

蔣介石指示胡宗南將軍，關於四川中部全般作戰部署。

十二月五日　中華民國代總統李宗仁自香港赴美國。

十二月七日　中華民國中央政府決定，從成都遷至台北辦公，並決定於成都設置防衛司令部，在西康省會西昌設置大本營。蔣介石以雲南省政府主席盧漢意存反覆，特命張群主任前往昆明曉諭，不意盧漢甘心降共，並將張群強制留住。

十二月十日　蔣介石自成都飛返台北。

十二月十日　中國國民黨中央黨部自成都遷至台北辦公。張群自雲南昆明脫險搭飛機到香港。

十二月十五日　中共主席毛澤東赴莫斯科，與蘇聯政府舉行談判。國民政府任命吳國禎為台灣省政府主席。

十二月廿七日　中共軍隊進入四川省會成都。

中華民國三十九年（一九五〇）

一月一日　蔣介石以中國國民黨總裁身分，發表告全國同胞書，號召全體軍民，反共到底。

中華民國第一屆國民大會代表七百六十餘人，在台北舉行會議，一致通過決議，敦請蔣介石復任總統。

一月五日　中華民國政府宣布與英國斷絕外交關係，因為英國承認北平（北京）中共政府。

一月八日　蔣夫人宋美齡女士自美啟程返台北。她係於一九四八年十一月廿八日赴美，其間蔣夫人在美國奔走呼籲美國政府與人民支持我國。

一月十一日　聯合國安全理事會通過決議，拒絕蘇聯所提出的立即排斥中華民國代表團的提案。蘇聯代表團退出會議表示抗議。

一月十三日　蔣夫人宋美齡女士自美國搭飛機經菲律賓返抵台北。

一月廿六日　蔣介石在國民黨中央常會中宣示，確保台灣與光復大陸的決心。

國民政府行政院公布「反共保民總體戰動員綱領」。

一月廿八日　國民政府外交部發表鄭重聲明，中華民國將不受中共政權與蘇聯簽訂之任何條約協議的約束。

二月二日　國民大會代表電請蔣介石復行視事。

蔣夫人宋美齡女士赴金門前線勞軍。

二月五日　國民政府住聯合國代表蔣廷黻在大會發言，指出蘇聯破壞一九四五年簽訂的中蘇友好同盟條約及違反聯合國憲章，要求聯合國譴責蘇聯及不承認北京中共政權。

二月九日　國民政府宣布，自一九五〇年二月十二日零時起，除已經宣布關閉的大陸沿海各港口外，增加關閉廣州灣及北海港口。

二月九日　美國國務院宣布，美國繼續援助中華民國政府，不承認中共政權，及台灣現在的地位絕對不容變更。

國民政府監察院大會決議，函覆代總統李宗仁，指斥其居住美國遙領國事之謬論，並且決議提請國民大會彈劾之。

代總統李宗仁對國民黨中央非

常委員會覆電，藉口遵醫囑不能遠行，拒絕返國。

二月十四日　中共主席毛澤東在莫斯科與蘇聯政府簽訂友好同盟互助條約。

二月十五日　國民政府立法院第五會期首次大會在台北市召開，立法委員三百八十餘人，聯名請求蔣介石復行總統職權。

台灣各縣市團體與機關首長，及海外僑團紛紛來電懇請蔣介石復行視事。

二月十九日　中國國民黨中央常務委員、中央監察委員、中央政治委員，及中央非常委員舉行聯席會議，以代總統李宗仁於上年十一月出國，中樞大計乏人主持，一致決議請求蔣介石復行總統職權，重行主持國政。

三月一日　蔣介石為順應輿情，挽救危局，於台北宣告繼續行使總統職權，領導全國軍民，進行反共復國之神聖戰爭。蔣總統發表文告，說明進退出處，一惟國民之公意是從，望海內外愛國同胞，精誠團結，務期掃除共黨，光復大陸。文告中揭示施政重點是：「第一，在軍事上鞏固台灣基地，進行光復大陸。第二，在國際上先求自力更生，再聯合民主國家共同反共。第三，在經濟上提倡節約，獎勵生產，推行民生主義。第四，在政治上保障民權，厲行法治。」

三月四日　中共主席毛澤東結束對蘇聯的訪問，自莫斯科飛抵北京。

三月十七日　國民政府行政院長閻錫山提出辭職。蔣介石總統提名陳誠為行政院長，獲得立法院大會投票同意。

蔣介石總統任命王世杰為總統府秘書長、周至柔為參謀總長、孫立人為陸軍總司令、桂永清為海軍總司令、周至柔兼空軍總司令、王叔銘為空軍副總司令。

三月廿六日　中共軍隊達十萬人圍攻西康省會西昌，西南軍政長官胡宗南及西康省政府主席賀國光，於夜間搭飛機撤離，西昌淪陷。（大陸地區至此全部落入共產黨手裡。）

四月五日　國民政府行政院會議通過「台灣省各縣市實施地方自治

綱要」，將在兩個月內開始舉行縣市長普選。

四月廿三日　國民政府軍隊自海口撤退。

五月二日　國民政府軍隊自海南島撤退，增強台灣澎湖防衛力量。

五月十六日　國民政府軍隊自舟山群島撤退，十五萬部隊及大量物資安全轉運到台灣。蔣介石總統為國軍自海南島及舟山群島撤退事件發表廣播演講，說明集中所有兵力，確保台灣即為反攻大陸、拯救同胞的基礎。

五月廿四日　美國國務院發表聲明，美國將繼續以經濟援華。

六月十日　國民政府前參謀次長吳石及前第四兵站總監陳寶倉，觸犯懲治叛亂條例，依法判罪，執行死刑。

六月十八日　前台灣省行政長官陳儀為勾結中共，經國防部高級軍法合議庭宣判死刑，今日伏法。

六月廿五日　北韓共黨軍隊突然越過北緯三十八度分界線進攻大韓民國，韓國戰爭爆發，聯合國安全理事會舉行緊急會議，通過決議要求北韓停戰。

蔣介石致電韓國總統李承晚，表示願對韓提供精神與道義援助。

六月廿七日　美國總統杜魯門宣布命令第七艦隊協防台灣，遏止共黨對台灣的任何攻擊，同時要求中華民國政府停止攻擊大陸。

六月廿八日　中華民國外交部長葉公超發表聲明表示，原則上接受美國協防台灣之建議，惟聲明：「美國之建議不影響中國政府對台灣之主權，或開羅會議關於台灣地位之決定；並不影響中國反抗國際共產主義及維護中國領土完整之立場。」美國第七艦隊軍艦駛入台灣海峽。

漢城陷落，南韓政府遷至大田。

六月廿九日　美國國務卿艾契遜在記者招待會中宣稱：「美國艦隊防護台灣，不涉及台灣地位」。

七月二日　台灣省地方自治開始實施，台灣東部的花蓮縣，首先舉行縣議員選舉。

七月八日　美國第七艦隊司令史樞波

將軍抵達台北，協商加強兩國聯繫事宜。

七月十一日　中共主席毛澤東第二次赴蘇聯訪問。

七月廿二日　中國國民黨中央常務委員會通過「中國國民黨改造案」，並通過以陳誠、張其昀及連震東等十六人為改造委員。

七月三十日　美國國務院任命卡爾・藍欽（Karl L. Rankin）為駐華公使。

七月卅一日　聯合國援助韓國最高統帥麥克阿瑟元帥，自東京抵達台北，與蔣介石總統舉行會談。會談之後，蔣介石總統發表談話說，他與麥帥的會談已奠定中美共同保衛台灣與軍事合作的基礎。麥帥亦發表聲明說：「關於台灣本島，包括澎湖在內，在目前情況下，不得遭受軍事進攻之政策，業經宣布。」他並說：「余更欽佩蔣總統不屈不撓抵抗共黨控制之決心。」

八月五日　中國國民黨中央改造委員會成立。

八月十日　美國公使藍欽抵達台北，擔任美國大使館代辦職務。

八月十六日　中華民國行政院會議通過台灣省各縣市行政區域調整方案，原劃分為八縣九市，經重劃為十六縣五市。

九月四日　蔣總統招待國民大會代表，說明第一屆國民大會臨時會議，因為在台灣的國大代表不足法定人數而暫緩召開。

九月十九日　聯合國第五屆會員大會，否決蘇聯及印度提出的使中共政權參加聯合國的建議案。

十月七日　中共宣布派軍隊進入西藏。

十月十日　蔣介石總統主持中華民國三十九年雙十國慶典禮，並發表國慶日告同胞書。

十月十九日　中共軍隊渡過鴨綠江，開赴前線協助北韓共軍作戰。

十月廿五日　台灣省光復五週年紀念日，蔣介石總統發表廣播講演，勉勵台灣同胞發揚反侵略愛祖國的民族精神，完成復興祖國的光榮任務。

十月廿五日　中共宣布以「抗美援朝志願軍」名義公開援助北韓共黨對聯合國軍隊作戰。

十一月九日　中共軍隊進入西藏首府拉薩。

十一月十三日　蔣介石總統對大陸同胞發表廣播演說，促使人民反共及不與韓境聯軍作戰。

十一月十七日　西藏的第十四世達賴喇嘛，遭受中共軍隊壓迫，逃亡印度。

十一月三十日　聯合國安全理事會否決蘇聯提出的「美國侵略台灣」案。

聯合國安全理事會通過決議，要求中共軍隊撤離韓國。

十二月五日　中華民國立法院改選，劉健群當選院長，黃國書當選副院長。

十二月廿七日　蔣介石總統根據行政院建議，以中華民國第一屆立法委員任期於民國四十年五月七日屆滿，現因無法辦理選舉，特咨請立法院贊同由現任立法委員於任期屆滿後，繼續行使立法權，其期間暫定一年。

中華民國四十年（一九五一）

一月一日　蔣介石總統主持中華民國開國紀念典禮，發表告全國軍民書，要求同胞自立自強，造成新風氣。

一月四日　中國國民黨各級黨部開始辦理黨員歸隊工作。

一月十五日　台北市舉行第一屆民選市長，吳三連當選首屆民選市長。

一月廿八日　台灣省各縣市完成縣議員及市議員普選，成立縣議會及市議會。

一月三十日　中國政府同意日本政府要求，允許日本派遣海外代表駐台北。

二月一日　聯合國大會通過決議，譴責中共為對韓國的侵略者。

二月六日　聯合國援韓最高統帥麥克阿瑟元帥，向美國參謀首長聯席會議建議，以中華民國軍隊用於韓國或其他地區。

二月二十日　美國第七艦隊司令史樞波將軍，第三次抵台灣訪問。

二月廿二日　美國第十三航空隊司令滕納將軍抵台灣訪問。

二月廿八日　中華民國行政院宣布，任命錢思亮為國立台灣大學校長。

三月一日　蔣介石總統復行視事一週年紀念，台灣各地舉行熱烈慶

祝活動。

三月廿四日　韓境聯軍最高統帥麥克阿瑟元帥發表聲明，主張將聯軍行動擴展到中國大陸境內。

四月六日　美國政府發表聲明，美國對華政策不變，但仍然反對使用在台灣的中華民國軍隊。

四月七日　美國政府發表對日本和約草案。

四月十一日　美國總統杜魯門下令，免除麥克阿瑟元帥一切職務，並任命李奇威將軍接替麥帥職務。

四月十三日　蔣介石總統在台北接見新任美國第七艦隊司令馬丁將軍，商談中美兩國合作事宜。

四月十九日　中國國民黨中央改造委員會通過，「中國國民黨從政黨員政治小組組織規程」。

四月廿一日　美國國防部宣布，派遣軍事援華顧問團到台灣，由蔡斯少將（William C. Chase）為團長。

五月一日　美國軍事援華顧問團長蔡斯少將抵達台北就任。

五月七日　中國青年黨主席曾琦在美國逝世，享年六十歲。
美國政府公布保密已久的前駐華美軍總司令魏德邁的「對華政策報告書」。

五月十八日　聯合國大會以四十七票對零票一致通過決議，對中共及韓共實施全球性的戰略物資禁運案。

五月十九日　美國政府致照會蘇聯，反對中共參加對日本和約。

五月廿三日　中共軍隊進入西藏首府拉薩，與地方政府簽訂「和平解放西藏協議」。

五月廿四日　中華民國交通部公佈施行「郵轉電報規則」。

五月廿五日　中華民國立法院會議，通過「三七五減租條例」案。
台灣省一人一元獻機委員會正式成立。

五月廿九日　中華民國駐美國大使顧維鈞會晤美國國務卿杜勒斯，就對日本和約問題再作商討。

五月三十日　中華民國外交部長葉公超與美國駐華大使藍欽會晤，重申我國對日本和約的立場。
立法院會議通過「財政收支劃分法」案。
台灣興建嘉南大圳全部竣工。

六月四日　中國國民黨中央改造委員會今通過，「中國國民黨海外

總支部（直屬支部）改造委員會組織通則」。

六月八日　美國第七艦隊司令柯拉克中將宣布，美國駐菲律賓空軍的一部分協防台灣。

六月十八日　日本外務省發表聲明說，中華民國政府為中國唯一合法政府。

六月廿三日　蔣介石總統應金門防衛司令官胡璉之請，親題「毋忘在莒」四字，鐫於太武山北海印寺前，以資激勵。

六月廿七日　中華民國與西班牙的佛朗哥政府恢復邦交。

七月六日　陸軍總司令孫立人將軍，為慶祝「七七」陸軍節，率全體陸軍將士上電蔣總統致敬。

七月八日　日本政府內閣會議，批准中日和平條約。

七月二十日　美國海軍軍令部長費克特勒上將，晉謁蔣介石總統，並發表談話說：「中美兩國共同努力，必能維護遠東安全」。

七月廿四日　中國國民黨中央改造委員會通過決議，自民國四十二年（一九五三）一月開始，推行「耕者有其田」政策（即限田政策），扶植自耕農。

七月卅一日　中華民國立法院投票批准中日和平條約。

八月二日　蔣介石總統簽署批准中日和平條約。

八月六日　中華民國行政院會議決議，孔子誕辰及教師節改為九月廿八日。
中華民國外交部宣布，撤銷駐日代表團，在東京設置大使館，以參事劉增華暫代館務。

八月九日　日本政府宣布，任命前外務大臣芳澤謙吉為駐中華民國大使。

八月十六日　蔣介石總統宣布，特任董顯光博士為駐日本大使。

九月一日　蔣介石總統率文武百官，在台北市圓山忠烈祠秋祭國殤，慰勉烈士遺族。

十月二日　蔣介石總統接受美國博俊大學贈送之名譽法學博士學位。

十月十日　中華民國國慶紀念，蔣介石總統主持中樞紀念典禮並檢閱三軍及發表告全國軍民書。
中國國民黨第七次全國代表大會，在台北市陽明山舉行揭幕儀式。（七全大會十八日第十

次會議，一致擁戴蔣介石連任總裁，並通過政綱。十九日第十四次會議，選舉陳誠、蔣經國等三十二人為中央委員。大會於二十日閉幕。）

十月廿五日　台灣光復七週年紀念，蔣介石總統發表告台灣省同胞書，各地舉行慶祝活動。

十月卅一日　中國青年反共救國團成立，蔣經國擔任主任。

十一月一日　中國國民黨中央委員會成立開始辦公，同時中央改造委員會宣佈結束。

十一月十五日　強烈颱風貝絲襲擊台灣，南部高雄、台南及屏東地區災情嚴重。

十一月十九日　胡適博士自美國返台。

十二月十一日　美國駐華大使司徒雷登，在美國因病辭職。

十二月卅一日　菲律賓航空公司一架客機，被共黨分子洪祖鈞劫持飛往大陸，在金門附近上空被國軍飛機截住，逼其在台灣機場降落。

中華民國四十一年（一九五二）

一月一日　蔣介石總統發表民國四十一年元旦文告，號召全國同胞推行社會、經濟、文化、政治四大改造，完成反共抗俄總動員。

一月廿一日　中華民國政府宣布，政府已草擬中華民國與日本間的雙邊和約草案。

二月一日　聯合國大會會議，以二十六票對九票，另十四票棄權通過中華民國提出的控告蘇聯違反中、蘇條約案。

四月廿八日　中、日和平條約在台北中華民國外交部舉行簽字儀式，由我國全權代表葉公超及日本全權代表河田烈分別代表兩國政府簽署。

六月廿七日　中華民國外交部宣布，中國與西班牙元首佛朗哥政府恢復外交關係。

七月三十一日　中華民國立法院會議表決通過「中、日和平條約案」。

八月六日　中華民國行政院會議通過決議，將至聖先師孔子誕辰及教師節改為每年的九月二十八日，並自今年起實施。

九月三日　英文中國郵報（CHINA POST）在台北市創刊。

十月十日　中華民國四十一年雙十國
　　　　慶，蔣介石總統主持中樞國慶
　　　　紀念典禮，並舉行檢閱三軍儀
　　　　式。

中國國民黨第七次全國代表大會，在
　　　　台北市陽明山舉行開幕典禮，
　　　　由蔣介石總裁親臨主持並致
　　　　辭。七全大會會期十天，預定
　　　　於二十日閉幕。

十月廿五日　蔣總統為台灣光復七週
　　　　年發表「告台灣省同胞書」，
　　　　並舉行台灣全省警察與民防部
　　　　隊檢閱儀式。

聯合國大會第七屆會議，以四十二票
　　　　對九票另九票棄權，通過美國
　　　　提案，否決親共國家提出的排
　　　　斥中華民國案。

十一月五日　美國大選結果揭曉，共
　　　　和黨員艾森豪當選總統，尼克
　　　　森當選副總統。

十一月十九日　旅居美國多年的胡適
　　　　博士返國觀光。

十二月廿六日　國防部宣布，為加強
　　　　軍事動員準備，台灣省已成立
　　　　四個師管區及十二個團管區司
　　　　令部。

中華民國四十二年（一九五三）

一月一日　中華民國開國紀念，蔣介
　　　　石總統發表元旦文告，勗勉全
　　　　國同胞，並提出「求新‧求
　　　　速‧求實‧求簡」四項新作
　　　　風。

一月五日　行政院長陳誠宣布民國四
　　　　十二年兩大施政：㈠實行耕者
　　　　有其田；㈡四年經濟建設計
　　　　劃。

一月十五日　中國國民黨中央常務委
　　　　員會通過「中國國民黨黨政關
　　　　係大綱」。

一月十七日　胡適博士離台返美。

一月二十日　蔣介石總統致電祝賀美
　　　　國總統艾森豪及副總統尼克森
　　　　就職。

一月廿八日　台灣省西螺大橋舉行通
　　　　車典禮，該橋長一千九百公
　　　　尺，為遠東第一大橋。

二月二日　美國總統艾森豪咨文美國
　　　　國會，決定解除「台灣中立
　　　　化」下令美國第七艦隊廢除台
　　　　灣海峽中立巡邏措施。
　　　　蔣介石總統為此發表聲明，確
　　　　認艾森豪總統此舉為合理而光
　　　　明之舉措。

二月八日　中華民國僑務委員會長鄭

彥芬，呼籲全球僑胞簽訂「反共救國公約」。

二月十三日　中國國民黨中央常務委員會決議廢止「中蘇友好同盟條約」。

二月十七日　大韓民國總統李承晚表示，反對中華民國軍隊參加韓國戰爭。

二月十八日　美國總統艾森豪提名藍欽（Karl C. Rankin）為駐中華民國大使。

二月廿四日　中華民國立法院大會通過，廢止「中蘇友好同盟條約及其附件」。

二月廿五日　蔣介石總統明令廢止一九四五年在莫斯科簽訂之「中蘇友好同盟條約及其附件」。

二月廿七日　日本政府發表統計說，日本全國各地共有華僑四萬二千四百六十七人。

三月一日　蔣介石總統復行視事三週年，台灣及海外僑胞均集會慶祝。

北京中央人民政府公布「全國人民代表大會及地方各級人民代表大會選舉法」。

三月五日　蘇聯共產黨領袖及政府總理史達林患癱瘓性中風逝世，年七十四歲（一八七九～一九五三）。

三月六日　中共人民政府發佈哀悼蘇聯總理史達林之命令，規定自七日至九日全國降半旗，並禁止各機關宴會與娛樂。

蘇聯政府改組，馬林可夫繼任總理及共黨第一書記。

三月九日　蔣總統夫人訪問白宮，艾森豪總統夫婦以茶會招待。

三月廿一日　蘇聯共黨宣布解除馬林可夫第一書記職務，由赫魯雪夫繼任。

三月廿五日　蔣總統夫人自美經菲律賓返回台北。

四月二日　美國駐華大使藍欽向蔣介石總統呈遞國書。

四月八日　台北市自立晚報奉令休刊七日。

四月十日　台灣省政府主席吳國禎辭職，行政院決議由俞鴻鈞繼任。

五月五日　中國國民黨第七屆中央委員會第二次全體會議在台北市陽明山開幕。（七日通過一九五四年國民大會召開第二次會議。）

五月廿二日　美國駐華大使藍欽離台

北返美述職。

六月二日　美國太平洋艦隊總司令雷德福上將晉見蔣介石總統。美國高壩水利工程專家薩凡奇晉見蔣總統。

六月十一日　中國國民黨中央常務委員會會議通過「黨員直接行使罷免權法」。

六月十五日　美國援華的首批 F-84 雷霆式噴射戰鬥機抵達台灣。

六月二十日　中華民國政府照會埃及政府，對埃及改建共和政體予以承認。

六月三十日　中共人民政府宣布，首次全國人口普查結果，人口總數計六○一、九三八、○三五人。

七月二日　在越南羈留四年久的中國難民及國軍共三萬餘人，已分批接運到台灣。留越南的國軍前第一兵團司令黃杰現在台灣。

七月十日　中華民國大法官會議，通過兩項憲法解釋案：㈠國民大會集會日期推算決定；㈡監察委員限制兼任公職。

七月十七日　國民政府閩海突擊隊自金門發動，突襲福建沿海的東山島共軍。

七月廿七日　韓國戰爭聯合國軍隊與共黨軍隊的停戰協定在板門店簽字。

七月三十日　美國太平洋艦隊新任總司令史敦普上將晉見蔣介石總統。

八月十一日　台灣省高級中學及大專學生實施軍訓，經行政院核定辦法，交由國防部頒佈施行。

八月二十日　中華民國國軍與美國第七艦隊部隊，舉行全島性的軍事訓練大演習。

九月十一日　中華民國國防部總政治部主任蔣經國赴美國訪問。

九月十五日　聯合國第八屆大會，以四十四票對十票另二票棄權的表決，拒絕蘇聯所提之使中共進入聯合國的要求。

九月廿七日　蔣介石總統採納行政院建議，依據憲法第二十八條規定，批准第一屆國民大會代表繼續行使職權，到次屆國民大會依法召集開會之日為止。
美國與泰國政府已經同意中華民國所提出之自緬甸境內撤出反共游擊隊的建議。

十月一日　蔣介石總統明令公布，國

民大會代表出缺遞補補充辦法。

十月五日　中華民國內政部發出公告：第一屆國民大會代表自十月十日起，至十二月底止，向該部聲報，逾期不報者，由候補人依法遞補，候補人逾期不報，即喪失候補人資格。

十月十日　蔣介石總統於中華民國雙十國慶日，主持中樞紀念典禮，發表告全國軍民書，並校閱三軍，接受二十萬民眾的歡呼。

十月二十日　中華民國國防部總政治部主任蔣經國，結束對美國的訪問返抵台北，並於離美前發表聲明表示「更比以前確信最後勝利是我們的」。

十月三十日　中國國民黨元老吳敬恆（稚暉）在台北逝世，享年八十九歲（一八六五～一九五三）。

十一月八日　美國副總統尼克森夫婦抵台灣訪問，與蔣介石總統兩度會談。

十一月十二日　中國國民黨第七屆中央委員會第三次大會，於國父中山先生誕辰在台北揭幕。

（蔣介石總裁十四日在大會發表手著「三民主義育樂兩篇補述」。）

十一月十七日　蔣介石總統命令，總統府秘書長王世杰免職。

十一月十八日　中華民國最高法院檢查署下令，通緝投共叛國有據之國民大會代表張治中等十八人。

十一月十九日　中國國民黨元老前行政院長吳鐵城在台北逝世，享年六十九歲（一八八五～一九五三）。

十一月廿三日　中華民國政府發表聲明，反對美國擬將釣魚台列島移交與日本。

十一月廿七日　大韓民國總統李承晚抵達台灣訪問，蔣介石總統親至機場迎接。（蔣總統與李總統於廿八日發表聯合聲明，籲請亞洲一切自由國家，共同組織聯合反共陣線。）

十二月四日　美國海軍部長安德森抵台北訪問。

十二月六日　中國共產黨中央宣布，高崗及饒漱石等因組織「反黨聯盟」已被整肅。

十二月九日　留在緬甸邊區的反共游

擊隊，已經撤回台灣十七批，共計兩千二百六十餘人。

十二月廿三日　中華民國政府立法院會議通過國民大會組織法第八條條文修正草案，將國民大會開議人數減為三分之一以上。

十二月廿六日　美國參謀首長聯席會議主席雷德福上將，與美國務院主管遠東事務助理國務卿勞勃森抵達台北訪問，與中美將領舉行會議。

十二月卅一日　蔣介石總統飭告各機關，中華民國四十三年元旦應舉行團拜，不再個別拜年，以符節約。

中華民國四十三年（一九五四）

一月一日　蔣介石總統發表元旦告全國軍民書，勗勉同胞要忍受更大的痛苦和犧牲，「自由是要我們的生命做代價，復國是要以我們的血肉來換取的」。

一月六日　中華民國國民大會秘書處正式通知海外及港澳地區國大代表，促請於二月十九日以前返國，出席第一屆國民大會第二次會議。

一月九日　蔣介石總統發佈命令，國民大會定於二月十九日在台北集會。

蔣介石總統應美國第七艦隊司令蒲賴德將軍邀請，於上午登該艦隊旗艦黃蜂號，參觀該艦隊在台灣海峽舉行的軍事演習。

一月十一日　韓國聯軍總司令赫爾將軍抵達台北訪問。

一月十三日　國民大會秘書長洪蘭友致電避居美國之副總統李宗仁，促其回國對監察院彈劾案提出答辯。

一月十三日　中華民國行政院會議決議，撥款興建台灣省石門水庫。

一月十五日　中國國民黨中央常務委員會會議通過，「各級黨部輔導農會工作要項」。

一月十九日　台北市自立晚報奉令，自民國四十二年十二月十九日停刊一個月期滿復刊。

一月廿一日　韓境聯軍統帥部宣布，反共戰俘重獲自由，中國反共義士一萬四千二百零九人，幾經險厄，終得分三批返回祖國。蔣介石總統特發表聲明稱許聯軍此一釋俘行動。

一月廿三日　一月廿三日為反共義士
　　　　「自由日」，自清晨零時一分
　　　　鐘起，全國各地響起自由鐘
　　　　聲，慶祝反共義士歸國。
一月廿四日　蔣介石總統為反共義士
　　　　獲釋事，特致電大韓民國總統
　　　　李承晚表示謝意。
一月廿五日　韓境反共義士第一批四
　　　　千六百八十七名平安返抵台
　　　　北，全國民眾熱烈歡迎。
一月廿九日　司法院大法官會議解
　　　　釋，在第二屆立法委員及監察
　　　　委員未能依法選出集會以前，
　　　　應仍由第一屆立法委員、監察
　　　　委員繼續行使其職權。
一月卅一日　中共人民政府宣布，北
　　　　京至蘇聯首都莫斯科的火車直
　　　　達列車通車。
二月二日　美國總統艾森豪宣布，美
　　　　國解除台灣「中立化」政策。
二月三日　蔣介石總統接見自韓國返
　　　　來的反共義士代表，備致慰
　　　　勉。
二月六日　中國共產黨召開七屆四中
　　　　全會，由劉少奇代表中共政治
　　　　局及毛澤東，向四中全會提出
　　　　政治報告。
二月九日　蔣介石總統接見美國第七

艦隊司令蒲賴德將軍。
　　　　第一屆國民大會第二次會議開
　　　　始辦理代表報到。
二月十一日　蔣介石總統以國民大會
　　　　代表身分，親臨台北市中山堂
　　　　辦理國大會議報到手續。
二月十四日　中華民國空軍飛機飛臨
　　　　上海市上空散發傳單，促使大
　　　　陸同胞奮起抗暴。
二月十五日　中國國民黨第七屆中央
　　　　委員會臨時全體會議，一致投
　　　　票選舉總裁蔣介石為中華民國
　　　　第二屆總統候選人。
二月十九日　中華民國第一屆國民大
　　　　會第二次會議在台北開幕，由
　　　　胡適博士擔任臨時主席。
二月廿二日　中華民國國軍舉行「軍
　　　　帖」演習，蔣介石總統親臨校
　　　　閱。
三月五日　美國海軍部宣布，美國將
　　　　在今年五、六、七等三個月
　　　　中，將十艘巡邏艇交與中華民
　　　　國。
三月七日　中國民主社會黨（原國家
　　　　社會黨）各級黨部會議決定，
　　　　推舉徐傅霖出任第二屆總統候
　　　　選人。
三月十一日　前台灣省政府主席吳國

禎自美國來電內容，經國民大會發表後，各方咸表憤慨，一致要求政府應予以嚴厲制裁。

三月十四日　台灣省山地居民九族中文名稱，由行政院內政部確定為：泰雅、賽夏、布農、曹、魯凱、排灣、卑南、阿美及雅美。

三月十五日　東北耆老莫德惠宣佈參加第二屆中華民國總統競選。

三月十七日　中國國民黨中央執行委員會決議，開除前台灣省政府主席吳國禎的黨籍。

三月二十日　留在雲南緬甸邊境的反共游擊隊第二期接運工作結束，共有三千四百五十一人平安抵達台灣。

三月二十日　第一屆國民大會第二次會議舉行第一次選舉大會，選舉中華民國第二任總統，因為候選人蔣介石、徐傅霖均未獲得法定當選票數，大會主席團宣布，定廿二日重行投票。

三月廿二日　第一屆國民大會第二次會議舉行第二次選舉大會，重行選舉第二任中華民國總統，蔣介石獲得一千五百零七票，當選為中華民國第二任總統。

三月廿二日　第一屆國民大會第二次會議舉行第三次選舉大會，選舉第二任副總統，陳誠獲得一千四百十七票，當選為中華民國第二任副總統。

三月廿五日　美國總統艾森豪，大韓民國總統李承晚等國元首，均來電祝賀蔣介石總統當選連任。

三月廿九日　台灣各界舉行青年節慶祝大會，蔣介石總統親臨致訓，八千多名大專學生同時宣誓參加中國青年反共救國團。

四月六日　美國贈送三艘巨型登陸艇自日本駛抵台灣。

四月十六日　中華民國行政院公布「赴美特別移民申請及審核辦法」。

四月十八日　由美國大使館管轄之美軍駐華軍事顧問團，將改組由美國太平洋艦隊司令直接指揮。

四月廿四日　中國國民黨駐菲律賓總支部，在馬尼拉舉行第十四屆代表大會。

四月廿八日　中華民國內政部公布「戒嚴期間新聞紙雜誌圖書管制辦法」。

四月三十日　蔣總統夫人宋美齡女士赴美國舊金山醫院就醫。

五月二日　台灣省第二屆臨時省議會議員，及各縣市長第二屆選舉，台北等十五縣市同時分別舉行。

五月七日　越南共產黨軍隊攻陷南越重鎮奠邊府。

五月十二日　中國國民黨元老、監察院監察委員丁惟芬在台北逝世，享年八十一歲（一八七四～一九五日）。

美國總統艾森豪特使符立德上將晉謁蔣介石總統，商談中美有關問題。

五月十八日　蔣介石總統命令，特任張群為中華民國總統府秘書長。

五月二十日　中華民國行憲第二任總統蔣介石、副總統陳誠，舉行宣誓就職典禮。蔣總統發表就職宣言：「第一，實現民主，爭取自由；第二，光復大陸，重建中華。」

五月二十日　蔣介石總統批准行政院長陳誠辭職，同時提名俞鴻鈞繼任行政院長，咨請立法院同意。

六月三日　中華民國新任行政院長俞鴻鈞首次主持政務會議，通過改組台灣省政府，任命嚴家淦為主席，連震東為民政廳長等人事案。

六月十六日　陸軍軍官學校建校三十週年校慶，蔣介石總統親臨鳳山主持校慶典禮，並致訓勉以恢復黃埔精神，喚醒黃埔靈魂。

六月廿一日　蔣介石總統發表命令，參謀總長周至柔任期屆滿，另有任用，著即免職，並特任桂永清為參謀總長。

六月廿四日　蔣介石總統發表命令，特任孫立人為總統府參軍長，黃杰為陸軍總司令、梁序昭為海軍總司令，王叔銘為空軍總司令，張彝鼎為國防部總政治部主任。

六月廿九日　日本劫掠中國名貴鑽石一、六三五粒，共重三六八‧一七克拉，經我駐日代表收回運抵台北。

六月廿八日　中華民國發表聲明，海軍在台灣海峽捕獲之蘇聯油輪「陶甫斯」號，船上載有對中共禁運之戰略物資。

七月一日　蔣介石總統發表命令，特任周至柔為國防會議秘書長，黃鎮球為國防會議副秘書長，黃仁霖兼代聯合勤務總司令。

七月六日　中華民國立法院會議通過「外國人投資條例」。

七月十六日　蔣介石總統發表命令，總統府設立光復大陸設計研究委員會，以副總統陳誠為主任委員。

七月廿一日　中華民國經濟部長尹仲容，在立法院報告關於水泥、紙業、工礦及農林四大國營企業移轉民營辦理情形。

七月卅一日　亞洲人民反共聯盟中華民國總會在台北正式成立，舉行會議通過會章，並選舉谷正綱等為理事。

七月卅一日　中共政府總理周恩來在蘇聯訪問後，已返抵北京。他於廿九日與蘇聯共黨領袖馬林可夫及赫魯雪夫會談。

八月二日　中國國民黨第七屆中央委員會第四次全體會議在台北市陽明山開幕。

八月四日　北京新華社報導，「全國縣級人民代表大會」已完成選舉，共選出省市級人民代表一六、八○七人。

八月五日　中國國民黨第七屆中央委員會第四次全體會議，通過「建立基層幹部制度綱要」。

八月八日　自美國駛回的「洛陽」、「漢陽」號兩艘驅逐艦，抵達台灣南部左營海軍基地，編入戰鬥序列。

八月十一日　北京中央人民政府第三十三次會議開幕，通過於今年九月十五日召開「全國人民代表大會案」。

八月十二日　中華民國參謀總長桂永清在台北逝世，享年五十五歲（一九○○～一九五四）。

八月十三日　蔣介石總統發表命令，任命副參謀總長彭孟緝代理參謀總長。

八月十八日　美國太平洋艦隊總司令史敦普上將抵達台北訪問。

八月廿四日　為改善台北鬧區交通秩序，中山北路天橋興工修建。

八月廿七日　台灣出版的「自由中國」等七十五家雜誌發表聯合聲明，響應文化清潔運動。
中華民國內政部下令，對「中國新聞」、「鈕司」、「新聞觀察」等十種誨淫誨盜雜誌，

分別處以定期停刊處分。

八月廿九日　蔣介石總統發表命令，任命黃珍吾為台北衛戍司令，羅友倫為憲兵司令。

九月三日　金門前線發生激烈砲戰，對岸共軍向國軍防地發射砲彈數千發。

九月五日　蔣介石總統任命蔣經國為國防會議副秘書長。

九月八日　中華民國噴射式機群首次出動，飛臨廈門上空作戰，另批機群協同海軍轟擊共軍陣地。

九月九日　美國國務卿杜勒斯抵台北訪問，晉謁蔣介石總統，會談三小時之久，就當前局勢及有關中美問題，廣泛交換意見。

九月十五日　中共政府「第一屆全國人民代表大會」在北京開幕，出席代表一千二百廿六人。（大會於九月廿八日閉幕，大會通過「中華人民共和國憲法，並選舉毛澤東為中央人民政府主席及朱德為副主席等案」。）

九月十七日　九月十七日為甲午中日戰爭六十週年紀念日，中華民國海軍總司令部官兵集會紀念。

九月廿一日　聯合國第九屆大會開幕，蘇聯提議以北京政府取代中華民國代表權，經大會以四十三票對十一票予以否決。

九月廿九日　浙閩沿海戰事，已擴大至馬祖方面，中共軍機空襲大陳島，被國軍擊落一架。蘇聯共黨首領赫魯雪夫及布加寧等抵達北京訪問。

十月九日　中華民國行政院公布「動員時期無線電器材管制辦法」。

十月十日　蔣介石總統主持中樞雙十國慶紀念典禮，發表「告全國軍民書」，並校閱三軍及接受各國駐華使節賀忱。

十月十六日　美國前駐華大使司徒雷登著《旅華五十年回憶錄》出版，頌揚蔣介石總統為中國人民意志的代表，自由中國的象徵。司徒雷登曾任北京燕京大學校長多年。

十月廿二日　蔣介石總統夫人宋美齡自美返抵台北。

十月廿三日　台灣省東西縱貫公路高級路面完工通車。

十月廿五日　台灣省各界慶第九屆光

復節。

十月廿九日　金門及一江山均發生砲戰。

十一月一日　中華民國行政院設置「國軍退除役官兵就業輔導委員會」，以嚴家淦為主任委員。

台灣省民防司令部在台北成立。

十一月三日　中國國民黨中央評議委員、前海南行政長官陳濟棠在台北逝世，享年六十四歲（一八九一～一九五四）。

十一月九日　蔣介石總統應美國第七艦隊普賴德中將邀請，乘美海軍潛水艇出海巡視。

中華民國行政院命令內政部，將「戰時出版品禁止或限制登載事項」暫緩實施，因該禁例內容尚欠明確具體，引起新聞界一致反對。

十一月十一日　北京政府「國家統計局」發表關於全國人口調查統計公報說，包括海外及邊疆人口在內，人口總數計六億五千六百六十三萬餘人。

十一月十二日　中國國民黨紀念國父中山先生誕辰及建黨六十週年，在台北市中山堂舉行慶祝大會。

十一月十四日　中華民國海軍太平號軍艦在浙海巡邏突遭共軍海軍擊沉。

十一月十七日　國軍太平號軍艦在浙海被共軍擊沉，獲救官兵乘艦返抵台灣南部海軍左營基地，全國各地紛紛響應獻艦復仇運動。

十一月廿四日　中國國民黨建黨六十週年紀念日，海內外舉行熱烈慶祝。

南京國立政治大學（原為中國國民黨中央政治學校），獲准在台北復校，由劉季鴻任校長，研究部正式開學。

十一月廿六日　中共軍隊以一百五十艘機帆船進攻烏丘島，被國軍艦隊擊退。

十一月廿九日　美國軍方將首批軍刀式噴射戰鬥機移交與中華民國空軍總司令部。

十二月一日　美國第七艦隊改隸美國太平洋艦隊，仍巡邏台灣海峽。

十二月三日　中美共同防衛條約在華府正式簽字，全文十條，在台

北及華盛頓同時公布。

美國國務卿杜勒斯解釋中美共同防衛條約履行程序說：「為應付共產黨侵犯危機，美國總統可斷然行動。」

十二月七日　北京中共政府總理周恩來發表聲明說，「美國與台灣當局簽訂的共同防衛條約是非法的無效的」。

十二月十四日　美國援助的第三批軍刀式噴射戰鬥機抵達台灣。

十二月十六日　中華民國行政院會議通過「中美共同防衛條約」。

十二月廿六日　中華民國司法部次長查良鑑自美返台，向政府報告控訴「毛邦初侵吞公帑案」經過情形。

十二月三十日　蔣介石總統與美國參謀首長聯席會議主席雷德福上將舉行軍事會議，檢討現行軍事情勢。

中華民國四十四年（一九五五）

一月一日　蔣介石總統主持中樞開國紀念典禮，並發表告全國軍民書，勗勉同胞「厲行戰時生活，發揚法治精神，齊向勝利目標前進」。

一月九日　中共飛機百餘架次空襲大陳列島，投彈三百餘枚，軍民多人傷亡，被國軍地面砲火擊毀兩架。

一月十四日　中華民國立法院會議，通過「中美共同防衛條約」。

一月十八日　中共陸海空軍猛攻大陳列島外圍島嶼一江山，國軍守軍英勇奮戰，苦撐至三晝夜，卒以一江山孤懸不敵，陷落共軍之手。國軍守軍自司令王生明、參謀長王日誥以次共七百廿人，全體壯烈成仁。

一月廿二日　美國航空母艦混合艦隊駛入台灣海峽。

一月廿七日　美國遠東空軍總司令部宣布，美空軍第十八戰鬥轟炸機航空隊，移駐台灣擔任臨時任務。

一月廿九日　美國會參議院大會以八十五對三票通過決議，授權艾森豪總統使用武裝部隊協防台灣澎湖有關地區。

一月三十日　美國太平洋艦隊總司令史敦普上將第三度訪問台灣。美國水利專家薩凡奇勘察石門水庫基地。

二月一日　大陳島有海空戰鬥，中華

民國空軍炸沉一艘大型中共軍艦。

二月二日　北京人民政府「文字改革委員會」發表「漢字簡化方案草案」。

二月三日　美國遠東空軍總司令柏楚琪上將抵達台北訪問。

二月五日　美國總統艾森豪下令美國第七艦隊協助中華民國自大陳島撤退軍民，並準備迎擊中共軍隊挑戰。

美國太平洋地面部隊總司令克拉克中將抵達台灣訪問。

二月七日　大陳島軍民開始撤退，中美強大聯合艦隊已通過台灣海峽駛抵大陳，從事掩護撤退。

二月八日　蔣介石總統對海內外同胞發表廣播演說，指出此次大陳駐軍之轉移地區，乃適應新戰略需要，並與友邦共同致力防衛西太平洋之配合行動。

二月九日　美國參議院以六十四票對六票表決通過「中美共同防禦條約」。

二月十日　大陳義民一萬四千四百八十三人，全部安全撤抵台灣基隆。

二月十七日　北京人民政府國務院會議通過「發行新人民幣方案」。（自三月一日起新人民幣正式發行，舊幣以一萬對一收回。）

二月廿三日　美國第五航空隊司令藍密中將抵達台北訪問。

三月一日　中國國民黨第七屆中央委員會第五次全體會議在台北市陽明山舉行。蔣介石總裁在會議中致辭，訓勉全體同志應提振革命精神，創造新風氣，勵行戰時生活，為社會民眾服務。

三月三日　中美共同防禦條約生效，由中華民國外交部長葉公超及美國國務卿杜勒斯代表兩國政府，在台北市中山堂互換批准書。

美國國務卿杜勒斯晉謁蔣介石總統，商談有關中美共同防禦條約實施之具體步驟。

三月七日　美國援助中華民國登陸艇二十二艘在高雄舉行交接儀式。

三月十六日　美國國務院公布一九四五年，美英與蘇聯簽訂之雅爾達會議密約全文。

三月二十日　美國第七艦隊司令蒲賴

德抵達台灣訪問。

三月三十日　美國總統艾森豪對記者招待會說：「為了不能損害自由中國的士氣，及斷絕他們的希望，美國決定協防金門、馬祖。」

四月三日　美國陸軍部長史蒂文森抵台北訪問，與蔣介石總統商談中美有關問題。

四月四日　美國空軍第十六軍刀式噴射機截擊隊，自琉球調駐台灣。

四月五日　美國遠東空軍總司令柏楚琪抵達台北訪問。

英國首相邱吉爾辭職，艾登繼任英首相。

四月十日　前台灣省政府財政廳長任顯群以掩護中共間諜罪被保安司令部逮捕。

四月廿四日　美國政府以台灣地區緊張情勢繼續存在，特命參謀首長聯席會議主席雷福德上將及國務院主管遠東事務助理國務卿勞勃森到台北，與蔣介石總統會商有關中美共同防禦條約實施問題。

四月廿六日　美國第七艦隊司令蒲賴德中將宣布，第七艦隊台灣聯絡中心正式成立。

四月廿八日　中華民國行政院會議通過防空疏散計劃，規定台灣省政府所屬各機關，在六個月內疏散到台灣中部。

五月一日　蔣介石總統核定，中華民國常備兵現役服役期間，自兩年縮短為一年四個月。

五月六日　中華民國國防部宣布，國軍已在各外島領海內佈設防禦性水雷。

五月七日　美國第七艦隊司令蒲賴德中將與美國援華軍事顧問團長蔡斯少將，首次到金門訪問。

五月九日　中華民國國防部宣布，定九月三日為「軍人節」，原有各軍種節日一律廢除。

美國太平洋艦隊總司令史敦普上將，第四度抵達台北訪問。

五月十四日　蘇聯與東歐七個附庸國家在波蘭首都華沙簽訂「安全條約」，並成立統帥部設於莫斯科。

六月五日　台灣省立師範學院奉令改制為國立師範大學。

六月十日　台灣省保安司令部公布，「前在大陸被迫附共分子辦理登記辦法」。

六月十四日　中華民國與美國在華盛
　　　　　頓舉行「原子能和平用途協
　　　　　定」初簽儀式。

六月二十日　蔣介石總統命令，特任
　　　　　彭孟緝為參謀總長，黃仁霖為
　　　　　聯合勤務總司令。
　　　　　美國軍事援華顧問團團長蔡斯
　　　　　少將退休，由史邁斯少將繼任
　　　　　團長。

六月廿七日　中華民國空軍巡邏機兩
　　　　　架，及復興航空公司「藍天
　　　　　鵝」客機一架，在台灣海峽上
　　　　　空，突遭中共噴射機八架圍
　　　　　攻，巡邏機一架中彈墜海，另
　　　　　一架受傷後仍安然返防，「藍
　　　　　天鵝」亦中彈百餘發，亦仍飛
　　　　　抵台北。

七月三日　美國空軍第六十七戰鬥轟
　　　　　炸噴射機中隊，由琉球調駐台
　　　　　灣。

七月五日　北京人民政府「全國人民
　　　　　代表大會」第一屆第二次會在
　　　　　北京開幕。

七月七日　美國遠東空軍總司令庫特
　　　　　上將、美國太平洋空軍司令史
　　　　　密斯，及美國第十三航空隊司
　　　　　令李威廉同行抵台灣訪問。

八月二十日　中華民國總統府參軍長

孫立人，因「中共間諜郭廷亮
案」，引咎呈請處分。蔣介石
總統命令予以免職，並令派陳
誠、王寵惠、許世英、張群、
何應欽、吳忠信、王雲五、黃
少谷及俞大維等九人組織調查
委員會，秉公徹查。
蔣介石總統命令任命黃鎮球為
總統府參軍長。

九月三日　中華民國第一屆軍人節，
　　　　　各地舉行敬軍勞軍等活動。

九月四日　金門前線發生激烈砲戰，
　　　　　廈門中共砲兵發射砲彈二五四
　　　　　發。

九月二十日　聯合國第十屆大會在紐
　　　　　約開幕，蘇聯又提出以中共政
　　　　　權取代中華民國代表權案，經
　　　　　大會以四十二票對十二票的表
　　　　　決加以否決。

十月一日　菲律賓外交部宣布，菲律
　　　　　賓駐中華民國公使館升格為大
　　　　　使館。

十月三日　中國國民黨第七屆中央委
　　　　　員會第六次全體會議在台北市
　　　　　陽明山開幕。

十月四日　北京政府國務院會議通過
　　　　　「漢字簡化方案修正草案」。

十月六日　中國國民黨第七屆中央委

員會第六次全體會議通過「對國際關係與外交之決議案」等要案後舉行閉幕儀式。

十月十日　中華民國國慶紀念日，蔣介石總統發表告全國軍民書，勗勉同胞承接辛亥革命精神，負起反共復國責任。

十月二十日　前總統府參軍長孫立人案調查委員會提出調查報告，蔣介石總統以孫立人抗戰有功，特准予自新，毋庸議處。（孫立人將軍自此遭幽禁達三十年之久，於一九九一年始獲得自由。）

十月廿一日　中華民國政府宣布，終止對德國（西德）的戰爭狀態。

十月廿五日　台灣省光復十週年紀念大會在台北總統府前廣場舉行，蔣介石總統偕夫人蒞臨總統府陽台接受二十萬民眾歡呼致敬。

北京人民政府發表聲明有權要求收回澳門，葡萄牙政府被迫取消明朝政府割讓澳門四百年週年紀念。

十月卅一日　美國新任第七艦隊司令殷格索中將抵台北訪問。

十一月一日　中華民國金門前線陸海空三軍部隊舉行聯合大演習。

十一月八日　中華民國立法院會議通過「華僑回國投資條例」。

十一月十二日　中華民國國父中山先生九十誕辰，蔣介石總統主持中樞紀念大會，全國各地均熱烈慶祝。

十一月十四日　中華民國住聯合國代表團發表聲明，堅決反對外蒙古參加聯合國組織。

十一月廿四日　中國國民黨中央委員會黨政關係會議改組為「中央常務委員會政策委員會」。

十二月一日　台灣省第一期甲種國民兵分別入營服役。

十二月十一日　美國陸軍部長布魯克抵台灣訪問。

十二月十三日　中華民國駐聯合國代表團長蔣廷黻，在聯合國安全理事會會議中投票否決外蒙古進入聯合國組織案。安全理事會進行表決新會員案時，蘇聯代表首先對南韓及越南入會案加以否決，中華民國即對外蒙古入會案加以否決。

十二月廿七日　日本新任大使崛內謙介向蔣介石總統呈遞到任國書。

十二月廿九日　金門前線發生激烈砲
　　　　戰。

中華民國四十五年（一九五六）

一月一日　蔣介石總統主持中樞開國
　　　　紀念典禮，並發表告全國軍民
　　　　同胞書，昭示今年中心工作為
　　　　反共復國心理建設的精神動
　　　　員。

一月四日　美國參謀首長聯席會議主
　　　　席雷福德上將抵台北，主持協
　　　　防台灣的軍事會議。

一月九日　中華民國國防部與美軍援
　　　　華顧問團發表聯合公報說，美
　　　　國協助國軍成立九個預備師。

一月十五日　中國國民黨台灣省黨部
　　　　第三次全省代表大會在台北開
　　　　幕，蔣介石總裁在開幕會議中
　　　　指示今後建設台灣之十項中心
　　　　工作。

一月卅一日　北京人民政府國務院公
　　　　布「關於漢字簡化方案的決
　　　　議」。

二月一日　台灣省鐵路局柴油特快火
　　　　車開始行駛，自台北到高雄只
　　　　需五小時半。

二月五日　中國陰曆丙申年新年，台
　　　　灣省各界慶祝農民節。

二月十六日　美國國務卿杜勒斯抵台
　　　　北訪問，主持中美協商會議。

三月一日　美國贈送之「咸陽」號軍
　　　　艦駛抵台灣高雄港。

三月二十日　中華民國駐美國大使顧
　　　　維鈞博士辭職。

四月一日　中華民國國防部宣布，為
　　　　保持國軍部隊戰力，決定實施
　　　　「官兵退除役總檢辦法」。

四月五日　中華民國行政院會議通
　　　　過，任命駐日本大使董顯光博
　　　　士為駐美國大使，接替顧維鈞
　　　　職缺。

四月十六日　中國青年黨實現團結後
　　　　的新中央黨務委員會舉行成立
　　　　儀式。

四月十八日　蘇聯共產黨中央宣布，
　　　　解散「共產國際情報局組
　　　　織」。

四月廿三日　北京人民政府宣布成立
　　　　「西藏自治區籌備委員會」。

四月廿八日　中共主席毛澤東提出
　　　　「百花齊放，百家爭鳴」方
　　　　針。

五月五日　中國國民黨第七屆中央委
　　　　員會第七次全體會議在台北市
　　　　陽明山開幕，蔣介石總裁訓勉
　　　　同志「反共復國戰爭為一革命

戰爭」。

五月十二日　中華民國國防部決定，在軍中全面推行國語注音符號教育。

五月廿三日　中華民國外交部照會菲律賓政府，重申南沙群島為中華民國領土。

六月三日　中華民國內政部自六月三日午夜零時開始舉行「戶口普查」試查。

六月六日　中華民國新任駐美國大使董顯光博士，在華府向美國總統艾森豪呈遞國書。

六月三十日　台灣省訓練團正式成立。

七月二日　中華民國國防部總政治部主任蔣堅忍就職。

七月七日　美國副總統尼克森偕夫人，自越南西貢抵達台北，對中華民國作友好訪問。尼克森向蔣介石總統面遞艾森豪總統函件並會談中美問題。

七月十日　蔣介石總統命令，公布「反共抗俄戰士授田憑據頒發辦法」。

金門、馬祖地區成立戰地政務委員會，福建省政府將遷駐台北市辦公。

七月二十日　馬祖北方海面上空發生激烈空戰，中華民國空軍飛機擊落中共米格式噴射機四架，並擊傷兩架。

七月廿五日　台灣省北部地區中華民國駐軍舉行首次聯合大演習，歷時一週，於今日結束。

七月廿七日　台灣省政府第一批疏散人員，決定於八月一日開始在中部城市辦公。

八月四日　中華民國國防部長俞大維，偕美國第七艦隊司令殷格索中將赴馬祖視察。

八月廿二日　中國共產黨舉行第七屆中央委員會第七次全體會議，討論有關召開第八屆全國代表大會問題。

八月廿七日　蔣介石總統手諭總統府秘書長張群，飭知各機關「切勿發起與祝壽有關之任何舉動，並嚴禁募款。」（蔣總統今年七十歲華誕）

九月三日　強烈颱風「黛納」來襲，在台灣花蓮、宜蘭地區登陸，使台灣北部受災頗重。

九月十五日　馬祖島前線發生砲戰，中共砲兵對高登、北竿兩島發射砲彈六百十發。

九月十七日　中央通訊社開始使用十
　　　　　瓩發報機，對美國播發中華民
　　　　　國的中英文新聞。

九月廿八日　中國共產黨第八屆中央
　　　　　委員第一次全體會議在北京集
　　　　　會，選出毛澤東為中央委員會
　　　　　主席，劉少奇、周恩來、朱德
　　　　　及陳雲為副主席，鄧小平為總
　　　　　書記，董必武為中央監察委員
　　　　　會主席。

十月四日　美國中央情報局長艾倫、
　　　　　杜勒斯抵台灣訪問。

十月十日　蔣介石總統主持民國四十
　　　　　五年中樞國慶典禮，發表告全
　　　　　國軍民書及檢閱三軍。

十月十一日　九龍毀旗事件擴大，騷
　　　　　動地區死傷多人，香港政府宣
　　　　　布實施戒嚴。港九僑胞慶祝雙
　　　　　十國慶，香港政府職員撕毀中
　　　　　華民國國旗，英警開槍殺人，
　　　　　因而釀成事件。

十月廿三日　匈牙利首都布達佩斯爆
　　　　　發反共革命，蘇聯軍隊開入大
　　　　　屠殺鎮壓。

十月卅一日　蔣介石總統七十歲華
　　　　　誕，全國軍民熱烈慶祝。友邦
　　　　　元首紛電蔣總統祝壽。

十月卅一日　中華民國台閩地區戶口

普查初步統計，接受普查總戶
數為一百六十八萬六千三百五
十七戶（國軍及駐外人員戶數
除外），常住人口總計為九百
八十七萬四千四百五十人，其
中男性計五百二十八萬二千三
百十七人，女性計四百五十九
萬二千一百卅三人。

十一月二日　台灣省政府舉辦全省戶
　　　　　口普查發表初步統計，常住人
　　　　　口計九百三十一萬餘人，其中
　　　　　男性比女性多十八萬餘人。

十一月二日　中華民國國軍在湖口舉
　　　　　行「紫宸」演習，蔣介石總統
　　　　　親臨校閱，參加的陸軍一師之
　　　　　眾，飛機兩百架，及空降部隊
　　　　　八百餘人。

十一月七日　蔣介石總統電賀艾森豪
　　　　　當選連任美國總統，陳誠副總
　　　　　統亦電賀尼克森當選連任美國
　　　　　副總統。

十一月十二日　中華民國國父中山先
　　　　　生九十一歲誕辰，全國各地盛
　　　　　大慶祝。中國國民黨中央委員
　　　　　會發表「告全黨同志書」。

十一月十四日　台灣省政府決定於十
　　　　　六日起，各廳處均疏遷往台灣
　　　　　中部的中興新村，於廿二日起

停止辦公五天，將自十二月一日起在中部恢復辦公。

十一月十六日　聯合國大會以四十七票對廿四票的表決，否決印度提出之使中共政府加入聯合國組織案。

十一月廿一日　中國國民黨中央常務委員會會議通過，「海外對中共鬥爭工作統一領導辦法」。

十二月一日　蔣介石總統手著「蘇俄在中國」一書今日出版，並將出版英、法、德、俄、日等文譯本。
美國國務院發表「中美外交關係文件」包括一九四二年起之八年期間檔案。

十二月二十日　中華民國海軍首次舉行原子彈防護演習。國軍四萬餘人退除役官兵，經政府予妥善安置就業。

中華民國四十六年（一九五七）

一月一日　蔣介石總統主持中樞開國紀念典禮，發表元旦告全國軍民同胞書。

一月三日　中華民國與美國協議，由美援撥款在台灣中部清泉崗修建新式軍用飛機場。

一月十一日　中華民國著名外交家顧維鈞博士當選國際法庭法官。

一月十四日　中國國民黨中央常務委員會通過「戰地政務實施綱要」。

一月十九日　美國第七艦隊新任司令畢克萊中將抵台灣訪問。

一月廿七日　畢克萊將軍接任美國第七艦隊司令，原司令殷格索專任美軍協防台灣司令。

二月十日　美國太平洋艦隊總司令史敦普上將，第七度訪華，與蔣介石總統會談。

二月廿六日　中華民國國防部總政治部擴大政工會議在台北舉行，會期三天。

三月四日　中國國民黨第七屆中央委員會第八次全體會議在台北市陽明山開幕，蔣介石總裁親臨主持，對大會講述「反攻復國的基本條件」。

三月十六日　馬祖前線高登島發生激烈砲戰，中共砲兵發射砲彈六百餘發，國軍無損傷。

三月十八日　美國海軍部宣布，任命陶艾爾中將為美軍協防台灣司令，接替殷格索的司令職務。

三月廿五日　西歐六國共同市場條約

在羅馬舉行簽字儀式，同時簽訂原子能共營條約。

四月二日　中華民國中央研究院遷台灣後之首次院士會議在台北舉行，國內外院士九人參加。

四月九日　中共黨報人民日報發表社論：「繼續放手貫徹百花齊放，百家爭鳴的方針」。

四月十日　美國駐華大使藍欽發表聲明說，美國軍人雷諾槍殺華人劉自然案必將合理解決。

四月十二日　美國第七艦隊司令畢克萊中將暗示，美國第七艦隊航空母艦已裝備原子武器，美艦在台灣海峽曾與中共潛水艇接觸。

四月廿一日　台灣省全省第三屆省議員及縣市長選舉同時舉行。

四月廿六日　台灣第一家製造汽車公司——裕隆機器廠——首批出廠吉甫車十輛，自台北出發駛往高雄，作四百公里的長途試車。

四月廿七日　中國共產黨中央委員會發表「整風運動指示」，開始全面整風。

五月六日　中共「統戰部」在北京召開黨派座談會。

五月八日　美軍「鬥牛士」式飛彈部隊已進駐台灣基地。此種戰術性飛彈可裝備原子彈頭。

五月十五日　中共「新民主主義青年團」召開第三次全國代表大會，通過新團章，改名為「共產主義青年團」。

五月廿一日　台北松山機場新跑道落成啟用，可供巨型民航客機起降。

五月廿三日　美軍顧問團軍事法庭審理美軍上士雷諾槍殺劉自然案判決無罪，中華民國司法行政部認為顯然有失公平。

五月廿四日　劉自然案判決事件引起台北市民憤慨，湧至美國駐華大使館抗議，將美使館搗毀，美國新聞處亦被破壞。

五月廿五日　劉自然案不幸事件，美國國會將加以調查。中國之友諾蘭參議員聞訊表示震驚。行政院召開臨時院會商討善後。美國駐華大使藍欽向美國務院報告稱，美大使館職員八人受輕傷。

中華民國駐美大使董顯光向美國務院表示道歉。行政院長及副院長及全體政務委員為此不

幸事件引咎辭職，經蔣介石總統予以慰留。

五月廿六日　中華民國行政院因劉自然案事件提出總辭已奉蔣總統慰留，行政院命令將三名治安官員撤職，並命令陸軍總司令黃杰兼任台北衛戍司令，吳志勛代理憲兵司令，及陳友欽代理台灣省警務處長。

五月廿九日　美國國務卿杜勒斯告訴記者會說，美國對華政策，不受台北劉自然案事件影響。

六月一日　蔣介石總統為五月廿四日台北意外事件告誡國人「應及時反省，在反共鬥爭中，必須明是非，辨敵友。」

六月二日　台灣省第三屆臨時省議會成立，黃朝琴任議長，謝東閔任副議長。（第三屆臨時省議會後改為第一屆省議會。）

六月三日　蔣介石總統接見訪華之日本首相岸信介，商談中日及世局有關問題。

六月五日　美國總統艾森豪對台北不幸事件評論說，美國對中華民國的友好關係，絕不因此有所變更。

六月廿二日　金門前線發生激烈砲戰，廈門中共砲兵發射砲彈一千餘發。

六月廿五日　蔣介石總統發佈命令，特任黃杰為總統府參軍長，王叔銘為參謀總長，彭孟緝為陸軍總司令兼台灣防衛總司令，陳嘉尚為空軍總司令，及黃鎮球為台北衛戍司令。

七月三日　蘇聯共黨內鬨，馬林可夫、莫洛托夫等人被整肅，赫魯雪夫獨攬大權。

七月五日　中國國民黨中央委員會秘書長張厲生發表聲明表示，國民黨在國外絕無政治活動，旨在澄清馬來亞聯邦首長對中國國民黨所發生之誤解。

七月十六日　蔣介石總統接見台北市報業公會十三家會員報紙主持人及十二家報紙報紙總主筆和總編輯等三十二人，指示兩點：提高警覺勿為中共所利用及社會新聞需著重教育意義。

七月廿二日　新任美軍協防台灣司令竇亦樂抵達台北，接替殷格索職務。

八月八日　蔣介石總統命令，任命周至柔為台灣省政府主席，嚴家淦為行政院政務委員。

九月六日　中華民國國防部發言人說：「我國空軍攔截偵察機，已經全部噴射式化。」

九月廿五日　聯合國大會否決印度提出之使北京政府進入聯合國組織案。

北京當局發表，武漢長江大橋工程全部完工，定於十月十五日開放交通。

十月一日　中華民國與美國定十月八日及十一月十四日，在台北及華府簽訂郵政匯兌協定，恢復辦理中美郵政匯兌服務。

十月十日　蔣介石總統主持中樞雙十國慶紀念典禮，發表告全國軍民同胞書，昭示六大自由與三項保證，號召大陸中共人員等參加反共革命大業。

中國國民黨第八次全國代表大會在台北市陽明山舉行開幕儀式，蔣介石總裁親臨主持開幕典禮並致辭講述「革命形勢和大會使命」。

十月十六日　台灣省政府新聞處宣布，台灣現有報紙二十八家，日出四十餘萬份，出版社書店三百餘家。

著名國畫家齊白石在北京逝世，享年九十五歲（一八六三～一九五七）。

十月十八日　中國國民黨第八屆全國代表大會，通過蔣總裁提議「本黨增設副總裁案」。（二十日通過蔣介石總裁連任案，並通過政綱及現階段黨務工作綱領。廿三日通過陳誠為副總裁案，以及陳誠、蔣經國等五十人為中央委員等案後閉幕。）

十月卅一日　中國科學家楊振寧與李政道兩教授，合作研究推翻「對等定律」，共同獲得諾貝爾物理學獎。

十一月四日　蔣介石總統發表命令，任命胡適博士為中央研究院院長，接替朱家驊職務。

十一月十一日　蔣介石總統偕夫人親臨美國第七艦隊航空母艦「個儻之李卻特」號參觀大演習，中華民國軍艦四艘亦參加大演習。

十一月十九日　美國空軍部宣布，美國空軍屠牛式飛彈部隊，十一月底派駐台灣。

十二月十日　中國科學家楊振寧與李政道，在瑞典京城斯德哥爾摩

接受諾貝爾物理學獎。

十二月十一日　中共政府國務院會議通過「漢語拼音方案」。

十二月十七日　美國務院正式宣佈，莊萊德為駐中華民國大使，接替藍欽的職務，藍欽已奉調任美國駐南斯拉夫大使。

十二月廿五日　北京人民日報報導說，「台盟總部」舉行多次會議後，宣布聲討「叛徒謝雪紅及其他台盟右派分子」。

中華民國四十七年（一九五八）

一月一日　蔣介石總統主持中樞開國紀念典禮，發表告全國軍民同胞書，昭示把握有利機運，爭取反攻勝利。

北京政府宣布，自陝西省寶雞至四川省會成都的寶成鐵路建成開放通車。

一月三日　蔣介石總統接見民社黨主席徐傅霖等人士。

一月十二日　中國民主社會黨主席徐傅霖病逝台北，享年七十九歲（一八七〇～一九五八）。

一月十九日　台灣省全省四百餘萬選民，參加投票選舉第四屆縣市議員。

一月二十日　美軍協防台灣司令竇亦樂中將對記者會宣布，中共若在台灣海峽挑釁，必將遭到飛彈報復。

二月一日　中華民國與英國協議恢復辦理郵政匯兌業務。

二月一日　中共「全國人民代表大會」第一屆第五次會議，通過展開所謂「大躍進運動」。

二月五日　中國國民黨台灣省黨部第四屆委員會召開首次會議，選舉任覺五為主任委員。

二月十四日　中華民國行政院長俞鴻鈞呈請辭去本兼各職。（蔣介石總統十六日批示慰留。）

二月廿六日　美國贈送中華民國軍艦十一艘，在台灣南部海軍基地移交與國軍。

三月八日　美國新任駐華大使莊萊德，向蔣介石總統呈遞到任國書。莊萊德在抗戰期間曾任美國駐成都總領事。

三月八日　中華民國政府宣布，將於本年七月一日開始實施公務人員保險辦法。

三月十四日　蔣介石總統與美國國務卿杜勒斯會談有關加強中美合作問題。

美國駐遠東使節會議在台北舉行，由杜勒斯主持。

三月十五日　中華民國司法院長王寵惠病逝台北，享年七十八歲（一八八一～一九五八）。

三月十七日　美國太平洋區總司令史敦普上將宣布，美國駐中華民國軍事機構實行改組合併，成立美軍駐台協防軍援司令部。

三月廿七日　蘇聯總理布加寧被罷黜，由共黨第一書記赫魯雪夫繼任。

四月三日　中華民國新任國史館長羅家倫宣誓就職。

四月六日　中國國民黨元老馮自由病逝台北，享年七十八歲（一八八一～一九五八）。

四月八日　新任中華民國中央研究院長胡適博士宣誓就職，並主持第三屆院士會議，蔣介石總統親臨致辭。

四月十五日　台灣全省各報紙代表九人至行政院陳情，要求將「出版法修正條文草案」自立法院撤回或函立法院暫停審議，以便廣徵各方意見，從容審慎研究。

四月廿二日　中華民國七十五位立法委員聯銜提案，要求政府撤銷報紙登記限制辦法。

四月廿五日　中國國民黨駐菲律賓支部第十六屆代表大會在馬尼拉開幕，蔣介石總裁頒書面訓詞。

五月一日　蔣介石總統召見台北市聯合報、徵信新聞、中國郵報、民族晚報及大華晚報五報社長，對出版法修正案問題表示關切，願採納新聞界意見。

五月十四日　蔣介石總統命令，特任陸軍二級上將黃鎮球為台灣警備總司令。

五月十五日　大批白米、日用品、傳單，由中華民國空軍飛機進行第四十次空投救濟大陸災胞，遍及浙江、福建、江西、湖南、廣西等五省三十二縣市的城鄉。

五月廿一日　蔣介石總統夫人宋美齡女士赴美國訪問。

六月一日　中共黨雜誌「紅旗」半月刊創刊號出版。

六月廿五日　中華民國立法院三讀通過出版法修正案，台北市報業公會發表聲明，表示以沈痛心情接受事實，以盡人民守法義

務，但表明「爭取新聞自由為
記者天責，不因修正案通過而
解除，仍將不斷要求當局再事
修正，以臻合理完善。」

六月三十日　中華民國行政院長俞鴻
鈞辭職照准，蔣介石總統提名
陳誠繼任，咨請立法院同意。

七月十四日　新任美軍顧問團長杜安
抵台北。

七月廿六日　新任美軍協防台灣司令
史慕德抵台北。

七月廿八日　前美國援華志願空軍飛
虎隊司令陳納德將軍在美國逝
世，蔣介石總統馳電慰唁。

八月一日　中華民國政府開始辦理全
國公務人員保險計劃。

八月十四日　蔣介石總統命令，特任
黃鎮球為總統府參軍長，黃杰
為台灣警備總司令。
馬祖島附近發生激烈空戰，中
華民國軍方說，國軍飛機擊落
三架中共米格十七式機。

八月二十日　蔣介石總統前往金門、
馬祖前線巡視三天後返抵台
北。蔣總統於十八日乘軍艦自
台灣南部基地啟程，十九日到
北竿、高登、馬祖，二十日到
金門和小金門巡視前線陣地。

八月廿一日　蔣介石總統發佈命令，
特任葉公超為中華民國駐美國
大使，接替董顯光職務。

八月廿三日　廈門方面中共軍隊砲兵
猛烈轟金門國軍防地，兩小時
內發射四萬五千餘發砲彈，造
成傷亡兩百餘人，房屋被毀六
十五幢。中華民國金門防衛司
令部中彈，副司令趙家驤、副
司令吉星文（蘆溝橋事變抗日
英雄）及副司令章傑三人不幸
重傷殉職。

八月廿四日　金門戰火激烈，中華民
國國防部稱，國軍擊落中共米
格式戰機三架。
美國國務卿杜勒斯間接警告中
共稱，中共如圖攫奪金門、馬
祖，將被視為威脅和平。

八月廿五日　美國第七艦隊奉命戒備
台灣海峽。

八月廿六日　中共砲兵對金門發射砲
彈五千餘發，國軍亦予猛烈還
擊。

八月廿七日　金門國軍砲兵發揮威
力，摧毀共軍砲兵陣地多處。
共軍整日發射萬餘發砲彈。

八月廿八日　美國派航空母艦一艘、
驅逐艦四艘增援第七艦隊實

力，美國在太平洋的空軍部隊
奉准可在台灣海峽追逐中共飛
機。

八月廿九日　金門國軍砲兵發揮威
力，擊毀共軍砲兵陣地三十餘
處。共軍砲兵七天來共對金門
發射砲彈十二萬餘發。

中共在大陸農村實行「人民公
社」制度。

八月三十日　美國陸軍部長布魯克訪
問台灣，與蔣介石總統晤談。

九月二日　中華民國軍艦在金門料羅
灣擊沉中共艇隻十一艘。中共
軍對金門射擊三千餘發砲彈。

九月四日　艾森豪總統警告中共，對
台灣安全如有必要，美軍立即
協防金門及馬祖。

北京人民政府發表聲明，聲稱
領海的範圍由三海里擴展至十
二海里，表示金馬台澎等為中
國內政問題。

九月五日　美國駐關島的戰略空軍部
隊，奉准攜帶原子炸彈，準備
隨時出擊。

九月六日　美國總統艾森豪在華府召
開重要會議，研討台海形勢，
並發表聲明，準備與中共恢復
會談，強調決不損及中華民國

權利，協防金馬決策不變。

九月七日　中共政府國務院總理周恩
來，發表「關於台灣海峽地區
局勢聲明」。

美國軍艦協同中華民國船團，
護航補給金門成功。第七艦隊
將持續執行護航任務，奉命如
遭攻擊即予還擊。

九月八日　廈門中共砲兵對金門發射
砲彈五萬餘發。

中華民國國防部稱，澄海以東
二十英里海面上空發生激烈空
戰，國軍飛機擊落中共軍機七
架。

蘇聯總理赫魯雪夫致函美國艾
森豪，要求美軍部隊撤離台灣
地區，以利「一項穩定的和
平」。

九月十日　台灣海峽海上運輸暫停，
對金門開始實行空投補給。

九月十一日　廈門中共砲兵對金門射
擊五萬餘發砲彈，國軍砲兵猛
烈還擊。

九月十二日　美國總統艾森豪發表聲
明稱，美國決不在台灣海峽退
卻。

九月十四日　美軍在台灣境內趕建飛
彈基地。

九月十五日　美國代表與中共代表在波蘭首都華沙開始舉行秘密會談。

九月十八日　中華民國國防部說，國軍飛機在金門上空擊落五架中共米格式機，海軍擊沉中共魚雷艇三艘。

美國將首批 F-100 超級軍刀式噴射機移交給中華民國空軍。

九月二十日　中華民國軍方以海空方式對金門列嶼補給，連日均能順利達成任務。

美國太平洋區總司令費爾特上將抵台北訪問。

九月廿一日　金門砲戰迄今將滿月，共軍共發射砲彈三十二萬四千餘發。

九月廿三日　聯合國第十三屆大會，以四十四票對八票的表決拒絕印度所提出的使中共進入聯合國案。

中、美軍事將領在台北舉行會議，檢討台灣海峽軍事情勢。

美國在華沙會談中，已拒絕中共提出的有條件台海停火建議。

九月廿四日　中華民國國防部說，澄海海外上空發生空戰，國軍飛機擊落中共十架米格式機。

九月廿六日　美國國務卿杜勒斯重申美國協防台灣海峽決策，表示若縱容中共進犯金門馬祖，必將危及整個亞洲。

九月廿九日　蔣介石總統告訴中外記者說，金門砲戰乃保衛戰，純為屏障台灣海峽，中共冒險趨向戰爭邊緣，必將導致反共革命。

北京外交部發言人說，中華民國空軍飛機使用美援「響尾蛇」式空對空飛彈擊落共軍飛機。

九月三十日　美國國務卿杜勒斯告記者會說，美國已與十國商討對中共實行經濟制裁，若台灣海峽獲得可靠的停火，美國將贊成中華民國自外島撤出一部分軍隊。

十月一日　蔣介石總統告訴美國記者說，中華民國反對減少外島駐軍。並說，對外傳杜勒斯國務卿談話，殊難置信。

十月二日　艾森豪總統表示，解決台海危機，希望避用武力，認為停火將可提供談判機會。

杜勒斯國務卿向中華民國提出

鄭重保證，美國對華政策無大改變。

十月五日　中共政府國防部長彭德懷發表「告台灣同胞書」，建議同台灣當局「舉行談判，實行和平解決」。同時宣布，從十月六日起，以七天為期停止砲轟金門。

十月六日　蔣介石總統答覆美國記者詢問稱，中共廣播與「我政府和談之說純係離間中美之騙局」。

十月八日　美國宣布美軍護送中華民國補給船到金門的工作已告中止，但聲明若中共再作砲擊，美即恢復護航。

十月十日　蔣介石總統發表雙十國慶告全國軍民同胞書，提示金門戰役意義，對國家民族前途顯示永不為暴力所屈服。
中華民國國防部宣稱，國軍空軍在馬祖海面上空擊落中共米格式機五架。

十月十二日　美國國防部長麥艾樂抵台灣訪問，重申美國對中共絕不姑息。
中共廣播宣布，共軍在金門繼續停火兩星期。中共解放軍總參謀長粟裕被免職，由黃克誠繼任。

十月廿三日　美國務卿杜勒斯再度訪華，與蔣介石總統會談後發表中美聯合公報說，雙方咸認在當前情況之下，金、馬、台、澎在防衛上有密切關係。「美國確認中華民國為自由的中國之真正代表，並為億萬中國人民之希望與意願之真正代表。」

十月廿五日　台灣光復節，蔣介石總統發表告台灣全省同胞書，勗勉以光復台灣之精神，為光復大陸而努力。
中共人民政府國防部宣布，共軍逢「單日」對金門砲擊，「雙日停火」。

十月三十日　美軍援助中華民國的新型「M41 與 M42」坦克車，在台灣基地舉行交接儀式。

十一月三日　中國國民黨中央常務委員會通過「粉碎共黨和談陰謀實施計劃要點」。

十一月五日　中華民國國防部宣布，金門國軍砲兵擊毀廈門共軍大砲十五門及一個彈藥庫，共軍對金門射擊砲彈五千餘發。

十一月十七日　中華民國國防部宣布，國軍飛機在九月廿四日的空戰中，首次使用美援的「響尾蛇」飛彈擊落中共的米格式戰機。

十一月廿三日　中華民國行政院會議通過，實施單一匯率制，公司進出口匯出匯入匯率定為新台幣三十六元三角八分兌美金一元。

行政院命令中國銀行與交通銀行在台灣恢復營業。

十二月三日　中國國民黨中央常務委員會會議通過「策進大陸反共革命運動案」。

十二月九日　廈門共軍對金門射擊砲彈三千餘發。

十二月十日　中國共產黨第八屆六中全會閉幕，通過推行「人民公社」基本方針。

十二月十三日　美國第七艦隊司令基維德抵台灣訪問。

十二月十九日　美國空軍宣布，發射重逾四噸的人造地球衛星成功，一百分鐘運行地球一週。

十二月廿七日　西藏人民掀起武裝抗暴，轉戰三個月殺死共黨分子達五萬人，康巴族苦戰結果藏民死亡萬餘人。

十二月廿九日　廈門共軍對金門發射砲彈一千七百餘發。

十二月三十日　中共政府宣布，截至本年十一月初為止，全國各地已成立「人民公社」二萬六千五百多個，公共食堂兩百六十五萬所。

中華民國四十八年（一九五九）

一月一日　蔣介石總統在元旦發表告全國軍民同胞書，重申六大自由、三項保證繼續有效；並以主義為先鋒，武力為後盾，作為全國共同努力的目標。

一月三日　金門發生激烈砲戰，廈門共軍對金門射擊砲彈七千餘發。

一月七日　廈門共軍對金門射擊砲彈三萬三千餘發，中華民國守軍還擊加以壓制。

一月廿九日　菲律賓華僑反共抗俄總會第一次代表大會在馬尼拉開幕。

二月十三日　中華民國前行政院長孔祥熙，向香港政府控告星島日報刊登誹謗文字，經香港法院審結宣判，孔祥熙獲勝，被告

星島日報賠償港幣一萬元。

二月十四日　美國國務卿杜勒斯前患癌症復發，自由世界人士一致表示關切。

二月十九日　美國太平洋艦隊總司令費爾特上將抵台灣訪問。

二月廿四日　日本政府提名井口貞夫為駐華大使。

三月九日　約旦國王胡笙抵達台灣訪問八天，並與蔣總統會談。

三月二十日　西藏人民在首府拉薩展開大規模反共抗暴行動，藏人起義者逾三十萬眾。

三月廿三日　中共軍隊攻陷拉薩。

三月廿六日　中華民國蔣介石總統發表告西藏同胞書：藏胞奮起反共抗暴，政府正予有效援助，號召海內外同胞一致支持。

三月廿八日　北京人民政府國務院下令西藏軍區鎮壓「叛亂」，並以班禪喇嘛替代達賴喇嘛職務。

四月三日　達賴喇嘛自西藏逃抵印度，印度政府宣布予以外交庇護。

四月八日　西藏抗暴軍宣布成立臨時性政權，擁護達賴喇嘛為領袖，繼續與中共戰鬥。

四月十五日　美國總統艾森豪宣布，國務卿杜勒斯因病辭職。

四月十八日　美國總統艾森豪提名赫爾為國務卿。

四月廿七日　中共宣布，劉少奇繼毛澤東為「中央人民政府主席」，朱德為「人民代表大會常務委員長」，周恩來繼任「國務院總理」。毛澤東改任「人民政協名譽主席」。

五月十三日　中華民國政府為保持三軍實力，決定提早役齡一年，滿十九歲即服常備兵補充兵役。

五月十五日　中國國民黨第八屆中央委員第二次全體會議在台北陽明山開幕，蔣介石總裁親臨主持開幕會議，會期三天。

五月十七日　中國國民黨八屆二中全會通過議案，「策進大陸反共革命」。全會決定以唐縱為中央委員會秘書長。

五月廿四日　美國國務卿杜勒斯因病逝世，享年七十二歲（一八八八～一九五九）。

六月十八日　蔣介石總統夫人宋美齡女士旅美國年餘後返抵台北。

六月廿四日　台灣省臨時省議會，正

式改稱為台灣省議會，黃朝琴
任議長。

六月廿九日　蔣介石總統命令，任命
彭孟緝為參謀總長。

七月一日　中華民國中央研究院院士
會議，選出周煒良等九位新院
士。

七月五日　中華民國空軍在馬祖以南
海面上空，擊落中共米格式機
五架。

七月十四日　台灣省鐵路管理局宣
布，台灣鐵路自七月十四日開
始使電氣化設備。

七月十八日　中華民國銓敘部長雷法
章宣布，公教人員保險全面實
施，十七萬人已辦妥保險手
續。

八月二日　中國共產黨第八屆中央委
員第八次全體會議在廬山開
幕，決議整肅國防部長彭德
懷、黃克誠「反黨集團」。

八月三日　日本航空公司新闢台北東
京間航線正式開航。

八月四日　中華民國立法院三讀通過
「戡亂時期軍人婚姻條例」。

八月七日　低氣壓帶來強風暴雨，台
灣中南部十三縣市洪水成災，
受害人民逾萬，為台灣六十年

來最大之水災。

八月八日　中華民國政府宣布調整新
台幣兌美元匯率，定為三十六
元三角八分兌美金一元。

八月十一日　中華民國政府緊急撥款
救濟南部災民，行政院撥款新
台幣二千萬元，台灣省政府撥
款四千三百萬元，全省自十二
日起禁屠八天。

八月十五日　美軍勝利女神力士型飛
彈及全部裝備，移交與中華民
國陸軍使用。

八月廿二日　中華民國國防部宣布，
一年來廈門中央砲兵對金門共
發射砲彈六十四萬三千餘發。

九月二日　台北市民營公論報停刊。

九月七日　印度報紙報導，中共軍隊
數千人侵入印度旁遮普省，拉
哈爾盆地居民四十人被擄去。

九月十七日　中共政府宣布，國防部
長彭德懷被黜，林彪繼任國防
部長，羅瑞卿接替黃克誠為參
謀總長。

九月廿二日　聯合國第十四屆大會，
以四十四票對二十九票及九票
棄權的表決，通過不討論中國
代表權問題。

九月廿八日　台北市民營公論報復

刊，由日出一大張擴增為一張
半。

九月三十日　美國國防部長麥艾樂，
　　　　偕美國空軍參謀長懷特上將等
　　　　一行七人，抵達台灣訪問三
　　　　天。

十月八日　蔣介石總統於十月三日到
　　　　八日期間，在台灣北部及南部
　　　　基地校閱三軍。

十月十日　蔣介石總統主持中樞國慶
　　　　紀念典禮，發表告全國軍民
　　　　書，昭示勝利在望，中共正趨
　　　　向全面崩潰邊緣。

十月十六日　中華民國外交部發言人
　　　　宣稱：「台灣歸還我國開羅會
　　　　議宣言早有明文，自從民國三
　　　　十四年光復之日起，即無所謂
　　　　台灣法律地位問題。」

十月十七日　美國前駐華特使馬歇爾
　　　　元帥，因腦血管等病併發逝
　　　　世，享年七十九歲。

十月廿五日　台灣光復第十四週年，
　　　　各界舉行盛大慶祝活動，省運
　　　　動會開幕。

十一月一日　榮民總醫院在台北市石
　　　　牌揭幕，開始為全國退伍軍人
　　　　服務。

十一月十一日　中華民國國防部宣

稱，國軍退除役官兵九萬餘人
獲得安置。

十一月十七日　印尼政府排華措施，
　　　　強迫華僑集體遷居，造成流血
　　　　事件。
　　　　菲律賓歧視華僑變本加厲，強
　　　　迫華籍旅客於兩週內離境。

十一月廿五日　美國太平洋艦隊總司
　　　　令霍伍德上將抵台灣訪問。

十二月七日　中國國民黨中央常務委
　　　　員會會議決議，重申不贊成修
　　　　憲主張。

十二月十二日　中華民國國營招商局
　　　　「海明」號輪船，自台灣開辦
　　　　美國東海岸港埠定期航線，為
　　　　國輪航行台美航線之始。

十二月十六日　中國國民黨元老吳忠
　　　　信在台北病逝，享年七十三歲
　　　　（一八八七～一九五九）。

十二月廿六日　菲律賓政府取銷華人
　　　　入境禁令，中菲關係恢復正
　　　　常。

中華民國四十九年（一九六〇）

一月一日　蔣介石總統發表告全國軍
　　　　民書，指出反共革命戰爭，在
　　　　武力的對比上，雖是以寡擊眾
　　　　的戰爭，但在人心的對比上，

實為以眾擊寡的戰爭。

北京政府宣布，蘭州至新疆的鐵路，已通車至哈密。

一月六日　蔣介石總統頒佈召集令，中華民國第一屆國民大會第三次會議，定於二月二十日在台北市集會，海內外代表一千五百七十六人，在二月十日起辦理報到手續。

一月十二日　中共空軍米格十五式飛機一架，飛來台灣在宜蘭近郊南澳墜毀。

一月十五日　越南總統吳廷琰抵達台灣訪問五天，蔣介石總統親迎國賓，兩國總統會談中越合作問題。

二月一日　台灣郵政管理局，開辦劃撥儲金匯票業務。

二月四日　中華民國行政院會議通過「台灣省議員選舉罷免規程」。

二月十二日　國民黨中央常務委員會決議，設置中山獎學金鼓勵青年出國深造。

司法院大法官會議議決：憲法所稱國民大會代表總額，在目前情形，應以依法選出而能應召集之國民代會代表人數為計算標準。

二月十三日　郵政儲金匯業局奉准在台灣恢復營業。

二月十六日　台灣海峽上空發生空戰，中華民國巡邏機一架，迎擊十餘架中共米格式機，共機一架中彈起火。同日，東山島附近空戰中，國軍飛機擊落一架中共米格十七式機。

三月一日　天主教樞機主教田耕莘返抵台北，在樺山堂接任台北署理總主教職務。

三月八日　美國核子動力潛水艇劍魚號抵台灣訪問，蔣介石總統應邀登艇參觀。

台灣省中部大旱，日月潭水枯，省政府決定限制用電，影響物價上漲。

三月十一日　國民大會通過修正臨時條款，決議在動員戡亂時期，總統副總統得連選連任。

三月十二日　中國國民黨第八屆中央委員於台北舉行臨時全體會議，會中一致提名總裁蔣介石為中華民國第三任總統候選人，陳誠為副總統候選人。

三月十六日　中華民國與美國海軍舉行「藍星」聯合大演習開始舉

行。

三月廿一日 中華民國第一屆國民大會第三次會議，舉行選舉投票，蔣介石當選中華民國第三任總統。

三月廿二日 國民大會舉行選舉投票，陳誠當選連任中華民國第三任副總統。

三月廿七日 大韓民國總統李承晚宣布辭職。

三月廿九日 青年節，台北市十萬青年舉行慶祝大會。
北京人民政府宣布，在大陸城市建立「人民公社」。

四月四月 美國第七艦隊司令葛利芬中將抵台灣訪問。

四月十日 太平洋區中華民國、大韓民國、美國、泰國、菲律賓及越南六國空軍首長，在台北舉行第三屆空軍首長會議。

四月十四日 中華民國政府公布「博士學位評定會組織條例」。

四月十五日 有關駐華美軍地位協定，美方具體對策已送達中華民國政府，有關當局正在研究中，可望即開始進行談判。

四月廿四日 台灣省舉行選舉，投票選出第二屆省議員及第四屆各縣市長與議員。

五月二日 菲律賓總統賈西亞夫婦抵台灣訪問五天，會商東南亞局勢與中菲兩國合作問題。

五月九日 台灣中部東西橫貫公路舉行通車典禮，由陳誠副總統主持儀式。蔣介石總統頒發訓詞，認為是建設台灣輝煌事蹟之一。公路共分三條，全長三百四十八公里又一百公尺，工程浩大，修築費達三億餘元新台幣。

五月十日 美國總統艾森豪重申協防台灣立場，若中共襲擊外島，美軍即參與防衛金馬。
美國空軍部長夏普抵台灣訪問。

五月十七日 美國援助的 F-104 星式戰鬥機，首批運抵台灣。

五月二十日 中華民國第三任總統蔣介石、副總統陳誠同時宣誓就職。

五月廿三日 中華民國總統府資政閻錫山病逝台北，享年七十八歲（一八八三～一九六〇）。

五月卅一日 中華民國與美國政府同時宣布，美國總統艾森豪定於六月十八日訪問中華民國。

北京中共政府與「蒙古」在庫倫（烏蘭巴托）簽訂「友好互助條約」。

六月二日　台灣省第二屆省議會舉行成立大會，黃朝琴當選為議長，謝東閔當選為副議長。

六月五日　台北市大華晚報與美國長堤世界小姐選舉大會簽訂合約，主辦中國小姐選拔，選出林靜宜為第一屆中國小姐，參加長堤選美大會。

六月八日　中國國民黨中央常務委員會通過，「中日合作經營電視廣播事業方案」。

六月十六日　美國總統艾森豪乘軍艦離開菲律賓，正在來中華民國途中。

六月十七日　美國總統艾森豪乘軍艦來華途中，第七艦隊護衛嚴密，隨時準備應付可能突襲。中共廈門砲兵於十七日夜間廿一時至五十五分，及十八日午夜零時至零時四十五分，兩次對金門射擊砲彈八萬餘發。

六月十八日　美國總統艾森豪蒞華訪問，蔣介石總統親臨機場迎迓，兩國元首保證更密切合作。艾森豪總統在總統府廣場對台北市五十萬民眾歡迎大會中致詞，讚揚中華民國的偉大成就。

六月十九日　中美兩國元首發表聯合公報，強調兩國必須更堅強團結，協同抵禦中共挑釁。
艾森豪總統離華前往大韓民國訪問，蔣介石總統親臨機場送行。
艾森豪總統訪華期間，廈門共軍砲兵三度轟擊金門，總共發射砲彈達八萬八千餘發，國軍砲兵均予還擊壓制。

六月廿三日　美國與日本簽訂的安全條約開始生效。

六月廿五日　西藏人民反共抗暴怒火已蔓延至後藏，拉薩通往新疆的公路交通已被切斷。

七月一日　台北市英文「中國日報」，由油印版改為鉛印報紙。

七月五日　中國國民黨中央邀集有關機關分赴台灣高山地區訪問山胞，研究改善山地同胞生活方案。

七月十六日　國父中山先生手創的美國舊金山華文少年中國晨報，慶祝創刊五十年社慶。

蘇聯共黨突然決定，通知北京中共人民政府稱，將在一個月內將在大陸的一千三百餘名蘇聯專家全部撤回蘇聯。

七月十八日　日本自由民主黨總裁池田勇人，當選為日本新首相，接替岸信介職務。

七月廿一日　中華民國行政院會議通過，「戡亂時期台灣地區入境出境管理辦法修正案」。

八月一日　雪莉颱風來襲，台灣中部地區豪雨成災，蔣介石總統令飭有關單位，採取防護搶救措施。

八月十八日　中華民國行政院決議，將故宮博物院與中央博物院文物自台中遷至台北市。

九月四日　台北市「自由中國」雜誌發行人雷震涉嫌叛亂，被提公訴。

九月六日　中華民國選手楊傳廣，參加在羅馬舉行的第十七屆世界運動會獲得十項運動亞軍獎。

九月八日　中華民國政府核准美國紐約花旗銀行、美國銀行及銀行信託公司來台灣設立分行。

九月十二日　台灣省政府新聞處對台北市公論報提出告誡，因該報刊出「海外人士對雷震案的看法」一文，觸犯出版法及戒嚴時期新聞紙雜誌圖書管理辦法之規定。

九月十九日　新任美國軍事援華顧問團長戴倫少將抵達台北。

九月廿八日　中國國民黨第八屆中央委員會第三次全體會議在台北市陽明山開幕，蔣介石總裁對大會講述：「黨的基本工作與發展方向」。

十月八日　台北市「自由中國」雜誌發行人雷震等涉嫌叛亂，經法院判處有期徒刑十年，劉子英判處徒刑十二年，馬之驌判處徒刑五年。

十月九日　聯合國第十五屆大會通過決議，將有關中共入會建議案再擱置一年。
中華民國宣佈與非洲剛果建立邦交。

十月十日　蔣介石總統發表雙十國慶文告，書告全國同胞，指出「亞洲與世界和平繫於我國之復興」。

十月十四日　台灣省政府新聞處以台北市公論報刊登「捫心看雷震案」一文，違反出版法規定予

以警告處分。

十月十七日　中國國民黨中央常務委員會決議，支持黨外賢能人物參加競選各縣市議員。

十月十八日　聯合國大會以四十二票對三十四票另廿二票棄權的表決，否決使中共政權進入聯合國的提案。

十月廿四日　中國銀行總管理處奉准在台灣恢復營業，辦理進出口外匯業務。

十月卅一日　蔣介石總統七四華誕，特往金門馬祖外島前線巡視，戰地軍民歡騰祝壽。

十一月八日　美國大選結果，民主黨候選人甘迺迪當選為第三十五任總統，詹森當選為副總統。

十一月十一日　台北市民營公論報改組發生糾紛提起訴訟，台北地方法院宣判被告李萬居敗訴。

十一月十六日　石門水庫正式開始導水，將水庫水全部導入後池，供桃園大圳灌溉農田之用。

十一月廿六日　台灣省政府決定興建白河水庫，預計三年完成，全部工程費預計新台幣一億八千八百萬元。

中華民國五十年（一九六一）

一月一日　蔣介石總統於中華民國開國五十週年紀念發表告全國同胞書，指出金、馬、台、澎為亞洲反共陣營中之中流砥柱，決心在險阻艱難中，貫徹反共復國全程。

一月十五日　台灣省各縣市舉行選舉投票，選出第五屆縣市議員。

一月二十日　美國第三十五任總統甘迺迪，副總統詹森宣誓就任。

二月一日　故宮博物院與中央博物院歷代藝術品兩百五十三件，將運往美國公開展覽。啟運之前，自本日起到八日止，在台北市舉行預展。

二月九日　中華民國行政院會議通過「台灣省縣市政府組織準則」。

二月二十日　中國國民黨中央常務委員會通過立法院長張道藩辭職，提名黃國書、倪文亞為立法院長副院長候選人。

二月廿三日　美國駐華大使莊萊德發表演說稱，美國新政府對華政策仍保持其一貫性，將繼續援助中華民國。

二月廿四日　去國十載的國民黨元老

陳立夫，自美國返台侍親。

二月廿八日　台灣省政府會議通過，籌辦台灣電視事業。

三月三日　中華民國游擊隊一千餘人，自緬甸退至泰國邊區，美通知中、緬、泰三國，表示願協助撤退游擊隊到台灣。

三月七日　美國與中共代表在華沙舉行談判，中共提出以美國撤出台灣為條件，拒絕釋放被拘禁之美國人或與美國交換新聞記者。

三月十五日　台灣中部的后豐大橋、東勢大橋及南雲大橋相繼動工興建。

三月廿六日　台灣省新聞處發表，台灣省現有廣播電台五十六家，以人口數字計，平均二十萬人有電台一家。

四月二日　台灣省政府預定下年度設立「中興大學」，擬以省立農學院為基礎擴建。

四月五日　高雄港十七號碼頭光隆號油輪發生爆炸事件起火燃燒近兩天，死亡九人，四十五人受傷。

四月十三日　美國總統甘迺迪表明美國立場，堅決反對中共進入聯合國組織，並且繼續履行對中華民國與人民之承諾。

四月十五日　美國第七艦隊司令葛里芬中將抵台灣訪問四天。

四月廿六日　中國著名鐵路工程家詹天佑百年冥誕，中國工程師學會在台北集會紀念。

五月二日　台灣省第一條高速公路「北基二路」動工興築。

五月三日　亞洲人民反共聯盟第七屆大會，在菲律賓首都馬尼拉開幕。

五月五日　美國參謀首長聯席會議主席李尼茲上將，抵達台灣訪問兩天。

五月六日　中華民國陸軍飛彈部隊，舉行首次實彈試射成功。

五月十四日　美國副總統詹森來中華民國訪問兩天。蔣介石總統與詹森三度商談反共大計。詹森推崇蔣總統為當代偉大領袖。

五月十五日　台北市大華晚報主辦第二屆「中國小姐」選美大會。本年共選出中國小姐三名：馬維君赴美國長堤參加「世界小姐」選美大會，汪麗玲赴美國邁阿密參加「環球小姐」選美大會，李秀英赴倫敦參加「世

界小姐」選美大會。

五月廿二日　秘魯總統浦樂多伉儷抵台灣訪問四天，與蔣介石總統會談，並將參觀中華民國陸軍的訓練演習。

六月一日　中華民國行政院宣布，改訂匯率為買賣均為新台幣四十元兌美金一元，為單一匯率之始。

台北市民營公論報，於停刊兩月餘後，本日復刊。

六月四日　台灣南部高雄市半屏山發生山崩慘劇，死傷達五十餘人。

台灣高雄至香港航線新輪船「天祥」號，在駛往香港途中遇暴風不幸沈沒，乘客及船員四十餘人罹難。

六月九日　美國正式通知中華民國外交部稱，美國與外蒙古進行建交談判。

台灣銀行宣布，開始發行面值一百元的新台幣大鈔。

六月二十日　台灣省政府會議通過，「愛國獎券發行辦法」。

六月廿八日　美國國務卿魯斯克宣稱，美國正在研擬方略，阻止中共進入聯合國組織，並重申

美國繼續支持中華民國。

七月一日　中華民國中央銀行在台北恢復營業。

中華民國政府主持的「陽明山會談」第一次會議舉行開幕儀式，副總統兼行政院長陳誠對會議強調，表示希望與會人士，共謀經濟發展，配合反共復國需要，重建國家。

七月十二日　中華民國國營民航空運公司，新購「超級翠華」號康維 880M 型噴射式客機，本日首次自台北飛往香港。

七月十八日　美國政府再度申明立場，堅決拒絕中共進入聯合國組織，並支持中華民國在聯合國的地位。

七月十九日　美國國務卿魯斯克邀約中華民國駐美大使葉公超及駐聯合國常任代表蔣廷黻，會商有關外蒙古及中共問題。

七月廿三日　中華民國外交部宣布，副總統兼行政院長陳誠應美國總統甘迺迪之邀，於本月底赴華府訪問。

七月廿八日　美國會參議院以七十六票對零票一致通過決議支持中華民國，並指責中共為最殘暴

的政權。

七月卅一日　中華民國副總統陳誠抵
　　　美京訪問，與甘迺迪總統作首
　　　次會談。

八月一日　中華民國副總統陳誠在華
　　　府接受甘迺迪總統國宴款待，
　　　並與美國務卿魯斯克會談。
　　　日本前首相岸信介抵台灣訪
　　　問。

八月四日　中華民國副總統陳誠訪問
　　　紐約，會晤麥克阿瑟將軍及紐
　　　約市長。

八月八日　陳誠副總統抵美國舊金山
　　　訪問，受到華僑熱烈歡迎。

八月十三日　陳誠副總統訪問美國後
　　　返抵台北。

八月廿三日　蔣介石總統發佈命令，
　　　任命劉安祺為陸軍總司令。

八月廿六日　中國石油公司台灣苗栗
　　　錦水礦場五十五號油井，噴出
　　　大量原油天然氣，該公司初步
　　　試氣，列入生產。

九月四日　廈門中共砲兵擾射金門國
　　　軍前線。

九月十五日　中共空軍飛行員邵希彥
　　　與高佑宗，駕機投奔自由，降
　　　落在南韓的濟州島。
　　　中華民國中央銀行委託台灣銀

行發行一元硬幣，以銅、鋅、
鎳之合金材料鑄成，銀色圓
形，直徑二十五公釐，重量六
公克。

九月廿五日　美國太平洋海軍總司令
　　　費爾特上將訪問台灣。

十月四日　台灣省六十七鄉鎮，開始
　　　實施「家庭計劃」，由省農會
　　　負責推行。

十月七日　美國慶祝中華民國建國五
　　　十年國慶，特別發行印有兩國
　　　國旗之紀念郵票。
　　　自大陸駕機投奔自由的義士邵
　　　希彥與高佑宗，自南韓抵達台
　　　灣。

十月十日　蔣介石總統為中華民國開
　　　國五十年國慶，對全國同胞發
　　　表文告，昭示應一致朝向民
　　　主、倫理、科學指標，從頭做
　　　起，重新建設，根除共黨赤
　　　禍，實現三民主義。

十月廿五日　台灣省第十六屆光復
　　　節，蔣介石總統書勉全國同
　　　胞，以光復台灣精神光復大
　　　陸，擁護國策，協助政府完成
　　　使命。

十月廿六日　聯合國安全理事會會
　　　議，通過允許「蒙古人民共和

國」進入聯合國，表決時中華民國代表退出會場。

十月廿七日　蘇聯舉行核子炸彈試驗，放射塵危害大陸西北地區人民，中華民國政府籲請各國聲討蘇聯罪行。

十一月一日　台灣省立中興大學在台中市成立。

十一月十二日　中華民國國父中山先生九十六歲誕辰，中樞舉行紀念典禮，社會各界舉行社教活動。

十一月十二日　中國國民黨第八屆中央委第四次全體會議在台北市陽明山揭幕，蔣介石總裁親臨主持，並講述「貫徹本黨的時代使命和革命任務」。

十一月十五日　聯合國第十六屆大會，以四十八票對三十六票的表決，通過拒絕中共進入聯合國案。

十一月十六日　國民黨八屆四中全會閉幕，大會選出蔣經國、張道藩、周至柔、黃朝琴及丘念台等十五人為中央常務委員。

十一月十八日　蔣介石總統發表命令，特任蔣廷黻為駐美國大使兼駐聯合國常任代表，原駐美大使葉公超調任行政院政務委員。

十一月廿八日　蔣介石總統在台灣南部校閱國軍舉行的「光武」演習。

十二月二日　國立清華大學原子科學研究所，完成中華民國第一座核子反應器裝置開始運轉。

十二月三日　台灣省政府舉辦全省農戶總檢查，計現有自耕農三十九萬一千二百四十戶。

十二月七日　中共政府指控印度在中印邊界挑釁，尼赫魯總理表示印度不惜一戰。

十二月十二日　美軍協防台灣司令史慕德中將，訪問金門發表談話，促使東南亞自由國家嚴防中共可能行動。

十二月十五日　聯合國大會以四十八票對三十六票另二十票棄權的表決，否決蘇聯提出之排斥中華民國建議案。

十二月廿二日　台灣省議會會議通過調整田賦徵實率，賦額每元徵穀十九點三七公斤。

十二月廿五日　台灣銀行開始發行面值五十元的新台幣鈔票。

中華民國五十一年（一九六二）

一月一日　蔣介石總統發表元旦文
告，昭示全國同胞以同仇敵
慨、矢志光復大陸的決心，為
拯救同胞、挽回世界劫運，保
衛人類自由而奮鬥。

一月六日　廈門中共砲兵射擊金門國
軍前線。

一月十六日　台灣省南部東西橫貫公
路第一期工程，舉行開工儀
式。

二月五日　本日為農曆壬寅年春節元
旦，上午發生日全蝕，太陽、
月亮、火星、土星、金星、木
星與地球排成一線，聚於摩羯
座。

二月九日　台灣證券交易所正式開始
營業。

二月十二日　美國太平洋陸軍總司令
柯林斯抵台灣訪問。

二月廿二日　中華民國國防部宣佈成
立戰地政務局。

二月廿四日　中華民國中央研究院第
五次院士會議，在台北市南港
召開，選出新院士何廉等七
人。中央研究院院長胡適博
士，在會議中發表演講之際，
心臟病突發逝世，享年七十二

歲（一八九一～一九六二）。

三月一日　美國總統甘迺迪核定美軍
協防台灣司令史慕德中將退
休，並且提名美國第一艦隊司
令梅爾遜中將繼任協防台灣司
令。

三月一日　台灣鐵路局開始行駛運報
專車，便利台北市報紙供中南
部讀者閱讀。

三月二日　中、日合作籌設「台灣電
視公司」，資本新台幣三千萬
元，中方佔百分之六十，日方
佔百分之四十，並預定今年雙
十節國慶日開播。
中央研究院故院長胡適博士遺
體大殮，靈柩暫厝該院會議
庭，然後擇期安葬。

三月三日　中共空軍飛行員劉承司少
校，駕駛米格十五式噴射機投
奔自由，降於台灣機場。

三月六日　美國總統甘迺迪批准美國
駐中華民國大使莊萊德辭職。

三月八日　美國政府宣布，十二年來
中華民國共獲得美國軍事援助
二十二億美元。

三月十四日　美國國務院主管遠東事
務助理國務卿哈里曼抵台北訪
問，晉謁蔣介石總統晤談。

三月十八日　中華民國國劇大師齊如山，因心臟病突發在台北市逝世，享年八十八歲（一八七五～一九六二）。

三月二十日　中華民國政府對甘迺迪總統宣布將琉球交還日本一節，表示不贊同。

三月廿三日　中共空軍飛機十六架，分四批侵入金門上空，其中一架被國軍高射砲擊傷。

三月廿七日　中共人民代表大會二屆三次會議在北京開幕，毛澤東、劉少奇、及周恩來等政要出席。

三月三十日　美國參謀首長聯席會議主席李尼茲上將抵台灣訪問。

四月四日　美國第七艦隊新任司令薛伊中將抵台灣訪問。

四月十三日　台北榮民總醫院宣布，蔣總統健康情形良好。

四月廿八日　中華民國第一家電視公司，台灣電視公司在台北市成立，係中、日兩國合辦。

五月一日　中華民國歷代藝術品在美國舊金山德揚博物館展出，僑胞及外籍觀眾擁擠。

五月三日　新任美軍協防台灣司令梅爾遜抵台北就職。

五月十二日　香港政府宣布，五月初旬自大陸逃亡湧入香港的難民，經香港政府予以收容者大約有一萬人。

五月十九日　國立清華大學校長梅貽琦博士在台北市病逝，享年七十四歲（一八八九～一九六二）。

五月廿三日　對於大陸難民湧入香港問題，英國政府擬加以控制。同時，邊界中共駐軍突然開槍制止難民逃亡。

五月廿七日　中共政府命令停售赴邊界深圳的火車票，引起廣州萬餘人的抗議行動，搗毀車站，共軍開槍鎮壓，十餘人傷亡，百餘人被捕。

五月廿八日　聯合國組織發表全球人口調查統計，共有三十餘億人。

五月卅一日　香港政府統計，五月份內共有大陸難民十餘萬人逃至香港和澳門。

六月十六日　中華民國內政部成立出版事業管理處。

六月廿一日　澳門政府正式宣佈，准許自中國大陸逃出的難民入境。

六月廿四日　日本政府法務省移民局發表統計，中華民國旅日僑民共有四萬四千餘人。

六月廿五日　大陸逃至香港的難民中，第一批三百餘人自香港啟程赴台灣。

六月廿七日　美國總統甘迺迪重申美國對防衛金馬外島政策，與艾森豪總統政府相同，並對台海情勢表示嚴重關切。

七月二日　美國新任駐中華民國大使柯爾克抵台北履新。

七月六日　中華民國國防部發言人說，金馬外島對岸中共軍隊已超過四十萬人，仍未停止調動。

七月廿八日　中華民國運往美國公開展覽的歷史藝術品兩百餘件，已由美國軍艦載運返台北。

七月廿九日　蔣介石總統發佈命令，蔣廷黻專任駐美國大使，任命劉鍇繼任駐聯合國常任代表。

七月卅一日　美國援華顧問團長戴倫少將宣布，他奉調美國第八軍團服務，由桑鵬少將繼任團長。

八月一日　中華民國郵政總局宣布，開始受理公眾申請代訂國外進口報刊，惟以西德、法國、義大利等國出版之自然科學或技術性刊物為限。

八月五日　強烈颱風「歐珀」襲擊台灣地區，北部三縣市災情嚴重。

八月九日　中華民國駐美國大使館文化參事處調查報告說，現在共有一千五百七十一位中國學者專家，在美國大專學校任教或從事研究工作。

八月廿四日　印尼政府拒絕中華民國及以色列參加第四屆亞洲運動會。亞洲體育協會發表聲明，禁止印尼主辦的雅加達運動會使用「亞洲運動會」名義。

九月二日　新加坡舉行公民投票結果，贊成與馬來亞合併，但希望教育方面有自治權。

九月九日　中華民國國防部發言人說，國軍一架美國造 U-2 型高空偵察機，由陳懷生駕駛，在大陸南昌附近上空偵察時失蹤。北京人民解放軍空軍宣稱，在大陸華東地區上空擊落一架台灣的美製 U-2 式高空偵察機。

九月十四日　北京人民政府發表聲

明，「抗議美國 U-2 型飛機
侵犯中國領空」。

九月十九日　聯合國第十七屆大會通
過牙買加、千里達、盧安達及
蒲隆地四國加入聯合國組織，
使會員國總數增至一〇八個。

九月廿四日　中國共產黨中央委員第
八屆第十次全體會議在北京開
幕。（九月廿七日閉幕）

九月三十日　明代先哲徐文定公（光
啟）四百歲誕辰，中華民國中
央研究院與國立台灣大學聯合
舉辦紀念會與學術演講。蔣介
石總統親臨參加會議。

十月一日　亞洲人民反共聯盟第八屆
大會在日本東京舉行，共有二
十一個代表團參加。

十月十日　蔣介石總統發表民國四十
一年國慶文告，書勉全國同
胞，激揚民族大義，消滅共黨
暴政，並手訂規約十條，號召
中共軍隊官兵起義。

十月十日　台灣電視公司開播，蔣介
石總統夫人宋美齡女士親臨按
鈕，自由中國進入電視時代。

十月十一日　第二屆梵諦岡大公會議
在羅馬開幕，中華民國天主教
主教團參加。

十月十八日　中、美兩國軍隊聯合空
降演習，在台灣南部基地舉
行。

十月二十日　西藏與印度邊界戰爭爆
發，中共軍隊兩萬人發動猛烈
攻擊，向印度境內推進。

十月廿三日　中華民國前行政院長孔
祥熙自美國返國，蔣介石總統
伉儷親臨機場迎迓。

十月廿四日　甘迺迪總統宣布，美國
對古巴實施海上全面封鎖，美
國駐全球各地陸海空軍奉命實
施戒備。

十月廿八日　中共人民日報發表社論
稱：「全世界人民動員起來，
支持古巴人民，粉碎美國戰爭
挑釁」。北京舉行反美集會。
蘇聯共黨領袖赫魯雪夫下令，
蘇聯撤走在古巴境內的攻擊性
武器（飛彈）。古巴危機緩
和。

十月三十日　聯合國第十七屆大會舉
行表決結果，以五十六票對四
十二票另十二票棄權否決蘇聯
提出的排斥中華民國建議案。

十一月五日　中國國民黨中央委員
會，邀集從政同志舉行有關政
治改革的座談會。

十一月九日　中華民國國軍自製的 T-2 型火箭，舉行試射。

十一月十二日　中國國民黨第八屆中央委員第五次全體會議在台北市陽明山開幕，蔣介石總裁親臨主持，並講述「復國建國的方向和實踐」。（全會於十五日閉幕。）

十一月廿二日　蔣介石總統發表命令，任命黃杰為台灣省政府主席，省主席周至柔調任總統府參軍長，並任命陳大慶為台灣警備總司令。

十一月廿五日　日本政府宣布，任命木村四郎七為駐中華民國大使，接替井口貞夫職務。木村曾任珍珠港事變前夕的駐美國特使。

十一月三十日　北京人民政府國防部宣布，中共軍隊自十二月一日開始自印度邊境全線撤退。

十二月六日　印度政府宣布，印度已關閉駐中共區的領事館。

十二月十二日　中華民國政府國軍退除役官兵就業輔導委員會主任委員蔣經國說，輔導會已經安置國軍退除役官兵十二萬餘人，節省國庫鉅額開支。

十二月二十日　中國國民黨宣布開始辦理黨員總登記。

十二月廿五日　中華民國政府宣布，十二月廿五日為行憲紀念日，自本年起定為國定紀念日。

中華民國五十二年（一九六三）

一月一日　蔣介石總統發表元旦文告，號召全國同胞投身反攻復國聖戰，完成建國任務，肅清共黨禍根，重啟人類和平。

一月三日　中華民國前中央研究院院長朱家驊因心臟病突發病逝於台北，享年七十一歲（一八九三～一九六三）。

一月八日　美國大使館新聞處宣布，為援助中華民國經濟發展，美援公署已完成全面改組，今後將積極鼓勵民營企業發展。

一月十四日　美軍太平洋總司令費爾特上將訪問台灣。

一月十六日　中華民國行政院通過台灣省議會組織規程。

一月廿三日　英國政府宣布與「蒙古人民共和國」建立外交關係。同時，美國政府聲明重申美國不承外蒙政權。

一月廿六日　中國女核子物理學家吳

健雄博士，證實向量不滅定
律，在核子物理學上為重大進
步。

二月二日　香港英文南華早報報導，
去年自大陸由水路與陸路逃入
香港的難民共達十四萬餘人。

二月七日　中華民國前行政院院長宋
子文博士，自紐約返抵台北。

二月十五日　中國國民黨中央宣布，
國民黨黨員總登記辦理已完
成。

二月十六日　台灣省政府宣布加速實
施六項農田水利建設計劃，預
期在十年內增加產糙米四十萬
噸。

二月廿五日　中國國民黨蔣介石總
裁，在擴大孫總理紀念週中，
親行黨員總登記宣誓，並手書
誓約：一、遵奉總理遺教。
二、實現三民主義。三、遵行
五權憲法。四、慎施命令。
五、盡忠職守。六、嚴守黨
紀。七、誓共生死。從茲永守
此約，至死不渝，如有二心，
甘受極刑。

三月一日　南極一山峰命名為「張氏
峰」，以紀念中國探險家張逢
鏗先生。

三月十五日　中、美兩國軍方聯合舉
行之「銀峰」兩棲登陸演習，
在台灣南部開始，為期八天。

三月廿一日　中華民國陳誠副總統，
代表蔣介石總統赴菲律賓訪問
三天。

三月廿四日　台灣省開發海埔新生
地，計有三萬餘公頃用作生
產，可安置十八萬人，生產總
額預計一年可達新台幣十二億
元。

四月一日　中華民國郵政總局宣布，
與西德恢復辦理郵政匯兌業
務，雙方來往匯款金額均用美
元，每張匯票最高限額為美金
一百元。

四月十一日　中華民國政府決定，四
月廿九日為鄭成功復台紀念
日，並舉行公祭儀式。

四月十二日　北京人民政府主席劉少
奇赴印尼等東南亞國家訪問。

四月十七日　蔣介石總統對中國國民
黨新聞工作會談全體同志講
話：「應團結合作，自律自
重，隨時注意新聞道德與革命
人格，以國家、主義、責任作
為良知標準。」

四月廿八日　台灣省全省舉行選舉，

投票選出第三屆省議會議員。

五月二日　中華民國郵政總局宣布，與義大利恢復辦理郵政匯兌業務，雙方來往匯款金額均用美元，每張匯票最高限額為美金一百元。

五月十二日　印尼發生排華運動，尤以萬隆地區為最嚴重。

五月十五日　印尼萬隆警方戒備，禁止排華示威。

五月廿二日　美國總統甘迺迪說，若中華民國發動反攻大陸將涉及美國，美國已向中華民國政府表示其意見，即在採取此項行動之前，中、美應先舉行磋商。

印尼排華行動已擴大到蘇門答臘等地。

五月廿四日　中華民國政府對印尼排華暴行至表憤慨正循各種國際途徑，促使印尼當局鎮壓暴行。

六月二日　台灣省議會第三屆議員就任，並選出謝東閔為議長，許金德為副議長。

六月五日　泰國國王蒲美蓬與王后詩麗吉，應蔣介石總統之邀，抵中華民國訪問三天。

北京政府說，中華民國空軍上尉飛行員徐廷澤，駕駛美造F86式噴射機飛降大陸。

六月廿一日　孟迪尼當選為羅馬天主教教宗，定聖號為保祿六世。

六月廿六日　行政院陳兼院長誠，因辛勞過度請辭院長兼職。蔣介石總統特准自七月一日起給假一個月，以資休養。

六月廿八日　台灣省北部地區舉行「天神」防空演習。

七月五日　中共與蘇聯共黨在莫斯科開始會談。中共首席代表為鄧小平。

七月二十日　中共與蘇聯共黨舉行之有關思想觀念之會談無結果而散，中共代表鄧小平離莫斯科返北京。

七月廿五日　蔣介石總統伉儷，應美國第七艦隊司令穆琳中將之邀，登美國海軍航空母艦「星座」號，參觀該艦隊之海空軍聯合「火海」演習。

七月廿九日　美援 M41A「猛犬型」戰車一批，移交與中華民國陸軍部隊使用。

八月十一日　新近完工的台灣桃園石門水庫開始放水，受益地區廣

一萬五千公頃。

八月十六日　中華民國國防部宣布，「國防部總政治部」奉蔣總統命令改稱「總政治作戰部」，各級部隊、學校「政治部」，亦一律改稱「政治作戰部」。美國援華公署宣布，美國援助中華民國貸款將自下年度起減少，並且在四年內中止援助。

八月廿二日　中華民國行政院會議通過，決定參加簽署核子禁試條約。

九月一日　中華民國行政院「美援委員會」奉令改組，更名「國際經濟合作發展委員會」。

九月六日　中華民國行政院政務委員蔣經國，應美國國務院邀請赴美國訪問十天。

九月十日　強烈颱風「葛樂禮」襲擊台灣省東北部地區，造成損失達十六億新台幣元。

九月十一日　蔣經國在華府晉謁甘迺迪總統。蔣氏對記者說，自由世界應阻止中共擁有核子武力。

十月七日　中共訪日代表團團員周鴻慶，投靠蘇聯駐日本大使館請求予以庇護，但蘇聯將他交與日本加以收禁。

十月十日　蔣介石總統發表雙十國慶文告，勗勉同胞實踐革命戰鬥責任，中共已陷絕境，短期內必可予以消滅。並在總統府前廣場舉行閱兵大典，校閱三軍。

十月十七日　香港成立「中文大學」，是為海外唯一以國語為主要授課語言之大學。

十月廿五日　蔣介石總統於台灣光復節發表告台灣省同胞書，勉全省同胞與大陸同胞攜手奮鬥，並肩作戰，隨時準備響應大陸上抗暴義舉。

十一月十二日　中國國民黨第九次全國代表大會在台北市陽明山開幕，會期十天，蔣介石總裁親臨主持。

十一月十七日　中共人民政府第二屆「人代會」第四次會議，與中共「人民政協」第三屆全國委員會，同時在北京召開，會期兩週。

十一月十八日　中華民國滿族國民大會代表，著名國畫家溥儒（心畬）在台北市病逝，享年六十八歲（一八九六～一九六

三）。

十一月廿一日　中國國民黨第九次全
　　國代表大會，一致推舉蔣介石
　　連任總裁，並通過「中國國民
　　黨政綱」及「中國國民黨現階
　　段工作綱領」等重要議案。

十一月廿二日　中國國民黨九全大會
　　通過陳誠連任副總裁，蔣經國
　　等七十四人當選為中央委員及
　　于右任等一百四十四人為中央
　　評議委員。

十一月廿二日　美國總統甘迺迪在德
　　克薩斯達拉斯城遇刺逝世，全
　　球為之驚震。副總統詹森同日
　　宣誓就任美國第三十六任總
　　統。

十一月廿三日　蔣介石總統電唁美國
　　總統甘迺迪之喪。

十一月廿七日　蔣介石總統民國五十
　　二年度，親臨校閱陸、海、空
　　三軍之「嵩山演習」圓滿完
　　成。

十二月四日　中國國民黨中央常務委
　　員會會議，通過副總統陳誠辭
　　去行政院長兼職，並提名嚴家
　　淦繼任行政院長。

十二月十日　中華民國立法院會議同
　　意嚴家淦出任行政院院長。

十二月廿七日　日本政府釋放投奔自
　　由的中共訪日代表周鴻慶，使
　　其落於中共手裡，中華民國政
　　府向日本提出嚴重抗議。

十二月廿八日　美國國務卿魯斯克再
　　度表示，美國對中國政策不
　　變。

十二月三十日　中華民國駐日本大使
　　張厲生奉准辭職，並且召回駐
　　日本大使館公使及參事等外交
　　官員，表示對日本迫遣周鴻慶
　　回大陸事件抗議。

中華民國五十三年（一九六四）

一月一日　蔣介石總統發表元旦告全
　　國同胞書，號召全國同胞團結
　　一切力量。

一月十日　中華民國政府宣布，暫時
　　停止中、日政府間之貿易，以
　　抗議日本將周鴻慶強迫送回中
　　共區。

一月十一日　中華民國政府行政院決
　　定，政府機關與公營事業機構
　　暫停向日本採購。

一月十四日　日本駐台北大使館，遭
　　中華民國愛國人士投擲石塊抗
　　議日本親中共行為。

一月廿一日　日本首相池田勇人稱，

日本政府仍維持與中華民國友好關係，但又說日本對中共「採取現實政策」。

一月廿三日　今日為韓戰反共義士回國「一二三」自由日十週年，台灣各界舉行盛大慶祝活動。

一月廿五日　法國總統戴高樂，派法國前駐華大使貝志高向蔣介石總統解釋法國承認中共政權事後已離台。

一月廿六日　台灣省舉行第六屆縣市議員及第五屆鄉鎮轄市長選舉。

一月廿七日　法蘭西共和國與中共政府同時宣布，雙方建立外交關係。
中華民國政府發表嚴正聲明，痛斥法國與中共勾結，並重申反共復國基本國策，及反對任何「兩個中國」觀念。

一月廿八日　法國政府發表聲明稱，無意與中華民國絕交。

一月卅一日　日本首相池田勇人稱，日本政府堅決遵守「一個中國」政策。

二月七日　中華民國外交部發表聲明，重申反對「兩個中國」謬論，並指斥法國總統戴高樂的中立政策是分期投降。

二月十日　中華民國政府宣布，與法國斷絕邦交，自巴黎撤回外交代表。

二月二十日　中華民國駐法國大使館代辦高仕銘下旗離巴黎返國。法國駐華大使館關閉，法國公使代辦薩萊德離台北返法。

二月廿五日　蔣介石總統與來訪之日本前首相吉田茂二度會談，對中、日基本問題廣泛交換意見，已為兩國恢復談判奠定基礎。

二月廿六日　美軍援華顧問團官員代表美國政府，將一批 F104 式噴射戰鬥機移交中華民國空軍使用。

二月廿九日　中國青年黨內部三派分裂已久，現簽定團結方案結束分裂情勢。

三月二日　日本首相池田勇人又發謬言，竟稱：「台灣並非中國領土，僅係屬於中國行政權之範圍。」

三月十二日　中華民國行政院會議通過，政務委員蔣經國兼任國防部副部長。
中國留美學人李卓皓博士宣

布，已發現減胖賀爾蒙。

三月廿四日　美軍協防台灣司令梅爾遜中將奉調為美國海軍大學校長，遺缺由美國第六艦隊司令蘭納中將繼任。

三月廿八日　中華民國外交部宣布，任命陳澤華為駐日本公使並代辦大使館館務。

四月三日　達賴喇嘛在紐約設立「西藏辦事處」。中華民國外交部發表聲明，重申政府光復大陸後，將允許西藏人民自決。

四月五日　麥克阿瑟元帥因病在美國逝世，舉世哀悼。蔣介石總統電唁麥帥之喪，並發表悼詞，推許麥帥智仁勇兼備，乃本世紀模範鬥士，足為正義公理象徵。

四月七日　美國前副總統尼克森抵達台灣訪問三天。

四月九日　美國報章載稱，麥克阿瑟元帥曾在韓國戰爭期間建議使用原子彈及使用中華民國軍隊在鴨綠江登陸作戰。

四月十日　美軍將新型鷹式地對空飛彈一批，移交與中華民國軍隊使用。

四月十五日　美國國務卿魯斯克偕助理國務卿曼寧及彭岱等官員抵台灣訪問三天。

四月十六日　美國國務卿魯斯克強調美國支持中華民國，此行三度晉謁蔣介石總統，就世界局勢及中美兩國共同利益，廣泛交換意見。

四月廿三日　中美兩國在台北簽訂「文化交流協定」。

四月廿六日　台灣選舉第五屆縣市長。

五月二日　台灣第一條高速公路（台北市到基隆市）——麥克阿瑟公路——順利完工，舉行通車典禮。

五月八日　中華民國教育部長黃季陸表示，教育部正在研究延長義務教育年限實施方案，並將先實行小學畢業生充分就學方案。

五月十三日　台灣省政府準備延長義務教育年限，明年可能試辦初中畢業生免試升學制度。

五月廿四日　味全公司台中奶粉工廠，今日正式開始生產，首創台灣省自製奶粉紀錄。

五月廿八日　中華民國行政院會議通過，修訂國外留學規程，再度

放寬免試出國資格。

美國國務院正式宣佈，美國對中華民國的經濟援助將於一九六五年中期停止，但軍事援助及農產品法案仍將繼續。

五月卅一日　中華民國海軍總司令黎玉璽說，美援軍艦七艘，即將移交與國軍海軍使用，使海軍實力更見加強。

六月十一日　中華民國行政院通過，任命前台灣省政府主席魏道明為駐日本大使，接替張厲生的職務。

六月十四日　耗資新台幣三十二億元，費時八年興建完成之台灣桃園石門水庫舉行竣工典禮，由陳誠副總統親自主持。

六月十六日　中華民國陸軍軍官學校慶祝建校四十週年，由蔣介石總統親自主持典禮並致辭指出，「今天的靜如山嶽，就是為明天的動如雷霆作準備。」

六月二十日　台灣民航空運公司一架客機，自台中飛往台北途中，在豐原上空發生爆炸事件，機上乘客五十七人全部罹難，其中包括參加亞洲影展會的馬來西亞代表團長陸運濤夫婦及香港、台灣等地的電影界人士。

六月三十日　中華民國立法院會議，通過「著作權法修正案」。

美國新任台灣協防司令耿特納抵台灣就任。

七月一日　中華民國國防部宣布，台灣軍管區正式成立，由陳大慶兼任司令。

台灣省開始實施都市平均地權細則，公告地價，以增收之地價稅金，作為推行民生主義社會福利政策財源。

七月三日　日本政府外務大臣大平正芳抵台灣訪問，晉見蔣介石總統交換有關中、日間問題意見。

七月七日　中華民國空軍總司令部宣布，國軍飛機一架在大陸華北地區失事。中共海軍防空部隊說，台灣一架 P2-V 型飛機被擊落。

七月十五日　蘇聯共黨宣布，蘇聯最高蘇維埃主席布里茲涅夫被免職，由米高揚繼任。

七月廿一日　新加坡馬來亞人與華人發生大規模嚴重衝突，迄今已有五人死亡，一九二人受傷。

八月十二日　中華民國總統府秘書長

張群赴日本及大韓民國訪問。

八月十三日　中共軍隊在福建廣東沿海舉行軍事演習。

八月十四日　台灣省今年第一期米穀產量，達糙米一百零九萬四千公噸，創下歷年同期產量最高紀錄。

八月廿五日　美軍太平洋三軍總司令夏普上將，抵達台灣訪問三天。

九月一日　中華民國成立各界「紀念國父百年誕辰籌備委員會」，公推蔣介石總統為名譽會長，陳誠為主任委員。

中華民國中央研究院院士會議，選出錢思亮等六人為新院士。

九月三日　中共人民政府五屆「人代會」第一次會議在北京召開，彭真當選為北京市長，萬里當選為副市長。

九月四日　新加坡馬來亞人與華人種族衝突再起，雙方死傷五十人左右。

九月五日　美國第七艦隊司令強生訪問中華民國，證實美國「北極星」核子動力潛水艇將進駐太平洋。

九月九日　谷鳳翔繼任中國國民黨中央委員會秘書長。

九月廿七日　美國政府發表「華倫委員會」對甘迺迪總統被刺案調查報告書，確認係兇手奧斯華・魯比的個人行為。

國立台灣大學政治系主任彭明敏等人，因秘密起草「台灣獨立宣言」罪名已被逮捕。

十月三日　美國報紙報導，美國儲存的戰略飛彈達一千零九十一個，可毀滅任何侵略國家。

十月八日　大韓民國總理丁一權抵台灣訪問，與蔣介石總統商談反共團結大計。

十月十日　蔣介石總統發表雙十國慶文告，呼籲亞洲國家應聯合一致，撲滅共禍，以解除亞洲所有國家受的威脅。蔣總統並在總統府前廣場舉行盛大閱兵典禮。

十月十六日　台灣省政府供應學童營養午餐計劃開始實施，並在桃園縣龜山鄉龍壽國民學校舉行開辦典禮，由省主席黃杰主持。

蘇聯官方「塔斯新聞社」正式宣佈，赫魯雪夫已被解除蘇聯

政府總理及蘇聯共產黨第一書記職務，並稱由柯錫金繼任總理及布里茲涅夫繼任共黨第一書記職務。

十月十六日　北京人民政府宣布，中共在新疆省羅布淖爾附近舉行首次核子試爆，其威力相當於兩萬噸黃色炸藥（T.N.T.）的爆炸。

美國總統詹森發表聲明稱，中共的核子試爆意義不大，對大陸的苦難人民乃一悲劇。

十月十七日　台灣省的澎湖跨海大橋動工興建，預定五年完成。

台灣省政府計劃，在省內尚無公路可通的鄉鎮，如平溪、泰安、吳鳳、大同等地，將分年分期修築公路以利交通。

十月廿二日　對於美國提出的「使北京參加核子禁試條約」的建議，中共政府加以拒絕。

十月廿五日　蔣介石總統於台灣省光復節發表文告，對全省同胞勉以恢宏建設績效，邁向反攻里程。

十一月四日　美國大選結果揭曉，民主黨人詹森當選連任總統，韓福瑞當選為副總統。

蔣介石總統電賀美國總統詹森當選連任。

十一月五日　中國國民黨第二次新聞工作會談在台北市召開，蔣介石總裁訓勉新聞工作人員，促進社會心理建設，加強國民精神武裝。

十一月五日　北京人民政府總理周恩來，飛往莫斯科參加共產黨最高階層會議。

十一月十日　中國國民黨元老、監察院長于右任，在台北病逝，享年八十六歲（一八七九～一九六四）。

十一月十五日　台灣苗栗縣鐵砧山開鑽油井，發現大量天然氣，中國石油公司擬定開發計劃。

十一月廿四日　中國國民黨慶祝建黨七十週年慶典及國民黨第九屆中央委員第二次全體會在台北市陽明山舉行。蔣介石總裁書勉全黨同志，應以三民主義為身體力行目標，開啟復國建國新機運。

十一月廿六日　國民黨九屆二中全會通過，「加強社會福利措施，增進人民生活實施方針」等議案，並選出蔣經國、嚴家淦、

謝東閔等十七人為中央常務委員，然後閉幕。

十二月八日　日本新任首相佐藤榮作表示，日本對中華民國政策不變。

十二月九日　中國國民黨中央常務委員會通過，任命現任駐巴拿馬大使馬星野為中央通訊社社長。

十二月十日　中華民國行政院會議通過，大學夜間部畢業生授「學士學位」。

十二月十三日　北京人民政府宣布，第三屆全國「人民代表大會代表」共為三○三七人。

十二月十七日　台灣省政府宣布，今年稻米產量計兩百二十三萬公噸，創新紀錄。

十二月十八日　北京人民政府國務院會議通過，撤銷達賴喇嘛的「西藏自治區籌備委員會主任委員」職務。

十二月廿一日　中共人民政府「人代會」三屆一次會議，與「人民政協」四屆一次會，同時在北京開幕，並預定明年一月五日閉會。

十二月卅一日　中華民國行政院發表，民國五十三年（一九六四）全體生產毛額達九百四十三億元。

中華民國五十四年（一九六五）

一月一日　蔣介石總統發表新年文告，昭示全國同胞「要以射擊戰來消滅核子戰，以討伐叛逆的義師，來消彌世界人類戰爭的悲劇。」

一月三日　中華民國經濟部長楊繼曾說，民國五十三年輸出額約四億五千萬美元，為實施經濟建設以來成就最大的一年。

一月三日　中共人民政府「人代會」選出劉少奇為中央人民政府主席，宋慶齡、董必武為副主席，及劉少奇任命周恩來為國務院總理。

一月七日　印尼總統蘇卡諾宣布，印尼退出聯合國組織。

一月十三日　蔣介石總統發佈命令，特任蔣經國為國防部長，接替俞大維的職務，閻振興為教育部長，接替黃季陸的職務，及李國鼎為經濟部長，接替楊繼曾的的職務。

一月廿四日　英國第二次世界大戰期

間的首相邱吉爾爵士因病逝世，享年九十一歲（一八七四～一九六五）。

一月廿九日　中華民國政府發表，一九六四年輸出額為四億六千四百六十四萬美元，輸入額為四億零九百五十萬美元，貿易順差為五千五百十三萬美元。

一月三十日　中華民國田徑運動女傑紀政在加拿大，創下六十碼女子低欄世界新紀錄，成績為七秒七分。

二月十一日　蘇聯總理柯錫金抵達北京，與中共政府總理周恩來會談。柯錫金在訪問北越共黨之後，於返回莫斯科途中在北京停留。他並與毛澤東會談。

二月廿二日　中國國民黨中央委員會在台北市舉行儀式，表揚各種黨部成績特優的示範小組長計一七九人。

二月廿四日　中華民國行政院會議通過，整頓國營輪船公司招商局辦法。

二月廿七日　中華民國副總統陳誠臥病，患有肝癌象徵。

三月三日　是日為中、美共同防禦條約生效十週年紀念，美軍協防台灣司令耿特中將指出，美國與中華民國的共同努力，已獲得顯著效果。

三月四日　蔣介石總統伉儷探視副總統陳誠病況。

三月五日　中華民國副總統陳誠，因患肝癌症逝世，享年六十九歲（一八九八～一九六五）。蔣介石總統親撰輓聯云：「光復志節已至最後奮鬥關頭，那堪弔此國殤，果有數耶？革命事業尚在共同完成階段，竟忍奪我元輔，豈無天乎！」

三月廿九日　中華民國外交部宣布，將澳門辦事處關閉。

四月一日　中華民國陸軍飛彈「神箭五號」演習，在淡水以北基地舉行首次實彈射擊，四枚飛彈全中目標。
中華民國中央通訊社開始使用新式文字傳真機，直接向國內各報社傳遞新聞。

四月二日　被控涉及秘密起草「台灣獨立宣言」案的台灣大學政治系主任彭明敏，被軍事法庭判處徒刑八年，魏廷朝被判處徒刑八年，及謝聰敏被判處徒刑十年。

四月六日　新任美國第七艦隊司令勃萊克本中將，抵達台灣訪問。

四月九日　中美兩國簽定經濟社會發展基金協定，今後五年內，美國每年供中國新台幣二十億元以資運用。

四月十二日　台灣省自本日開始，分期換發國民身分證，預定兩年內全部換發完成。

四月十六日　中共政府總理周恩來及外長陳毅等抵達印尼首都雅加達，參加萬隆會議十週年慶祝活動。

四月廿三日　美國詹森總統特使洛奇訪問台灣，與蔣介石總統商討越南反共情形。

四月廿六日　中華民國與日本簽定一億五千萬美元長期貸款協定，在台北簽字換文。
中國國民黨宣布成立新聞事業機構黨部。

五月一日　中華民國國防部宣布，海軍一一九號軍艦在東引海面擊沉中共艦艇四艘，並擊傷兩艘。

五月七日　天主教阮樂化神甫領導的越南華僑反共據點海燕特區，遭受越共軍隊的猛烈攻擊。

五月十四日　居留日本多年主張「台灣獨立」的廖文毅，決定放棄獨立運動，返回台灣參加反共大業，受到朝野各界的熱烈歡迎。
北京人民政府宣布，舉行第二次核子爆炸試驗。

五月十七日　新近自日本返國的廖文毅博士發表談話，促使海外迷途人士放棄愚昧的獨立幻想，參加反共大業。

五月二十日　居留日本的「台灣民政黨」領袖鄭萬福，宣布解散黨組織並放棄台獨主張。

五月廿四日　中共人民政府宣布，自六月一日起廢除「軍銜制度」，並改變共軍軍帽徽領章和軍服式樣，換用新式樣。

五月廿七日　中國國民黨召開第十次黨務工作會議，蔣介石總裁訓勉全體同志，認識大局，加強團結。

五月廿八日　中華民國政府宣布「外僑護照簽證辦法」，並決定自八月一日起實施。
台灣省出入境管理限制予以放寬，手續再予簡化。

五月卅一日　台灣省政府會議通過，

決定實施國民學校學生志願升學方案。

六月四日　美國太平洋空軍總司令哈瑞斯上將抵台灣訪問。

六月六日　廖文毅宣佈放棄「台獨」主張返回台灣後，蔣介石總統宣布依法赦免廖文毅，並且發還其被沒收的財產。

六月十六日　陸軍軍官學校慶祝建校四十週年校慶，蔣介石總統親臨高雄縣鳳山該校主持盛典。陸軍官校原名國民黨中央軍官學校，蔣介石為創校校長。

六月十七日　中華民國行政院通過修正護照簽證辦法，自八月一日起生效，觀光簽證有效期間為一個月。

六月十八日　美國宣佈，首次出動巨型 B-52 式戰略轟炸機襲擊北越共軍地區。

六月廿五日　中華民國國防部宣佈，國防部奉蔣介石總統指示，全面革新國軍福利制度，每年三大節，官兵各增發薪餉一個月，自本年七月一日起實施。

六月廿七日　蔣介石總統發佈命令，特任彭孟緝為總統府參軍長，黎玉璽為參謀總長，接替彭孟緝職務。

六月三十日　中華民國政府宣佈，國家外匯存底已逾三億美元，今後經濟及貿易將不受美援停止的影響。

七月一日　中華民國政府發表，在近十六年期間，共接受美國援助十四億美元。

七月十六日　中華民國前副總統李宗仁在美國居住多年，現已離開美國前往歐洲，將被中共誘惑返回大陸。

七月十九日　中華民國監察院會議通過修改院長選舉辦法，監察委員有三分之一出席，即可選舉院長及副院長。

七月二十日　中華民國前副總統李宗仁與夫人李德全，返抵北京變節投靠中共政權。

七月廿四日　美軍在華地位協定，經美國與中華民國雙方歷時將近十年久談判，現終獲協議，即將正式簽訂生效。

八月三日　中國青年黨領袖余家菊，陳啟天等發表談話，促請政府早日反攻大陸。

八月四日　中華民國政府宣佈，已經批准聯合國組織憲章修正案。

八月六日　中華民國國防部發表，金門島南方海面發生海戰，國軍兵艦擊沉中共艦艇五艘，國軍砲艦一艘電訊中斷，海空軍正搜索中。

八月九日　新加坡政府宣佈退出馬來西亞聯邦並宣告獨立，但與馬來西亞仍維持軍事及經濟合作。

八月十六日　越南總理阮高祺抵台灣訪問，與蔣介石總統會談加強中，越竑共合作事宜。

八月十七日　美軍援華顧問團新任團長江霖少將抵台北。

八月廿一日　中華民國政府宣佈，任命王雲五為國立故宮博物院管理委員會主任委員，將復璁為故宮博物院長。

八月廿二日　蔣介石總統夫人宋美齡女士赴美國訪問。

八月廿五日　太平洋美軍總司令夏普上將抵台灣訪問，中美高級將領舉行會議，討論加強兩國軍事合作事宜。

八月廿八日　美國前副總統尼克森抵台灣訪問，認為美國越南的堅定政策，足以贏得戰爭勝利。

八月三十日　蔣介石總統發佈命令，特任高魁元上將為陸軍總司令，馮啟聰中將為海軍總司令，唐守治上將為國防部總政治作戰部主任。中國與美國代表在台北市簽訂「美軍在中華民國地位協定」。

九月七日　蔣總統夫人宋美齡女士抵華盛頓訪問。

九月九日　北京人民政府宣佈，「西藏自治區」正式成立。

九月十二日　馬來西亞華人要求以華語作為馬來西亞聯邦的國語，但馬來西亞「巫統」人民反對。

九月十九日　蔣總統夫人宋美齡女士，在華府與美國前總統艾森豪夫婦晤談。中華民國國防部長蔣經國離台北赴美國訪問。

九月廿三日　中華民國國防部長蔣經國晉謁美國總統詹森，討論當前世界問題。

九月廿八日　中華民國國防部長蔣經國，在華府獲得美國前總統艾森豪授權，駁斥投靠中共的李宗仁離間中美關係之謊言：「美國在四十四年（一九五五）擬推翻中華民國。」

十月四日　中華民國國防部長蔣經國

自美國返抵台北。

十月九日　中華民國前駐美國大使及駐聯合國常任代表蔣廷黻，在紐約病逝，享年七十一歲（一八九五～一九六五）。

十月十日　蔣介石總統發表雙十國慶文告，書勉全國同胞：「要以國父先烈開國的堅毅精神來國；要以北伐打倒軍閥的奮鬥精神來討毛；要以八年抗戰的犧牲精來光復大陸；要以建設台灣的實踐精神來重建各省。」

十月十二日　美國空軍參謀長麥康納爾上校抵台灣訪問。

十月十三日　北京人民政府宣佈，批准將僮族改稱「壯族」，將廣西省僮族自治區改稱「廣西壯族自治區」。

十月十五日　二次大戰期間曾任中國戰區美軍總司令魏德邁將軍訪問台灣，蔣介石總統設宴款待。

十月廿五日　台灣省光復二十週年，全國各界熱烈慶祝，蔣介石總統訓勉同胞為光復大陸而努力。

十月廿九日　前中華民國立法院長及

行政院長孫科自美國返抵台北。

十一月六日　華僑救國聯合總會第三次代表大會在台北市開幕，會期三天。

十一月十日　中國國民黨中央常務委員會會議決定，國民大會臨時會議定於明年二月一日召開。中共黨報解放日報總編輯姚文元，在上海文匯報發表「評新編歷史劇海瑞罷官」，對作者北京副市長吳晗發動清算的文章。

十一月十一日　中共空軍飛行員李顯斌、李財旺及康保生三人，駕駛蘇聯造伊留申二八型噴射轟炸機一架，自杭州起飛投奔自由，降落在台灣。

十一月十三日　烏坵附近海面發生海戰，中華民國國防部說，國軍兵艦擊沉中共艦艇四艘，擊傷一艘，國軍損失掃雷艇一艘。

十一月十六日　蔣介石總統在台灣南部基地，校閱三軍聯合舉行之「重慶演習」。

十一月十七日　聯合國第二十屆大會，以四十七票對四十六票另二十票棄權的表決，否決使中

共政權進入聯合國的建議案。

十一月廿七日　中國國民黨邀請青年黨及民主社會黨人士，於十二月間舉行兩次座談會，將廣泛交換國是意見。

十二月一日　中華民國政府公佈「姓名條例」修正案。

十二月二日　美國第七艦隊司令勃萊克辭職，由郝蘭德將軍繼任。

十二月二日　中華民國內政部宣佈說，台灣的瘧疾已絕跡。世界衛生組織官員稱讚台灣防瘧的成功。

十二月九日　美國將一批 F-5A 型超音波噴射式戰鬥機移交給中華民國空軍使用。
　　蘇聯共黨主席米高揚辭職，由包戈尼繼任。

十二月十九日　中國國民黨中央倡導節約，新年不拜年，不寄賀年片。

十二月廿二日　蔣介石總統發佈召集令，中華民國國民大會定明年二月一日在台北市舉行臨時會議。

十二月廿五日　中華民國政府決定全面推行家庭計劃，提高國民的生活水準。

十二月廿九日　美國參謀首長聯席會議主席惠勒上將，抵台灣訪問。

中華民國五十五年（一九六六）

一月一日　蔣介石總統發表元旦告全國同胞書，指出今年為國民革命決定性關頭。勗勉萬眾一心，內外夾擊，予中共以徹底消滅。

一月三日　中華民國行政院決定，撥款興建公寓住宅，配給中央級公務人員使用。

一月七日　中華民國政府頒發獎金給駕飛機投奔自由祖國的中共空軍人員：黃金兩千兩給李顯斌，黃金一千兩給李財旺，另一千兩為康保生遺屬保留。

一月九日　蔣介石總統頒發召集令，中華民國第一屆國民代表大會第四次會議定於二月十九日舉行。

一月十二日　企業鉅子董浩雲在日本新建造的巨型油輪「東亞巨龍」號舉行下水典禮，使中華民國商船總噸位已逾百萬噸。

一月十四日　中華民國行政院公佈「檢肅共諜聯保辦法」。

一月二十日　反共報人前香港大公報
　　　　督印人周榆瑞，自倫敦返台灣
　　　　觀光。

一月廿六日　國際聞名的作家林語堂
　　　　博士，自紐約返國訪問四天。

一月廿八日　中華民國立法院會議通
　　　　過「處理在華美軍刑案條
　　　　例」。

一月廿九日　美國空軍第五十運兵機
　　　　中隊，進入台中市公館機場。

二月一日　中華民國國民大會臨時
　　　　會，在台北市中山堂開幕，蔣
　　　　介石總統對大會致詞，勗勉代
　　　　表同仁以光復大陸為準繩，重
　　　　視憲法尊嚴，貫徹共同責任。
　　　　大會預定二月八日閉幕。

二月七日　中華民國國民大會臨時會
　　　　通過，修正「動員戡亂臨時條
　　　　款」，並決議接受不修訂憲法
　　　　之建議。

二月八日　中華民國國民大會臨時會
　　　　通過「兩權行使辦法」後宣告
　　　　閉幕。

二月九日　中華民國第一屆國民大會
　　　　第四次會議，開始辦理代表報
　　　　到手續。

二月十二日　中國共產黨中央批准
　　　　「文化革命五人小組關於當前

學術討論的匯報提綱」（簡稱
二月提綱）。

二月十五日　大韓民國總統朴正熙伉
　　　　儷抵達台北訪問四天，與蔣介
　　　　石總統會談兩國有關問題。

二月十九日　中華民國第一屆國民大
　　　　會第四次會，在台北市中山堂
　　　　開幕，蔣介石總統親臨致詞，
　　　　指出「中共偽政權已陷於孤立
　　　　絕境，我十六年來軍經建設已
　　　　奠定基礎，拔除禍根，具必勝
　　　　信念」。

二月廿二日　美國第七艦隊司令郝蘭
　　　　德抵台灣訪問。

二月廿六日　中華民國行政院宣佈，
　　　　軍公教人員待遇今年起調整，
　　　　每年加發薪兩個月。省轄市鄉
　　　　鎮比照實施。

三月七日　中國國民黨九屆三中全會
　　　　在台北市陽明山開幕，會期四
　　　　天，蔣介石總裁親臨致詞，講
　　　　述「本黨在反共革命大形勢中
　　　　的責任」。

三月九日　中國大陸發生強烈地震，
　　　　震央在河北省刑台，強度達九
　　　　級，北京地區亦達六級。

三月十二日　印尼總統蘇卡諾下台，
　　　　陸軍總司令蘇哈托接收政權，

並宣佈解散共黨組織。

三月十四日　蔣介石總統應美國海軍邀請，登美國核子動力航空母艦「勇往」號參觀。

三月二十日　中國郵政創辦七十週年紀念，郵政總局在台北新建的郵政博物館正式開放。

三月廿一日　國民大會第四次會議，選舉蔣介石連任中華民國第四任總統。

三月廿二日　國民大會選舉嚴家淦為中華民國第四任副總統。

三月廿六日　中國國民黨宣佈，大陸反共組織已匯成巨大力量，最近有六位國民黨同志在大陸殉難。

四月五日　中共官方人民日報發表專文：「海瑞罵皇帝」和「海瑞罷官」是「反黨反社會主義的兩株大毒草」。

四月七日　印尼境內兩萬名華裔人舉行反中共示威。

四月十二日　在日本居留多年的鄭萬福，宣佈解散「台灣民政黨」，自東京返回台北。

四月十六日　美國國務卿魯斯克，提出十項美國對華政策，其中包括：尊重對中華民國防禦條約

的承諾，支持中華民國在聯合國的地位，美國無意進攻中國大陸，及增加美國與中共的非官方接觸。

四月廿一日　菲律賓首都馬尼拉的華僑商店，在菲政府吊銷營業的威脅下，將中文招牌取下。

四月廿三日　緬甸境內親中共的華文學校，已被緬方下令關閉。

五月一日　美國軍事援華顧問團成立十五週年，蔣介石總統設盛大茶會款待美國顧問團官員。

五月三日　中華民國政府表示，歡迎美國任命馬康衛為美國駐中華民國新大使。

五月五日　菲律賓首都馬尼拉市長修改發佈的命令，允許華人商店的中文招牌可以繼續使用。

五月九日　中共政府宣佈，在新疆舉行第三次核子爆炸試驗。

五月十日　美軍太平洋總司令夏普上將抵台灣訪問兩天。

五月十六日　北京中共發表「關於無產階級文化大革命的決定」。

五月二十日　中華民國第四任總統蔣介石、副總統嚴家淦就典禮在台北市中山堂隆重舉行，全國軍民熱烈慶祝。

五月廿七日　中華民國副總統兼行政
　　　院長嚴家淦宣佈新內閣組成，
　　　新任副院長黃少谷，新任外交
　　　部長魏道明，新任內政部長徐
　　　慶鐘等。

六月三日　北京中共政府宣佈，「北
　　　京市委員會第一書記」彭真被
　　　撤免，由李雪峰繼任。同時彭
　　　真黨羽吳晗、鄧拓、廖沫沙
　　　（即吳南星集團）均遭整肅。
　　　北京大學校長陸平，被中共指
　　　為反黨分子。

六月六日　中共宣佈，中共北京市委
　　　決定改組「北京日報」、「北
　　　京晚報」，及暫時停刊「前」
　　　雜誌。

六月九日　台灣省各地豪雨不止，河
　　　川暴漲，堤坊告急，為近數十
　　　年來僅見。

六月十二日　中共連日藉「文化大革
　　　命」幌子進行政治大整肅，南
　　　京大學（原中央大學）校長及
　　　武漢大學副校長等相繼被整
　　　肅。

六月十六日　中華民國監察院會議通
　　　過，孫科任考試院長，程天放
　　　任考試院副院長。

六月廿五日　中國國民黨中央舉行國
民黨示範小組長表揚大會，蔣
　　　介石總裁親臨主持儀式。訓勉
　　　同志提供更大貢獻，強化基層
　　　組織。

六月廿六日　中共實施整肅聲中，原
　　　子科學家錢學森等四十餘人，
　　　被控從事反毛活動。

七月三日　美國國務卿魯斯克抵華訪
　　　問，蔣介石總統兩度接見，就
　　　世界局勢及中美共同利益問題
　　　舉行會談。魯斯克發表聲明，
　　　強調美國總統詹森對華政策絕
　　　不受姑息分子影響。

七月八日　中國青年反共救國團主任
　　　蔣經國對青年集合講話，促使
　　　堅定反共復國信念，鍛鍊技
　　　能，研習科學。

七月九日　中共宣傳部長陸定一被整
　　　肅，由陶鑄接任。中共中央宣
　　　佈，任命陳伯達為中共中央委
　　　員會「文化革命小組組長」。

七月廿四日　中華民國中央研究院舉
　　　行第六次院士院會議，選出胡
　　　世楨、鄧昌黎及何炳棣等八人
　　　為新院士。蔣介石總統以茶會
　　　款待回國學人與中央研究院院
　　　士。

八月三日　中國國民黨中央常務委員

會會議修正通過，「中共駐海
外工作人員立功起義來歸獎勵
辦法」。

八月八日　中共中央發表「關於無產
階級文化大革命的決定」。

八月十日　毛澤東在北京會見「文化
大革命」群眾，要求他們「關
心國家大事，把文化大革命進
行到底」。

八月十二日　中國共產黨中央委員八
屆十一中全會閉幕發表公報。
全會自一日開始在北京舉行。
中共中央正式成立「文革小
組」，陳伯達任組長，江青為
第一副組長，張春橋等為副組
長，姚文元等九人為組員。

八月十三日　西德總理艾哈德鄭重表
示，西德絕不與中共政權建立
邦交。

八月十六日　北京中共宣佈，林彪任
中央委員會副主席及中央軍事
委員會副主席。

八月十八日　中共權力鬥爭揭曉，林
彪升為中共第二號頭目，劉少
奇被打垮，排名降到第八。中
共號召「文化大革命」利用青
年「紅衛兵」開始暴亂，要打
倒四舊（文化、習慣、風俗、

思想）。
中共在北京天安門廣場舉行
「文化大革命」群眾大會，由
陳伯達主持，毛澤東、林彪、
周恩來、鄧小平、劉少奇等參
加。

八月二十日　毛澤東在北京首次接見
「紅衛兵」，利用無知少年，
打倒異己，大陸陷於混亂。

八月廿二日　中華民國僑務委員會通
告海外僑胞，協助中共駐外人
員起義投奔自由。
中國青年黨領袖左舜生自香港
返回台灣。

八月廿五日　中華民國行政院會議通
過，任命陳之邁為駐日本大
使。日本政府已任命島津久大
為駐中華民國大使。

八月廿六日　中共「紅衛兵」在大陸
各地發動暴亂，破壞古蹟文
物，迫害教會修女，驅使二十
萬青年舉行反蘇聯示威遊行，
並迫使「民主同盟」關閉在北
京的總部。
蘇聯外交部向中共駐莫斯科大
使館抗議「紅衛兵」的反蘇聯
挑釁行為。

八月廿八日　廣州市「紅衛兵」，搗

毀黃花岡七十二烈士墓頂頂端的自由神像。

北京市「紅衛兵」在蘇聯大使館前示威，高喊反對修正主義。

八月廿九日　中共「紅衛兵」到處暴行，外商機構無以生存，英商怡和公司宣佈自大陸撤出。

八月卅一日　毛澤東在北京接見「紅衛兵」和「革命師生」群眾，由林彪代表毛澤東講話，聲稱決心鬥垮「走資派」的當權派。

中共「紅衛兵」愈演愈烈，東德共黨向中共提出嚴重抗議，使中共下令約束「紅衛兵」暴行。

九月二日　中共「紅衛兵」在大陸各地遭到地方中共幹部的反對，使大陸陷於混亂動盪局面。

九月九日　美國國院發表聲明，重申美國對中華民國的承諾，支持中華民國在聯合國的代表權。

九月十二日　中共中央宣佈改組，劉少奇常委職位被剝奪。

中共「紅衛兵」在北京開始發行「紅衛兵報」，毛澤東為紅衛兵「最高司令」，林彪為副最高司令。

九月十五日　中共被迫要求「紅衛兵」暫停在農村的暴行。日本宣佈禁止日本青年前往中共地區。

北京的「大公報」被改名為「前進報」。

毛澤東、林彪、周恩來、鄧小平、劉少奇等再度出現於北京天安門，接見「紅衛兵」，並且由林彪代表講話。

九月十七日　蔣介石總統發佈命令，任命余伯泉為總統府參軍長，接替彭孟緝職務。

九月二十日　中共政府宣佈，北京到法國首都巴黎的飛機航線正式開航。

聯合國第二十一次大會，以五十七票對四十六票另十七票棄權的表決，否決關於排斥中華民國代表權的建議案。

九月廿一日　上海市民眾反對「紅衛兵」暴亂，再度發生衝突，造成流血事件。

九月廿二日　美國空軍部長布朗抵達台灣訪問。

九月廿四日　中共「紅衛兵」的大字報，開始攻擊劉少奇。

九月廿五日　中共「紅衛兵」掘毀北京市郊的外國人墓地，英國、法國等向中共政權提出嚴重抗議。

九月三十日　大陸影劇導演文逸民、演員伍秀芳等投奔自由，自香港抵達台北。

十月一日　中共政府在北京天安門廣場舉行「十一」國慶，以「紅衛兵」為中心的群眾大會，由林彪代表毛澤東講話，公開攻擊蘇聯東德等共產國家。

十月十日　蔣介石總統於中華民國雙十國慶日發表文告，揭發毛澤東的陰謀與罪惡，號召中共黨軍幹部接應國軍反攻，先行起義，聲明於推倒毛酋後，實行普選。蔣總統並發表告全國同胞書，指出亞洲的共禍起於中國大陸，自必終於中國大陸。

十月十九日　蔣介石總統在台灣北部基地，親臨校閱三軍的「南昌」演習。

十月廿二日　蔣總統夫人宋美齡女士，在美國舊金山發表演講，指出毛澤東狂妄一如德國的希特勒，並嚴辭斥責「兩個中國」謬論。

十月廿六日　蔣總統夫人宋美齡女士訪美經年後返抵台北。
中國國民黨元老陳立夫自美國返國。

十月廿七日　北京師範大學及人民大學「紅衛兵」，張貼「大字報」批評劉少奇及鄧小平。

十月卅一日　是日為蔣介石總統八十歲壽誕，全國歡欣慶祝，「蔣總統思想言論集」出版。

十一月三日　蔣介石總統接見美國主管遠東事務助理國務卿彭岱，聽取在馬尼拉舉行之越南戰爭七國高階會議報告，並將中華民國對世局意見告知彭岱。
毛澤東、林彪等在北京第四次接見「紅衛兵」。中共宣稱「紅衛兵」有兩百多萬眾。

十一月七日　中共「紅衛兵」大字報，攻擊中共中央宣傳部長陶鑄及副總理李先念。

十一月九日　美國太平洋陸軍總司令畢治上將、美國空軍副參謀長哈羅威上將及美國空軍戰術司令狄索威上將訪華，晉謁蔣介石總統會談。

十一月十日　香港中共「文匯報」編輯主任兼採訪主任劉粵生投奔

自由抵達台北。

十一月十一日　毛澤東於十日及十一日連續兩天，在北京檢閱「紅衛兵」兩百多萬人。

十一月十二日　是日為中華民國國父孫中山先生一百零一歲誕辰。在台北市陽明山中山樓興建之中華文化堂正式落成，蔣介石總統親臨主持儀式。蔣總統並宣佈將國父誕辰定為中華文化復興節。

在台北市士林鎮外雙溪興建之中山博物院舉行落成典禮，政府決定易名為「故宮博物院」。

十一月十五日　美國總統詹森特別代表布萊克抵台北訪問四天，與中華民國官員商談亞洲區域經濟合作問題。

北京的「北京大學」紅旗戰鬥組的聶元樟說：「劉少奇、鄧小平是黨內資產階級當權派的代表。」

十一月十六日　中共中央下令，自十一月廿一日起到明年四月止的期間，禁止「紅衛兵」赴北京。

十一月廿一日　美國駐聯合國代表高德柏重申立場，美國無法接受排斥中華民國代表權的任何建議。

十一月廿二日　中華民國駐聯合國代表劉鍇及駐美國大使周書楷，先後向美國申明堅決反對義大利國所提出的建議：「要求聯合國大會設立委員會研究中國代表權問題」。

十一月廿六日　毛澤東、林彪、周恩來、朱德等在北京第八次接見二百五十萬「紅衛兵」。

十一月廿九日　聯合國第二十一屆大會，以六十票對三十四票棄權的表決，拒絕義大利等六國提出的排斥中華民國代表權建議案。

十二月一日　佐藤榮作當選日本自由民主黨總裁及日本政府首相。

十二月二日　中華航空公司新開闢的台北至越南西貢直達客機航線，今日起飛行。

中華民國前國防部長白崇禧上將在台北病逝，享年七十四歲（一八九三～一九六六）。

十二月四日　中共「紅衛兵」宣佈，彭真、萬里，作家田漢與夏衍等被逮捕。

十二月七日　美國國務卿魯斯克抵達台北，與中華民國副總統嚴家淦舉行會談。魯斯克發表談話，強調美國對華政策不變。

十二月八日　中共「紅衛兵」大字報攻擊劉少奇為中國的赫魯雪夫，並列舉劉的「十大罪狀」。

十二月十一日　中共出動海軍艦艇恫嚇，要求澳門葡萄牙國當局禁止反共人士活動，澳門宣佈接受中共的要求。

十二月十二日　是日為張學良與楊虎城發動之「西安事變」劫持蔣介石委員長三十週年紀念，台灣沒有任何舉動。

十二月十四日　中華民國選手吳阿民，在曼谷第五屆亞洲運動會榮獲十項全能運動金牌獎。

十二月十六日　中華民國舉行的全國戶口與住宅普查工作，已告完成。

十二月二十日　中共內爭面臨攤牌，北京市面出現大批要求罷黜劉少奇及鄧小平的標語。

十二月廿一日　中共「紅衛兵」宣佈，公審鬥爭中共前宣傳部長陸定一等八名幹部。

十二月廿三日　澳門葡萄牙當局對中共完全屈服，反共團體遭受迫害。
北京「紅衛兵」大字報透露，中共政權前總參謀長羅瑞卿已被拘捕。

十二月廿六日　中國國民黨九屆四中全會在台北市陽明山揭幕，會期四天，蔣介石總裁親臨主持儀式。

十二月廿七日　毛澤東、林彪等以「全國紅色工人造反者聯合會」名義接收總工會，並下令「工人日報」停刊。
中共政府宣佈，在大陸西部地區舉行第五次核子試驗，其威力相當於數十萬噸的黃色炸藥（TNT）。

十二月廿九日　中國國民黨九屆四中全會今日舉行閉幕典禮，全會通過「改進本黨組織適應戰鬥需要方案」、「中華文化復興運動推行方案」等案及改選蔣經國、謝東閔等十九人為中央常務委員。

十二月卅一日　蔣介石總統核准將台北市改制為院轄市，行政院成立小組負責籌劃台北市改制事

宜。

中華民國五十六年（一九六七）

一月一日　蔣介石總統元旦發表告全國同胞書，強調唯有中國人才能解決中國問題，亦唯有從中國問題的解決上，才能求得亞洲與世界禍亂問題的解決。

一月二日　中華民國政府新設動員戡亂機構，定名為「國家安全會議」，由黃少谷任祕書長，下設建設、動員、政戰、科學發展四會。

一月三日　澳門葡國當局下令禁止懸掛中華民國國旗。

一月五日　毛澤東指名批評劉少奇與鄧小平抗命，揭露過去八年期間中共內閧真相，說明毛澤東係被逼迫辭去中共黨主席職務。

中共中央宣傳部長陶鑄，被紅衛兵拖往街頭遊行公審。

一月六日　中華民國政府宣佈，一九六六年對外貿易總值輸出輸入額達十一億五千餘萬美元，其中輸出額佔五億六千二百萬美元，輸入額佔五億九千餘萬美元，入超計兩千七百餘萬美元。

一月七日　中國大陸各地紅衛兵暴亂情勢不斷擴大，據報導南京市有十萬工人與紅衛兵發生衝突。

昆山工人亦起暴亂，使京滬鐵路交通中斷。

一月九日　上海市數萬反毛工人罷工，全市陷於混亂狀態。中共內鬥亦尖銳化，傳「文化革命小組」內部告分裂。

一月十一日　澳門葡國當局下令關閉中華民國大陸救災總會辦事處，外交部命令召回駐葡萄牙使館代辦吳文輝以示抗議。

一月十二日　台灣耆宿丘念台在日本東京病逝，享年七十四歲（一八九四～一九六六）。

一月十三日　蔣介石總統發佈命令，任命高玉樹為台北特別市（亦稱院轄市）首任市長。

金門島東北部上空發生激烈空戰，中華民國國防部稱，中共米格十九式飛機兩架被國軍飛機擊落。

一月二十日　中華民國空軍人員完成架設第一座氣象衛星收報站已開始使用，使今後氣象預報的

準確性大為增高。

一月廿七日　北京傳說，中共以「美
　　國特務」罪名下令逮捕投靠中
　　共的中華民國前副總統李宗
　　仁。

二月一日　蔣介石總統發佈命令，設
　　置動員戡亂時期「國家安全會
　　議」，特派黃少谷為秘書長，
　　同時命令將「國防會議」撤
　　銷。

二月三日　中共宣佈，親毛派成立
　　「北京市人民公社籌備委員
　　會」。

二月五日　中共宣佈，「上海市人民
　　公社」成立，張春橋為主任，
　　姚文元為副主任。

二月十八日　中華民國行政院訂定中
　　央與地方機構權責劃分方案，
　　行政院將成立人事、事物、法
　　制及研究四機構。

二月廿五日　中共宣佈，「上海市人
　　民公社」改稱為「上海市革命
　　委員會」。

二月廿八日　是日為一九四七年台北
　　市發生「二二八事變」二十週
　　年紀念日，未有任何舉動。

三月一日　蔣介石總統接見美國駐聯
　　合國常任代表高德柏，討論世
界局勢。高德柏前來亞洲訪問
　　中華民國、大韓民國、越南及
　　菲律賓等四國。

三月八日　美國太平洋三軍總司令夏
　　普上將，抵達台灣訪問四天。

三月十一日　台北市興建之「土地改
　　革紀念館」舉行落成典禮，由
　　副總統嚴家淦主持儀式。

三月十九日　中華民國內政部與台灣
　　省政府，進行全面修訂地方自
　　治法規。。

三月廿三日　法國政府宣佈，將中華
　　民國在巴黎的駐聯合國文化教
　　育組織的兩幢房屋移交與中共
　　方面。

三月廿七日　泰國總理他農將軍偕夫
　　人抵達台灣訪問四天。

四月四日　澳大利亞總理荷特夫婦抵
　　達台灣訪問三天，與蔣介石總
　　統就世局及亞洲情勢交換意
　　見。

四月七日　中華民國外交部在台北召
　　開駐外使節會議，旨在強調外
　　交主動，籲友邦聲援中國大陸
　　的抗暴運動。

四月十日　美國前副總統尼克森抵台
　　北訪問，晉謁蔣介石總統致
　　敬。

四月十二日　美國政府宣佈，中國著
　　　名音樂家、大陸「中國音樂學
　　　院」院長馬思聰已投奔自由，
　　　安全抵達美國。

四月十九日　中華民國內政部公佈新
　　　聞用紙辦法，由每日出版兩大
　　　張放寬為兩大張半。台北市與
　　　台灣省大部份報紙將擴版。

四月二十日　國防部宣佈，中華民國
　　　傘兵部隊實施空降演習，證明
　　　有能力一旦下令反攻大陸，可
　　　在三小時內空降大陸作戰。

四月廿九日　中華民國女童子軍舉行
　　　第一次檢閱大會，蔣總統夫人
　　　宋美齡女士親臨檢閱，並致詞
　　　勉勵全體女童子軍忠於國家實
　　　踐人生以服務為目的銘言。

四月三十日　中共各地紅衛兵又湧入
　　　北京市內。

五月一日　蔣介石總統偕夫人舉行茶
　　　會款待美軍駐華官員。

五月七日　中華民國副總統嚴家淦，
　　　在東京與日本首相佐藤榮作會
　　　談，就中共情勢及越南問題交
　　　換意見，並與日本前首相吉田
　　　茂會晤。

五月八日　台北市改制為院轄市，自
　　　七月一日起實施新制。景美、

木柵、內湖、南港、士林及北
投等六個台北縣的鄉鎮併入，
面積計二七二點一平方公里，
較原市區面積六六點九八平方
公里擴大三倍，人口總數增至
一百四十六萬。

五月九日　中華民國副總統嚴家淦訪
　　　問華府，與美國總統詹森就中
　　　國大陸現狀、東南亞局勢及中
　　　華民國經濟情況等問題舉行會
　　　談。

五月十六日　中共中央宣佈，撤銷文
　　　化大革命「五人小組」，另設
　　　立委員會，隸屬於中央「政治
　　　局」。

五月二十日　香港與九龍各界百餘自
　　　由團體發表聲明，支持香港政
　　　府平亂措施。中共在北京舉行
　　　十萬群眾反英大會。

五月廿七日　蔣介石總統接見嚴家淦
　　　副總統，聽取嚴氏報告訪問美
　　　國經過情形。

五月三十日　投奔自由的著名音樂家
　　　馬思聰，在美國國會作證中
　　　說，中共的核子試爆裝置為法
　　　國製造的。

六月一日　加拿大蒙特利爾的博覽會
　　　中華民國館，於五月三十日失

火焚毀，行政院會議決定儘速
重建開放。

六月五日　中東以色列與阿拉伯國家
戰爭爆發，埃及封鎖蘇彝士運
交通，使中華民國石油運輸價
受影響。

六月七日　中國國民黨中央委員會，
在台北市舉行五十五年度示範
小組長表揚儀式。

六月十二日　台灣造船公司全部自力
建造的第一艘巨型貨輪「銀
翼」號，舉行命名下水典禮，
由副總統嚴家淦親臨主持儀
式。

六月十五日　美國軍事援華顧問團新
任團長戚烈拉少將抵台北就
職。

六月十七日　北京人民政府宣佈，
「在大陸西北地區上空爆炸第
一顆氫彈成功」。

六月廿八日　蔣介石總統發佈命令，
任命黎玉璽為總統府參軍長，
高魁元為參謀總長，陳大慶為
陸軍總司令，賴名湯為空軍總
司令及劉玉章為台灣警備總司
令。

七月一日　台北市正式改制為院轄市
（特別市），院轄市市政府及

臨時市議會舉行成立典禮，市
長高玉樹及市議會議長張祥傳
同時就職。

七月四日　美國海軍軍令部長穆勒上
將，抵台北訪問。

七月七日　是日為蘆溝橋「七七事
變」三十週年紀念日。

七月九日　中華民國外交部次長楊西
昆，自台北啟程赴非洲作第十
九次友好訪問。
香港政府英國當局表示，決不
向中共的暴力行為低頭。

七月十一日　香港的親中共分子在鬧
區縱火，投擲炸彈，情勢嚴重
英國當局宣佈實施全面戒嚴。

七月十三日　中共「革命委員會」在
北京召開「動員大會」，號召
集中力量徹底批鬥彭真集團與
其背後支持者。

七月十四日　美軍協防台灣新任司令
邱約翰中將，抵達台北就職。
中華民國外交部在西班牙首都
馬德里召開駐歐洲各國使節會
議，會期三天。

七月十六日　香港政府出動大批軍
警，逮捕親中共暴亂分子五百
餘人。

七月十九日　美國國務卿魯斯克發表

談話，斥責中共好戰，對鄰邦不存善意，對於受中共核子威脅的國家，美國考慮予以防衛保證。

七月廿四日　天主教樞機主教（紅衣主教）田耕莘，因病在嘉義聖瑪爾定醫院逝世。羅馬天主教教宗保祿六世、蔣介石總統等皆致電唁。

七月廿七日　中華民國教育部擬就九年義務教育學區劃分原則：每四萬人口為一學區，設一所學區國民初中，鄉鎮地區，每一鄉鎮設一所學區國民初中。

七月廿八日　中華文化復興運動推行委員會，在台北正式成立，請蔣介石總統兼任會長，並通過綱要及組織章程。
　　香港政府英國當局為對付親中共分子，通過緊急法令，授權軍警打擊暴亂活動，拘人限期由二十四小時延長至一年。

七月廿九日　台灣南部高雄市港口擴建第二港口工程，正式開工實施。

七月卅一日　中共黨「人民日報」及「解放軍報」，發表社論「祝建軍四十週年」，抨擊彭德懷、羅瑞卿等進行反毛運動。

八月三日　中華民國駐美國大使周書楷奉召返國，磋商有關聯合國代表權問題。

八月七日　蔣介石總統提名林紀東、黃正銘、曾繁康、李學燈等十五人為大法官。

八月九日　中國國民黨中央常務委員會會議通過行政院所訂之「九年國民教育實施方案」。

八月十日　中華民國海外華文文教會議在台北市開幕，蔣介石總統親臨主持典禮，訓勉僑胞實踐三民主義民族文化，強化海外文教機構。

八月十一日　香港政府下令，將九龍全部邊界加以封鎖，以阻止中共暴亂分子越界滋事。

八月十五日　中華民國總統府資政、前行政院長孔祥熙博士在美國紐約病逝，享年八十八歲（一八八〇～一九六七）。

八月十七日　蔣總統夫人宋美齡女士偕蔣緯國將軍乘專機赴美，參加孔祥熙博士葬禮。蔣介石總統除致電弔唁外，並手撰「孔庸之先生事略」、題頒「為國盡瘁」輓額，以申悼念。

八月十七日　第十七屆東方學者國際會議，在美國密西根州安阿堡舉行，中國學者三百四十人參加。

香港政府下令，將「香港夜報」、「新午報」及「田豐日報」等親中共報紙加以封閉。

八月廿二日　台灣省議會通過決議，凡公職候選人必須經檢核合格。

八月廿六日　中華民國立法院會議通過「教育部文化局組織條例」，將成立文化局。

九月一日　中共北京市「革命委員會」召開擴大會議，號召加強鎮壓「地、富、反、壞、右」五類分子破壞活動，並堅決取締「五、一六兵團」。

九月五日　反共義士莊榮金等十二人，殺死中共幹部奪船起義投奔台灣。

太平洋美軍總司令夏普上將抵台灣訪問三天。

九月八日　日本內閣總理大臣佐藤榮作兩度晉謁蔣介石總統，商討中、日兩國共同問題，並就當前世局及大陸中共情勢交換意見。佐藤於七日抵達台北。

九月十日　中共當局為報復日本首相佐藤榮作訪問中華民國，下令將日本「每日新聞」、「產經新聞」及「東京新聞」三家報紙駐北京記者驅逐出境。

九月十一日　台北市改為院轄市的新市議會，舉行首次會議。

九月十四日　中華民國行政院會議通過，「修正台灣省各縣市實施地方自治綱要」等六種法規。

九月十六日　蔣介石總統親自主持國家安全會議第四次會議，決定「民國五十八年度（一九六九）國家建設重點草案」。

九月十九日　中華民國駐越南大使館，遭越共恐怖分子投擲炸彈，館內職員一人死亡，另廿七人受傷。同時，大使館新聞參事鍾道，在越南首都西貢堤岸被共黨分子射擊兩槍受傷。

九月二十日　越南首都西貢警察廳長宣佈，對中華民國駐越南大使館投擲炸彈的暴徒已被逮捕。

九月廿四日　北京新華通訊社報導說，毛澤東最近曾赴華北、華東、中南等地區視察文化革命現況「提供最新指示」。

九月廿五日　世界反共聯盟第一屆大

會在台北市舉行，共有六十七個國家及十三個反共組織的代表參加。蔣介石總統親臨大會致詞，強調根除亞洲禍亂，必須首先解決中共，並促自由世界應聯合戰鬥擊敗分裂的共黨集團。

西藏流亡印度的達賴喇嘛抵日本東京訪問。

九月廿七日　亞洲華商貿易會議第五屆大會在台北開幕，會期四天。

北京消息，劉少奇發表廣播演說，誓言「推翻毛澤東」。

九月廿八日　中國至聖先師孔子誕辰及教師節，蔣介石總統親宴優良教師，宣示決心改進教育，貫徹實施九年國民教育制度。

九月三十日　亞洲人民反共聯盟第十三屆大會在台北開幕，會期兩天。

十月一日　中共宣佈，北京舉行五十萬人大集會，慶祝中共「人民政府」成立十八週年，林彪發出「鬥私批修」的號召，攻擊蘇聯，七國的共黨代表退出國慶大會會場。

十月二日　美國國會眾議院會議通過，將一艘驅逐艦租借給中華民國海軍使用。

十月四日　印尼棉蘭市一萬五千餘華僑，宣佈放棄中共發給的護照。

十月七日　蘇聯莫斯科電台廣報導說，中共已將劉少奇逮捕拘禁。同時，蘇聯「黨生活雜誌」說，史達林整肅期間，共黨黨員七十九萬七千人死亡。

十月九日　中國國民黨中央宣佈，台灣各縣市議員及鄉鎮長改選，國民黨內提名登記完成。

十月十日　蔣介石總統於民國五十六年雙十國慶節發表告全國同胞書，號召一切反毛反共力量，「從文化政治上結合，從軍事行動上會師，弔民伐罪，一鼓勘平共亂」。

十月十八日　強烈颱風「解拉」襲擊台灣，帶來暴風豪雨，在宜蘭、基隆地區造成重大損失。

滿清末代皇帝溥儀（年號宣統），以患尿毒症不治，在北京逝世。

十月十九日　中華民國行政院會議通過，修正「外交、教育及經濟三部組織法」。

行政院指定台北院轄市，作為「實施都市平均地權條例」實行區域。

十月廿三日　中日合作策進委員會第十二屆會議在東京開幕，會期六天。中華民國代表張群對大會演說「營救東方文化，清除共產毒素」。

十月廿五日　台灣省光復節，各界熱烈慶祝。蔣介石總統書勉同胞，擴大台灣省三民主義建設成果，提早完成光復大陸神聖使命。

十月廿七日　蔣介石總統在台灣南部海域，親校陸海空三軍聯合兩棲突擊登陸作戰的「南京演習」。並在高雄縣鳳山主持陸海空三軍官校聯合畢業典禮。北京人民政府宣佈，與印尼斷絕外交關係。

十月卅一日　蔣介石總統八秩晉一華誕，全國同胞及海外僑胞展開熱烈祝壽活動。

十一月二日　中華民國對外貿易委員會主任委員徐柏園宣稱，今年台灣省輸出總額預計約六億五千萬美元，創光復以來的最高額。

十一月七日　台灣土地開發公司計劃投資新台幣三億元，在新店、桃園、內壢、頭份、潭子等五個工業區從事開發事業。

第二次世界大戰期間駐華美軍總司令魏德邁將軍（已退休）抵達台灣訪問。

十一月十二日　中國國民黨九屆五中全會在台北市陽明山開幕，蔣介石總裁在典禮中訓勉全體同志，要知恥反省，力圖精進，滅共復國。行政院長嚴家淦對全會作政治報告，指出中共「情勢瀕臨崩潰，國際情勢對我有利」。

十一月十五日　北京中共新華通訊社報導說，最近考古家在周口店又發現新「北京人」的骨骼。

十一月十九日　中華民國中央銀行為應付英鎊貶值，採取緊急措施，命令暫停收兌英磅、港幣、馬來亞幣及新加坡幣。

十一月廿三日　中國國民黨九屆五中全會，在通過對政治報告決議文與四項慰問電文後，圓滿閉幕。全會選出嚴家淦、蔣經國、謝東閔等十九人為中央常務委員。

十一月廿四日　台灣省台中市長張啟
　　仲被公務員懲戒委員會予以撤
　　職並停止任用一年。

十一月廿五日　中華民國政府，正在
　　積極編製「第五期四年經濟計
　　劃」。

十一月廿七日　中國國民黨第九次婦
　　女工作會議在台北揭幕，蔣總
　　統夫人宋美齡女士親臨主持。
　　國防部長蔣經國訪問日本，與
　　日本首相佐藤榮作舉行會談。
　　蔣氏說，中、日兩國應加深瞭
　　解合作。
　　聯合國第廿二屆大會以五十九
　　票對四十五票另十七票棄權的
　　表決，否決使中共進入聯合國
　　建議案。

十一月廿九日　中華民國行政院局部
　　改組，蔣介石總統命令，任命
　　俞國華為財政部長，查良鑑為
　　司法行政部長，孫運璿為交通
　　部長。
　　考試院副院長程天放博士，以
　　患血癌症在美國逝世，享年六
　　十九歲。

十二月三日　中國科學家李卓皓博
　　士，自美國返台，作為期四週
　　的講學，他係內分泌學權威。

十二月六日　中華民國政府為適應經
　　濟發展，擬定十年能源開發計
　　劃。
　　香港的三十三所親中共學校學
　　生約兩萬人實行罷課，抗議香
　　港政府查封親北京的「中華中
　　學」及拘捕該校校長黃祖芬。

十二月八日　美國將最新式的戰車一
　　批，贈給中華民國陸軍部隊使
　　用。

十二月十日　日本前首相岸信介抵台
　　灣訪問，蔣介石總統予接見並
　　款宴。

十二月十三日　中華民國國防部長蔣
　　經國，與美國太平洋三軍總司
　　令夏普上將舉行會談，雙方討
　　論台灣情勢，防衛計劃，中美
　　合作及軍援等問題。

十二月十四日　中華民國行政院會議
　　通過，指定中華航空公司與印
　　尼有關當局商談有關雙方通航
　　問題。

十二月十八日　台灣省政府定民國五
　　十七年（一九六八）元旦公佈
　　國民小學課程標準，內容著重
　　九年一貫制與職業教育。
　　印尼政府命令，強迫華僑改名
　　歸化，並且禁止華僑慶祝中國

農曆新年（春節）。

十二月廿一日　中華民國教育部宣佈
　　　修訂國外留學政策，擬定近
　　　程、中程、遠程三項目標，培
　　　植建設人才。

十二月廿四日　美國原子能委員會宣
　　　佈，中共在新疆省羅布泊地區
　　　舉行第十七次低能量的核子裝
　　　置試爆。

十二月廿五日　是日為中華民國行憲
　　　二十週年日，蔣介石總統在紀
　　　念大會中致詞稱：「憲法精神
　　　在實行三民主義思想，反共復
　　　國鬥爭，即捍衛憲法聖戰。」

十二月廿九日　中華民國國防部宣
　　　佈，金門防衛司令部下令，民
　　　國五十七年元旦停止對廈門砲
　　　擊三天。

中華民國五十七年（一九六八）

一月一日　蔣介石總統於元旦發表告
　　　全國同胞書，指示加速倫理、
　　　民主、科學建設，以奠定「先
　　　戰之戰」的必勝基礎。蔣總統
　　　元旦文告並自金門飄傳往大
　　　陸。

一月二日　航行於台灣與香港間航線
　　　的貨輪「興中」號，在澎湖附

近海面不幸觸礁沉沒。

一月三日　中華民國空軍飛機，深入
　　　大陸地區空投散發反共傳單。

一月五日　中華民國外貿當局說，民
　　　國五十六年度，對外貿易輸出
　　　額高達十五億美元，較五十五
　　　年度增加三億一千萬美元，輸
　　　出與輸入額相抵，計出超兩千
　　　六百萬美元。
　　　台灣省政府糧食局說，去年全
　　　年產糧為糙米兩百四十萬四千
　　　六百餘公噸，創歷年來之最高
　　　紀錄。

一月七日　台灣省政府訂定公務人員
　　　退休三年計劃，自今年起開始
　　　實施。

一月八日　台灣省政府報告，去年漁
　　　業生產總值達四十億元，產量
　　　達四十五萬三千噸。

一月九日　中華民國教育部決定，統
　　　一編印國民中學教科書。

一月十一日　中華民國行政院會議通
　　　過，修正私立學校規程。

一月十二日　台灣省政府交通處計
　　　劃，在高雄港興建貨櫃輸運輪
　　　專用碼頭。

一月十三日　世界銀行宣佈，以一千
　　　七百五十萬美元貸款給予台灣

省鐵路局，供其購買鐵路機車。

一月二十日　中華民國內政部宣佈，立法委員劉景鍵、徐君佩、姚連芳，監察委員于鎮洲、孫玉琳、郝遇林，及國民大會代表周烈範，因被法院判刑而喪失中央民意代表資格。

一月廿二日　台灣省舉行選舉二十個縣市的議員及鄉鎮長完成，投票率高達百分之七十七點八。

一月廿三日　台灣省印刷業公會發起自律運動，簽訂公約，不印刷不良書刊及賭具。

一月廿四日　中華民國行政院擬定，「促進婦女地位十年長期發展計劃方案」，以提高婦女地位。

一月廿五日　中華民國行政院核准，將不合時宜的法規三十三種予以廢止。

一月廿八日　中國國民黨中央常務委員會會議通過，台灣省第六屆縣市長及第四屆省議員國民黨候選人人選。

一月卅一日　台灣省政府為謀求改善山胞生活，決定舉辦山地經濟情況調查。

二月二日　中華民國行政院命令，將「台灣省土地代書人制度」予以廢止。

二月七日　非洲馬拉威、上伏塔、史瓦濟蘭及象牙海岸四國的十三位農業技術人員，到台灣接受農業講習。

二月九日　台灣省政府與台北院轄市政府官員，會商行政區域勘界測量計劃，因為台灣省台北縣原屬之數鄉鎮已劃歸台北市市區。

二月十二日　太平洋區旅行協會第十七屆年會開始在台北市舉行，會期六天，共有三十個國家及地區代表參加會議。

二月十六日　中華民國民航空運公司（C.A.T.）客機，自香港飛來台北途中，在台北縣林口出事墜毀，機上二十一人罹難，四十三人生還，出事原因正在調查中。

二月二十日　中華民國行政院長嚴家淦在立法院會議中報告說，國家經濟穩定成長，國民個人所得折合二〇九美元。

二月廿五日　中華民國教育部核准，國立中央大學在台灣復校，校

址設於中壢市。

二月廿九日　中美兩國軍隊聯合演習，在台灣南部基地舉行。

三月一日　中國國民黨台北院轄市第一屆委員會成立，主任委員梁興義及各委員宣誓就職。

中共在上海市發動文藝界大整肅運動，于玲、葉以群、豐子愷、周信芳等人均遭整肅。

三月四日　中國青年黨宣佈，青年黨人士黃順興、黃振之，決定參加台灣省第六屆台東縣及屏東縣長選舉。

三月七日　中華民國對外貿易委員會主任委員徐柏園說，民國五十六年度（一九六七）對外貿易總值共達十四億五千九百萬美元，較前年增加百分之廿六，創歷年最高紀錄。

三月九日　中國著名之數學家華羅庚，在北京遭中共鬥爭。

三月十日　中共中央宣佈，「紅旗雜誌」停刊。

三月十五日　美國第七艦隊新任司令布蘭格中將抵台北訪問，將晉謁蔣介石總統。

三月廿一日　中華民國行政院會議通過「行政院賦稅改革委員會工作計劃綱要」，以改進賦稅結構及稅務行政。

三月廿五日　中華民國國產第一艘巨型貨輪，三萬五千噸的「永祥」號在基隆港舉行下水典禮，將懸掛青天白日滿地紅國旗從事遠洋貨運。

三月廿八日　中華民國行政院決定撥款九百三十五萬元，就台灣海峽海底地質與重砂，進行全盤查勘，籌組探測小組負責執行。

中華民國教育部討論初中學校改制問題，原則是改為國民中學。

三月三十日　台灣省政府宣佈，修正統一發票案辦法，自四月一日起施行，將免用發票標準提高，省轄市改為六萬元新台幣以下，縣改為五萬元以下。

四月一日　中華民國參加第十九屆世界運動會籌備會選拔委員會正式成立，著手擬訂選拔辦法和標準。

投奔自由的著名音樂家、北京「國立音樂學院」院長馬思聰，偕夫人自美國回國訪問。

四月三日　中華民國行政院會議決

定，台北市公共汽車開放民營，已核定市區公車民營申請辦法。

美軍援助 F-5A「自由鬥士」新型戰鬥機大批運抵台灣，空運總司令部舉行新機換裝結訓典禮。

交通部民用航空局宣佈，民運航空公司國際航線班機自四月十日起全面停航。

美國政府宣佈，新移民法自今年七月一日起生效，中國移民人數配額與其他國家相同，每年為兩萬人。

四月四日　中華民國陸軍飛彈部隊，舉行「神箭八號」演習。

四月五日　中華民國國防部宣佈，全省自本年七月一日起開始辦理戶口配米，憑戶口名簿向米商購米。

台灣省政府決定出售省有房地產，並舉辦對承購者予以貸款。

四月九日　台北市政府擬訂整建地區計劃。

星馬航空公司指責中華航空公司減價競爭，宣佈將雙方航線予以停止飛行。

四月十日　中國國民黨中央常務委員會會議通過，修正「國民生活須知」、「建立討毛救國聯合陣線初步計劃要點」。

四月十二日　中華民國行政院決定，自今年七月一日起，香蕉、洋菇、電話、電力分別增加捐稅。

四月十四日　中華民國立法院通過「證券交易法」。

四月十九日　台東縣長濱鄉八仙洞，發現史前遺址，台灣大學考古隊地質學教授木朝棨認為係新石器時代中期或舊石器時代末期遺址。

四月廿一日　台灣省各縣市舉行選舉第四屆省議員第六屆縣市長結果發表，國民黨當選省議員有六十一人（總數七十一席），國民黨員當選縣市長者有十七人（總數二十人）。

四月廿二日　中國國民黨中央指示各級黨部，負責督促黨選黨員，履行競選諾言，團結地方，造福桑梓。

台灣省第四屆省議員及第六屆縣市長選舉投票率達選民總人數之百分之四十七強。

四月廿五日　中共中央發起「三查
　　（查叛徒、查特務、查走資
　　派）運動」，以清除異己的反
　　毛派分子。

四月廿六日　中華航空公司與星馬航
　　空公司同時宣佈，中、馬星航
　　線班機定五月二日起恢復航
　　行。

四月廿九日　台省灣政府會議通過，
　　縣市政府教育科一律改稱教育
　　局。

五月一日　蔣介石總統伉儷舉行茶
　　會，款待在華美國軍官眷屬。

五月四日　中華民國教育部編列預算
　　四百萬元新台幣，供編譯世界
　　名著及編印科學辭典之需。
　　台灣省政府衛生處，訂定「加
　　強查緝偽劣禁藥辦法」。

五月十日　中華民國國防部三軍總醫
　　院，在台北新建之大樓揭幕，
　　由蔣總統夫人宋美齡女士蒞臨
　　主持剪綵儀式。

五月十一日　中華民國內政部宣佈，
　　將醫事人員出國申請案件予以
　　凍結。

五月十三日　中華民國政府準備在十
　　年內，投資新台幣四十二億
　　元，改善台灣鐵路的營運。

五月十六日　著名音樂家馬思聰夫婦
　　離台返美國僑居。

五月十七日　美軍協防台灣司令邱約
　　翰及美國軍事顧問團長戚烈
　　拉，稱讚國軍精良，足可阻止
　　中共的攻擊。

五月廿一日　歷年投奔自由的反共義
　　士義胞，在台北舉行集會，紀
　　念「五月難民潮」。

五月廿二日　中華民國立法院財經委
　　員會決議，開徵香蕉、洋菇、
　　蘆筍臨時捐，為期一年。
　　美國副國務卿卡心白說，美國
　　決堅守對中華民國承諾，履行
　　協防台灣義務。

五月廿七日　國立台灣大學附設醫
　　院，順利完成中華民國醫學界
　　史上第一次腎臟移植手術。

五月廿九日　台灣省政府決定，因實
　　施九年國民教育制度，暫行禁
　　止私人創辦初中學校。

六月一日　台灣省第四屆省議會正式
　　成立，並選舉謝東閔為議長及
　　蔡鴻文為副議長。

六月三日　中華民國興建第一座原子
　　能發電廠計劃，政府業已定
　　案，可望於民國六十三年（一
　　九七四）開始供電。

六月四日　台灣省政府衛生處發表統計報告說，台灣省民國五十六年（一九六七）人口出生率，已下降到每千人為二十八點五人。

六月五日　台灣省政府公路局籌建南北直達公路案，經亞洲銀行完成初步調查，政府將向亞洲銀行申請貸款新台幣一百億元作為興建基金。

六月九日　中華民國行政院決定，簡化台灣入境手續，爭取觀光旅客來台，海外各地華僑團體回國手續，政府授權各地使館辦理。

六月十日　台灣省政府主席黃杰表示，由於已實施九年國民教育制度，今後政府將不准創辦私立小學與初中。

六月十二日　中華民國前立法院長張道藩在台北市病逝，享年七十四歲（一八九五～一九六八）。

六月十三日　中華民國行政院會議通過，「徵兵規則體位區分標準」修正案。

六月十六日　陸軍軍官學校建校四十四週年校慶，蔣介石總統在高雄縣鳳山該校主持校慶祝紀念大會，舉行盛大閱兵，並致辭訓勉師生發揚黃埔精神。該校最初設於廣東黃埔，通稱「黃埔軍校」，後改稱「中央陸軍軍官學校」。

六月二十日　蔣介石總統接見美國太平洋軍隊總司令夏普上將，舉行會談。

六月廿一日　美國國務卿魯斯克談話強調，美國無權出賣台灣，美國與中共關係難改善。

六月廿三日　台灣省政府決定動用新台幣一億元，開發東部土地資源，化河川地山坡為水旱田桑地，預定在四年內完成三萬公頃。

六月廿六日　中國國民黨第十三次黨務工作會議在台北市陽明山開幕，會期五天。

六月廿九日　中華民國政府決定解決公教人員退休問題，公教福利互助金，最高可獲得新台幣十萬元。

七月一日　中華民國立法院通過國際禁止核子武器擴散條約。
中共中央宣佈，黨辦「紅旗雜誌」經改組後復刊。

七月五日　中華民國立法院修正通過「勞保條例」，擴大保險範圍，取消住醫院期限，增加門診給付與失業保險。

七月六日　中華民國外交部次長楊西昆啟程赴希臘首都雅典，主持七月九日到十五日駐歐洲及中東地區使節會議，然後將訪問非洲二十三個國家。

七月七日　台灣省政府發表，台北市改制為院轄市後，台灣省各縣市所轄面積減少到三萬五千六百八十九點〇七〇平方公里。

七月十一日　中華民國政府決定調整軍公教人員方租津貼，並增列子女助學金，均自今年七月一日起實施。
交通部長孫運璿在立法院報告說，政府將在今後四年期間，投資新台幣十八億五千萬元，發展民用航空事業。

七月十六日　菲律賓移民局宣佈，中國旅客在菲國只能停留六十天。

七月十七日　中國民主社會黨內部爭執三方面人士，在台北市舉行座談會，商討黨內團結問題。

七月十八日　中華民國中央研究院舉行院士選舉結果，王兆振、郭廷以、盧致德及魏火曜當選為新院士。

七月二十日　世界人民反共聯盟第一屆會員代表大會，亞洲人民反共聯盟中國總會第十四屆代表大會，在台北市中山堂揭幕。

七月廿五日　中國石油公司與台灣造船公司簽訂合約，在基隆建造兩艘十萬噸級巨型油輪，每艘造價美金八百五十萬元。

七月廿八日　中華民國中央研究院訂定十年發展計劃，撥款新台幣六億元，擴增十一個研究所，負擔訓練與研究雙重任務。

七月卅一日　台北中國擴播公司電台第一座調頻電台（FM），正式開始廣播。

八月一日　中華民國行政院會議通過，公立大專院校主管採實施任期制度。

八月七日　中國國民黨中央委員會秘書長谷鳳翔辭職，由張寶樹繼任秘書長。

八月十四日　中華民國經濟部核定，修正簡化「華僑及外國人投資申請書」格式。

八月十六日　中華民國行政院賦稅改

革委員會主任委員劉大中，告訴工商界領袖說，改革賦稅的目的是求經濟穩定。

美國海軍軍令部長穆勒上將抵台訪問。

八月廿二日　中華民國行政院核定，今後建造三層樓以上之樓房，一律改為「鋼筋混凝土」構架，五層樓以上必須使用「R.C. 構架」。

八月廿三日　中華民國國防部發表統計說，台海「八二三」砲戰廿三日屆滿十週年，中共砲兵向金門馬祖群島共射擊砲彈九〇〇、一四八發。

國防部長蔣經國為金門砲戰十週年發表告「毛共官兵書」，號召覺悟奮起，反共討毛，自救救國。

八月廿六日　第一屆國際華學會議在陽明山華崗揭幕，由張其昀主持，參加學者共二一七人，分別來自二十個國家地區，共提出論文一七五篇。

九月一日　台北市「徵信新聞報」，改名為「中國時報」，內容加以擴充。

中華民國參加第十九屆世界運動大會（奧林匹克運動會），共有八個項目，核定四十三名選手參加比賽。

九月九日　台北市長高玉樹、市議長張祥傳、市教育局長劉先雲，代表台北市全體市民向蔣介石總統呈獻金盾，感謝蔣總統明令實施九年國民教育的德意。台灣省及台北市同時實施九年國民教育制度。

九月十二日　中華民國行政院會議決議，成立交通法庭及修訂「道路交通管理條例」。

九月十五日　美國太平洋空軍總司令艾德門中將抵台灣訪問。

九月十六日　中國青年黨元老左舜生自香港返台北。

九月廿一日　美國海軍台灣海峽巡邏司令勒普少將抵台北訪問。

九月廿六日　中華民國行政院會議通過，採取「原地高架」方式改善台北市區內的鐵路。

十月一日　強烈颱風襲擊台灣，帶來豪雨災害，計有二十九人喪生，二十人失蹤，房屋倒塌五百間及發生七處山崩。

十月三日　中華民國行政院會議決議，核定「改善民間祭典節約

辦法」。

十月九日　中華民國國防部宣佈，金門防衛司令部下令，雙十國慶節，國軍停止對廈門砲擊一天。

十月十日　蔣介石總統於雙十慶日發表文告，號召海內外同胞及大陸反共志士，共同討毛救國，光復中華，並接見各地返國參加國慶之僑領，告以復國前途光明，堅忍奮鬥必定勝利。

十月十一日　中華民國教育部次長鄧傳楷說，「對於國際奧林匹克委員會通過我國正名為中華民國案感到興奮。」過去十年間，因受國際姑息分子影響，中華民國被迫使用「台灣」字樣參加奧會活動，曾經多次抗議。

十月十三日　中國共產黨中央委員八屆十二中全會在北京開幕，會期十八天。

十月十五日　中華民國行政院長嚴家淦在立法院答覆立法委員質詢時說，今後政府將援助勸導官員少打「高爾夫球，尤其不應該為此影響公務。」

十月十六日　耗資新台幣七千五百萬元的台北市郊華江大橋業已建造完成，定十二月一日通車。

十月十八日　蔣介石總統接見中央研究院院士語文學家趙元任博士與其夫人楊步偉女士，垂詢其近況及最新著作。趙元任旅居美國四十年，最近返國訪問。中華民國田徑運動女選手紀政，在第十九屆世界運動會女子八十公尺低欄決賽中，以十秒四成績打破十秒六的世運紀錄，為中華民國獲得本屆世運第一面獎牌（銅牌）。

十月十九日　新加坡政府說，自明年開始，新加坡中小學公民歷史將採用華文。

十月廿四日　中華民國第一屆圖書雜誌展覽會在台北市揭幕，會期兩週。

十月廿六日　蔣介石總統在台灣北部陸軍基地，校閱部隊舉行的「光華演習」。

十月廿七日　台灣省政府為維護國民健康，定下月核換兩萬五千餘家的營業執照。

十月廿七日　中華民國奧林匹克委員會主席楊森，接獲國際奧林匹

克委員會主席布倫達治正式通知，該會決定自十一月起，恢復中華民國在國際奧會的正式名稱「中華民國」而非「台灣」。

十月廿九日　中華民國空軍總部展出自製的「介壽號」飛機，作為慶祝蔣介石總統八十三歲華誕壽禮。

十月卅一日　中國國民黨中央委員會出版的「中央半月刊」，改為月刊，調整內及版面，擴大發行。

十一月一日　中國國民黨第十屆代表大會，定於明年三月廿九日召開，以集中全黨智慧，開拓反攻復國機運，加速完成討毛救國革命任務。

十一月三日　位於台北市郊的中山博物院（後改為故宮博物院），政府決定加以改建，並加強在海外的宣傳。

美國太平洋艦隊總司令郝蘭德將軍抵台灣訪問。

十一月六日　美國太平洋陸軍總司令海恩斯將軍抵台灣訪問。

美國舉行大選結果，共和黨候選人尼克森當選為總統，安格紐當選為副總統。

十一月十一日　台灣電力公司宣佈，十年電源計劃已告定案，將投資新台幣五百二十億元（其中半數已有著落），將增加電量三百八十萬瓩。

中國國民黨中央常務委員會會議通過，行政院所擬「孔子誕辰紀念」改稱「大成至聖先師孔子誕辰紀念」。

十一月十四日　中華民國行政院會議通過「戶警合一方案」，並決定由內政部擬定實施辦法，試辦一年。

十一月十五日　中華民國行政院命令台灣省政府，防止物價建材上漲，並經常注意供應調節。

十一月十八日　台北市政府宣佈，台北市統計人口共有一百五十六萬八十八人。

世界中文報業協會在香港正式成立，由香港星島日報胡仙擔任首屆主席，台北市聯合報王惕吾擔任副主席。

十一月十九日　蔣介石總統分別接見田徑運動教練楊傳廣，世界運動會選手紀政，及旅日本圍棋國手林海峰，殷切予以嘉勉。

亞洲銀行宣佈撥款五十萬美元，供台灣興建南北高速公路之需。

十一月二十日　聯合國第十九屆大會，以五十八票對四十四票，另二十三票棄權的表決，否決排斥中華民國的建議案。

十一月廿四日　台灣省政府報告說，去年全省交通事故死亡共計一萬四百七十九人。

十一月廿七日　中華民國政府將循立法途徑，建立工人退休制度，在新訂勞工法中，將予明確規定。

十一月廿八日　蔣介石總統接見世界中文報業協會代表回國訪問團胡仙（香港星島日報）等二十一人垂詢各僑地情況及中文報業發展情形。

十二月二日　香港傳說，中共重要領袖劉少奇曾試圖逃亡，曾遭槍傷。

十二月九日　「亞洲鐵人」楊傳廣與「田徑女傑」紀政，宣誓入中國國民黨，由國民黨中央委員會秘書長張寶樹分別發給國民黨員證書。

十二月十日　中華民國教育部，修正「大學研究所招博士班辦法」。

台北市政府撥款新台幣五千萬元，充實美化位於圓山的兒童樂園，分訂近程、遠程計劃，預定三年內完成。

十二月十二日　高雄市的小港機場，由國內航線機場升格為國際航線機場。

十二月十五日　台灣的遠東航空公司宣佈增開國內航線的夜航班機便利乘客。

十二月十七日　中華民國交通部觀光局發表，今年來台灣的觀光旅客已逾三十五萬人。

十二月十八日　台北市民政局呼籲市民，節省「耶誕節」浪費，移作慈善事業。

中國國民黨中央委員會為加強推行生活革新，改造社會風氣，邀集各有關機關主管，檢討研訂「簡發賀年片及簡化拜年實施辦法」。

十二月廿七日　美國原子能委員會宣佈，美國測知中共於本日下午在新疆羅布泊舉行核子爆炸試驗，為北京舉行的第八次核子試驗。

十二月廿九日　中共政府宣佈，興建
　　的南京長江大橋全面完工，開
　　放交通。

中華民國五十八年（一九六九）

一月一日　蔣介石總統發表元旦告全
　　國同胞書，指出中共黨內部分
　　崩離析，號召軍民加強復國準
　　備，強調政治，經濟再建設、
　　再發展，社會、文化再動員、
　　再革新。
　　中華民國經濟部成立國際貿易
　　局，由經濟部次長汪彝定兼任
　　局長。
一月二日　中華航空公司一架客機，
　　在自台東飛往高雄途中，在大
　　武山第二高峰撞山失事。
一月四日　中華民國國防部發表，羅
　　友倫繼唐守治擔任總政治作戰
　　主任。
一月五日　中華民國交通部民用航空
　　局決定，將台北市松山國際機
　　場加以擴建以應發展需要。
一月六日　中華民國行政院宣佈，公
　　教人員俸給制度自今年七月起
　　實施，暫不取消實物配給及教
　　育補助計劃。
一月七日　中華民國外交部發表統

計，全世界一百三十八個國家
中，六十七國與中華民國有邦
交。
一月十日　中華民國經濟部發表，去
　　年對外貿易總值計十七億五千
　　萬美元，較前年增長百分之十
　　七。
一月十一日　台灣省政府民政廳發
　　表，台灣省現住人口總計一千
　　二百零一萬六千餘人，男性多
　　於女性。
一月十五日　中國國民黨第十次全國
　　代表大會秘書處成立，大會秘
　　書長為張寶樹，副秘書長為秦
　　孝儀、謝然之及薛人仰。
一月廿二日　國畫家張大千將臨摹敦
　　煌壁畫六十二幅捐贈給故宮博
　　物院珍藏。
　　蔣介石總統電賀尼克森就任美
　　國第三十七屆總統。
一月廿三日　中華民國行政院決定，
　　對政府機關大印制度將作有限
　　度改革，所屬單位行文不蓋大
　　印。
一月廿五日　中華民國田徑運動女傑
　　紀政，以七秒八成績創新式女
　　子六十碼高欄世界紀錄。
一月廿六日　中華民國交通部宣佈，

中華民國與美國間越洋長途電
話實施自動撥號制度。

一月廿九日　中國國民黨中央委員會
所屬各單位工作檢討會揭幕，
會期預定三天。

一月三十日　中共宣佈，投共的前中
華民國副總統李宗仁在北京逝
世，享年七十八歲。

二月一日　明代末年堅守台灣的鄭成
功的後裔鄭審一在日本逝世。

二月七日　蔣介石總統接見台灣曾文
水庫建設委員會副主任委員廖
文毅，垂詢水庫建設情形及地
方民間生活情形。廖文毅在日
本宣佈放棄台灣獨立運動後返
回台灣。

二月十日　中華民國工業展覽會在台
北市新公園揭幕。

二月十六日　中華民國行政院發表國
民所得統計說，民國五十七年
（一九六八）平均每人所得初
步估計為新台幣九千四百八十
七元，較上年的八千四百九十
四元增加百分之十一點七。

二月廿三日　中國民主社會黨（原名
中國國家社會黨）主席張君勱
（原名張嘉森），在美國病
逝，享年八十三歲（一八八七

～一九六九）。

二月廿四日　台灣遠東航空公司一架
客機，在自高雄飛往台北途中
失事焚毀。

二月廿六日　中華民國國史館館長羅
家倫辭職，蔣介石總統命令特
派黃季陸繼任國史館館長。

二月廿七日　中華民國教育部發表，
民國五十七年度（一九六八）
全國學生人數計三百六十一萬
四千七百六十七人。

二月廿八日　美國進出口銀行宣佈，
貸款七百一十七萬美元給中華航
空公司，資助其購買波音七〇
七型噴射式客機兩架。
第二次世界大戰期間，曾任中
國戰區美軍總司令及蔣介石委
員長顧問的魏德邁將軍抵台灣
訪問。

三月一日　中國國民黨中央黨部通令
各級黨部，審慎選舉代表出席
國民黨第十屆全國代表大會。

三月十三日　中華民國行政院核定，
在台灣省桃園縣境內擴建國際
飛機場。

三月十五日　中共與蘇聯雙方軍隊，
在東北的珍寶島再度發生流血
衝突。

三月二十日　中華民國行政院核定，將高雄縣小港機場開放為國際航線貨運站，並作為技術降落站。

三月廿一日　中華民國行政院決定，中央級民意代表增補選舉原則決定，國民大會代表將辦增選補選，立法委員與監察委員只辦增選。

三月廿二日　中國國民黨中央委員會秘書長張寶樹稱，國民黨第十屆全國代表大會籌備完成，定三月廿九日揭幕，出席與列席人員將達一千二百人。

三月廿四日　中國國民黨黨務工作檢討會議開幕，由中央常務委員嚴家淦主持，致詞勉各同志求新求變，開創新局面。會期預定三天。

三月廿八日　羅馬天主教教宗保羅六世宣佈，晉昇三十三位樞機主教（紅衣主教），中國南京教區總主教于斌名列第一。

三月廿九日　中國國民黨第十次全國代表大會，在台北市陽明山中山樓舉行開幕典禮，蔣介石總裁親臨主持，演講：「革命歷史的啟示和革命責任的貫徹，

並提示三大任務：㈠全面革新，鞏固復興基地；㈡團結一致，剷除匪共；㈢重建倫理、民主、科學的三民主義新中國。

三月卅一日　中華民國國防部長蔣經國代表蔣介石總統，在華盛頓參加美國前總統艾森豪元帥的喪禮。

美國總統尼克森接見中華民國國防部長蔣經國。

四月一日　中華民國司法院命令各級法院成立交通法庭，並自四月七日起受理案件。

中國共產黨第九次全國代表大會在北京開幕，由毛澤東主持，出席代表一五一二人。

四月四日　中國國民黨第十次全國代表大會第十二次大會通過「中國國民黨黨章修正案」，全文分十二章四十七條（現行黨章為十二章六十五條）。

四月五日　國民黨十全大會第十四次及十五次大會，通過「現階段的建設案」及「中國國民黨政綱案」。

四月八日　國民黨十全大會第十八次大會，全體代表一致通過，擁

戴蔣介石先生繼續擔任中國國民黨總裁。第十九次大會，蔣介石總裁提出中央委員候選人名單，由出席代表無記名圈選七十九名（中央委員名額為九十九人，候補為五十一人，由代表選出中央委員七十九名，候補中央委員四十一人。總裁遴選委員二十名候補十名）。

四月九日　中國國民黨第十次全國代表大會舉行第二十次大會，大會秘書長張寶樹宣讀當選第十屆中央委員九十九人，候補中央委員五十一人名單（中央委員嚴家淦、蔣經國、谷正綱等九十九人，候補中央委員鄺景福等五十一人）。

十全大會舉行閉幕典禮，由蔣介石總裁主持儀式，並訓勉全黨同志加強革命組織，完成復國大業，開拓光明前途。

四月十三日　中華民國外交部決定嚴格執行內外互調政策，預定在一年內調動一百名官員。

四月十四日　中共宣佈，中國共產黨第九次全國代表大會主席團秘書處發表新聞公報稱，「九大」已通過林彪提出的政治報告及中國共產黨黨章，並正式提名林彪為毛澤東的繼承人。

四月十七日　中華民國國父孫中山先生第一位外籍軍事顧問荷馬李將軍夫婦靈骨運抵台北市，安葬在台北市陽明山公墓。蔣介石總統特頒給「永懷風義」橫額，以紀念其對中國革命之貢獻。

四月廿二日　中華民國教育宣佈，修訂國外留學規程，將延長留學期限，以利高深研究。

四月廿三日　中華民國與日本雙方代表，在台北市簽訂「修訂中、日空運協定」，將台灣省南部的高雄市列入兩國間的航線。

四月廿八日　中共宣佈，中國共產黨九屆中央全會第一次會議，選出毛澤東為主席，林彪為副主席，並選出毛澤東等五人為中共中央政治局委員，及紀登奎等人為候補委員。

五月三日　中華民國內政部發表統計說，大專學生中男生佔百分之六十五強，女生佔百分之三十四。

五月十一日　中華民國內政部宣佈，將現行的禮儀規程加以修訂。

五月十五日　中華民國行政院命令公佈，「戡亂時期台灣地區戶政改進辦法」，實行戶警合一制，自民國五十八年（一九六九）七月一日起試行一年。

美國商務部長史丹斯抵台北，與中華民國政府官員商談有關紡織品銷美的問題。

五月三十日　中華民國行政院會議通過，電力和電燈臨時捐自本年七月一日起停止徵收。

五月三十日　越南總統阮文紹偕夫人抵達台北，預定訪問三天，與蔣介石總統舉行首次會談。

六月七日　中國南京區天主教總主教于斌，在凡諦岡接受樞機（紅衣）主教榮銜後，自羅馬返抵台北。

六月九日　中國國民黨黨務工作會議在台北開幕，會期預定四天，蔣介石總裁訓勉黨工同志深入民間，了解民情，貫徹國民黨十全大會決議。

六月十日　台北市政府授權陽明山管理局，地方自治業務、人事行政大部份可自行決定。

六月十五日　陸軍軍官學校四十五週年校慶，蔣介石總統親臨高雄縣鳳山該校主持校慶典禮，並致詞訓勉國軍官兵鍛鍊鋼鐵般的意志，體能、和紀律，以行救國、救民、救世之大仁。同時，該校校史已編印完成，作為校慶獻禮。

六月二十日　中國國民黨第三次新聞工作會議在台北召開，會期三天，會中研討八個中心議題。

六月廿九日　台灣省政府教育廳決定，考選兩百名山地居民學生，保送高級農業學校受教育。

七月一日　中華民國行政院本日公佈，「動員戡亂時期自由地區中央公職人員增補選辦法施行細則」。

新任行政院副院長蔣經國正式就職。

中華民國財政部宣佈，台灣省基隆、台北及高雄三個海關正式成立。

七月七日　台灣省瑞三煤礦發生瓦斯爆炸事件，礦工不幸傷亡八十餘人，有關當局正在調查中。

七月八日　美國首都國會圖書館舉行，「中文藏書百年展覽」，獲得中外人士好評。

七月十三日　台灣省政府為促進人事
　　　新陳代謝，已核定公務人員兩
　　　千餘名，自本月起辦理退休。
七月十四日　中國國民黨台北市黨部
　　　宣佈，開始受理國民黨員競選
　　　台北院轄市第一屆市議員登
　　　記。
七月十六日　中華民國行政院規定，
　　　公務人員因為貪污行為而科刑
　　　者，不得再任公職。
　　　中國青年黨元老左舜生，自香
　　　港返國協調青年黨各派系召開
　　　該黨代表大會。
七月十七日　中華民國中央公職人員
　　　增補選舉事務所成立，舉行首
　　　次會議決定，中央公職人員增
　　　補選定於本年十二月二十日舉
　　　行。
七月十九日　中華民國教育部長鍾皎
　　　光在立法院會議中說，留學政
　　　策作重大改進，自費留學一律
　　　考試，教育部已擬定六項改進
　　　辦法。
七月廿一日　美國太空人駕登月小
　　　艇，於台灣時間清晨四時十八
　　　分降於月球表面，十時五十
　　　分，太空人阿母斯壯首先踏上
　　　月球表面，圓滿完成太空人登

月歷史任務。
　　　中國青年黨全國代表大會在台
　　　北市開幕，會期五天。
七月廿三日　中華民國教育部說，今
　　　年海外華僑學生申請回國升學
　　　者有三千多人。
七月廿五日　清代末期革新運動重要
　　　人物康有為的夫人梁隨覺，在
　　　台北市病逝，享年九十歲。
七月卅一日　台北市政府偽藥品禁查
　　　緝中心發表統計說，民國五十
　　　四年（一九六五）至五十八年
　　　（一九六九）六月期間，台灣
　　　全省查獲地下藥廠五十四家，
　　　偽藥一五八件。
八月二日　美國國務卿羅吉斯訪問中
　　　華民國，晉見蔣介石總統會
　　　談。羅吉斯邀請行政院副院院
　　　長蔣經國於明年春天赴美國訪
　　　問。
八月六日　美援首批 OH-6 型直升飛
　　　機，移交中華民國陸軍部隊使
　　　用。
八月七日　中華民國中央公職人員增
　　　補選舉事務所發表，立法委員
　　　增選十一名，經決定台灣省選
　　　出七名，台北市選出四名。
八月八日　美國國務卿羅吉斯於訪問

亞洲各國後返美途中，在澳洲坎培拉發表談話稱，「中華民國與中國存在都是現實的。」

八月十一日　中華民國中央銀行宣佈，自八月十二日起，修訂法國貨幣法郎牌價，買進為新台幣七元二角，賣出為新台幣七元二角二分。

八月十六日　中國國民黨駐美國總支部第十六屆全美代表大會，在美國舊金山開幕，蔣介石總裁特頒書面訓詞，勗勉強化基層黨務組織。

八月十七日　美國環球航空公司新開闢中，美定期航線，首班客機抵達台北。

八月二十日　美國國務卿羅吉斯發表談話，重申美國無意主張「兩個中國」政策。

八月廿六日　中國國民黨台灣省黨部，在台北市召開黨政工作檢討會，會期四天。

九月一日　中華民國僑務委員會宣佈，規定應聘出國人員身份學歷必須符合職務。

九月四日　中共廈門砲兵射擊金門城區，四名女童受傷。

九月六日　中華民國空軍總部，與美國空軍當局簽訂合約，擔任代美國修理四十架 C-47 式飛機和十六架 F-100 式戰鬥機。

九月十一日　中華民國行政院核定，中華民國與印尼交換航空權合約，雙方航線劃定，已經簽字生效。

九月十二日　中國國民黨中央常務委員會通過，馬超俊等五位高齡幹部依例退休，希望從政同志響應此項號召，促進黨政機構新陳代謝功能。

九月十三日　中華民國政府為配合全面政治革新，鼓勵公務人員依例退休，年滿六十歲或任職二十五年即合格。考試院已擬訂公務人員依例自退實施辦法。

九月十八日　中華民國行政院原子能委員會，決定擴大現行組織，並改名為「國家原子能委員會」。

九月廿二日　中國明朝前期孤本笈散佚國外者頗多，中華民國中央圖書館商洽，以交換方式攝製微捲底片回國度藏。

九月廿四日　第七屆世界華商貿易會議在台北開幕。

九月廿七日　中國國民黨中央委員會

公佈，台北市第一屆市議員選
舉國民黨候選人提名人選名
單，計林挺生等四十三人。

九月三十日　中華民國國防部發表，
廈門中共砲兵射擊金、馬國軍
前線，居民死傷二十四人。

十月二日　中華民國舉行中央公職人
員增補選舉，應選名額正式宣
佈，計國民大會代表十五名，
立法委員十一名，及監察委員
二名。

十月三日　強烈颱風「芙勞茜」帶來
豪雨災害，台灣省北部地區發
生嚴重水災。

十月五日　中共新華通訊社報導說，
中共最近曾舉行氫彈試驗爆炸
及首次地下核子試爆。

十月六日　中共宣佈，董必武擔任北
京人民政府代理主席。

十月七日　中華民國與大韓民國開闢
民航路線，韓國航空公司首班
客機飛抵台北。

十月八日　金門防衛司令部宣佈，雙
十國慶紀念日，中華民國部隊
停止對廈門共軍的砲戰。

十月十日　蔣介石總統於國慶日發表
文告，指出中共分崩離析，形
成癱瘓狀態，中華民國生聚教

訓，已立於不敗之地。

中國國民黨營的台北中國電視
公司，今日起開始試播。中國
電視是中華民國的第二家電視
台，台灣電視公司為第一家電
視台。

十月十一日　台灣的中國航運公司使
用六艘萬噸貨櫃輪船開闢台灣
與美國間的航線服務。

十月十六日　中國青年黨創黨元老之
一的左舜生在台北市病逝，享
年七十七歲（一八九三～一九
六九）。

十月廿五日　蔣介石總統於台灣光復
二十四週年紀念日發表文告，
勗勉全體同胞，弘揚光復台灣
的歷史意義，開拓國家民族的
光明前途。

十月卅一日　中華民國內政部重申禁
止使用糖精的命令，塞克拉邁
與德爾精皆禁止製售，薩卡林
可用於醫藥及外銷食品。

十一月一日　中國國民黨中央委員會
公佈，國民黨提名的中央公職
人員增補選國民大會代表與立
法委員候選人二十名，全為台
灣省與台北市籍的國民黨員，
並表示希望友黨人士參加競

選。

中國民主社會黨全國臨時代表大會在台北市開幕。

十一月二日　美國戰略空軍總司令哈羅威上將夫婦，及美國太平洋陸軍總司令海恩上將抵達台北訪問。

十一月三日　世界中文報業協會第二屆年會在台北開幕，會期預定三天。

十一月十一日　聯合國大會本屆大會投票表決，以五十六票對四十八票，另二十一票棄權將建議中共入會案加以否決。

十一月十二日　台北市「國父紀念館」，於國父中山先生誕辰興工建造。

十一月十三日　中華民國內政部召開會議決定，今後將嚴格禁止製造與使用家用 D.D.T.。

十一月十五日　台北市改制後第一屆市議員選舉結果，四十八位市議員順利選出，其中國民黨提名的四十三位候選人全部當選。

十一月廿一日　美國與日本發表聯合聲明稱，琉球群島將於一九七二年由美國交還給日本。美軍於二次世界大戰末期攻佔琉球。

中華民國外交部發表聲明，重申政府對琉球歸屬問題立場不變，指出根據二次世界大戰同盟國宣言及舊金山和約，應由有關國家協商決定琉球問題。

十一月廿三日　中國民主社會黨（原名中國國家社會黨）在台北市舉行臨時全國代表大會，通過黨章臨時條款，選出十一位委員並發表宣言，共赴反共大業。

十一月廿四日　中國國民黨建黨七十五週年紀念大會在台北市中山堂舉行，國民黨黨史委員會主任委員黃季陸對大會演講：「中國國民黨與台灣」。中國國民黨黨史委員會，與中華民國國史館合辦之「中華民國史料研究中心」在台北市郊之青潭正式成立。

十一月廿七日　中華民國行政院鄭重宣佈：「我國發展核子能限於和平用途，決遵守一切國際協定。」

十二月一日　中華民國教育部公佈，最新修正之「國外留學規

程」，及新訂之「國外留學生甄試辦法」，定明年元月一日起施行。

十二月二日　台灣省政府決定，將石門水庫水位降低為二三六點五公尺，以提高防洪功能，減少台灣北部地區積水威脅。

十二月五日　中華民國財政部說，去年對外貿易輸出總值超過十億美元，對美國貿易出超五千餘萬美元。

十二月八日　中國著名外交家顧維鈞博士偕夫人，自美國返台灣度假。

十二月十六日　國際新聞學會中華民國分會成立，推舉聯合報發行人王惕吾為分會會長。

十二月十八日　中華民國第一座國際衛星通信地面電台，正式展開對美國、日本及泰國的通信業務。

十二月十九日　美國國務院宣佈，自本年十二月廿三日開始，美國有限度開放對中共非戰略物資的禁運。

十二月二十日　中華民國自由地區舉行中央公職人員增補選投票，共選出國民大會代表十五人，

及立法委員十一人。

十二月廿三日　中華民國光復大陸設計研究委員會第十六次大會在台北開幕，會期預定兩天。

十二月廿五日　中華民國前國史館長羅家倫，因病在台北市逝世，享年七十三歲（一八九八～一九六九）。
中國道教六十三代天師張恩溥，因病在台北市逝世。

十二月廿六日　中華民國國防部發言人說，中、美基本條約未變，美國軍艦仍巡邏台灣海峽。

十二月廿九日　中華民國中央公職人員增補選舉投票，台北市議會選出監察委員兩名。

十二月三十日　菲律賓新總統馬可仕宣誓就任。

中華民國五十九年（一九七〇）

一月一日　蔣介石總統元旦書告全國同胞，應從精神、生活、行動、觀念上，政治、經濟、教育、文化等方面再革新、再進步，開創倫理、民主、科學三民主義新中國的新運。

一月二日　美國副總統安格紐抵台灣訪問，兩度晉見蔣介石總統會

談。

一月三日　美國情報人員協助主張「台灣獨立」的彭明敏自台灣逃出，後轉往美國。彭明敏原為台灣大學政治系主任，與謝聰敏、魏廷朝被控從事台獨運動。

歸化中國的美國女傳教士艾偉德在台北病逝。有「小婦人」之稱的艾偉德在中國山西傳教的事蹟，經好萊塢拍攝成電影「六福客棧」。

一月五日　台灣省政府民政廳報告說，台灣山地同胞民國五十六年度（一九六七）個人所得平均為新台幣三千二百二十一元。

一月十日　美國國務院宣佈，美國將以一個中隊十八架 F-104 星式噴射型戰鬥機援助中華民國空軍。

一月十一日　中華民國新聞局發表，國軍退除官兵輔導委員會統計，十五年來已安置退除役官兵十八萬五千八百二十三人。

一月十四日　蔣介石總統接見來華訪問的美國空軍部長席曼斯晤談。

中華民國教育部公佈，經認可的留學美國大學名單計二二九校，較前增加五十一所，而且原名單中所列的神學院已加以刪除。

佐藤榮作擔任日本新首相。

一月十五日　中華民國財政部宣佈，去年度對外貿易總額逾二十二億美元，其中對日本負逆差鉅大。

中華民國行政院會議通過，修正「旅客出入國境攜帶金錢外幣限制辦法」第二條條文，將其中外幣限額美金二百元提高為四百元。

美國國院重申支持中華民國的政策，警告中共勿圖攻擊金門、馬祖，並且說明美國與中共在華沙會談的動機。

一月二十日　中國國民黨中央委員會召開工作檢討會。中華民國交通部電信總局決定，設立國際電話交換中心。

一月廿八日　美國舊金山的中文「世界日報」，於出版七十餘年久後，將予以出售或停刊。

一月三十日　中華民國立法院宣佈，在舉行立法委員增選後，立法

委員總額為七百八十四人，出席立法院院會法定人數應為一百五十七人。

一月卅一日　美國國防部宣佈，以 F-100 型軍刀式噴射戰鬥機三十四架贈給中華民國空軍，並撥贈維護費五百二十萬美元。

二月二日　中華民國中華航空公司新闢橫越太平洋中美航線，使用波音七〇七型噴射式客機，今日首航飛往舊金山。

日本新任首相佐藤榮作表示，日本對中華民國立場不變，反對所謂「兩個中國」政策。

中華民國教育部說，民國五十八年度（一九六九）共有外籍學生一一九名接受獎勵，來中華民國深造。

二月七日　中華民國交通部核定，在今後兩年內訂造五艘一萬五千噸級全貨櫃商輪。

聯合國人口委員會宣佈，今年全世界人口總數將達三十六億二千二百萬人。

二月十二日　台灣新竹與竹北間鐵路發生重大車禍事件，觀光號列車追撞平等號快車，兩節車廂翻覆，十人不幸喪生，另有四十七人受輕重傷。

二月十六日　台灣郵政管理局正式創設第一個台北夜間郵局，營業時間自每晚九時至翌晨，為公眾服務。

二月二十日　中華民國教育部宣佈，全國各級學生總數達三百八十一萬人，教育經費達新台幣七十二億元。

二月廿一日　台灣遠東航空公司一架專運台北市各報紙到台灣中南部的飛機，在台北市郊福壽山山頂撞毀失事。

二月廿三日　中華民國內政部宣佈，去年全國共查扣不良出版品四百二十三萬餘件。

二月廿六日　美國海軍部宣佈，美國第七艦隊司令易人，新司令為魏納斯中將。

三月一日　中華民國紅十字會台灣省分會宣佈，該分會所屬十一個血庫今日起一律改稱「血液銀行」。

三月二日　中華民國經濟部長孫運璿說，由於政府推行十項措施，策進經濟建設，去年國民總生產額達新台幣一千九百零四億元，較十七年前增加十倍。

三月五日　美國軍事援華顧問團新任團長泰萊少將抵達台北履新。

三月七日　中華民國與泰國雙方代表長在台北松山國際機場舉行之修訂中，泰航空協定談判，達成協議。

談判自六日開始舉行。

三月十日　台灣省台北縣石碇鄉文山煤礦發生瓦斯爆事件，礦工七人不幸喪生。

三月十四日　台灣中國石油公司，在日本建造的第二艘十萬噸油輪軒轅號，在日本吳港舉行下水典禮。

三月十七日　台北市孔子廟產權代表人辜振甫表示，願意將孔廟全部產權捐獻給國家。

三月二十日　中華民國第二十三屆郵政節，交通部郵政總局新創之郵遞區號制度開始實施，作為節慶獻禮。

三月廿三日　台灣省政府審計處發表，民國五十八年（一九六九）國民所得為，新台幣一三三二億三千六百萬元，平均每人為九千五百五十四元。

美軍太平洋空軍總司令納薩若夫婦乘專機抵達台北訪問兩天。

菲律賓政府宣布，馬尼拉出版的親中共「華僑商報」社長于長城，及總編輯于長庚被菲國當局下令拘捕。

三月廿九日　中國國民黨中央委員第十屆二全中會，在台北市陽明山開幕，蔣介石總裁親臨主持，並以「為復國建國」為題訓勉全黨同志。

三月三十日　亞洲開發銀行通過決定，對中華民國貸款一千八百萬美元，資助修建台北市至楊梅間的一段高速公路。

四月一日　中國國民黨十屆二中全會第五次大會通過，「改進基層政治風氣及司法風氣案」。

四月二日　中國國民黨十屆二全中會，通過「現階段加強國民就業輔導工作綱領」與「全面實踐國民生活須知，貫徹社會革新」兩項議案，並選舉二十一名常務委員後宣告閉幕。當選常務委員的為嚴家淦、蔣經國、謝東閔等二十一人。

四月八日　中國國民黨中央常務委員會決議，設五個督導組，負責對國民黨十全大會及十屆二中

全會各項決議案，作全面長期性督導考核，以期徹底執行。

四月十三日 中華民國行政院修正三軍軍官服役條例草案，送請立法院審議。草案規定，軍官服役十年後，得依軍事需要延長三至五年。

四月十五日 美國第七艦隊司令魏斯納中將抵台灣訪問。

四月十八日 中華民國行政院副院長蔣經國搭機飛往美國，作為期十天的訪問。

四月十九日 中華民國行政院副院長蔣經國，在美國舊金山告訴華僑說，政府決心光復大陸。

四月廿一日 蔣經國副院長在華盛頓，與美國國務卿羅吉斯會談中、美有關問題。

四月廿二日 美國總統尼克森在白宮款待蔣經國副院長，並舉行會談。尼克森重申中、美兩國之友好關係及美國對華條約義務之堅定立場。

四月廿三日 蔣經國副院長六十誕辰（農曆三月十八日），華府的中國記者特前往其訪美行館布萊爾賓館獻禮祝賀。

中華民國行政院會議通過決定，命令國防部公布「台灣地區戒嚴時期出版物管制辦法」。

四月廿四日 美國國務院發表聲明稱，蔣經國副院長華府之行，曾商討中、美兩國共同安全事項、台灣經濟發展，中華民國對非洲、亞洲及拉丁美洲國家技術援助計劃，以及區域合作，國際及東亞局勢，中、美均獲裨益。台灣茶葉外銷量去年高達二千一百五十萬公斤，創歷年來之最高紀錄。

中共宣布，發射一個人造衛星進入地球軌道。

四月廿四日 中華民國行政院副院長蔣經國，今午在紐約市布拉薩大飯店，參加美國工商協會午宴發表演說之際，突有兩名暴徒謀刺，其中一人開槍，立即被美國安全人員制服，蔣副院長安然無恙。兩嫌犯皆為來自台灣的留學生。

美國總統尼克森、國務卿羅吉斯及紐約市長林賽，皆向蔣經國表示為其被狙擊事件而致歉意。

四月廿六日 行政院副院長蔣經國在

紐約被謀刺消息傳抵台灣後，各界紛電慰問。

元朝太祖成吉斯汗（鐵木真）大祭典禮，蔣介石總統特派蒙藏委員會委員長郭寄嶠代表主祭。

四月廿八日　台灣省政府規定，建築物因用途特殊，凡高度超過三十五公尺者，須隨時向內政部申請許可。

四月廿九日　中華民國行政院副院長蔣經國，結束在美國訪問十天行程後，於晚間搭機飛抵日本，預定停留兩天。

五月一日　美國國防部宣布，任命鮑伯格中將為美軍協防台灣司令。

行政院副院長蔣經國完成訪美任務返抵台北。

五月六日　蔣介石總統發佈命令，特任錢思亮為中央研究院院長。

孟子二千三百四十二年誕辰，孟氏在台後裔舉行祭禮，由亞聖奉祀官孟繁驥主祭。

五月八日　英國新任駐中華民國領事戴飛抵台北，接替卸任領事勃雷的職務。

五月九日　天文奇觀「水星凌日」，

在台灣時間中午十二時十九分至二十時十三分為止。

五月十一日　中華民國行政院副院長蔣經國應越南總統阮文紹邀請，赴越南訪問三天，與阮文紹總統及陳善謙總理會談，就中南半島情勢交換意見。

五月十三日　中華民國行政院核准修正「人民出國探親辦法」，自本年七月一日起公布實施。

五月十六日　世界銀行總裁麥納瑪拉抵達台灣訪問，代表世界銀行簽訂「台灣電力發展計劃」與「中華開發信託公司」兩項貸款合約共六千二百五十萬美元。

五月十八日　上月在紐約企圖謀刺行政院副院長蔣經國的兩名嫌犯黃文雄和鄭自才，被紐約州最高法院大陪審團以非法持有武器，企圖謀殺罪起訴。

五月十九日　中華民國地方自治法規修改委員會決定，台灣省縣市議會議員名額，今後將作適當限制，各縣市議員最低為十九名，最高為五十七名。

中國國民黨中央委員會民國五十九年（一九七〇）業務研討

會在台北市開幕，會期五天。

五月二十日　中華民國交通部民用航空局，與美商派森斯公司簽訂合約，委託該公司設計桃園新國際機場。

五月廿一日　蔣介石總統接見美軍太平洋總司令馬侃上將及太平洋總部政治顧問柯寧。

五月廿四日　中華民國駐菲律賓首都馬尼拉大使館，於凌晨三時遭暴徒投擲一顆土製炸彈，館舍玻璃窗及冷氣機受損壞，幸無人傷亡。

五月廿五日　中華民國行政院決定，將田賦徵收標準予以降低，以減輕農民負擔。

五月廿八日　中華民國立法委員郭國基因病逝世，享年七十歲。郭係台灣省籍，有「郭大砲」之稱。

五月卅一日　中華民國教育部公布，修正「留學生回國服務辦法」。

六月一日　美國太平洋艦隊總司令郝蘭德上將抵台北訪問三天，中華民國政府頒贈大綬雲輝勳章一座。

六月十日　英國政府公布，在日本侵佔中國東北的「九一八」瀋陽事變後，中國、日本及英國三國間關係的歷史文件。

六月十五日　中華民國經濟部決定，今後華僑及外國人士來台灣投資的最低金額，限定為二十萬美元。

六月十六日　第三屆亞洲作家會議在台北市開幕，會期四天，參加會議的計十八個國家一百三十多位代表。

六月十七日　中華民國政府有關當局決定，積極推廣綜合養豬計劃，預計在三年內產豬千餘萬頭。

六月十八日　國際中國古畫討論會在台北市故宮博物院揭幕，蔣總統夫人宋美齡女士以名譽會長身分在大會致詞，指出中國畫深涵詩意與靈感，勉創造更新意境。

六月廿四日　中華民國教育部公布，新修正的「大陸來台學生學籍處理及輔導就學辦法」。

六月廿八日　台灣省政府為提高國民就學率，命令嚴禁工廠雇用未滿十四歲的童工。

六月廿九日　蔣介石總統發佈命令，

特任陸軍一級上將高魁元為總統府參軍長，及空軍二級上將賴名湯為參謀總長。

七月六日　中華民國副總統兼行政院長嚴家淦，赴日本訪問抵達東京，會晤日本首相佐藤榮作，討論中、日有關問題，並主持世界博覽會「中國日」典禮。

七月十日　中華民國行政院命令，派旅美學人李志鐘出任國立中央圖書館館長。

七月十二日　美國太平洋空軍總司令納薩若上將偕隨員八人抵台灣訪問。

七月十四日　前新疆省政府主席盛世才在台北市病逝，享年七十六歲（一八九五～一九七〇）。日本政府宣布，決定將「日本」的發音統一規定為「NIPPON」而非「NIHON」。

七月十六日　美國陸軍參謀長魏摩蘭上將，抵台灣訪問四天。

七月廿二日　中國國民黨中央常務委員會會議決定，將電影娛樂稅率降低，國產影片自原來的百分之四十降為百分之三十，並且通過將電影事業納入「文化事業」範圍。

七月廿六日　中華民國中央研究院舉行第九次院士會議，選出八位新院士，並且對七項議案獲得結論。

七月廿八日　中華民國內政部公布，閩台地區人口統計結果，共有一千四百五十五萬四千零五十人，其中男性計七百六十六萬九千一百八十三人，女性計六百八十八萬四千八百六十七人。

七月卅一日　中國青年黨新推選的「幹事」陳翰珍就任新職。

八月一日　台北市新成立的「中華電視台」正式開播。該台為中華民國軍方支持的電視台。

八月八日　中國國民黨中央文化經濟事業管理委員會正式成立。

八月十日　日本對中華民國台灣省北部的釣魚台群島（即尖閣群島），提出主權異議。

八月十二日　美國駐日本大使館發言人宣稱，釣魚台群島「是琉球群島的一部分，美國政府已決定歸還日本」。

台灣中華航空公司一架客機，於自花蓮飛往台北途中，在台北市郊撞山失事，計有十三人

不幸喪生，一人失蹤，另十七人受輕重傷。

八月廿一日　中華民國外交部發言人宣稱，台灣以北大陸礁層資源，中華民國有權探勘開採，以示釣魚台群島（即尖閣群島）主權屬於中國。

八月廿二日　中華民國外交部長魏道明在立法院報告說：「我國對釣魚台群島立場已明告日本，根據國際法及一九五八年大陸礁層公約，我國有探勘開採之權。」

八月廿三日　金門砲戰（「八二三砲戰」）十二週年日，金門前線軍民利用各種氣球空飄，將大批青天白日滿地紅國旗、蔣介石總統文告及安全證等傳單飄向大陸。
中國共產黨中央九屆二中全會在北京開幕。

八月廿六日　蔣介石總統接見美國副總統安格紐，會談有關世界局勢及中、美特別問題。

八月卅一日　中國國民黨中央委員會成立業務綜合檢查組，對各省級黨部進行業務檢查。

九月三日　抗戰勝利紀念日。蔣介石總統親臨台北市圓山忠烈祠主持秋祭革命先烈大典。

九月五日　國際貨幣基金會通過，將新台幣之平價定為每元折合零點零二二二一六八克純金，及新台幣四十元折合美金一元。

九月七日　強烈颱風襲擊台灣省，造成嚴重災情，四十一人不幸喪生，四十五人失蹤，三十三人受傷，房屋倒塌千餘間。

九月八日　美軍協防台灣司令部新任司令鮑格伯中將抵達台北就職。

九月九日　北京新華通訊社報導，中國共產黨中央九屆二中全會，在通過「關於加強戰備工作報告」後閉幕。全會於八月廿三日至九月六日在北京舉行。

九月十二日　美國第七艦隊司令魏斯納中將抵金門前線訪問。

九月十八日　亞洲人民反共聯盟第十六屆大會在日本京都開幕。

九月十九日　美國開發總署署長韓納抵達台北，與中華民國政府官員會商。
中華民國教育部發表，已將「大專畢業生徵集常備兵服役規定」通知各大專院校，其中

規定大專畢業生服役期限，陸軍一律為兩年，海空軍皆為三年。

九月二十日　中華民國國防部發言人稱，日本巡邏艇在釣魚台群島水域阻擾「我國漁船作業」。

九月廿一日　中美兩國聯合軍事演習在台海舉行，中華民國參謀總長賴名湯、海軍總司令宋長志及空軍總司令陳衣凡，參觀美國最新型攻擊航空母艦「美利堅號」，及視察兩國聯合演習進行情形。

九月廿三日　中國國民黨台灣省第八屆全省代表大會在台中市召開，蔣介石總裁書勉台省國民黨同志，貫徹革新要求，使台省黨務邁進新境界。

九月廿五日　中華民國教育部宣布，中美基金會撥款二百九十五萬元，補助八所大專院校擴充科學設備。

九月廿七日　中華民國釣魚台作業漁船四百艘，遭受日本巡邏艇干擾，基隆與宜蘭漁業界人士請求政府保護。

美國加利福尼亞州州議會通過，以中國孔子誕辰九月廿八日為教師節。加州舊金山市政府先於九月廿五日宣布，孔子誕辰九月廿八日為該市教師節。

十月三日　中華民國政府宣布，全面實施平均地權課稅標準，地價稅累進級距、累進稅率，最高為千分之七十，最低為千分之十五。

台灣造船公司為中國石油公司建造之十萬噸油輪「有巢號」，在基隆市舉行下水典禮。

十月六日　中華民國外交部說，已正式照會日本表示「我國不能同意日本對釣魚台群島主權的敘述與主張。」

十月七日　中華民國第一屆雜誌展覽，在台北市中央圖書館開幕，展出各類雜誌三百多種。

十月十日　蔣介石總統發表雙十國慶告全國同胞書，切望秉持誠摯純潔的革命精神，完成復國建國的大業。

十月十三日　中共人民政府與加拿大政府發表建交公報，將在六個月內互換大使。

中華民國宣稱與加拿大斷絕外

交關係，因為加拿大承認中共政權。

美國政府官員認為，加拿大與中共政權建立外交關係，將不致改變美國在聯合國的政策，也不改變美國不承認中共政權的政策。

前中華民國駐加拿大大使薛毓麒自加拿大抵美國談話說，加拿大外交部長夏普曾保證，加國政府將本過去中、加友誼及尊重人權原則，處理旅加國華僑問題。

十月十四日　中國國民黨中央常務委員會通過，調任林金生為中央委員會副秘書長。林金生係台灣省籍國民黨員，原任台北市黨部主任委員。

十月十九日　中華民國副總統兼行政院長嚴家淦抵紐約出席聯合國成立廿五週年紀念大會，發表聲明稱，中華民國為聯合國組織創建國之一，決盡力維護聯合國憲章義務。

十月廿二日　嚴家淦副總統在華府會晤美國副總統安格紐，商談中、美共同問題，盼美國加強援助亞洲盟邦。

十月廿三日　中華民國政府與歐洲共同市場簽訂協定，台灣紡織品可以輸往歐洲。

十月廿五日　中華民國副總統嚴家淦會晤美國總統尼克森，廣泛商討世局，盼中、美兩國加強合作。尼克森總統告嚴副總統，美國決堅守對華承諾。

台灣省與台北市各界，分別在台中市及台北市舉行台灣光復二十五週年慶祝大會。校址設在台北市北投的政工幹校，奉命改名為政治作戰學校。

十一月一日　美國空軍部長席曼斯抵台北訪問。

十一月六日　中共政權與義大利政府發表「建交」聯合公報，聲明在三個月內互換大使。

中華民國政府嚴正宣布，義大利與中共建交嚴重「損害我國權益，與義大利斷絕邦交，一切後果由義大利單獨負責。」許紹昌大使在關閉大使館後啟程返國。

十一月十日　美國波音七四七式巨型噴射客機，安然降落台北松山國際機場，為中華民國航空史上寫下新頁。同時，松山機場

實施擴建，預定明年四月間完成，計劃包括延長跑道等七大工程，動支新台幣兩億餘元。

十一月二十日　聯合國第二十五屆大會，就有關中國代表權問題建議案舉行投票，表決結果以六十六票對五十二票另七票棄權，通過「重要問題案」，並以五十一票對四十九票另二十五票棄權，將中共入會案加以否決。

十二月三日　中華民國行政院公布，退休公務員退休金優惠存款辦法。

十二月十五日　日本前首相岸信介及前駐華大使井口貞夫抵台灣訪問。

十二月廿三日　台北市長高玉樹對英文中國日報發表談話，被指為「公然蔑視監察權」，監察委員表示憤慨。

十二月廿五日　中共主席毛澤東在北京接見美國記者史諾。史諾為著名的中共支持者，以「一顆紅星在中國」一書出名。

十二月廿七日　中華民國田徑運動女傑紀政，本日在台北市與其美國籍教練瑞爾舉行結婚典禮，

當晚即偕同飛往日本渡蜜月。

十二月三十日　中華民國財政部稱，今年對外貿易總額達三十億美元。

中華民國六十年（一九七一）

一月一日　蔣介石總統發表元旦告全國同胞書，勉以同舟共濟，堅忍淬勵，導發大陸上再一次辛亥革命之來臨。

一月四日　中國國民黨台灣省委員會第八屆委員及候補委員舉行宣誓就職典禮。

一月五日　中華民國外交部宣布，因為智利政府承認中共政權，中華民國與智利斷絕邦交，關閉駐智利大使館，並撤退駐智利農業技術團。

一月六日　中華民國行政院國際經濟合作發展委員會初步估計說，去年國內生產毛額約達新台幣兩千一百七十八億元，平均國民所得每人為新台幣一一、六八四元折合美金二九二元」。

一月九日　蔣介石總統接見來華訪問的美國太平洋陸軍總司令羅森上將。

一月十日　中華民國前駐美大使董顯

光博士在美國加利福尼亞州病逝，享年八十五歲（一八八七～一九七一）。

北京新華通訊社報導，中共上海市第四次代表大會，選出張春橋、姚文元為市委會第一及第二書記，王洪文、馬天水等為市委會書記。

一月十三日　中華民國經濟部報告，民國五十九年（一九七〇）對外貿易總值為三十億零七千萬美元，及輸出與輸入相抵，計出超三千萬美元。

一月十五日　中華民國總統府國策顧問劉峙在台北市病逝，享年八十歲（一八九二～一九七一）。

一月廿七日　中國農曆春節，蔣介石總統關懷前線三軍將士，特派參謀總長賴名湯上將前往慰問。

一月三十日　中華民國留美學生，在紐約、華盛頓、芝加哥等城市遊行，反對日本對釣魚台群島的無理要求，並擁護政府維護主權、領土完整的嚴正立場。

二月一日　中華民國行政院戶口普查處公布，去年台閩地區常住人口接近一千五百萬人，總戶口超過二百六十三萬八千戶。

二月二日　中華民國第一座完全由國內科學家與工程師自行設計的微功率核子反應器（亦稱原子爐），自本日起開始正式運轉。

二月六日　台灣省政府警務處發表統計說，台灣省現住人口總數為一千二百八十九萬八千八百六十人。人口密度為每平方公里三六一人（此項統計不包括台北市人口數字）。

二月九日　中國國民黨中央文藝工作研討會在台北市召開，會期三天，討論文藝工作之改進。

二月十二日　北京消息，「主席劉少奇」、「國防部長彭德懷」及「北京市長彭真」等均被中共軟禁。

二月十三日　中華民國公務員懲戒委員會，對台北市長高玉樹移付懲戒案，決定成立四人小組，展開調查。

二月十五日　中華民國內政部發表，台閩地區農漁業普查完成，總計共有農漁戶九十八萬九千九百餘戶。

英國政府宣布，英國開始採用圓、角、分的十進位新英鎊幣制，並廢止沿用八百年久的鎊、先令、便士為單位的舊幣制。

二月廿五日　美國總統尼克森發表第二個年度外交政策報告中，關於中國問題部分，表示美國尊重對中華民國的承諾，並盼改善與中共的關係，而且強調撤軍並非有意退出亞洲。中華民國外交部發言人魏煜孫說，對尼克森總統外交政策報告中有關對中共之想法「我們不能同意」。

三月一日　中國國民黨台北市黨部本日召開第二次代表大會，討論北市黨務問題。

三月三日　美國國防部宣布，中共於本日晚間八時十五分，自大陸西北部之雙井子基地發射第二個人造地球衛星。

中華民國當局下令逮捕並驅逐在台灣從事「台灣獨立」活動的日本人。（次日逮捕並驅逐和「台獨」分子有聯繫的美國傳教士。）

三月四日　中華民國駐美國大使周書楷，為尼克森總統在其世局咨文中使用不當措辭事，向美國政府表示強烈反對。

美國總統尼克森堅決表示，支持中華民國在聯合國的地位，絕不以中華民國的合法席次示惠中共。美國助理國務卿葛林，亦說明美國對華政策不變。

中華民國行政院會議通過，修正「廣播及電視無線電台設置及管理規則」。

三月五日　中國童子軍創建六十週年舉行慶祝大會，副總統嚴家淦對大會訓勉擴大推行日行一善運動。

三月十五日　美國政府宣布，美國解除美國人民赴中共地區的旅行限制，但對北韓、北越及古巴的旅行限制仍不解除。

三月十九日　中華民國外交部發言人魏煜孫發表聲明，再度表明中華民國政府立場：反對「兩個中國」謬論，既定國策絕不改變。

三月廿五日　自中國大陸逃出的著名音樂家馬思聰，在美國國會眾議院安全小組委員會作證，歷

陳大陸中共迫害知識分子的實況。

三月廿六日　台灣省澎湖跨海大橋舉行通車典禮。該橋為國人自力完成的大橋，全長二千二百六十公尺，為遠東第一長橋。

三月廿九日　中華民國外交部嚴正聲明，與中東的石油國科威特斷絕外交關係，因為科威特承認中共政權。

三月卅一日　蔣介石總統發佈命令，特任前駐美國大使周書楷為外交部長，調外交部長魏道明為總統府資政。

四月二日　印尼航空公司開闢中、印航線，印尼航空公司首航客機飛抵台北市，展開雙方民航事業新頁。

四月八日　美國國務院宣布，美國邀請中共桌球（乒乓球）隊赴美國訪問，美國桌球隊亦將訪問中共大陸。此舉被稱為「乒乓外交」之始。

中華民國行政院會議通過，任命沈劍虹為駐美國大使，接替周書楷的職缺。

四月九日　美國國務院發表聲明，擬將釣魚台群島主權交與日本，中華民國政府堅決反對，向美國提出嚴重交涉。為保衛釣魚台主權，舊金山的中國留學生舉行遊行示威。

四月十日　中華民國政府重申堅定立場，維護釣魚台主權，對美國國務院的建議，提出嚴重交涉，及在「我國海域探油工作決不受影響」。

四月十四日　台北市台灣大學學生數十人，為維護釣魚台主權，特向美國大使館抗議。同時，台北市政治大學學生為維護釣魚台主權，在校內舉行遊行及座談會。

四月十六日　中華民國國防部發言人說，廈門中共軍隊對金門前線發射三十九發砲彈。

四月二十日　美國駐華大使馬康衛表示，對於釣魚台主權問題，美國政府決不偏袒。

四月廿一日　中華民國教育部長羅雲平表示，盼大專學生對維護釣魚台主權問題，信賴政府嚴正立場，不宜再有遊行抗議行動。

日本駐華大使館說，已將各大專院校對有關釣魚台主權問題

之抗議書轉達東京日本政府。

四月廿五日　中華民國前行政院長宋子文博士在美國病逝，享年七十七歲（一八九四～一九七一）。

四月廿六日　北京新華通訊社報導，中共主席毛澤東發表紀念「五一」國際勞動節口號三十二條，其中有「解放台灣」。

四月廿八日　美國國務院發言人布瑞宣稱，美國主張中華民國與中共政權直接談判，並且表示台灣地位「仍未解決」。

四月廿九日　中華民國教育部核定，台灣省立成功大學（校址在台南市），及中興大學（校址在台中市），自今年七月一日起改制為國立大學。

美國總統尼克森在記者招待會中表示，所謂中華民國與中共政權舉行「直接談判完全不切實際。」

四月三十日　中華民國新任外交部長周書楷召見美國駐華大使馬康衛，促其轉達美國政府澄清美國對台灣澎湖的立場。

台北市長高玉樹違法失職案，公務員懲戒委員會決定予以申誡。

五月一日　美國駐華軍援顧問團慶祝成立二十週年。

中華民國國立中央圖書館，創設國家聯合書目制度。

北京人民日報發表專文稱：「中國領土主權不容侵犯」。此為毛澤東政權對釣魚台主權問題之首次正式表示意見。

五月四日　中華民國文藝團體舉行文藝節慶祝大會，並頒發文藝獎金。五月四日原為青年節，係用以紀念中華民國八年發生的「五四」運動，後青年節改為三月廿九日，用以紀念黃花崗七十二烈士事件。

五月五日　歐洲貨幣市場情勢混亂，西德政府宣布停止吸進美元，黃金價格創每盎司四十元美金的最高峰。

中華民國行政院通過「國防研究院組織條例」草案。

美國國務院發言人布瑞四月廿八日所作有關台灣主權尚未解決的聲明，未經白宮認可，美國務院承認錯誤。

五月七日　中華民國有關當局統計表示，台灣地區人口密度達每平

方公里四百零七人，居世界首
位。

五月十四日　中國國民黨中央常務委
員會通過，國民黨黨史委員會
主任委員由杜元載繼任。

五月十七日　台灣警備總司令部發言
人宣布，日本籍不良分子小林
正來台灣從事「台獨」活動，
攜來傳單，謀圖不軌，被警備
總部逮捕遞解出境。

五月十九日　蔣介石總統與沙烏地阿
拉伯國王費瑟舉行會談，廣泛
交換對世局意見。費瑟國王並
參觀中華民國軍事演習，稱讚
軍隊精良。

五月二十日　台北市議會通過臨時動
議案，建議政府將居住台灣地
區的國民籍貫，採用「原籍」
與「現籍」兩欄記載方式，以
溝通地域觀念，加強國人團結
心理，厚植反攻力量。
中華民國行政院通過「交通部
觀光事業局組織條例草案」，
送請立法院審議。

五月廿五日　台灣造船公司建造之第
二艘十萬噸巨型油輪「神農」
號，在基隆港舉行下水典禮。

五月廿七日　中華民國外交部發言人

表示對奧地利政府放棄中立政
策而承認中共政權，表示遺
憾。

六月一日　中國國民黨民國六十年
（一九七一）度工作革新研討
會，自今日起分三期進行。

六月二日　美國總統尼克森表示，他
將在六星期以內決定美國對聯
合國的中國代表權問題所採取
之立場。

六月四日　中華民國駐美國大使沈劍
虹會晤美國助理國務卿葛林，
商談有關中、美兩國共同利益
問題。

六月五日　第十七屆亞洲影展在台北
市揭幕，預定九日閉幕。

六月九日　美國國務卿羅吉斯與日本
外相愛知揆一，在法京巴黎對
美國將琉球群島移交給日本之
簽字日期達成協議。

六月十一日　中華民國政府發表聲
明，對美國擅自將琉球移交日
本至為不滿，釣魚台列嶼為中
華民國領土之一部分，對美、
日間轉移堅決加以反對。

六月十五日　蔣介石總統主持國家安
全會議，訓示：「我們國家的
立場和國民的精神」，激勵國

人：「莊敬自強，處變不驚，慎謀能斷」。

台灣省議會發表聲明，表達全省同胞服膺蔣總統訓示之決心，保證擁護政府決策，團結一致，堅強奮鬥。

美國國務院發表聲明稱，美國將琉球行政權交還日本，至於釣魚台主權事，仍待中華民國與日本洽商解決。

六月十七日　美國及日本兩國分別在華府及東京簽署琉球群島移轉協定，美國仍將保留島上主要軍事基地。

六月廿一日　美國太平洋總司令馬侃上將抵台灣訪問。中國國民黨中央常務委員會通過實踐蔣總裁訓示方案，期盼全國黨政軍民身體力行。

六月廿四日　台灣電力公司獲得美國貸款一億三百八十萬美元，再建一座核子電廠，美國民間基金佔貸款的一半。

七月一日　中華民國中央氣象局，在台北正式恢復建制。台灣省立成功大學及中興大學，今日起改為國立。

七月十日　美國總統尼克森派國家安全顧問季辛吉秘密通過巴基斯坦進入中國大陸，將與中共政權總理周恩來舉行會談。

美國國務院宣布下年對中華民國軍事援助，將逾一億美元。

七月十一日　中華民國外交部發言人，重申南沙群島為中華民國固有領土。

美國反共社團發起之「自由中國週」運動，今日開始活動，呼籲輿論界認清中共真面目，堅決反對中共進入聯合國組織。

七月十五日　美國與中共政府發表公告，宣布美國總統尼克森（尼克松）將在一九七二年五月之前赴中國大陸訪問。

美國國務卿羅吉斯在尼克森總統宣布前往中國大陸訪問之前半個小時，以電話告知中華民國駐美國大使沈劍虹。

七月十六日　中華民國代理外交部長楊西昆召見美國駐華大使馬康衛，為尼克森總統將訪問大陸事，提出嚴重抗議。外交部命令駐美大使沈劍虹為尼克森訪問中共事提嚴重抗議。

美國總統尼克森的國家安全事

務顧問季辛吉與白宮新聞秘書齊格勒舉行記者招待會，特就季辛吉秘密訪問北京及其與中共總理周恩來會談內容作公開之說明。

七月十八日　全美國各地華僑促使美國總統尼克森對其訪問中共區計劃再加考慮。

中華民國國防部發言人說，廈門中共軍隊對金門前線射擊砲彈四十八發。

七月十九日　美國國務卿羅吉斯與中華民國及日本等九個亞洲國家駐美國大使會晤，就尼克森總統將訪問中共事有所交談。

七月二十日　中華民國九所大專院校學生代表三十六人，集聚在台北美國大使館前，抗議尼克森總統訪問中共計劃。

中華民國外交部發言人說，美國總統尼克森曾專函蔣介石總統，保證美國尊重中、美共同防禦條約之承諾。

日本首相佐藤榮作說，日本將繼續對中華民國提供經濟援助，以加強其經濟開發與穩定。

七月廿一日　台灣省議員黃光平等建

議政府，修改戶籍法，加註「祖籍」一欄，以建立數典不忘祖與來台無分先後之健康心理。

在美國國會參議院外交委員會通過廢止一九五五年的「台灣決議案」後，美國政府再度向中華民國保證信守其防衛條約承諾。

七月廿六日　中華民國總統府秘書長張群，在東京會晤日本首相佐藤榮作，商談一小時半。

七月卅一日　中華民國駐美國大使沈劍虹及駐聯合國常任代表劉鍇，訪晤美國國務卿羅吉斯，商談有關中華民國在聯合國的代表權問題。

中共黨的「兩報一刊」發表聯合社論：「紀念八一建軍節」，要求美軍從亞洲撤退及「解放台灣」。

八月二日　中華民國外交部就所謂聯合國中國代表權案發表聲明，促使各會員國奮起挽救聯合國的厄運。

美國國務卿羅吉斯宣稱，美國贊成中共於今秋進入聯合國，但將反對排除中華民國的任何

行動。

八月四日　土耳其共和國宣布，與中共建立外交關係，建交公報在巴黎簽字。

美國駐聯合國常任代表布希，為安排中共進入聯合國同時防止排擠中華民國爭取會員國支持其提案，邀請二十個會員國的代表舉行會商。

八月五日　中華民國外交部發言人宣稱，為使駐各國使節明瞭政府今年如何因應所謂聯合國中國代表權問題，決定分別舉行簡報。

外交部發言人並說，因為土耳其宣布承認中共政權，中華民國政府宣布與土耳其中止外交關係。

八月六日　中華民國外交部說，駐亞洲太平洋地區各國使節會議今天上午在台北市的台北賓館舉行。

八月十日　中華民國中央銀行宣布，修訂「小額匯款申請結匯須知」。

八月十五日　中華民國教育部宣布，今年大專院校聯合招生入學考試放榜分發完畢，錄取名額共兩萬七千九百三十五人，錄取率為百分之三十五點四，比去年高百分之零點六十三。

八月十七日　中華民國外交部發表聲明，嚴重抗議伊朗承認中共政權，並關閉駐德黑蘭大使館斷絕外交關係。

八月二十日　中華民國外交部宣布，因非洲獅子山國承認中共政權，自即日起與獅子山國斷絕外交關係，關閉駐獅國大使館及撤退農耕隊。

中共政權外交部發表聲明，表示反對美國有關聯合國中國代表權之提案。

八月廿六日　中國青年黨中央黨部主席李璜宣布辭職。

日本政府宣布，日圓對美元採取浮動匯率制。此項行動表示日圓已經升值。

八月三十日　美國舊金山華僑社會宣言，為保存中華文化傳統，決心抵制美國政府的「混校」計劃。

九月一日　中華民國聯勤總部的光華兵工廠的巨型砲彈廠落成開工生產，表示兵工生產邁進一大步。

九月四日　台灣省政府教育廳新招考
　　　國語推行員一批，待訓練完畢
　　　後將介紹至各縣市擔任國語推
　　　行工作。

九月十日　美國政府宣布，加州州長
　　　雷根將以尼克森總統特使身分
　　　來華參加中華民國建國六十年
　　　雙十國慶。

九月十一日　美國與日本會談結果，
　　　日本拒絕接受美國所提日圓升
　　　值的建議，並拒絕連署美國的
　　　防止中華民國被從聯合國排除
　　　的提案。

九月十三日　中共政權宣布，中共中
　　　央委員會副主席林彪與其妻子
　　　葉群及兒子林立果等人，「發
　　　動反革命政變未遂」，乘飛機
　　　外逃，飛機在外蒙溫都爾汗附
　　　近墜落，機毀人亡。

九月十五日　中華民國外交部長周書
　　　楷，率領代表、顧問等人員，
　　　從台北赴紐約出席聯合國第廿
　　　六屆大會。聯大會議定於廿一
　　　日揭幕。

九月十六日　美國總統尼克森宣布，
　　　美國贊成中共進入聯合國並獲
　　　得安全理事會席次，但保持中
　　　華民國的聯合國會員國資格。

美國駐聯合國大使布希，向三
十餘國盟邦駐聯合國代表解釋
修改「中國代表權問題」草
案，建議將聯合國安全理事會
常任席次給予中共政權。

中華民國外交部長周書楷，在
華盛頓會晤美國國務卿羅吉
斯，商討中華民國在聯合國的
情勢及其他外交事務。

九月十九日　中華民國外交部長周書
　　　楷在美國電視訪問談話中表
　　　示，中華民國在聯合國安全理
　　　事會中的常任理席位載明於聯
　　　合國憲章內，絕對不容侵奪。

九月廿一日　聯合國第二十六屆大會
　　　在紐約揭幕，共有一百零八件
　　　議案。

全美國各地華僑約一萬人，集
聚在紐約聯合國總部廣場示
威，反對中共進入聯合國。同
時，舊金山市的華僑亦舉行遊
行示威，反對中共進入聯合
國。

外國電訊報導，中國大陸最近
發生重大事故，其主要跡象
是：中共政權「十一」國慶籌
備工作突然停止；中共軍用飛
機在九月十三至十五日停飛。

各方揣測紛紜。

九月廿二日　美國向聯合國大會提出所謂「中國代表權」問題兩項議案：一為「重要問題案」另一為「代表權案」。

九月廿五日　中共報紙文章強烈攻擊美國在聯合國大會提出的所謂中國代表權問題案，並宣稱，除非中華民國被排出聯合國一切機構，否則中共不可能進入聯合國。

九月廿六日　中華民國新聞局發表僑生回國升學數字統計，二十年來已達三萬一千七百九十八人，其中畢業於國內各大學者有一萬五千五百四十三人。

九月三十日　中華民國行政院公布實施「台灣省議會組織規程」及「台灣省議會議員選舉罷免規程」。

蘇聯塔斯新聞社報導說，中共一架噴射機「侵入蒙古領空並墜毀，九人死亡」。

十月一日　中共「十一」國慶，毛澤東等均未參加慶祝活動，亦未舉行遊行，情況異常冷淡。

十月五日　美國政府宣布，尼克森總統的國家安全顧問季辛吉將前往北京，安排尼克森訪問中共計劃。

中華民國外交部長周書楷為季辛吉再赴大陸問題，在紐約與美國國務卿羅吉斯晤談。

十月七日　中國著名作家巴金（以「家」、「春」、「秋」等小說聞名），及曹禺（以「日出」、「北京人」、「雷雨」等劇本聞名）等，遭中共迫害下放，受長期勞改。

十月九日　美國加利福尼亞州州長雷根、大韓民國國會議長白斗鎮等抵台北參加中華民國六十年國慶。

十月九日　美國紐約、波士頓等城市，宣布十月十日為「自由中國日」慶祝中華民國六十週年雙十國慶。

十月十日　蔣介石總統發表雙十國慶告全國同胞書，訓勉同胞要「獨立自強，苦撐堅忍，戒懼而不恐懼，鬥志而不鬥氣」，發揚國父「有志竟成」精神，再造辛亥光輝勝利。蔣總統伉儷蒞臨總統府陽台，接受廿五萬民眾熱烈歡呼致敬。

十月十二日　宗聖曾子二千四百七十

六年誕辰，各界在台北市舉行大牢大典。

十月十五日　美國太平洋軍總司令馬侃說，中共大陸地區的軍事與民用航空業務仍陷於停頓狀態。

十月十六日　美國總統尼克森的國家安全事務顧問季辛吉再度前往中國大陸，安排尼克森訪問中共事宜。

十月十八日　中華民國外交部長周書楷在聯合國大會辯論所謂中國代表權問題時，發言駁斥排擠中華民國的謬論，特別指出若阿爾巴尼亞的容納中共案獲得通過，即為聯合國組織末日的開始。

美國國會參議院三分之二多數參議員發表聲名，支持維護中華民國在聯合國的地位。

十月廿六日　聯合國大會第二十六屆大會對所謂「中國代表權」問題案舉行表決，大會以五十九票對五十五票另十五票棄權的票比，將美國所提中國代表權為「重要問題案」加以否決。於是，在大會表決阿爾巴尼亞所提接受中共進入聯合國案之前，中華民國出席大會代表團長外交部長周書楷對大會宣布中華民國退出聯合國組織，並率領全部代表團人員離開會場。接著，大會以七十六票對三十五票另十五票棄權的票比，通過阿爾巴尼亞等二十三個國家提出的要求「恢復中華人民共和國在聯合國的一切合法權利和排除蔣介石的代表」案。

中華民國總統蔣介石為退出聯合國發表告全國同胞書，指出聯合國向暴力屈膝，已成為罪惡的淵藪，並嚴正聲明：「恢復大陸同胞的人權自由，乃是整個中華民族的意願，乃是我們決不改變的國家目標，和必須完成的神聖責任。無論國際形勢發生任何變化，我們將不惜任何犧牲，從事不屈不撓的奮鬥，絕不動搖。」

十月廿六日　美國國務卿羅吉斯說，將中華民國排出聯合國，對聯合國的前途將有不利的影響，是一項令人遺憾之行動。他並說，中華民國為國際社會中受尊敬之一員，「與我們之間的

關係，不受退出聯合國的影響」。

中華民國外交部發言人宣布，因為比利時承認中共政權，中華民國聲明與比利時中止外交關係。

十月廿八日　中國國民黨第十屆中央委員舉行臨時全體會議，聽取外交報告並且決議，「我退出聯合國決策正確，我決不承認聯合國之非法決議。」蔣介石總裁訓勉全黨同志團結奮鬥，莊敬自強，不為一時的國際變局所搖撼。美國國會參議院會議，以四十三票對四十票的表決拒絕廢止外島決議案。（按參院外交委員會曾表決通過廢止一九五五年通過之授權美國總統採取行動以防止中共可能攻擊中華民國外島之決議，現再予以恢復。）

十月廿九日　美國參議院會議通過決議，終止美國援外法案，此項行動與聯合國承認中共政權有關。

十月三十日　台灣省第二十六屆運動大會在台北市開幕，共有三千四百餘名選手參加競逐錦標。

聯合國教育科學文化組織通過決議，接納中共政權取代中華民國政府。

十一月一日　中國國民黨中央委員會，舉行對一千餘位績優婦女義務幹部頒獎儀式。

美國駐中華民國大使馬康衛晉謁蔣介石總統有所報告。

十一月二日　中共政權宣布派外交部副部長喬冠華出席聯合國大會，並派黃華為駐聯合國常任代表及安全理事會代表。

十一月十日　中東國家黎巴嫩宣布承認中共政權，中華民國外交部宣布與黎巴嫩終止外交關係。

美國會參議院批准美國將琉球群島交還日本的條約。美國於第二次世界大戰末期攻佔琉球群島，統治迄今二十七年之久。

十一月十二日　美國駐聯合國代表團宣布，美國國務院已決定對中共駐聯合國代表團人員加以旅行限制。規定到紐約市半徑廿五英里以外地區旅行，必須在四十八小時前通知美方，同時有若干地區完全禁止前往。此等限制與對蘇聯代表團人員的

限制相同。

十一月十四日　美國副國務卿強生偕夫人抵台灣訪問，發表談話強調中、美兩國應繼續增強合作。

十一月十五日　美國國務卿羅吉斯重申美國繼續維持與中華民國的外交關係，並履行其條約義務。

十一月十九日　墨西哥政府宣布承認北京中共政權，中華民國宣布與墨西哥斷絕邦交。

十一月廿二日　美軍太平洋總司令馬侃上將，與中華民國行政院副院長蔣經國及國防部長黃杰等會晤，就美軍協防問題交換意見。

十一月二十日　台灣中華航空公司的第八二五班機，於自台北飛往香港途中，在澎湖縣附近失事墜海，交通部正在調查中。

十一月三十日　美國政府與中共政權同時宣布，美國總統尼克森將在明年二月廿一日開始訪問中共。

十二月一日　中華民國第一屆國民大會第五次會議秘書處本日成立開始辦公。

十二月二日　中華民國行政院會議核定，「戡亂時期台灣與金門、馬祖地區往返申請處理辦法」，並通過「兒童福利法草案」。

十二月八日　冰島政府與中共政權代表，在丹麥首都哥本哈根簽署「建交」聯合公報。

十二月十五日　中華民國政府公布，將「中國銀行條例」名稱修正為「中國國際商業銀行條例」，依公司法設立開放民營。

十二月十六日　招商局輪船公司本日慶祝創建一百週年紀念。該局成立於清代末葉。

十二月十八日　聯合國秘書長宇譚擅自取消中央通訊社駐聯合國兩名記者的採訪資格，中華民國中央通訊社社長馬星野向聯合國提出強烈抗議。

十二月廿二日　美國國務卿羅吉斯重申美國立場，指出尼克森總統與中共接觸，絕不損害盟國利益，並且強調未作自台灣撤軍承諾。

中國國民黨中央委員會決定，明年三月六日至十日召開十屆

三中全會，推選總統副總統候選人。

十二月廿三日　台灣省議會議員、縣市長、縣市議員、鄉鎮長、縣轄鄉鎮市長及鄉鎮市民代表共五項地方選舉，行政院核定延期辦理，由內政部與台灣省政府另訂選期。

美國軍事援華顧問團新任團長巴恩斯少將抵台北履新。

十二月廿五日　全美國中國同學會在華府，舉行反共愛國會議，表示堅決支持中華民國政府共赴時艱。

十二月廿六日　美國出動兩百架軍機，大舉攻擊北越共區目標，傳美國計劃擴大對越共的空中攻擊。

十二月廿七日　中國國民黨台灣省黨部，在台中市召開農業問題研討會，會期預定三天。

十二月廿八日　全美國中國同學會在華府舉行的反共愛國會議，今日圓滿閉幕，決定成立反共愛國聯盟。

十二月廿九日　中共政權發表，美國與中共雙方政府商訂，以美國總統尼克森的國家安全事務助理亞歷山大・黑格准將為首的先遣組，將於明年一月三日開始訪問中國大陸，為尼克森總統訪問中共事進行技術安排。

十二月三十日　社會名流王雲五先生發表「國是芻言」，建議政府召開臨時反共建國會議。

中華民國六十一年（一九七二）

一月一日　蔣介石總統發表元旦文告，訓勉全國同胞，堅持理想，鐵立如山，知恥發憤，並又鄭重宣示，「與中共勢不兩立，絕無任何妥協餘地。」

一月二日　美國總統尼克森表示，美國將維持與中華民國間的關係及防衛條約。

一月廿五日　台灣出版的「大學雜誌」，連續發表陳鼓應等人的文章，表示反對國民黨的統治、反對蘇聯、反對台獨，要求開放「學生愛國運動」。

二月七日　中國國民黨中央常務委員會核定中華民國第五任總統、副總統黨內候選人提名選舉辦法。

二月十六日　美國政府公布，尼克森總統訪問中共行程。

二月二十日　中華民國第一屆國民大會第五次會議，在台北市中山堂揭幕。蔣介石總統蒞臨致詞，勉全體代表善盡重開國家新運之責任，「匯合智慧，以我之治，制敵之亂；集中力量，以我之實，擊敵之虛。」

二月廿一日　美國總統尼克森搭乘專機「七六精神」號，於上午十一時廿八分降落於北京機場，開始其史無前例的「和平之旅」。尼克森的專機自關島起飛，經過上海，在晴冷的天氣裡抵達中國首都北京。同來的包括美國國務卿羅吉斯及國家安全事務顧問季辛吉等人。尼克森的訪問行程預定二月廿八日結束。

二月廿八日　中國與美國雙方在上海簽訂「聯合公報」即「上海公報」。中、美雙方在公報中闡明各自的立場。中國政府重申：「中華人民共和國政府是中國的唯一合法政府，台灣是中國的一個省，解放台灣是中國的內政，別國無權干涉。」美國政府聲明，「美國認識到在台灣海峽兩邊的所有中國人都認為只有一個中國。」聯合公報強調指出雙方同意以和平共處五項原則處理國與國之間的關係。「上海公報」由中國總理周恩來與美國總統的國家安全事務顧問季辛吉，分別代表雙方簽署。（「上海公報」英文全文見本書英文部分。）中華民國外交部就美國總統尼克森與周恩來發表之「聯合公報」發表聲明，重申中共為叛亂集團，無權代表中國，美國與中共的任何協議一律無效。

三月六日　中國國民黨第十屆中央委員會第三次全體會議，於本日在台北市陽明山中山樓開幕，蔣介石總裁親臨主持並致辭，勉全黨同志，堅定信心意志，衝破艱難險阻，開創勝利契機。

三月九日　中國國民黨十屆三中全會，接受中央評議委員會建議，一致推選蔣介石總裁為中華民國第五任總統候選人，並且通過由蔣總裁提名嚴家淦為副總統候選人。

三月廿一日　中華民國第一屆國民大會第五次會議，投票選舉蔣介

石連任第五任中華民國總統。

三月廿二日　中華民國國民大會第五次會議，選舉嚴家淦為中華民國第五任副總統。

三月廿五日　中華民國第一屆國民大會於本日閉幕，蔣介石總統親臨致辭：「誓竭忠藎之力，以內除毛賊，外致和平。」

四月一日　中華民國國父紀念館舉行落成典禮，同時，國父銅像亦舉行揭幕儀式。國父紀念館館址位於台北市東區仁愛路，建築相當雄偉。

四月十九日　中國國民黨中央常務委員會決議，撤銷國民黨內部的五個督導組，以符合精簡組織的原則。

四月廿六日　中國國民黨中央常務委員會會議通過，提名倪文亞為立法院院長，劉闊才為副院長。

五月二日　中華民國立法院舉行選舉，倪文亞當選為院長，劉闊才當選為副院長。

五月十五日　中國國民黨中央常務委員會會議通過精簡組織後的秘書長以下各單位人選。國民黨中央委員會秘書長張寶樹對記者招待會說明，國民黨中央調整組織的目的是起用新人。中華民國監察院長李嗣聰因病在台北市逝世，享年七十五歲。

五月十七日　中國國民黨中央常務委員會通過決議，請蔣介石總裁身分徵召蔣經國同志出任行政院長。旋經蔣總裁俯允提名，並依法咨請立法院同意。

五月二十日　蔣介石於中華民國第五任總統及副總統就職大典中，即席昭告海內外同胞，指出政府既要力足以推進廉能之治，又要力足以恢宏志士之氣，完成其討賊復國的使命，追求再北伐的勝利，創造再統一的光榮。蔣介石連任第五屆總統，嚴家淦連任第二屆副總統。

五月廿六日　中華民國立法院投票同意蔣介石總統提名前行政院副院長蔣經國為行政院長。蔣經國為蔣介石的長公子，獲得三八一張同意票。

五月三十日　中華民國新任行政院長蔣經國及副院長徐慶鐘以次各部會新任首長宣誓就職，由蔣介石總統親臨主持監督並致辭，勉以激揚「爭生存，決存

亡」的精神，完成再北伐，再
統一的誓願。

六月一日　中華民國新任行政院長蔣
　　　　經國主持首次行政院會議，會
　　　　議通過任命謝東閔為台灣省政
　　　　府主席，張豐緒為台北市長。

六月五日　希臘政府宣布承認中共政
　　　　權，而與中華民國斷絕外交關
　　　　係。

七月十日　美國助理國務卿葛林抵台
　　　　灣訪問，與中華民國政府首長
　　　　交換有關中、美共同問題及世
　　　　局之意見。

七月廿二日　中華民國蔣介石總統感
　　　　染感冒，午後引發肺炎，嗣經
　　　　診治，日內可痊。

八月六日　蔣介石總統移入榮民總醫
　　　　院繼續療養。

八月二十日　中華民國青少棒球隊美
　　　　和，在美國比賽榮獲世界冠
　　　　軍。

八月廿七日　中華民國少年棒球隊，
　　　　在美國舉行的比賽中榮獲冠
　　　　軍。

八月三十日　中國國民黨中央常務委
　　　　員會會議決定，將中國通史及
　　　　中國現代史列為大學共同必修
　　　　課程。

九月三日　中華民國八千餘位大專院
　　　　校教授發表聯合宣言，堅決反
　　　　對日本與中共往來的聲明。

九月十五日　蔣介石總統於午間又感
　　　　不適，嗣經診治，即迅速恢復
　　　　正常。

九月十七日　日本政府派遣特使椎名
　　　　悅三郎抵台灣訪問，中華民國
　　　　各界群眾舉行示威，抗議日本
　　　　首相田中角榮親近中共的言
　　　　行。副總統嚴家淦、行政院長
　　　　蔣經國先後接見椎名悅三郎，
　　　　重申中華民國政府立場，反對
　　　　日本與中共交往，強調必須尊
　　　　重中、日和約，如日本背信，
　　　　即等於再度為敵。

九月廿二日　中華民國外交部就日本
　　　　政府宣布日本首相田中角榮定
　　　　於廿五日訪問中共事，發表聲
　　　　明指出，中華民國政府行使全
　　　　國主權，日本與中共的任何協
　　　　議，均屬非法無效。

九月廿五日　日本首相田中角榮及外
　　　　相大平正芳抵達台北京訪問，
　　　　與中共總理周恩來舉行會談。

九月廿七日　中共主席毛澤東接見日
　　　　本首相田中角榮晤談。田中已
　　　　與周恩來舉行多次會談。

九月廿九日　中國與日本簽署「中華人民共和國政府、日本國政府聯合聲明」，雙方決定，自該聲明簽署之日起，中、日兩國建立外交關係並盡快互換大使。日本政府承認中華人民共和國政府是「唯一合法政府」，台灣是中國不可分割的一部分。

中華民國外交部以日本與中共達成協議，發表所謂「聯合公報」，片面撕毀中、日和約，與中共建交，有負蔣介石總統在戰後以寬大政策拯救日本扶植其復興的德意，特於廿九日鄭重聲明「我國與日本斷絕外交關係」。

十月十日　蔣介石總統於雙十國慶紀念日書勉全國軍民同胞，精誠團結，力排橫逆，自謀自備，再開新局。蔣夫人款接歸國僑胞，勉以伸張正義，抗拒邪惡，為國家民族而奮鬥。

十月廿五日　慶祝台灣光復廿七週年紀念，蔣介石總統書勉全體同胞，應懷「莊敬自強」的真義，奮發「憂勞興國」的熱忱，協力同心，創造更進一步的建設成果。

台灣省南部東西橫貫公路，全部修建完成，正式開放通車。

十一月十二日　中華民國選手獲得在澳洲墨爾本舉行的世界高爾夫球賽冠軍。

十一月三十日　中華民國行政院會議通過，第六期四年經濟建設計劃。

十二月二日　中華民國的四十五位工商業領袖，組織「東亞關係協會」，負責處理在中華民國於九月廿九日宣布與日本絕交後雙方間經濟文化交流事務。日本方面成立「交流協會」。

十二月六日　中國國民黨中央常務委員會決議，要求外交部適應國際情勢，展開總體外交。

十二月廿一日　中華民國外交部發表聲明，宣布與澳大利亞斷絕外交關係，因澳國承認中共政權。同日，紐西蘭政府亦宣布承認中共政權。

十二月廿三日　中華民國動員戡亂時期自由地區增加中央民意代表名額選舉、及台灣省第五屆省議員與第七屆縣市長選舉，在閩台地區分別舉行投票，計選

出國民大會代表、立法委員、省議員與縣市長共一八二人，其中中國國民黨提名候選人當選者計一五一人。

十二月廿五日　蔣介石總統於中華民國行憲紀念日，頒詞勗勉國民大會代表，維護民主憲政法統，結合全民力量，實現主義目標。

十二月廿六日　中華民國「東亞關係協會」與日本「交流協會」簽訂協議，保證中、日兩國在非政府階層上的協調工作。

中華民國六十二年（一九七三）

一月一日　蔣介石總統發表元旦文告，書勉全國同胞，秉持忠肝熱血，苦撐堅忍，對世局逆流制變。並指斥毛共反人性，無祖國，乃是貌似而實異的非中國人。

二月一日　台灣省第五屆省議會成立。

二月十五日　中華民國行政院公布，新台幣對美元匯率改為三十八元新台幣兌換美金一元，台幣升值百分之五。

二月十七日　中華民國治安當局拘捕參加「民族主義座談會」的台灣大學教授陳鼓應等人士。

二月二十日　中華民國外交部對美國與中共發表「聯合公報」將互設所謂「聯絡辦事處」一事，發表嚴正聲明，指出中共係叛亂集團，無權代表中國人民，美國與中共的任何協議「我政府絕不承認」。

三月六日　中華民國行政院長蔣經國，在立法院提出八點有關政治與社會革新事項，呼籲各界共同推動，實踐力行。

三月七日　中國國民黨中央常務委員會決定，提名余俊賢為監察院院長，周百鍊為副院長。

三月九日　中華民國外交部發表聲明，宣布中華民國與西班牙斷絕外交關係，因西班牙承認中共政權。

四月一日　中華民國的中央通訊社，奉命改組為公司組織以有利其在國外的工作。中央社係國民黨創建於一九二四年。

四月十七日　第十一屆國際攝影展覽在台北市舉行，波蘭、捷克、及匈牙利等國家參加。

四月廿二日　孔孟學會在台北市召開

年會，蔣介石總統書勉與會人士，須明禮、守法、行仁、踐義，發揚倫理、民主、科學精神。

五月一日　台灣省第八屆縣市議會分別成立。

五月九日　中華民國與沙烏地阿拉伯王國簽訂協定，中國將派遣更多專家赴沙國參與技術合作計劃工作。

五月卅一日　中華民國行政院命令，將「經濟合作委員會」改組為「經濟設計委員會」，並任命張繼正為主任委員。張繼正係總統府秘書長張群之子。中華民國青年反共救國團主任蔣經國辭職，由李煥繼任主任。

六月七日　中華民國外交部發表聲明警告日本，若日本改變中、日航空協定，中華民國將對日本民航事業採取「強烈措施」。

六月十五日　陸軍軍官學校第四十九週年校慶，蔣介石總統特派行政院長蔣經國赴高雄縣鳳山該校主持校慶典禮。

六月廿七日　中國國民黨中央常務委員會舉行會議，研討當前世界局勢及美國與蘇聯舉行高階層會議事，會議決定不受國際多元政治影響，並堅持不與中共、蘇聯接觸的反共國策。

七月廿三日　美國商務部長丹特宣布，美國計劃於明年在台北設立貿易中心。他說，貿易中心將於明年春季開幕，約有十五家美國工業與科學公司參加展覽會。

八月二日　中華民國行政院批准四億四千四百萬美元預算計，共修建台灣南北高速公路第一與第二階段工程之需。

八月七日　中華民國立法院會議通過，「動員戡亂時期貪污治罪條例修正案」。

九月一日　中華民國軍方人士說，美國已開始撤退美國在台軍隊的空運單位。空運單位約佔美軍部隊的百分之六十。

九月十三日　中華民國考試院長孫科，因心臟病在台北市逝世，享年八十二歲。孫科係中華民國國父孫中山先哲嗣。

九月三十日　國民黨元老李石曾病逝台北，享年九十四歲。

十月十日　蔣介石總統書告全國同胞，沉著果決，堅持信心，內

不為憤心所移，外不為形勢所
劫，衝破橫逆，再造新局。

十月三十日　台灣省規模最大的水庫
曾文水庫，於蔣總統華誕完
成，呈獻祝嘏。同時，台中港
建港工程舉行開工典禮。

十一月十二日　中國國民黨中央委員
十屆四中全會，在台北市陽明
山中山樓開幕，蔣介石總裁書
勉全體同志。全會預定十五日
閉幕。

十一月十五日　中國國民黨中央委員
十屆四中全會，於通過「本黨
對現階段黨的建設與奮鬥之提
示」，「本黨對現階段政治革
新政治建設之提示」等中心議
題，及選出嚴家淦、蔣經國及
謝東閔等廿一人為中央常務委
員後，宣告閉幕。

十一月廿二日　中華民國行政院會議
通過能源節約四項原則，其中
規定所有機構一律減少能源消
耗量百分之二十五。

十二月十日　台灣省政府宣布，台灣
北迴鐵路（蘇澳至花蓮），定
於十二月廿五日動工修築。

十二月廿二日　蔣介石總統健康情況
日佳，於廿二日自榮民總醫院
返回士林官邸休養。

中華民國六十三年（一九七四）

一月一日　蔣介石總統發表元旦文
告，勉全國軍民同胞，「接受
時代嚴格考驗，人人各盡責
任，創造明天的成就。」
中華民國行政院長蔣經國對美
國紐約時報發表談話說，中華
民國將永遠不與中共談判。

一月十八日　中華民國外交部發表聲
明，重申中華民國對南沙（史
普拉特萊）及西沙（巴拉賽
爾）列島的主權。

一月廿七日　中華民國行政院發表，
「穩定當前經濟措施方案」，
目的在鞏固經濟發展基礎，並
照顧大眾生活利益。

一月廿九日　美國國務院助理國務卿
殷格索抵台灣訪問，與中華民
國政府首長就中、美共同問題
交換意見。

二月一日　中華民國國防部發言人證
實，中華民國已經派軍隊駐防
南沙列島。

二月十一日　中華民國外交部已照會
菲律賓，重申中華民國對南沙
列島的立場。

二月十五日　美國總統尼克森提名李納德·安克志為新駐中華民國大使，將接替現任大使馬康衛的職務。馬康衛將返美國退休。安克志現任美國駐泰國大使。

三月廿二日　中國國民黨台灣省黨部召開黨政工作研討會，會期兩天。

四月十五日　中華民國交通部發言人表示，交通部準備與日本斷絕航空服務後的各種措施。

四月十七日　中國國民黨中央常務委員會決議，為反對日本與中共簽訂航空條約，中華民國於必要時須對日本航空業務採取斷然措施。

四月二十日　日本政府與中共政權在北京簽訂「民航協定」，雙方將開闢民航客機路線。

中華民國發表聲明稱，日本與中共簽訂所謂「民航協定」，中華民國政府宣布與日本斷絕航空服務。外交部聲明中說：「日本田中政府屈從中共無理要求，罔顧我政府曾向日方迭次表明的堅決公正態度，破壞中日航線之現狀，並在日外相大平正芳所發表之荒謬談話中，否定中華民國之國旗，嚴重損害我國之尊嚴與權益，再度傷害中日兩國人民在戰後協力建立之友誼，特對日本宣布採取斷航措施。」

中華民國中華航空公司與大韓民國的空運服務，亦於二十日中止，但華航飛美國班機改經關島路線，仍照常服務。

五月二日　中華民國行政院長蔣經國說，政府的穩定經濟措施已有顯著成效。

五月五日　中華民國政府積極鼓勵拓展輸出，今日起降低外銷貸款利率並且放寬融資。

五月廿八日　亞洲太平洋市長協會第三屆大會在台北市開幕，來自二十個國家的代表約一百二十人參加會議。

六月十日　中華民國行政院長蔣經國說明台灣經濟建設的四大目標是：政治修明、國防堅強、經濟繁榮、治安良好。

六月十六日　中華民國陸軍軍官學校創建五十週年校慶，蔣介石總統特派行政院長蔣經國前往高雄縣鳳山該校主持慶典，並頒

發書面訓辭「黃埔精神與革命大業的再推進」。

七月一日　中華民國政府宣布與泰國中止外交關係，因泰國承認中共政權。

七月十六日　中華民國外交部長沈昌煥透露，中華民國與美國合作，製造 F-5E「自由」型噴射戰鬥機和直升飛機。

七月廿五日　中國國民黨中央委員會黨務工作會議在台北市開幕，由中央委員會秘書長張寶樹報告當前局勢。

八月三日　中華民國與南美洲的巴拉圭簽訂一項將來廣泛合作的協議。

八月五日　日本出版的「產經新聞」說，該報將自八月十五日起，連載「蔣總統秘錄——中日關係八十年之證言」一書的全文。「產經新聞」並將於十五日對蔣總統的健康情形加以詳細報導。

八月廿四日　中華民國的少年棒球隊，在美國舉行的一九七四年比賽中獲得冠軍。這是中華代表隊連續四年榮獲冠軍。

八月廿六日　美軍協防台灣司令部新任司令史奈德海軍中將抵達台北履新。他係接替退休的畢夏尼中將的職務。

九月三日　中華民國經濟部長孫運璿說，中華民國將與沙烏地阿拉伯合作，投資一億三千萬美元，在沙國建造一個煉油廠及一個肥料廠。

九月六日　中華民國的中華航空公司說，由於財政理由，決定退出國際航空運輸協會，將自九月十七日起生效。

九月十五日　聯合國秘書長華德翰受到中共的壓力，將中華民國贈予聯合國之題有孔子「禮運大同篇」之綠色大理石碑，自聯合國大會大廳外外牆移走。

九月廿八日　強烈颱風襲擊台灣北部地區，基隆、宜蘭等地豪雨成災。行政院長蔣經國命令台灣省政府妥辦善後工作。

十月六日　台灣省政府費時五年，耗資新台幣五十億元興建之德基水庫大壩正式竣工，開始發電。

十月十日　蔣介石總統發表雙十國慶文告，勖勉全國同胞投身獻力大建設，須知志氣齊一，決心

堅定，行動一致，力量集中，則任何暴君奸賊，終難逃我我文化斧鉞。

蔣總統夫人宋美齡女士款待回國參加慶典的僑胞一千餘人。

十月十二日　中華民國財政部長李國鼎說，美國進出口銀行已經同意貸款九億三千四百萬美元，資助中華民國興建十項基本發展計劃之需。

十月廿五日　慶祝台灣光復節，蔣介石總統頒發訓辭，勗勉台灣全省同胞攜手併肩，勇往邁進，達成復國建國的時代使命。

十月廿八日　美國總統福特簽署廢除「台灣決議案」法案。「台灣決議案」即「總統使用美國武裝部隊保護台灣及澎湖列島權力」法案。

十月卅一日　蔣介石總統八秩晉八華誕，全國各界紛獻建設成果祝壽。

十一月三日　由中華民國經濟部長孫運璿率領的經濟貿易代表團，啟程赴南美洲各國訪問與促進貿易業務。

十一月廿四日　中國國民黨建黨八十週年，蔣介石總裁發表紀念詞，期勉全黨同志承擔救國救民職志，人人自立自信，自發自強，即內不致為一時艱困環境所撓，外不致為國際形勢衝擊所惑，以完成國父與諸先烈「肫肫其仁浩浩其天」創黨革命的遺志大願。

中國國民黨第十屆中央委員第五次全體會議，與國民黨創建八十週年紀念大會，於廿四日在台北市國父紀念館同時舉行。蔣介石總裁對全黨同志發表「國父建黨八十週年紀念詞」。稍後，國民黨五中全會移往陽明山中山樓繼續進行。

十一月廿七日　中國國民黨中央委員十屆五中全會，在先後通過「本黨現階段政治革新政治建設之檢討與策進」、與「本黨現階段黨的建設工作之檢討與策進」三大中心議題與建黨八十週年宣言，以及選舉嚴家淦、蔣經國、謝東閔等廿一人為中央常務委員後，宣告閉幕。

十二月一日　蔣介石總統又感不適，經醫師診治後，肺炎減輕，胸腔積水亦減少。

十二月二日　中華民國外交部長沈昌煥說，海外華僑若持有中共政權發給之護照必須先將其現有護照拋棄，始得請領中華民國護照。

十二月十九日　台灣省政府及台北市政府設立平價供應中心，供售公教人員生活必需品。

十二月二十日　中華民國行政院發表，國民收入數字今年平均約達七百美元，較一九七三年的四百七十美元增加相當多。

十二月廿五日　蔣介石總統於行憲紀念日發表文告指出，只要一切行動對準敵人，一切力量投入反共，就能加速摧毀共黨的暴力統治，確實保障民主憲政的常新永盛。

十二月廿七日　蔣介石總統清晨攝護腺炎復發，並有心律不規律現象發生。

十二月卅一日　中華民國行政院長蔣經國談話，提出新年經濟發展五項工作重點，強調繼續在穩定中求進步。

中華民國六十四年（一九七五）

一月一日　蔣介石總統發表元旦文告，勗勉全國同胞，一致奮發其道德的信心和勇氣，並貢獻出道德信心和道德勇氣所凝聚而成的合成心力，以我們自己基地建設戰備的力量，來討伐奸匪毛賊邪惡罪孽，重建三民主義新中國。

一月九日　蔣介石總統脈搏一度轉慢，投以藥石而癒，惟仍有輕度之寒熱未盡去。

一月九日　中華民國經濟部發表，去年對外貿易總額超過一百廿五億美元，較一九七三年增加百分之五十五左右。國民平均每人所得估計約達新台幣兩萬六千六百元，折合美金七百元。

一月十七日　中華民國行政院長蔣經國，命令教育部及司法行政部等單位提高教育素質，及發展職業教育等。

一月廿五日　國際新聞學會理事會決議，恢復中華民國分會的會籍。國際新聞學會於一九七二年因菲律賓華僑報人于姓兄弟案，將中國分會會籍停止。

二月四日　中國國民黨中央常務委員會決定，簡化春節拜年要點。

二月五日　中華民國行政院長蔣經

國，於春節期間飛臨金門、澎湖慰問軍民，並轉達蔣總統關懷之至意。

二月五日　中華民國行政院說，一九七四年的經濟成長率降到百分之零點六左右，這與全球性的經濟情勢衰退有關。

二月十四日　中華民國政府對越南政府的「白皮書」發表聲明稱，中華民國「對西沙群島及南沙群島的固有主權，是不容置疑，不可侵犯的」。

二月十七日　中華民國的中國鋼鐵公司，與美國伊利諾大陸國民銀行及芝加哥信託公司，簽訂兩億美元的貸款合同，資助中鋼公司在高雄建造一座鋼鐵廠之需。

二月十八日　中國國民黨中央常務委員會，命令從政黨員勵行節約。

二月十九日　中國國民黨中央常務委員會會議通過，立法院「增額立法委員」任期屆滿，依法改選。

三月三日　中國國民黨中央邀請台灣工商企業與學術文化界人士舉行早餐會，對國家重要政治問題交換意見。

三月二十日　中國國民黨中央黨史委員會主任委員杜元載在台北市病逝，享年七十歲。

三月廿四日　中華民國政府自本日開始舉行為期三天的國家經濟會議，為未來的經濟發展政策預作籌畫。出席的政府官員、工商企業領袖及經濟專家等共有一百廿位。

三月廿八日　中華民國行政院長蔣經國發表專文「為國獻身，為民獻心」，反共復國政策不變。中華航空公司要求政府批准優待機票價計劃，歡迎美國西海岸旅客來台灣觀光，雙程票價為美金七百五十元，低於正常票價一千一百六十二元。

四月二日　中國國民黨中央常務委員會通過「現階段心理建設執行計劃案」。

四月五日　中華民國總統蔣介石，以突發性心臟病於今日下午十一時五十八分在台北市士林官邸逝世，享年八十九歲（一八八六～一九七五）。（據蔣公年表初稿說：「公自民國六十一年（一九七二）七月下旬罹患

肺炎，遂不得不從事醫治療
養，且原已日漸康復，詎料今
年春間，攝護腺炎復發，經醫
悉心診治，已有進展，不幸於
五日夜間因突發性心臟病，急
救罔效，竟於十一時五十分崩
殂。當日為民族掃墓節，亦即
農曆清明，午夜迅雷震電，颶
風疾雨，如山頹，如野哭，雖
鼎湖箕尾，天道難知，顧奠牆
裡，人類允同也。」「先是，
公於三月廿九日預立遺囑。當
公彌留之際，蔣夫人及副總統
嚴家淦、行政院長蔣經國、立
法院長倪文亞等接環侍在側，
於遺囑上敬謹簽字。公遺體隨
即於子夜奉移榮民總醫
院。」）

四月六日　中國國民黨於今日清晨七
時，召開中央常務委員會臨時
會議決議，接受蔣介石遺囑：
「實行三民主義，光復大陸國
土，復興民族文化，堅守民主
陣容，誓達目的，毋怠毋
忽。」並決議「依中華民國憲
法規定，總統缺位時，應即由
副總統嚴家淦同志繼位。」嚴
氏當於同日上午十一時宣誓，

繼任中華民國總統。

四月十六日　美國副總統洛克斐勒與
參議員高華德率領的代表團等
二十個外國弔喪代表團，來台
北參加中華民國故總統蔣介石
的葬禮。

美國副總統洛克斐勒，將美國
總統福特的信函面交與行政院
長蔣經國，信中重申在蔣介石
總統逝世後，美國繼續支持中
華民國。

四月廿六日　越南前總統阮文紹，恰
在越共軍隊攻陷首都西貢之前
搭飛機抵達台北。阮文紹係被
反對派逼迫辭職。

四月廿八日　中國國民黨第十屆中央
委員會舉行臨時全體會議，通
過決議保留黨章中的「總裁」
一章，用以紀念蔣介石總裁，
並且修改國民黨中央組織條
例，增設主席一職，蔣經國當
選為首任國民黨主席。

五月三日　中華民國政府在高雄市設
立一處難民接待中心，為自越
南逃出之華僑提供臨時的居住
場所。據估計將有大約一千四
百名華僑自越南及高棉撤退到
台灣。中華民國政府在西貢淪

陷之前，特派海軍船隻赴越南接運華僑難民。

五月七日　中華民國行政院長蔣經國，以新任中國國民黨主席身分首次主持召開國民黨中央常務委員會會議，表示決為貫徹國民黨「革命任務」效命致力。

五月三十日　中華民國新任總統嚴家淦，首次主持總統府國父紀念月會，及陸軍總司令馬安瀾、空軍總司令徒福、聯合勤務司令羅友倫、及國防部總政治作戰部主任王升等宣誓就職典禮。

五月卅一日　中華民國總統嚴家淦發佈命令，公佈「中央政府建設公債發行條例」。

六月九日　中華民國政府宣佈與菲律賓共和國中止外交關係，因菲律賓承認中共政權。

六月十日　中國國民黨主席蔣經國命令，要求國民黨中央及省級幹部要「開大門，走大路，擔大任，成大業」。

六月十八日　中國國民黨中央常務委員會會議通過，「黨員從寬恢復黨籍黨權實施要點」。

六月十九日　中華民國與沙烏地阿拉伯王國，在沙京利雅德簽訂協定以進一步加強兩國間的經濟及技術合作，將成立一個聯合委員會負責合作計劃。

七月一日　中華民國宣佈與泰國斷絕外交關係，因泰國承認中共政權。

七月九日　中華民國的「亞東關係協會」與日本的「交流協會」雙方代表，在台北市簽訂一項非官方民航協定，將中斷十七個月久的兩國間民航服務予以恢復。

七月十四日　中國國民黨中央委員會核定，將二百六十名曾被停止黨權人士的黨籍予以恢復。

七月十六日　台灣南部高雄市第二個港口工程興建完成開放使用，可容納船舶七萬五千噸。興建費用達新台幣十四億元，費時九年。

七月廿七日　中國國民黨本年度黨務工作會議在台北市陽明山開幕，會期三天。

八月九日　中華民國行政院長蔣經國建議，將原訂之第六個「四年經濟發展計劃」改訂為「六年

經濟發展計劃」。

八月十日　中華民國與日本間的民航服務於今天恢復，中華航空公司飛往美國舊金山的第〇〇二號班機，於下午自台北飛往東京轉飛美國。

九月十七日　蔣宋美齡女士搭飛機赴美國就醫。

九月廿二日　南美洲巴拉圭總統史楚尼抵達台北，對中華民國作為期四天的訪問。

九月廿三日　中華民國行政院長蔣經國在立法院報告時說：「決不隨波逐流，決不搖擺遊移，絕不與中共和談，也絕不與蘇聯有所來往」，將「關閉這兩個大門」。

十月十日　中華民國雙十國慶紀念，嚴家淦總統發表國慶文告，並在總統府前廣場舉行盛大閱兵儀式。上次閱兵儀式在一九六四年國慶日舉行。

十一月三日　中華民國全國教育會議在台北市舉行，三百餘位教育專家參加，討論重要的教育問題。中共中央宣佈，「批鄧、反擊右傾翻案風」運動在大陸展開

十一月十七日　中華民國經濟計劃委員會說，中華民國的經濟成長率已經自一年百分之六點五回升到百分之七點五。

十一月十九日　中華民國國策顧問前廣西省政府主席黃旭初在香港病逝，享年八十四歲。

十一月廿四日　中國國民黨主席蔣經國，在一九七五年度國民黨示範小組長表揚會上說，要「引導國民向復國建國目標邁進」。

十二月一日　美國總統福特飛抵北京訪問。

十二月三日　美國國會眾議院通過一項議案，要求政府不能作任何有損中華民國自由的行為。此決議獲得眾議員總數四百卅五席中的二百十八席支持。

十二月五日　中華民國外交部發言人對美國總統福特訪問中共之行評論說，中華民國堅決反對美國承認中共政權。

十二月九日　美國主管遠東太平洋事務的助理國務卿哈比布抵達台北，就美國總統福特最近訪問中共之行的結果，向行政院長蔣經國提出說明。哈比布向蔣

院長保證，美國維持與中華民國友好關係的政策仍然不變。

十二月二十日　中華民國舉行「增額立法委員」選舉投票。增額立法委員任期為三年。

十二月廿六日　中華民國立法院會議通過無線電廣播電台與電視台法案，其中規定廣播電台與電視台的商業廣告不得多於播出時間總數的百分之十五。

十二月廿七日　中華民國警政當局，命令台灣省籍人士康寧祥、張俊宏主辦的「台灣政壇」雜誌停刊。

中華民國六十五年（一九七六）

一月八日　中國共產黨中央發佈訃告稱，中共中央副主席、國務院總理、政協全國主席周恩來，因患癌症在北京逝世，享年七十八歲（一八九八～一九七六）。台北的中共問題專家相信，周恩來的逝世，對於中共領袖的接班問題及中共的對外政策都不致有重大的影響。由於周恩來的逝世，中共宣佈任命華國鋒為「代理國務院總理」。

一月十三日　台灣省政府報告，在推行家庭計劃政策後，人口出生率逐年下降，及男女的平均壽命延長到六十六點七二歲。

二月十九日　中華民國行政院會議通過第一個六年經濟發展計劃，自今年起實施。

二月廿一日　中華民國的中華航空公司及遠東航空公司獲得政府的支援，將以大約九千五百萬美元基金從美國購買七架新型飛機參加營運。華航將購五架波音式客機，遠東將購兩架波音式客機。

二月廿七日　中華民國行政院長蔣經國在立法院施政報告中說，要將所有力量來「反共救國」。他並且嚴辭駁斥關於「台灣獨立」的論調。他強調，「要求台灣分離出去的分子是毀滅自己」。

三月八日　中華民國與沙烏地阿拉伯王國的經濟及技術合作會議今日在台北開幕，會期預定五天。據估計，今年兩國的雙邊貿易總額將達四億五千萬美元。

三月十三日　中華民國政府以全力支

援工商業，擴大出口貿易，並於今年投資新台幣五千億元，用於擴建基隆、高雄、台中、花蓮及蘇澳等港口設施。

三月十九日　中華民國外交部發言人就越南共黨新地圖將中國領土西沙及南沙群島劃為其領土間題發表聲明，重申該群島為中國固有領土。

三月廿六日　中國名作家林語堂在香港病逝，享年八十一歲。

四月五日　中共發表消息說，北京天安門廣場發生大規模悼念周恩來，反對「四人幫」的群眾活動，遭到鎮壓。中華民國的共黨問題專家相信，天安門廣場的暴亂事件是效忠鄧小平的分子發動的，這表示是資本主義路線派對江青集團極端派反攻的開始。

四月六日　在北京天安門暴亂事件的次日，中華民國行政院長蔣經國發表談話，號召大陸同胞為爭取自由而戰。

四月十四日　中國國民黨中央常務委員會決定，於本年十一月十二日召開第十一屆全國代表大會。

四月廿六日　第四屆亞洲作家會議在台北市開幕，參加的各國作家約八十位。

中華民國與南非共和國達成協議，將兩國的外交代表互升為大使館級。

五月十日　中華民國行政院長蔣經國在國父紀念週的講話中，要求貫徹故總統蔣介石遺囑的「行動綱領」，建立清明廉能的民主政治。

五月卅一日　中華民國治安當局以「意圖顛覆政府」為由，逮捕高雄地區「台獨」分子顏明聖及楊金梅，並分別判處無期徒刑及有期徒刑十二年。

六月一日　台灣的中國石油公司，決定開採高雄海岸外的天然瓦斯場，據估計每天的產量可達五千萬立方公尺。

六月九日　中華民國行政院宣佈局部改組，新任內政部長張豐緒、財政部長費驊、參謀總長宋長志、海軍總司令鄒堅。

七月一日　中華民國經濟計劃委員會宣佈，政府將以大約三千六百八十億美元的基金實施「六年經濟計劃」。此計劃係自今年

開始。

七月十七日　中華民國奧林匹克委員會今天決定，中華民國退出在加拿大蒙得婁舉行的奧林匹克運動會，因為國際奧林匹克委員會最後決定要求中華民國選手以「台灣」代表隊而非中華民國代表隊參加奧運比賽。

七月廿八日　中國大陸河北省唐山地區發生空前強烈的大地震，造成生命與財產的嚴重損失。地震發生於廿八日凌晨三時四十二分五十六秒，強度為芮氏地震儀的七點八級。

七月三十日　台北的大陸救災總會決定儘快對唐山大地震提供救濟協助。

八月四日　紐約時報報導說，美國將以價值三千四百萬美元的精密雷達防空系統供應中華民國，並將以六十架 F-5 噴射式戰鬥機援助中華民國空軍部隊。

八月十六日　中華民國中央氣象局測出，大陸寧夏省中衛附近發生大地震，強度為芮氏地震儀的七級。外電報導說，四川北部受到影響。

八月二十日　非洲的中非共和國宣佈承認中共政權。

八月廿一日　非洲的史瓦濟蘭王國的總理德拉米親王夫婦，抵達中華民國作為期七天的訪問。

八月廿五日　中華民國的美國僑民商會已起草一項聲明，要求美國政府停止考慮承認中共政權。

九月一日　中華民國新聞局發表聲明，否認美國報紙所傳中華民國已開始秘密處理廢鈾燃料製造核子武器。聲明認為該項報導為「邪惡的虛構」。

九月九日　中共中央宣佈：中共中央主席、中共中央軍事委員會主席、政協全國委員會名譽主席毛澤東在北京逝世，享年八十三歲（一八九三～一九七六）。毛澤東字潤之，湖南省湘潭縣韶山沖人士，一八九三年出生。

毛澤東在北京逝世的消息今日下午傳抵台北，中華民國人民感到欣喜，許多地方聽到電台廣播或口傳消息時，紛紛燃放炮竹。

九月廿一日　中國國民黨台灣省黨部第十次全省代表大會在台中市開幕，會期預定三天。

十月六日　中共中央宣佈，中共中央
　　已拘禁審查江青、張春橋、姚
　　文元、王洪文，「四人幫」被
　　粉碎。

十月十日　中華民國雙十國慶紀念
　　日，各界歡欣慶祝。台灣省政
　　府主席謝東閔在家裡收到一個
　　郵包，發生爆炸，左手被炸
　　傷，治安當局正在調查中。

十月廿一日　中華民國行政院會議通
　　過「經濟建設六年計劃」，自
　　今年起到一九八一年，將投資
　　達美金四千六百六十三億元之
　　鉅。

十一月十二日　中國國民黨第十一次
　　全國代表大會在台北市陽明山
　　中山樓開幕，會期預定七天。

十一月十四日　國民黨十一全大會會
　　議通過，「中國國民黨黨章修
　　正案」及「中國國民黨政綱
　　案」。

十一月十六日　國民黨十一全大會，
　　選舉蔣經國為國民黨主席。

十一月十八日　中國國民黨第十一次
　　全國代表大會，於通過「反共
　　復國行動綱領案」後宣告閉
　　幕。

十一月十九日　中國國民黨第十一屆

中央委員第一次全體會議在台
北市陽明山舉行，會議通過國
民黨主席蔣經國提名的廿一名
常務委員後閉幕。

十一月廿四日　中國國民黨中央常務
　　委員會會議通過中央委員會各
　　處會主管名單：秘書處主任陳
　　水逢、組織工作會主任李煥
　　等。

十二月十二日　是日為民國廿五年張
　　學良與楊虎城發動之「西安事
　　變」四十週年紀念日。

十二月二十日　中華民國政府批准電
　　力加價方案，平均提高百分之
　　二十，自今日起實施。

中華民國六十六年（一九七七）

一月二日　中國國民黨主席蔣經國發
　　表新年談話，要求「嚴格黨政
　　分野」，「黨政幹部雙向交
　　流」，及「本黨徹底精簡人
　　事」。

一月十八日　中華民國行政院宣佈，
　　「平均地權條例」完成立法程
　　序，將全面推廣土地改革政
　　策。

一月卅一日　中華民國國策顧問萬耀
　　煌在台北病逝，享年八十七

歲。

二月七日　科威特的油輪保爾格號載有原油三萬公噸（價值兩百萬元美金），在台灣基隆港外海面發生觸礁事件，原油流失台灣北部海灘，殺害無數海洋生物。

二月廿八日　是日為一九四七年發生的台灣「二二八事件」三十週年紀念日，台灣民間有私下紀念活動。

三月十六日　中華民國經濟計劃委員會預計，今年的經濟成長率將達百分之八點五，國民平均收入將增加到新台幣三萬四千一百廿七元，折合美金八百九十八元。

三月廿六日　中華民國的海洋研究船「海空號」，於赴南極地區從事一百十五天久的探險工作後，今日返抵基隆港。

四月八日　中華民國政府宣佈與中東的約旦王國斷絕外交關係，因約旦承認中共政權。

四月九日　中華民國內政部宣佈加強督導掃除社會四害：職業賭徒、走私、流氓、烟毒。

四月十二日　是日為中國國民黨於民國十六年宣佈「清黨」五十週年紀念。

四月十九日　中華民國教育部長蔣彥士，因蘇澳發生翻船學生死亡事件引咎辭職。

五月十八日　中華民國的中華航空公司，使用最新型的波音七四七廣體噴射式客機，開始飛行台北到美國舊金山的直達航線。

五月廿七日　中華民國外交部發言人，對越南共黨企圖將西沙與南沙群島列入其版圖問題再度發表聲明，重申西沙與南沙群島為中國固有領土之一部分，其主權不容置疑。

六月三日　中國造船公司為美國歐斯威柯公司建造的超級油輪安得夫爾號，在台灣高雄港舉行下水典禮。該艘四十四萬五千噸的油輪，為今日全世界居第三位的大輪船。

六月十六日　中華民國舉行五項公職人員選舉投票，參加競選的中國國民黨員候選人共有三千四百餘人。

七月七日　中華民國行政院長蔣經國，在「七七事變」對日抗戰四十週年紀念日發表談話，號

召全國同胞發揚「八年抗戰精神」，並表示堅決反對美國與中共關係正常化企圖。

七月九日　中華民國總統嚴家淦應沙烏地阿拉伯王國國王卡立德邀請，搭機前往訪問三天。這是嚴家淦自一九七五年四月蔣介石總統逝世後繼任總統以來，首次出國訪問。

七月廿五日　強烈颱風「齊爾瑪」襲擊台灣南部高雄地區，狂風暴雨造成驚人的財物損失。據初步估計高雄等地區損失達新台幣一百億元之鉅。

八月十日　中國國民黨中央常務委員會核定，台灣省第八屆縣市長、第六屆省議員及第三屆台北市議員國民黨員候選人部分名單。

八月十二日　中共中央宣佈，中國共產黨第十一次全國代表大會在北京開幕，出席代表一千五百十人，代表全國三千五百餘萬共產黨員。大會由華國鋒代表中央委員會主持。大會預定十八日閉幕。

八月十六日　台灣基督教徒長老會，在「台灣教會公報」上發表「人權宣言」，聲稱中華民國當局要面對現實，採取措施，使台灣成為一個「新而獨立的國家」。基督教長老會是宗教團體中一個主張「台獨」的教派。

八月廿六日　美國國務院主管遠東太平洋事務助理國務卿賀布魯克抵達台北，向中華民國政府說明美國國務卿范錫與中共官員會談的事情。賀布魯克與行政院長蔣經國會談約一小時五十分鐘之久，但官方對會談內容保持緘默。

八月廿九日　中共宣佈，華國鋒當選中共中央主席。

九月十九日　太平洋的東加王國國王杜普六世偕王后瑪泰荷，抵達台灣作為期一週的訪問。

九月三十日　中華民國國防部長高魁元說，中華民國軍隊能夠在奉到命令後三個小時內登上大陸。

十月一日　中華民國自美國海軍獲得兩艘驅逐艦，進一步加強其防衛實力。兩艦是中華民國利用美國提供之軍售信貸購得的。

十月五日　中華民國政府決定將以新

台幣兩百二十億元，實施四項重大交通建設計劃，其中包括完成台灣環島鐵路計劃。

十月二十日　中華民國政府宣佈降低田賦徵實標準，規定一般土地按每賦元徵收稻穀十三公斤，三七五出租地為每賦元徵十公斤。

十月廿八日　台灣的第一座地熱電廠開始試行發電。電廠設在宜蘭縣清水鎮。

十一月五日　台灣警備總司令部今天宣佈破獲一個顛覆組織「人民解放陣線」，有三名嫌疑分子被捕法辦。由於此案十分嚴重，警總特以一百萬元新台幣獎金發給提供破案線索之人。

十一月十六日　中華民國今日啟用第一座核子發電機發電，使其進入核子電力時代。

十一月十九日　中華民國舉行五項地方公職人員選舉投票，桃園縣中壢鎮發生意外事件，大批群眾包圍警察分局引起警民衝突，有八輛汽車被燒毀，警局門窗被破壞，造成「中壢事件」。

十二月一日　中華民國政府宣佈任命行政院政務委員周書楷為駐梵諦岡教廷大使，接替現任大使陳之邁的職務。

十二月二十日　台灣省第六屆省議員宣誓就職，第六屆省議會正式成立。

中華民國政府宣佈，今年的經濟成長率為百分之八點一，低於去年的成長率百分之十一點五，原因是投資額較小及產品出口成長率較低之故。

十二月廿八日　中國國民黨中央常務委員會會議決定，國民黨十一屆二中全會定於明年二月十四日召開，會期預定兩天，全會將決定第六任總統及副總統的國民黨候選人。

中華民國六十七年（一九七八）

一月七日　中國國民黨中央常務委員會會議通過中央委員會人事調整案，邱創煥任中央委員會副秘書長，沈之岳任社會工作會主任，楚崧秋任文化工作會主任，及潘振球任台灣省黨部主任委員。

一月七日　中國國民黨中央常務委員會召開會議，決定接受嚴家淦

總統建議，提名行政院長蔣經國為今年總統選舉的國民黨候選人。

一月九日　嚴家淦總統今天發佈命令，定期召開國民大會第六次會議，選舉行憲第六任總統及副總統。國民大會將於二月十九日開幕，預定三月廿五日閉幕。

二月十四日　中國國民黨第十一屆中央委員第二次全體會議，今日在台北市陽明山開幕，會期預定兩天。

二月十五日　中國國民黨第十一屆中央委員第二次全體會議通過，提名行政院長蔣經國為中華民國第六任總統的國民黨候選人，並通過提名台灣省政府主席謝東閔為副總統的國民黨候選人。二中全會發表宣言後宣告閉幕。

二月十六日　中華民國非國民黨籍的立法委員黃順應在接受訪問中說，盼台灣與大陸的統一早日實現。

二月十九日　台灣省籍的非國民黨員地方人士余登發，發表談話，呼籲台灣與大陸應該統一。

二月廿六日　中共中央宣佈，中共第五屆全國人民代表大會第一次會議，選舉華國鋒為國務院總理，鄧小平為副總理。

三月廿一日　中華民國國民大會第六次會議，選舉行政院長蔣經國為行憲第六任總統，任期六年。

三月廿二日　中華民國國民大會選舉台灣省政府主席謝東閔為副總統。

四月十三日　中華民國政府發表聲明，重申釣魚台列島為中國領土。

四月廿五日　中華民國行政院會議通過，「卸任總統、副總統禮遇條例」。

五月三日　中國國民黨中央常務委員會決定，由王任遠出任中央組織工作會主任，接替趙自齊的職務。

五月二十日　蔣經國總統與謝東閔副總統，今日上午在台北市國父紀念館舉行的典禮中宣誓就任為期六年的任期。約有兩千六百位政府首長、外國使節、貴賓、華僑僑領袖及各界人士等參加歷時僅二十五分鐘的隆重

儀式。蔣經國總統發佈命令，任命蔣彥士為總統府秘書長，及馮啟聰為總統府參軍長。

中國國民黨中央常務委員會會議決定，由孫運璿出任行政院長。

五月廿六日　中華民國立法院投票同意蔣經國總統提名前經濟部長孫運璿為行政院長，表決結果為三二九票對十二票通過。

蔣經國總統發佈命令，任命郝伯村為陸軍總司令，鄭為元為國防部副部長。

五月廿九日　中國國民黨中央常務委員會決定，前台北市長林洋港出任台灣省政府主席，及前行政院政務委員李登輝出任台北市長。

六月十六日　中華民國總統蔣經國主持國民黨北伐統一全國五十週年紀念典禮致詞說，要完成「再北伐，再統一」。

六月三十日　國際貨幣基金會宣佈，中華民國獲列為全世界第二十五位的大貿易國家。

七月十日　中華民國中央銀行宣佈，政府決定將新台幣升值百分之五點二，並將新台幣對美金的匯率改為三十六元（原為三十八元）對美金一元。

七月廿五日　美國國會參議院以九十四票對零票通過決議案，警告卡特總統說，在政府對已有廿四年久的美國與中華民國間的共同防衛條約作任何改變之前，須先與參議院磋商。

七月廿九日　蔣經國總統重申中華民國的基本政策是，「絕不與任何共產黨政權接觸」。他說，散佈「台北與北平談判」或「台北與莫斯科合作」一類荒謬言詞的人，是那些陰謀破壞中華民國國家利益的分子。

八月十六日　中國唯一的天主教樞極（紅衣）主教于斌，在羅馬梵諦岡教廷病逝，享年七十七歲。宗教人士說，于斌因心臟病突發，兩小時後不治。

八月廿三日　中華民國行政院會議通過「改進警政工作方案」，並決定立即付諸實施。

新聞報導說，美國政府有意退出已有三十年久的中美農村經濟復興聯合委員會。

九月廿五日　中華民國內政部與經濟部合辦的全國勞資關係研討會

在台北市舉行，蔣經國總統出席致詞。

十月十日　中華民國雙十國慶紀念日，蔣經國總統主持有一萬二千名部隊參加的閱兵儀式，最受人注意的是中華民國自行製造的「橫風六號」飛彈。

十月十一日　中國國民黨中央常務委員會會議決定，「增額國民大會代表」及「增額立法委員」的國民黨候選人名單。

十月十六日　美國政府通知中華民國說，美國將終止與中華民國的「經濟援助協定」及「農村復興聯合委員會」協議。

十月卅一日　台灣省境內共有高速公路三百七十七公里開放交通。

十一月九日　中華民國行政院會議決定，高雄市將自一九七九年七月份起升格為院轄市（特別市）。

十一月十八日　中華民國的大約二十名非國民黨籍的地方人士，發表「聯合政見」，內容要點包括「召開國民會議」、「言論出版自由化」、「開放政黨」、「解除戒嚴令」及「反對省籍歧視」等。

十一月三十日　中華民國體育界人士發表聲明宣稱，他們堅決拒絕接受中共邀請他們以中共代表團的一部分參加亞洲運動會。

十二月十六日　美國總統卡特於美國時間星期五晚間宣佈說，美國將於一九七九年一月一日與中華人民共和國建立正式外交關係，並終止與在台灣的中華民國的正式關係。卡特總統在經由美國駐台北大使安格爾面交蔣經國總統的信件中說，美國政府不久將派遣一名高級官員赴台北，與中華民國政府討論在外交關係斷絕後調整中美間的關係。

美國政府在聲明中「承認中華人民共和國政府是中國的唯一合法政府」、「承認只有一個中國，台灣是中國的一部分。」美國聲明說，美國將繼續出售武器給中華民國，但是台北的採購項目將依據「選擇基礎」加以批准。美國並將於一九七九年一月一日正式通知中華民國說，美國意欲不繼續在一九五四年簽訂的中美共同防禦條約。

中國國民黨中央常務委員會召開緊急會議，討論美國承認中共政權問題。蔣經國總統發表嚴正聲明，責斥美國「背信毀約」，並宣稱絕不與中共談判。蔣經國並且發佈三項緊急處分事項：全面加強軍事戒備、維持經濟穩定及延期舉行增額民意代表選舉。

十二月十八日　中國國民黨召開第十一屆中央委員第三次全體會議，有人在會中提出「聯俄」建議，蔣經國表示反對說，「聯俄是錯上加錯」。

十二月二十日　中國國民黨中央為貫徹十一屆三中全會的決議，決定成立工作組，由常委嚴家淦擔任召集人。

十二月廿七日　由美國副國務卿克理斯托夫領導的美國六人代表團抵達台北，與中華民國政府官員舉行兩天的會議，討論有關美國於明年一月一日承認北京政權後重行調整美國與中華民國關係問題。克理斯托夫抵達時，受到憤怒的民眾強烈抗議。

十二月廿九日　美國副國務卿克理斯托夫與中華民國政府官員舉行兩天的會談並未達成任何協議，於今日按照預定日程離台返美。不過，中美雙方同意將於未來數月繼續在台北及華府舉行商談。

十二月卅一日　中華民國政府對美國通過「中止中美共同防禦條約」一舉，向美國政府提出最強烈的抗議。

中華民國六十八年（一九七九）

一月一日　美國與「中華人民共和國」建立外交關係。

中國人民代表大會常務委員會發表「告台灣同胞書」，提出與台灣盡快實現通航、通郵、發展貿易及文化交流等問題。同時，中共宣佈從即日起，停止對金門馬祖砲擊。

一月三日　中華民國總統蔣經國在中國國民黨中央常務委員會會議中宣稱，對中共的「和平統一」號召「絕不能信，也絕不能上當」。

一月七日　中華民國政府宣佈，派遣外交部次長楊西崑赴華盛頓，與美國政府就中美斷絕外交關

係後的安排事宜進行第二回合會談。

一月十六日　美國政府宣佈成立「美國在台協會」，負責處理美國與中華民國之間的非官方往來事務。

一月廿一日　中華民國治安當局，將主張「和平統一」的台省籍地方人士余登發余瑞言父子兩人逮捕。

一月廿八日　中國國務院副總理鄧小平應美國總統卡特邀請赴美國訪問九天。

二月十五日　中華民國政府宣佈設立「北美事務協調委員會」，負責處理中華民國與美國之間的非官方往來事宜。

二月廿三日　中華民國與美國達成協議，自三月一日起「北美事務協調委員會」將為中華民國在華盛頓的代表，及「美國在台協會」將為美國在台北的代表。

三月一日　中華民國駐美國的大使館及美國駐中華民國大使館都正式關閉。

三月十日　中華民國新聞局發表聲明，指出台灣的「民主運動」是受了中共統戰所致，號召民眾應提高警覺。

四月八日　中華民國奧林匹克委員會主席沈家銘說，中華民國奧林匹克委員會不反對國際奧林匹克委員會對中華民國奧會名稱問題所作的一項裁定。國際奧會在南美烏拉圭京城的會議中決定，仍然維持承認中華民國奧會名稱，同時承認設在北京的「中國奧林匹克委員會」。

四月十日　美國總統卡特簽署經美國國會參議院與眾議院通過的「台灣關係法案」，其中規定在美國與中華民國斷絕外交關係後，仍允許繼續維持兩國間的商業及文化關係，並且將對中華民國提供能夠保持自衛能力所需的防衛物資。

四月十六日　台灣警備總司令部軍事法庭宣佈，將被控圖謀以暴力推翻政府的吳春發判處死刑，及將其同謀分別判處八年有期徒刑至無期徒刑。軍事法庭同時宣佈，將前高雄縣長余登發判處八年有期徒刑，因其知情未檢舉吳春發圖謀叛亂案及散佈中共宣傳言論。

四月廿二日　約有兩百名台灣省籍人士舉行集會，表示抗議治安當局對他們的「迫害」行動。

四月三十日　美國宣佈自台灣撤退最後一批軍事人員。

六月六日　中國國民黨中央常務委員會決定，任命陳時英為中央委員會秘書處主任，及蕭天讚為社會工作會主任。

六月八日　中華民國交通部宣佈，將鐵路火車、公路汽車及公共汽車的免費票制度一律取消，以節省開支。

六月二十日　中國國民黨中央常務委員會會議決定，沈昌煥出任國家安全會議秘書長。

七月一日　中華民國政府宣佈，將台灣南部的高雄市升格為第二個院轄市（特別市）。台北市為台灣省的第一個院轄市。

七月十七日　中華民國立法院通過法案，授權政府在新竹縣境內設立「科學公園」，以吸引高科技工業的投資。

七月廿八日　台灣省籍的地方人士在台中市集會，表示抗議治安當局對他們的迫害，與警方發生衝突事件。

八月四日　中國民主社會黨主席團主席蔣勻田與夫人自台灣回大陸觀光，在北京會晤「人大常委會委員長」葉劍英。

八月十六日　中國民主社會黨主席團在台北召開臨時會議，討論該黨主席團主席蔣勻田前往大陸事件，經會議決定開除蔣勻田的黨籍並解除其主席團主席職務。

九月六日　中華民國政府宣佈，決定將台灣四周兩百英里的範圍劃為經濟區，並將中華民國的領海範圍自三英里擴大到十二英里。

九月八日　台灣省籍的政界人士許信良、張俊宏、黃信介等，在台北市創辦「美麗島」雜誌。

九月十五日　中華民國行政院長孫運璿啟程赴中東沙烏地阿拉伯王國訪問三天。這是孫氏就任院長十五個月來首次出國之行。

十月五日　是日為農曆中秋節，蔣經國在寓所舉行中秋節茶會，款待一九三六年發動「西安事變」的張學良與夫人趙一荻女士。

十月十日　中華民國各界慶祝雙十國

慶，張學良參加國慶大會，這是他在台灣首次出現於公共場所，特別引人注意。

十月十四日　美國在台協會理事長丁大衛宣佈，美國已與北美事務協調委員會簽訂協定，美國繼續供應中華民國能源燃料。

十一月二日　中華民國行政院長孫運璿抵達漢城，代表中華民國政府參加大韓民國總統朴正熙的葬禮，朴正熙於十月廿七日遭謀殺。

十一月十六日　中華民國與美國代表結束四十天久的修訂航空協定談判。依據雙方發表的備忘錄，中華民國將開闢台北至美國紐約、西雅圖、達拉斯及關島等城市的民航空運路線，及美國的航空公司也將擴大對中華民國的民航業務。

十二月十日　台灣省籍政界人士主辦的「美麗島雜誌」發動的抗議活動，在高雄市造成警民激烈衝突事件，結果有一百八十多人受傷。騷亂首領分子大部分被警察逮捕法辦。與事件有關的「美麗島」、「八十年代」等黨外人士主辦的雜誌被有關當局勒令停刊。

十二月十四日　中國國民黨十一屆中央委員第四次全體會議，於通過「加強在海外對敵鬥爭工作案」、「以復興基地建設經驗，策進光復大陸重建國家案」後宣告閉幕。國民黨中央委員會秘書長張寶樹辭職，由蔣彥士繼任秘書長職務。

十二月廿五日　由於國際汽油價格暴漲的影響，中華民國政府宣佈提高汽油、柴油及燃料油的價格，平均漲價率為百分之三十七，及電力增加百分之十八，新價格均自一九八○年一月一日起生效。

中華民國六十九年（一九八○）

一月三日　美國政府通知中華民國政府說，在中止一年時間後，美國將恢復對中華民國出售大約兩億八千萬美元的武器。

二月二十日　台灣警備總司令部軍事法庭宣佈，對高雄「美麗島」暴亂事件八名領導分子提出叛亂罪嫌控告，及將其他三十七名在押分子案件移轉普通法庭處理。

二月廿一日　中華民國行政院宣佈批准中央銀行自二月廿五日起，發行面額新台幣五百元與一千元的新鈔票。

二月廿八日　因為涉入高雄「美麗島」暴亂事件被捕的台灣省議員林義雄的母親與兩個女兒在家中遭人殺害，大女兒受傷，造成驚震全台的林宅血案。是日適逢「二二八事件」三十三週年紀念日。

二月廿九日　中共中央宣佈，中共中央決定對中共黨主席劉少奇冤案「平反昭雪」。

三月五日　中華民國的北美事務協調委員會與美國的在台協會，正式簽署兩國間的空運協定。

四月一日　中共中央宣佈，中國銀行在國內發行外幣兌換券。

四月四日　為紀念故總統蔣介石興建的「中正紀念堂」今日舉行落成典禮，紀念堂所在地廣達二十五公頃的公園同時完成開放。

四月十七日　國際貨幣基金會在華盛頓舉行的會議中表決通過，接納中華人民共和國為會員國，使中華民國失去國際貨幣基金會的會籍。

四月十八日　中華民國台灣警備總司令部軍事法庭宣佈對高雄「美麗島」雜誌叛亂案重要被告的判決，立法委員兼「美麗島」雜誌發行人黃信介判處有期徒刑十四年，「美麗島」雜誌總經理施明德判處無期徒刑，其他被告姚嘉文、張俊宏、林義雄、呂秀蓮、陳菊等各判處有期徒刑十二年。

四月廿三日　中華民國政府對美國國務院對「美麗島」案的評論，深表不滿。

五月六日　中華民國立法院會議通過公職人員選舉罷免條例，為今年下期將舉行增額中央民意代表選舉之先聲。

五月十三日　中華民國總統蔣經國在財經會談中致辭，要求研究能源問題的對策，以消除預期漲價的心理。

六月五日　中國國民黨中央常務委員會會議決定，在本年內恢復舉行「增額中央民意代表選舉」。

六月十一日　中國國民黨中央常務委員會及國家安全會議決定三項

增額中央民意代表總名額為二
〇五名，較一九七八年原定名
額增加八十一名。一九七八年
原定的選舉，因為美國承認中
共政權而延期。

六月三十日　中華民國政府宣佈，將
英國前駐台灣淡水領事館舊址
予以收回。該舊館址通稱為
「紅毛城」，係於一八六七年
由滿清政府與英國政府訂約
「永久租借給英國」。

七月四日　中華民國中央選舉委員會
會議決定，增額立法委員及國
民大會代表選舉投票於今年十
二月六日舉行，但監察委員選
舉日期尚未決定。

七月廿三日　中華民國行政院長孫運
璿在國家建設研究會致詞說：
「偏安不能自保，分裂必將滅
亡」，促使國人團結努力，達
成復國建國目標。

八月廿五日　中華民國經濟部發表聲
明，嚴格禁止台灣廠商與大陸
方面進行間接或直接貿易，違
者將依法議處。

八月廿九日　中華民國行政院長孫運
璿，啟程赴中美洲三國作為期
十五天的訪問。

九月四日　中華民國與美國簽訂「科
學與技術合作協定」。

九月十日　中共政府公佈，中華人民
共和國國際法。

九月廿五日　中共中央發出公開信，
號召全國青年提倡一對夫妻只
生育一個孩子。

十月二日　中華民國的北美事務協調
委員會與美國在台協會理事
會，在華盛頓簽訂「權益與豁
免協定」，這表示該兩個非官
方機構駐在對方的代表人員將
享受幾乎與正常外交官員相同
的權益。

十月十日　中華民國雙十國慶紀念，
全國各界熱烈慶祝。

十月十三日　南非共和國總理鮑沙偕
夫人抵達中華民國訪問三天。
鮑沙總理係應中華民國行政院
長孫運璿邀請來台北訪問。

十一月四日　中華民國總統蔣經國主
持財經會議，要求切實檢討物
價上漲原因，研定對策，穩定
經濟情勢。

十一月十八日　中國國民黨中央要求
國民黨員，在未來的公職人員
選舉中，要做到絕對的「公
正、誠實、守法與負責」。

十一月二十日　中共宣佈，中國最高
　　　人民法院特別法庭正式開庭，
　　　公審林彪、江青「兩個反革命
　　　集團」的十名共犯。

十一月廿九日　荷蘭政府批准鹿特丹
　　　一家公司，將兩艘海軍潛水艇
　　　與其他設備出售給中華民國。

十二月六日　中華民國舉行增額中央
　　　民意代表選舉投票順利進行，
　　　選舉結果國民黨候選人獲得大
　　　多數席次。在改選的七十席立
　　　法委員中，國民黨獲得五十六
　　　席，在改選的七十六席國民大
　　　會代表中，國民黨獲得六十三
　　　席。非國民黨籍人士共獲得三
　　　十三席立法委員及國大代表。
　　　此次選舉的投票率約佔全部合
　　　格選民中的百分之六十八。

十二月二十日　荷蘭國會通過將兩艘
　　　潛水艇出售給中華民國，潛艇
　　　與其他裝備共值美金約五億
　　　元。

十二月廿八日　中華民國舉行自一九
　　　六五年以來規模最大的一次全
　　　國人口普查，普查地區包括南
　　　沙群島與西沙群島的居民。普
　　　查順利進行，於今日上午圓滿
　　　完成。一九八〇年人口普查結

果，全國人口總數計有一千七
百八十萬五千零六十七人，人
口密度為每平方公里四百九十
五人，人口增長率為千分之二
十二。

中華民國七十年（一九八一）

一月一日　中華民國開國紀念，全國
　　　各界歡度新年。

一月九日　荷蘭在台北設立荷蘭協
　　　會，以促進荷蘭與中華民國間
　　　的貿易。
　　　蔣經國總統接見自美國返台的
　　　大戰期間美國空軍援華「飛虎
　　　隊」司令陳納德將軍的遺孀陳
　　　香梅女士。陳香梅隨美國共和
　　　黨領袖史蒂文生在北京訪問後
　　　抵達台灣訪問。

一月十日　中華民國中央銀行宣佈，
　　　截至一九八〇年底為止，中華
　　　民國的外匯存底已累積到美金
　　　七十四億元之鉅。

一月十二日　蔣經國總統主持軍事會
　　　議時宣稱，「絕不與中共談判
　　　是中華民國永不改變的政
　　　策」。

二月十八日　蔣經國總統在國民黨中
　　　央常務委員會會議中講話，指

示要進一步挖掘人才，努力貫徹考試制度。

三月四日　中國國民黨中央宣稱，已完成國民黨「強化組織，加強行動草案」。

三月十一日　中國國民黨中央常務委員會決定，由余俊賢出任監察院長，及黃尊秋出任監察院副院長。

三月十五日　台灣省政府主席林洋港赴日本訪問。他在東京發表談話說，中華民國永遠不與中共談判或接觸。

三月十七日　中華民國的非國民黨籍的立法委員費希平及康寧祥等聯名向行政院提出書面質詢，建議解除戒嚴令、開放黨禁、尊重言論自由等。

三月廿五日　中華民國的台灣省籍政界人士林正杰等在「縱橫」月刊創刊號上發表文章，提出與大陸統一問題的意見。

三月廿九日　中國國民黨第十二次全國代表大會在台北市陽明山開幕，由國民黨主席蔣經國主持開幕典禮並致詞，大會預定四月五日閉幕。蔣經國說，中華民國的七十年代，「是三民主義勝利與光復大陸的時代」。

四月二日　國民黨十二全大會選舉蔣經國連任國民黨主席。

四月五日　國民黨十二全大會於通過「修改黨章案」、「貫徹以三民主義統一全國案」及「黨務工作報告決議」案，並選出中央委員一百五十人及中央評議委員二百廿七人後，宣佈閉幕。

四月六日　中國國民黨十二屆中央委員第一次全體會議在台北市陽明山舉行，會議通過由蔣經國主席提名的中央常務委員嚴家淦、謝東閔、孫運璿、王昇及李登輝等二十七人。

四月廿三日　中華民國新任北美事務協調委員會主任委員蔡維屏離台北赴華盛頓就任新職。蔡維屏原任外交部次長。

四月廿九日　中國國民黨中央常務委員會決定，由關中擔任國民黨台北市黨部主任委員。

五月四日　第一屆歐洲產品展覽會在台北市揭幕，來自一百廿三個歐洲國家的二百九十三家公司參加展出。

五月六日　中國國民黨中央常務委員

會決定，由倪文亞出任立法院長。

五月廿九日　中共中央發表公告說，中華人民共和國名譽主席宋慶齡，因患慢性淋巴細胞性白血球病在北京逝世，享年九十歲。中共中央決定為宋慶齡舉行國葬。宋慶齡治喪委員會致電宋慶齡在美國、台灣、香港的親屬宋美齡、蔣經國、蔣緯國等，並歡迎他們來參加葬禮，葬禮定六月四日在上海舉行。宋慶齡是中華民國國父孫中山先生的遺孀，宋美齡的長姊。

六月十七日　中華民國經濟計劃發展委員會說，該會預估自一九八二年起的四年期間，中華民國的經濟成長率將為百分之八。中國國民黨中央決定由台灣電力公司董事長楊金宗出任高雄市長，接替現任市長王玉雲的職務。

七月三日　台灣的留美學生陳文成，因涉嫌在紐約圖謀槍殺蔣經國案，被台灣警備總司令部約談後突然死亡事件引起各方注意。

七月七日　中華民國政府在台北召開第十一次國家建設研究會，與會的留美學人等提出有關政府對大陸政策等問題。

八月八日　中共官員宣佈，中華民國空軍的少校軍官黃植誠駕飛機降落大陸。

八月十二日　中華民國中央銀行宣佈，將美金與新台幣的匯率加以調整，由美金一元兌新台幣三十六元改為美金一元兌新台幣三十八元，新台幣貶值約百分之五。

八月廿三日　中華民國交通安全當局決定成立調查委員會，負責徹查遠東航空公司波音七三七式客機失事事件。空難發生於台灣苗栗上空，造成一百十人喪生的慘劇。

八月廿五日　中華民國歷史研究會在台北市開幕，有一百四十位國內外學人參加，會期預定三天。

九月三日　台灣省中部與南部地區遭到近三十年來最嚴重的水災，造成二十三人喪生，財物損失估計高達新台幣二十三億元以上。台灣省政府緊急撥款五十

億元供賑災之需。

九月十三日　中央銀行說，中華民國的外匯存底已劇增到美金約八十億元之鉅。

九月三十日　中共宣佈，中國人民代表大會常務委員會委員長葉劍英發表談話，說明台灣回歸祖國，實現和平統一的「九點方針政策」。

中華民國新聞局長宋楚瑜發表談話，斥責葉劍英的聲明「基本上還是統戰宣傳」。

十月七日　中國國民黨主席蔣經國在國民黨中央常務委員會會議中再次宣稱，「永遠」不與中共談判，並且「決為三民主義統一全國奮鬥到底」。

十一月十四日　中華民國舉行縣市長及議員選舉，參加投票的合格選民在一千萬人以上。選舉結果，國民黨候選人在十九個縣市長中贏得十五名縣市長。在台灣省議員選舉中，國民黨候選人當選七十七席中的六十席，獨立競選人士獲得十七席。在台北院轄市議員選舉中，國民黨員在五十一席中獲得三十八席，在高雄市議員選舉中，國民黨員在四十二席中獲得三十二席。

十一月廿一日　中華民國各界舉行三民主義統一中國研討會，決議成立「三民主義統一中國大同盟」。

十一月廿五日　中華民國行政院實施局部改組，新任行政院副院長邱創煥、國防部長宋長志、參謀總長郝伯村、內政部長林洋港、台灣省政府主席李登輝。

十二月八日　中華民國行政院長孫運璿率領高級官員一行前往印尼作為期五天的訪問。據外國新聞社報導說，中華民國以飛彈等武器供應印尼政府。

十二月二十日　台灣省第七屆省議會成立，高育仁當選為議長，黃鎮岳當選為副議長。

十二月廿八日　前廣東省政府主席余漢謀上將在台北市病逝，享年八十六歲。

中華民國七十一年（一九八二）

一月八日　一九八二年國際羽毛球比賽會在台北市開幕，來自世界各地的羽毛球選手參加比賽，會期預定一週。

一月十一日　美國國務院宣布，美國決定以武器售給中華民國。北京外交部發言人表示對美國此舉提出嚴重抗議。

一月十二日　中華民國外交部發言人發表聲明，對美國宣佈恢復對中華民國供應武器的決定表示歡迎。

一月二十日　蔣經國總統在國民黨中央常務委員會會議中講話，要求當選公職的國民黨員「人人做公僕，為民服務」。

一月廿三日　世界自由日大會在台北市開幕，由世界人民反共聯盟榮譽主席谷正綱主持。大會發表宣言，號召世界自由國家團結一致，「擊敗共黨奴役勢力」。

二月三日　中國國民黨主席蔣經國在國民黨中央常務委員會會議中講話，指示國民黨員發揚革命精神、開拓統一中國道路，推翻中共政權。

二月十三日　中華民國政府下令，禁止一千五百項日本產品進口，並且命令在一年期間不准進口日本製造的七噸以上的大卡車及大巴士。

二月十八日　中華民國行政院長孫運璿在立法院第六十九屆會期中說，中華民國現正準備製造坦克車，艦艇等精密武器與軍事裝備品。

三月廿二日　中國國民黨中央常務委員會副秘書長陳履安一行九人前往大韓民國作友好訪問。陳履安是故副總統陳誠之子。

三月廿八日　美國檀香山僑胞集資興建的興中會紀念堂，今日舉行開幕典禮。中國國民黨中央黨史委員會主任秦孝儀等專程自台北赴檀香山參加典禮。華僑興建紀念堂為了紀念中華民國國父孫中山先生於一八九四年（清代光緒二十年甲午）十一月廿四日在檀香山成立興中會，開始致力於革命事業。

四月二十日　中國青年黨及中國民主社會黨高層黨務人員應邀參加國民黨在台北市召開的座談會，表示一致支持國民黨提出的「三民主義統一中國政策」。

五月七日　美國副總統喬治・布希抵達北京從事三天的友好訪問。

五月廿九日　前廣東省政府主席李漢

魂與太太吳菊芳抵北京訪問。

六月二日　中國國民黨主席蔣經國在中央常務委員會會議中發表講演，促使國民黨同志發揚精神力量，克服困難。

七月八日　中華民國行政院長孫運璿在答覆立法委員質詢中說，「台灣獨立聯盟是叛亂組織」。

七月廿四日　中共「全國人代大會常務委員會副委員長廖承志」以信件給中國國民黨主席蔣經國，要蔣經國「負起歷史責任，毅然和談達成國家統一」。信中並邀請蔣經國訪問大陸。廖承志是國民黨左派人物廖仲凱之子。

七月三十日　中華民國教育部次長李模發表聲明說，中華民國政府對日本文部省修改中學歷史教科書，歪曲日本侵略中國史實，表示嚴重關切，促日本慎重檢討處理。

八月十七日　蔣宋美齡女士在美國發表致北京廖承志的公開信，嚴斥廖承志致國民黨主席蔣經國信中的謬論。

八月十八日　中國國民黨主席蔣經國在國民黨中央常務委員會會議席間發表講演，要求國民黨同志「堅強奮鬥，不為世局困擾」，不受中共「統戰眩惑」，「貫徹反共復國國策」。

九月十八日　中華民國的歷史學會，為紀念「九一八事變」日本侵略東北五十一週年，舉行座談會，發表嚴正聲明，斥責日本篡改史實謬行。同時國民黨黨史會舉辦「九一八」日本侵華圖片、資料展覽，供各界參觀。

十月十日　中華民國雙十國慶紀念，各界歡愉慶祝。

十月十五日　中華民國行政院長孫運璿在立法院答覆質詢時說，中共「未放棄犯台企圖，戒嚴令不容取消」，絕不與中共舉行談判。

十月十六日　一九七〇年諾貝爾文學獎得主蘇聯作家蘇斯尼辛，應中華民國文藝基金會主席吳三連邀請抵達台北訪問。

十月廿二日　「三民主義統一中國大同盟」在台北正式成立，會議通過盟章、綱領，並發宣言，

決定開始推動活動。

十一月十七日　中國國民黨主席蔣經國在國民黨中央常務委員會會議中指示，從政的「國民黨員協助工商界克服困難，及嚴查處分仿冒商標不法分子」。

十一月廿四日　是日為中華民國國父孫中山先生於一八九四年在美國檀香山創立興中會八十八週年紀念，中國國民黨特舉辦各項紀念活動。

中華民國政府宣佈，任命錢復為北美事務協調委員會駐美國代表，接替蔡維屏的職務。

十二月九日　中國國民黨中央委員會，舉行「三民主義論文比賽」優勝者頒獎儀式。

十二月廿三日　中華民國政府宣佈，已選定與日本最大汽車製造公司本田合作，在台灣生產小客車，雙方聯合投資五億四千萬美元。當局預計在開工後的八年內的生產量達到每年三十萬輛客車。

中華民國七十二年（一九八三）

一月一日　蔣經國總統發表民國七十二年新年獻辭，重申必須推翻中共政權，中國統一必須依據憲法。

一月四日　中華民國國策顧問蔡培火病逝，享年九十五歲，他是台省籍的政界元老之一。

一月十四日　中華民國立法院三讀通過商標法修正案，新法規定將侵害註冊商標案犯者的處罰提高到最重五年徒刑。

一月十七日　中華民國行政院提出一九八三年度施政方針，強調繼續加速各項建設，擴大對大陸的領先差距。

二月十六日　荷蘭的瑪迪納航空公司客機飛抵台北，為台灣與荷蘭間民航服務的開始。

三月三日　中華民國行政院長孫運璿在立法院作報告時宣稱，政府對於「叛亂」組織的活動絕不姑息。

三月二十日　中華航空公司自本日起開闢台北與紐約間的客機航線，每週飛行兩班。全程飛行時間為十五個小時，中途在阿拉斯加州的安克拉治停留加油。

三月廿四日　中華民國與所羅門（群島）國建立外交關係。所羅門

位於南太平洋海域，包括多個火山岩島嶼，總面積約五百六十平方英里。

三月廿八日　中國國民黨中央政策委員會邀立法委員舉行座談會，就選舉法修正案進行協調，與會立法委員均表示支持修訂監察委員選舉辦法。

四月二日　國畫大師張大千因病在台北市逝世，享年八十五歲。

四月十二日　中華航空公司今日起開闢台北到荷蘭阿姆斯特丹的定期客機航線，這是中華航空公司發展環球民航服務的第一步。

五月九日　中華民國總統蔣經國發佈命令，任命王昇為國防部聯訓部主任，許歷農為總政治作戰部主任，及劉和謙為海軍總司令。

六月十日　蔣經國總統特派林洋港、連震東等十四人為中央選舉委員會委員，並以林洋港為主任委員。

七月十二日　台北市內鐵路地下化工程今日舉行破土典禮，此項計劃將把台北市內自林森北路到廣州街的二點八公里的鐵路軌道移於地下道內，旨在改善市內的交通情勢，全部工程預算為新台幣一百七十二億元，預定於一九九一年完成開放交通。

七月十三日　中華民國政府發表聲明，指出中共政權為一「叛亂集團」，其與英國間的任何有關香港未來地位之談判，以及可能達成的任何協議，「均屬無效」。

八月卅一日　中國國民黨中央常務委員會會議核定國民黨立法委員候選人名單，共有五十七人。

九月三日　中華民國交通部命令，禁止菲律賓航空公司客機飛到台北，由於菲律賓民航局已禁止中華航空公司班機飛到馬尼拉。禁飛問題與菲律賓反對派領袖艾奎諾事件有關。

九月十四日　中華民國行政院命令，任命林清江為台灣省政府教育廳長。

菲律賓政府民航局宣佈撤銷不准中華航空公司班機飛到馬尼拉的禁令。同日，中華民國交通部宣佈撤銷不准菲律賓航空公司班機飛到台北的禁令。

九月十六日　中華民國中央研究院院長錢思亮，因心臟病突發在台北市台灣大學附設醫院逝世。錢氏曾任台灣大學校長多年。

九月廿五日　中華民國孔孟學會在台北市師範大學舉行第廿三次會員大會，由理事長國民黨元老陳立夫主持。

十月八日　中國國民黨中央委員會秘書長蔣彥士說，關於充實中央民意代表機構問題，仍應依據憲法臨時條款辦理，不宜擴大選舉範圍。

十月十日　中華民國雙十國慶紀念，蔣經國總統發表國慶祝詞，宣稱「反共鬥爭，必須堅持到底，不與中共妥協」。

十月廿五日　慶祝台灣光復節，中華民國行政院長孫運璿在慶祝大會中演講時說，努力建設台灣復興基地，迎接三民主義世紀勝利，及「慶祝光復大陸之日，為期不遠」。

十月卅一日　台北市郊的關渡大橋興建完工，宣布開放交通。橋長八百零九公尺，費時三年完成，工程費達新台幣七億元之鉅。

十一月一日　科學家吳大猷博士在台北市南港中央研究院蔡元培廳，宣誓就任中央研究院院長新職。他是接替上月病逝的錢思亮的院長職務。

十一月廿三日　中國國民黨中央常務委員會會議，通過「行政院一九八四年施政方針案」，決定繼續加強社會安全與福利事項。

十二月一日　中共政府商務部宣布，全國開放對棉布、絮棉敞開供應，取消布票制度，這是近三十年來大陸人民首次可以不需布票購布。

十二月三日　中國國民黨在今天舉行的增額立法委員選舉中獲得重大的勝利，在七十一席立法委員中，國民黨候選人獲得六十二席。反對派人士獲得六席，獨立人士獲得三席。曾擔任反對派領袖十四年久的立法委員康寧祥但此次選舉中失掉席位，使人很感意外。

十二月廿五日　蔣經國總統主持行憲紀念日大會致詞說：「只要中華民國憲法存在，中華民國法統必然存在」，他並且列舉一

九八三年的十大成就。

十二月廿八日　中國國民黨中央常務委員會會議決定，將本年增額立法委員選中，違紀競選或助選的國民黨員雷渝濟等二十一人開除黨籍。

中華民國七十三年（一九八四）

一月一日　中華民國開國紀念日，蔣經國總統發表新年獻詞，再度宣稱，要「完成反共復國大業，再創中華民國新機運」。

一月十一日　中國國民黨中央常務委員會會議決定，二月十四日與十五日舉行國民黨中央委員十二屆第二次全體會議，以決定中華民國第七任總統及副總統的國民黨候選人。

一月十四日　中華民國新聞局宣布，新聞局決定准許今年一年內進口日本電影片，試行一年。政府自一九七三年起一直禁止進口日本攝製的電影片。

高雄港的海底隧道修建完成，將於五月間開放交通。

一月十五日　設在澎湖的「漁民廣播電台」已開始廣播節目，為全國六十萬眾的漁民服務。漁民電台每天廣播時間自清晨六時開始，至夜間十二時為止。

一月廿九日　中華民國行政院經濟建設委員會報告說，由於外貿出超不斷增長，中華民國的外匯存底已累積到一百三十七億美元之鉅的空前高紀錄。

一月卅一日　蔣經國總統於中國國民黨召開十二屆二中全會的前夕，特派國民黨中央常務委員谷正綱與倪文亞，分別邀請中國青年黨及中國民主社會黨領袖晤談，徵詢兩黨的意見。

二月九日　中華民國行政院長孫運璿，要求各部會今年做好四項重要工作：加速工業升級、改革賦稅、維持社會秩序、改善醫療設施。

二月十四日　中國國民黨十二屆中央委員第二次全體會議，今天在台北市陽明山開幕，會期兩天。國民黨主席蔣經國在開幕式中致詞宣稱，要以「三民主義統一中國」。

二月十五日　中國國民黨十二屆中央委員第二次全體會議，推選黨主席蔣經國為中華民國第七任總統的國民黨候選人，稍後並

推選李登輝為副總統候選人。全會在通過蔣經國主席提名的三十一名中央常務委員後宣告閉幕。新常委包括嚴家淦、謝東閔、孫運璿、李登輝、王愓吾、林洋港及許水德等人。

三月廿一日　中華民國第一屆國民大會第七次會議在台北市中山堂舉行的大會中，選舉蔣經國連任任期六年的中華民國第七任總統。他獲得出席大會的一千零二十名國大代表中的一千零十二票的支持。

三月廿二日　中華民國第一屆國民大會第七次會議，在今天的大會中選舉台灣省政府主席李登輝為中華民國第七任副總統。他獲得出席大會的九百九十九位國大代表中的八百七十三票的支持。

三月廿七日　中華民國立法院舉行選舉，倪文亞當選為院長，劉闊才當選為副院長。

中華民國首次製造的 AT-3 式雙座噴射教練機出廠，係中山理工學院設計的。

四月十日　蔣經國總統主持財經座談會，提出五點指示，其中包括經濟建設的規劃、人才的培育和運用以及守法習慣與環境保護觀念的確立等。北京當局宣布，中國成功的發射第一個試驗通信地球衛星。

四月十二日　中華航空公司的一架波音型 COM1 班機，自桃園國際機場起飛前往紐約，開始華航的歷史性環球飛行服務。該機將在阿拉斯加州的安克拉治加油後直飛紐約，然後由紐約續飛至荷蘭的阿姆斯特丹，乘客可自阿姆斯特丹搭乘華航的例行班機飛往台灣。

四月廿六日　美國總統雷根（里根）偕夫人搭飛機抵達北京，開始對中國大陸的六天訪問。

五月二十日　蔣經國於上午九時在台北市陽明山中山樓宣誓就任中華民國第七任總統。稍後，李登輝宣誓就任第七任副總統。

五月廿一日　中華民國總統蔣經國提名經濟計劃發展委員會主任俞國華為行政院長，咨請立法院予以同意。

五月廿五日　中華民國立法院會議投票同意俞國華為行政院院長，原任行政院長孫運璿獲蔣經國

總統聘任為總統府資政。

五月三十日　蔣經國總統發佈命令，任命張繼正為中央銀行總裁，陳履安為國家科學委員會主任委員。張繼正是國民黨元老張群之子，而陳履安是故副總統陳誠之子。

六月一日　新任中華民國行政院長俞國華舉行首次記者招待會，提出新內閣施政三大目標：促進社會和諧發展、擴大經濟發展功能、與開展國家現代化的前途。

六月二日　蔣經國總統發佈命令，任命邱創煥為台灣省政府主席。

六月五日　蔣經國總統發佈命令，任命沈昌煥為總統府秘書長，汪道淵為國家安全會議秘書長。

六月十八日　蔣經國總統發佈命令，聯合勤務總司令蔣緯國任參謀本部聯合作戰訓練部主任，並任命溫哈熊為聯合勤務總司令。

六月二十日　中國國民黨中央常務委員會會議通過蔣經國主席交議的國民黨中央人事案：吳俊才任革命實踐研究院副主任，梁孝煌與馬英九任中央委員會副秘書長，宋時選任組織工作會主任，鄭心雄任海外工作會主任、關中為台灣省黨部主任委員，陳金讓為台北市黨部主任委員。

六月廿七日　中國國民黨元老張靜愚在台北市病逝，享年九十一歲。

七月二十日　中華民國立法院會議通過「基本勞工標準法案」。

八月十七日　蔣經國總統發佈命令，特任孔德成為考試院長，林金生為副院長。

九月廿六日　在中共與英國政府簽訂「香港前途的協議」後中華民國行政院長俞國華發表聲明說，中華民國政府與人民對香港的居民表示十分關切。他提出對香港中國居民的十一項援助保證。

十月三日　中國國民黨中央常務委員會會議，對中共與英國間的香港問題談判作成五項決議，宣稱不承認中共與英國簽訂的「香港前途的協議」。

十月廿三日　台灣省政府主席邱創煥在台灣光復節前夕發表談話，宣稱要建立祥和的社會。

十一月三日　蔣經國總統主持財經會談，強調中華民國的經濟朝著自由化、國際化方向發展。

十一月十二日　中華民國治安當局採取強有力措施，嚴厲打擊有組織的罪惡集團，在第一天的行動中逮捕五十多名地下罪惡首要分子。

十一月廿四日　是日為中國國民黨建黨九十週年紀念日。國民黨主席蔣經國於黨慶前夕發表專文「貫徹國民革命的全程任務」。國民黨中央黨部在台北市舉行慶祝建黨九十週年大會，前總統嚴家淦在會中致詞，宣稱要以「三民主義統一中國」。中華民國國父孫中山先生，於一八九四年（清光緒二十年）十一月廿四日，在美國檀香山創立興中會，開始致力於革命事業，迄今屆滿九十年。

十二月十九日　中共宣稱，中國總理趙紫陽與英國首相撒切爾，分別代表中、英兩國政府在北京簽訂「中華人民共和國政府和大不列顛及北愛爾蘭聯合王國政府關於香港問題的聯合聲明」。聲明中規定，中國政府於一九九七年七月一日對香港行使主權。

十二月廿六日　中國國民黨中央常務委員會會議，蔣經國主席指示，要全力支持貫徹執行十四項經濟建設計劃。

中華民國七十四年（一九八五）

一月一日　中華民國內政部戶政司報告說，台灣及澎湖群島的人口總數已增加到一千九百萬眾。

一月八日　中華民國行政院香港事務小組決定，簡化出入境申請手續、放鬆外匯管制，並採取鼓勵措施等，以吸引香港的大型企業及金融機構遷到中華民國來。

一月廿一日　中共宣布，第六屆人民代表大會常務委員會決定，自一九八五年開始，每年九月十日為「中國教師節」。

二月六日　中國國民黨中央常務委員會會議通過蔣經國主席提議，中央委員會秘書長蔣彥士辭職照准，由馬樹禮繼任秘書長職務。

二月十一日　中華民國財政部命令，

台北市第十信用合作社因有違法貸款及舞弊行為，指定由台灣省合作金庫加以監管。

二月十二日　中華民國財政部發言人表示，台北市第十信用合作社案有關人員蔡萬春、蔡辰洲等二十八人已奉令限制出境與禁止財產轉移。

二月十三日　中國國民黨中央常務委員會會議，蔣經國主席發表談話，宣稱在新的一年裡，要堅持「不退卻、不灰心」的態度來克服種種困難。

二月廿七日　中華民國治安當局逮捕涉嫌在美國舊金山殺害劉宜良（筆名江南）的陳啟禮（一名陳虎門）、吳頓及董桂森三人，並依法提起公訴。劉宜良自台北去美國讀書，在舊金山漁人碼頭觀光區經營商店。

三月一日　中華民國立法院舉行秘密會議，同意治安當局逮捕現任立法委員台北市第十信用合作社理事會主席蔡辰洲。

三月六日　蔣經國總統在國家安全會議中致詞，強調要整頓財稅金融及經濟各方面現有的各種問題。

三月十一日　中華民國行政院宣布，由財政、法務兩部會同調查台北市第十信用合作社舞弊案。

三月十三日　中華民國政府批准經濟部長徐立德辭職，因其在一九八○到一九八四年任職財政部長期間，處理台北市第十信用合作社案受到各方批評。

三月二十日　中國國民黨中央常務委員會會議通過蔣經國主席交議人事案，將郭哲調任為中央委員會副秘書長。

三月廿九日　北京光明日報報導說，繼發現秦代兵馬俑之後，秦始皇陵考古隊最近又探明秦始皇陵地宮等重要建築，發現證實歷史家司馬遷關於秦墓中以水銀為「江河大海」的記載。

四月十六日　中華民國的第一個試管嬰兒在台北市榮民總醫院出生。

四月十九日　中華民國國防部軍法局高等審判庭，對美國舊金山華人劉宜良（筆名江南）被謀殺案宣布判決。被告汪希苓判處無期徒刑、胡儀敏與陳虎門各判處有期徒刑兩年半。

四月廿四日　中華民國前教育部長黃

季陸病逝，享年八十七歲。

四月廿五日　中華民國行政院長俞國華召集財經會議，決定成立臨時性的「經濟革新委員會」。

五月二日　中華民國行政院正式成立經濟革新委員會，此新單位將在六個月內提出新經濟政策方案。

五月十六日　中華民國財政部成立專案小組，負責徹查台北市第十信用合作社的舞弊案。

中華民國的中山科學技術院說，中華民國科技人員已完成發展第一種地對空的飛彈計劃，並已於三月二十日舉行「天弓一號」飛彈試射成功，該院現計劃在一九八八年十二月舉行「天弓二號」型飛彈試射。

五月十七日　台灣省議會十四名非國民黨籍的省議員提出集體辭職書，表示對省議會強行通過省政府下年度預算案一事的抗議。

五月廿二日　中國國民黨中央常務委員會會議決定，由許水德出任台北市長，及蘇南城為高雄市長。

六月十日　中共宣布，中國政府決定，將中國人民解放軍員額減少一百萬人，一百萬人相當於總兵力的四分之一。

六月十六日　中美洲的宏都拉斯共和國外交部長巴尼加，在台北主持宏國駐中華民國大使館的開幕典禮。

六月廿八日　中華民國立法院三讀通過「版權法修正案」，新法旨在打擊出版界的盜印劣風，擴大保障版權的範圍，並加重對侵害版權犯者的處罰。其中也規定，外國作家必須先向中華民國有關當局辦理著作物登記始能享受版權保障。

六月廿九日　中國國民黨中央黨史委員會召開專家研討會，紀念對日本抗戰勝利四十週年，及回顧八年抗戰的經驗，用以激勵後進。

七月五日　中華民國政府新聞局長張京育發表聲明，重申禁止與大陸作間接、直接貿易的政策。

七月七日　是日為中國對日本抗戰「七七事變」紀念日，抗戰蒙難同志會舉行紀念會，同時紀念抗戰勝利四十週年。

七月三十日　中國國民黨中央常務委員會會議，核定國民黨員一百五十七人為台灣地方公職人員選舉的候選人。

八月二日　中華民國中央研究院近代史研究所，舉辦中華民國「抗戰建國史研討會」，邀請國內外學者專家參加。

八月十四日　中華民國政府公布，對台北市第十信用合作社舞弊案調查結果，對涉案的十五人予以申誡、記過、記大過的處分。財政部長陸潤康被免職。

八月廿一日　中國國民黨中央常務委員會會議核定，由中央銀行副總裁錢純出任財政部長，接替因台北市第十信用合作社舞弊案被免職的陸潤康的職務。

九月三日　中華民國各界在台北市國父紀念館隆重舉行對日本抗戰勝利四十週年紀念大會，由當年在首都南京代表政府接受日本降書的何應欽將軍主持並致詞。同時，蔣經國總統發表談話，號召國人要發揚抗戰八年的精神。

九月八日　黃埔軍校出身的著名軍事將領何應欽上將發表談話，促使海內外及大陸上的黃埔校友，一致發揮團結犧牲精神，共同致力於「三民主義統一中國」。

九月九日　中華民國副總統李登輝偕夫人，啟程赴中美洲作為期廿一天的訪問。他將訪問巴拿馬、哥斯達黎加和瓜地馬拉三個友邦。

九月十五日　台灣最大的明湖水力發電廠正式啟用發電。該工程費時六年完成，建造費達新台幣兩百七十億元之鉅。據估計，此水力發電廠每年可發電達十七億六千九百萬 KWH（千瓦小時）。

十月十日　中華民國雙十國慶紀念，蔣經國總統發表國慶談話，再度宣稱要堅持反共到底。

十月三十日　外交部宣布，任命王肇元為中華民國駐南美洲烏拉圭大使。

十一月十日　中華民國政府決定接受香港及九龍的效忠中華民國的教師於「緊急情勢」下移居台灣。行政院並未特別說明緊急情勢的性質為何，但顯然係指一九九七年中共接收港九地

區。

十一月十六日　中華民國今日舉行四項地方公職人員選舉，約有一千四百萬名合格選民參加投票，選舉二十一名縣市長（候選人有五十四人），七十七席台灣省議會議員（候選人有一百五十八人），台北市議會議員五十一席（候選人有七十四人），及高雄市議會議員四十二席（候選人有七十一人）。

十一月二十日　蔣經國主席主持國民黨中央常務委員會會議講話，指示要「誠懇、踏實、虛心、革新」。

中華民國立法院已通過商標法修正案，其中規定外國公司可以對侵害其商標權益的中國人提出控告，即使他們的商標未向中華民國有關當局辦理登記。

十一月廿九日　中華民國行政院長俞國華對香港「光華雜誌」發表談話說，為了贏取三民主義對共產主義競賽的勝利，中華民國政府已擬定長期發展目標，並且有信心克服「中共對經濟及社會各方面的挑戰」。

十二月四日　中國國民黨中央常務委員會會議決定，於一九八六年三月廿九日舉行十二屆中央委員第三次全體會議。

十二月七日　中華民國外交部宣布，中華民國政府決定與中美洲的尼加拉瓜國斷絕外交關係，因尼國政府承認中共政權。

十二月十六日　蔣經國總統發佈命令，任命宋心濂上將為國家安全局長，原局長汪敬煦上將調任總統府參軍長。

十二月十九日　台北地方法院對台北市第十信用合作舞弊案宣布判決，共有五十四名被告判刑，其中原理事會主席蔡辰洲被判處徒刑十二年，加上其他罪行，他前後共被判刑期超過一百年。

十二月廿五日　蔣經國總統在行憲三十八週年紀念大會中宣稱，他的蔣家人「不能也不會」競選下屆中華民國總統。蔣總統並且保證，中華民國將沒有軍事統治。

中華民國七十五年（一九八六）

一月一日　中華民國開國紀念日，全

國各界歡度假期。

一月廿三日　蔣經國總統對美國「讀者文摘」雜誌發表談話說，統一中國的具體途徑就是「只要大家實行三民主義，必能達到與台灣經濟同樣的水準」。

二月五日　中國國民黨主席蔣經國在國民黨中央常務委員會會席間講話，要求國民黨員多交朋友，克服困難，渡過難關。國民黨中央委員會秘書長馬樹禮說，本年黨務工作重點是積極籌備第十二屆三中全會。

三月八日　中國國民黨中央政策委員會舉行外交問題研討會，決議強化外交陣容、開創外交機勢，對付中共統戰陰謀。

三月廿九日　中國國民黨十二屆中央委員會第三次全體會議在台北市陽明山開幕，由蔣經國主席主持並致詞，再度強調以「三民主義統一中國」。三中會會期三天。

三月卅一日　中國國民黨十二屆中央委員第三次會議在通過數項重要議案及通過三十一名中央常務委員人選後宣告閉幕。中央常務委員名單中有嚴家淦、謝東閔、李登輝、沈昌煥、郝柏村等。

四月廿三日　國立台灣大學附設醫院順利完成分割出生十四天的連體嬰兒手術，救了兩個女嬰中的一人。這是醫學界第一宗分割出生時間最短的孿生手術。

四月廿四日　中華民國外交部長朱撫松與巴拉圭外交部長沙迪華，代表兩國政府在台北市簽訂引渡條約。

五月三日　中華民國的中華航空公司波音七四七型貨機駕駛員王錫爵駕機自台北起飛，降落於廣州白雲機場，要求在大陸定居。大陸民航局以電報通知台北，邀請中華航空公司派人商談辦理接回貨機及該機其他人員事宜。

五月廿三日　中華航空公司及大陸民航局代表，在香港完成有關華航降落廣州的貨機與人員交接工作。

五月廿六日　中華民國交通部宣布調查中華航空公司飛行員王錫爵駕貨機降落大陸事件，將追查有關失職人員予以處分。

六月十一日　中華民國總統蔣經國發

佈命令，特命吳伯雄等十四人為中央選舉委員會第三任委員。

六月十五日　中國國民黨中央委員會秘書長馬樹禮，在國民黨台灣省代表大會中說，當前黨務工作的重點是「健全組織，貫徹革命」。

八月二十日　中國國民黨中央常務委員會會議核定，增額國民大會代表及立法委員的國民黨籍候選人名單。

九月廿三日　中華民國外交部長朱撫松發表聲明，再度申明中華民國對中共的基本立場是，堅守「不接觸、不談判、不妥協」三大原則。

九月廿五日　中華民國在退出亞洲奧林匹克委員會十三年後，重獲准加入亞洲奧林匹克委員會。

十月六日　中華民國經濟部宣布，決定增加投資新台幣十二億元，在今後三年期間用於發展防污染技術工業。

十月九日　蔣經國總統在中華民國雙十國慶前夕發表談話說，在國家遭逢艱難之際，需要「堅定沉著，決不衝動，意氣用事」。

蔣經國總統對美國記者發表談話說，政府可以在短期內宣布解除戒嚴令，但是新政黨必須遵守憲法，支持反共政策。

十月十二日　中共宣布，英國女王伊麗莎白二世抵達北京訪問。這是英國元首歷史上第一次到中國作正式訪問。

十月十五日　中華民國中央研究院院士李遠哲，獲得一九八六年諾貝爾化學獎。

中國國民黨中央常務委員會會議通過，「動員戡亂國家安全法令」與「動員戡亂時期民間社團組織」兩項議案。

十一月八日　中國國民黨中央委員會秘書長馬樹禮對記者訪問談話中，對解除戒嚴與開放黨禁兩項議案提出解答與說明。他說：「這是履行憲政最具體的行動」，「希望無黨籍人士認清本黨的誠意」。

十一月十日　中華民國的台灣省籍政界人士宣布組織「民主進步黨」，舉行首次代表大會，並通過黨章、黨綱及選舉主席等措施。

中華民國內政部長吳伯雄對無黨籍人士宣布組織「民主進步黨」一事發表聲明說，「此類活動在政府完成組織政治團體立法之前自屬不法，政府不能承認。」

十一月十八日　中國國民黨台灣省黨部主任委員關中發表談話，呼籲選民應以「健康理念」參與選舉。

十二月四日　中華民國經濟部發言人說，由於最近發生一連串不安事件，影響外人對台灣投資的意願。

十二月三十日　中華民國教育家曾約農因病逝世，享年九十五歲。他是清代名臣曾國藩之孫。

十二月卅一日　中國國民黨主席蔣經國在國民黨中央常務委員會會議中講話，要求全體國民黨員努力追求革新，加強黨員與黨的仁義關係，做好以服務代替領導。

中華民國七十六年（一九八七）

一月一日　中華民國開國紀念日，全國同胞歡樂慶祝。

一月十六日　中共宣布，中共中央政治局召開擴大會議，會議批准胡耀邦辭去中共中央總書記職務。會議發表公報說，胡耀邦在會議上檢討他擔任黨中央總書記期間，「違反黨的集體領導原則」。

二月一日　中共宣布，中國銀行首次發行「人民幣長城信用卡」。

四月十三日　中共宣布，中國國務院總理趙紫陽，與葡萄牙國總理席爾瓦分別代表兩國政府，在北京簽訂中華人民共和國政府與葡萄牙共和國政府關於澳門問題的聯合聲明。聲明中宣布，中國政府於一九九九年十二月二十日對澳門「行使主權」。

六月廿三日　中華民國立法院會議，通過「動員戡亂國家安全法令」及「動員戡亂時期民間社團組織」兩項議案。在法案生效後，台灣及澎湖地區的「緊急命令」將予以解除。

七月十五日　中華民國政府宣布，台灣及澎湖地區的緊急命令予以解除，國家安全法令開始實施，以及外匯管制加以放寬。

八月一日　中華民國行政院宣布，行

政院設立勞工事務委員會。

九月十五日　中共政府宣布，台北市自立晚報記者李永得和徐璐，自台北經過日本抵達北京，他們是三十八年來首次到大陸採訪的台灣新聞記者。

九月廿七日　中共政府宣布，西藏自治區首府拉薩市，發生少數人遊行示威事件，其後又發生多次騷亂事件。

十月十四日　中國國民黨中央常務委員會會議，通過台灣居民赴大陸探親方案，從而結束海峽兩岸同胞中斷往來三十八年久的歷史。

十月廿五日　中共宣布，中國共產黨第十三次全國代表大會在北京開幕，出席代表一九三六人，及特邀代表六十一人。

十一月二日　中華民國紅十字會宣布，今日起開始接受希望赴大陸探親的居民的申請登記。

十一月十日　中華民國與美國代表開始舉行智慧財產權談判。

十二月三十日　中國大陸出現第一家「當舖」，名稱是「成都華茂典當服務商行」，開始營業。

中華民國七十七年（一九八八）

一月一日　中華民國政府宣布，自今年一月一日起，取消新報紙出版的登記限制，並且取消報紙每天出版張數的限制。台北市數家重要報紙開始擴充，展開激烈的競爭。

一月十一日　中華民國立法院會議通過，「動員戡亂期間集會遊行法」，其中規定三項基本原則。

一月十三日　中華民國第七任總統蔣經國，因患心臟病及內出血，於今日下午三時五十分在台北市逝世，享年七十七歲（一九一一～一九八八）。行政院宣布在三十天的國喪期間禁止示威活動。蔣經國在其父親蔣介石去世後三年即一九七八年當選總統，並於一九八四年當選連任總統，任期六年尚未屆滿。

一月十三日　中華民國總統蔣經國今天因心臟病突發逝世，享年七十七歲。中國國民黨中央常務委員會在緊急會議中決定，依據憲法規定，由副總統李登輝繼任中華民國總統。李登輝即

日宣誓就任總統。現年六十四歲的李登輝，成為出任總統的第一位台灣省籍人士。李登輝將任滿蔣經國第二屆總統剩餘的任期（蔣經國的第二屆任期自一九八四年到一九九〇年）。

三月三日　中華民國行政院經濟計劃發展委員會通過，以十一億元美金設立國際經濟合作基金，用於協助發展中的國家。

三月十日　中國北京醫科大學宣布，大陸的第一個試管嬰兒在醫科大學附屬第三醫院出生。

三月廿四日　中華民國國防部與新聞局發表聲明，重申中華民國永遠不從事發展核子武器政策，美國政府對此事加以證實。
中共政府宣布，中國人民政治協商會議第七屆全國委員會第一次會議在北京開幕，出席政協委員一千九百十五名。

三月廿五日　中共政府宣布，第七屆全國人民代表大會第一次會議在北京開幕，出席代表兩千九百七十名。

四月八日　中共政府宣布，第七屆全國人民代表大會第一次會議，

選舉楊尚昆為中華人民共和國國家主席，並且決定李鵬為國務院總理。

四月十八日　中華民國紅十字會，開始為台灣地區居民的信件轉遞到大陸各地。

四月廿八日　中華民國代表團參加亞洲開發銀行，在菲律賓首都馬尼拉召開的年度大會。

七月八日　中國國民黨第十三次全國代表大會在台北市開幕，代理國民黨主席李登輝當選為國民黨主席。李登輝在蔣經國於一月初逝世後，繼任中華民國總統並代理國民黨主席職務。

七月廿八日　中華民國行政院會議通過關於自共黨控制地區進口「出版品、電影片、電視及廣播電台節目管理辦法」。

八月十八日　中華民國行政院會議決定，設立「大陸工作小組」，為一切與大陸有關事務政策的主管機構。

八月三十日　中華民國與美國代表在華盛頓開始舉行財政金融談判。中華民國代表同意將台灣的信用卡公司市場對美國開放並同意擴大對外國銀行的信

貸。

九月五日　中華民國行政院發言人宣稱，中華民國已完成「雄風二號」長程飛彈的發展，不久將正式列入國軍裝備中。

九月七日　中共官方宣布，中國科學家在山西省太原衛星發射中心，順利發射一個試驗性氣象衛星「風雲一號」。

九月十四日　中共官方宣布，中國的核子動力潛水艇，從水下發射載運火箭的試驗已獲成功。

十月廿三日　中華民國政府宣布實施農民健康保險制度，增加農人社會福利。

十一月三日　中華民國行政院大陸工作小組修改法規，准許大陸同胞來台灣探視親屬病人或參加親屬葬禮。

十一月十七日　中華民國行政院會議通過，准許私人安裝小型碟型天線，可以收視日本的「NHK」電視台節目。

十二月一日　中華民國行政院公布，關於非官方參加在大陸舉行的國際學術會議、文化及體育活動等管理原則，以及在海外的大陸人士學生等赴台灣訪問管

理原則。

中華民國七十八年（一九八九）

一月一日　中華民國開國紀念日，各地人民歡度假期。

一月十日　中華民國與巴哈瑪共和國共同宣布建立外交關係。巴哈瑪群島位於大西洋西部，原為英國殖民地，於一九七三年獨立建立巴哈瑪共和國，為聯合王國成員之一。

一月二十日　中華民國立法院會議通過「民間團體成立辦法」。

一月廿六日　中華民國立法院會議通過中央民意機構年長代表志願退休辦法。

三月六日　中華民國總統李登輝偕夫人，搭機抵達新加坡從事為期四天的訪問，與新加坡總統李光耀等官員舉行會談。

三月廿七日　中華民國中央銀行宣布，自今年四月三日開始，取消新台幣對美元匯率浮動的限額。

四月七日　中華民國奧林匹克委員會宣布，中華民國的運動員和體育機構將以「中華台北」名義參加在大陸舉行的體育活動。

四月十五日　中共宣稱，中國共產黨中央總書記胡耀邦因病逝世，北京與全國各地群眾及高校學生舉行一系列的悼念活動。北京大學等高校學生舉行示威遊行，在天安門廣場和新華門前靜坐抗議。

四月十七日　中華民國行政院大陸工作小組通過決議，准許公立學校教師和職員赴大陸探親。

四月十八日　中華民國行政院大陸工作小組決定，准許人民前往大陸從事採訪新聞及拍攝影片。

四月廿六日　中共人民日報發表社論「必須旗幟鮮明的反對動亂」。文中指出，起於北京高校的學潮，在北京和一些地方成為「有計劃、有組織、有預謀的政治動亂」。

五月十三日　先後約有三千多名北京學生，聚集在天安門廣場開始實行絕食運動。

五月十五日　蘇聯共產黨中央委員會主席及政府總理戈巴奇夫率領代表團抵達北京訪問。

五月廿二日　中共宣布，中共中央和國務院決定，在北京市部分地區實施戒嚴。

五月廿八日　中華民國科技人員自行發展與製造的「經國號」戰鬥機，順利完成首次試飛。

五月卅一日　中華民國的學生百萬之眾舉行空前盛大的示威集會，表示支持大陸上發生的民主運動。

六月一日　中國國民黨中央委員會秘書長李煥，宣誓就任中華民國行政院院長新職。中國國民黨中央委員會秘書長由宋楚瑜繼任。

六月四日　中共宣布，六月三日晚間，「奉命向北京城內開進的各部隊先後進入市區，但在各主要路口都受到嚴重的阻攔。運送武器裝備的軍車被攔截，戰士遭襲擊，戒嚴部隊迫不得已，採取強制措施平息暴亂。在有些地段發生衝突，軍事博物館、木樨等地響起槍聲。六月四日晨五時左右，戒嚴部隊進駐天安門廣場，廣場上的學生和其他人同時撤走。」（根據人民日報登載消息）但美國電視及報紙的報導與此訊大不相同，事件真相有待將來澄清。

六月四日　中華民國總統李登輝發表聲明，嚴詞譴責中共在北京天安門廣場屠殺參加爭取民主自由運動的純潔青年學生和無辜民眾。

六月六日　中華民國行政院大陸工作小組決定，台灣居民可以直接向大陸撥發電話，並且可以直接給大陸親友寫信交郵，不再需要經紅十字會收轉。

六月十九日　中華民國行政院香港澳門工作小組宣布，政府計劃簡化香港及澳門公司遷到台灣的手續，並且協助兩地公司遷往第三國。

六月廿三日　中共宣布，中國共產黨第十三屆中央委員會第四次全體會議在北京舉行，選舉江澤民同志為中共中央總書記。全會並且通過「關於趙紫陽同志在反黨反社會主義的動亂中所犯錯誤的報告。」

七月十一日　中華民國立法院會議通過，將銀行法加以部分的修改，主要是完全廢除對銀行利率的管制制度。新法自七月十九日起生效。

七月二十日　中華民國政府宣布，中華民國與格倫納達共和國建立外交關係。格倫納達島位於大西洋加勒比海，原為英國殖民地，於一九七四年獨立建國。

九月四日　中美洲的瓜地馬拉共和國總統阿芮法洛，在台北與李登輝總統發表聯合聲明，強調加強兩國間的關係。

九月十五日　多米尼加共和國總理瑪麗·查爾斯抵達台北，開始對中華民國作六天訪問。

九月廿五日　中華民國國防部發言人說，中華民國科技人員自行發展與製造的「天弓」飛彈系統，已經正式列入防禦武器系統內。

九月廿六日　中華民國行政院宣布，中華民國與非洲的賴比瑞亞共和國恢復外交關係。

十月二日　中華民國政府宣布，中華民國與中美洲的比利齊共和國建立外交關係。比利齊原為英國殖民地「英屬宏都拉斯」，於一九八一年獨立建國。
非洲史瓦濟蘭王國國王莫斯威特三世，抵達台北，從事五天的訪問。

十二月二日　中華民國立法委員、台

灣省議會議員、台北與高雄院轄市市議員，以及各縣市議會議員選舉同時舉行投票。

十二月廿六日　中共宣布，中華人民共和國環境保護法開始實施。

中華民國七十九年（一九九〇）

一月十四日　中華民國總統李登輝與中美洲的海地共和國總統艾維爾發表聯合聲明，宣稱決加強雙邊合作關係。

一月十六日　中華民國政府宣布，低級公務人員可以前往大陸探視親友，及在一九四九年以前移居大陸的台省籍人士亦可以返台灣訪問。

二月十三日　中華民國行政院大陸工作小組決定，准許台灣的演藝人員赴大陸作商業性演出，也可以參與中共主辦的各種活動。

二月廿六日　中華民國總統李登輝與薩爾瓦多共和國總統布克德發表聯合聲明，宣稱決加強兩國的雙邊合作。

二月廿八日　是日為一九四七年台灣發生的「二二八」事變紀念日，台灣政界人士舉行私下紀念活動。

三月一日　中華民國行政院通過，准許中華民國與蘇聯及阿爾巴尼亞兩個共產黨國家之間從事直接貿易活動。

三月十七日　數千名大學生在台北市中正紀念堂廣場集會，抗議國民大會代表擴大職權。

三月廿一日　中華民國第一屆國民大會第八次會議在台北市中山堂舉行第八任總統選舉，國民黨候選人李登輝當選為中華民國第八任總統，任期六年。

三月廿二日　中華民國第一屆國民大會第八次會議，舉行副總統選舉，前教育部長李元簇當選為中華民國第八任副總統。

三月廿七日　中華民國第一屆國民大會第八次會議通過決議，規定未出席大會的國民大會代表，應於一九九〇年七月底以前退休。

四月五日　中華民國政府宣布，中華民國與非洲賴索托王國恢復外交關係。

四月八日　中華民國經濟部長陳履安與新加坡工商部長李顯龍，舉行兩國間的首次經濟合作會

議。

四月十八日　中共官方宣布，中共中央與國務院核准，上海市政府加速進行浦東地區開發計劃。

四月三十日　中華民國政府決定，各級議會民選人員，可以在休會期間赴大陸作私人訪問，在政府遷到台北以前留於大陸的退伍軍人，可以申請移居台灣。

五月十六日　中國國民黨中央常務委員會會議，同意行政院長李煥與全體閣員辭職。

五月二十日　李登輝與李元簇在總統府舉行就任總統與副總統的宣誓典禮。

李登輝宣誓就任總統，發佈特赦命令，獲特赦的政治異議人士包括許信良及施明德等人。

五月廿六日　中華民國政府宣布，中華民國與非洲幾內亞比紹共和國建立外交關係。幾內亞比紹原為葡萄牙殖民地，於一九七三年獨立建國。

五月廿九日　中華民國立法院會議通過李登輝總統提名原國防部長郝柏村為行政院長，接替李煥的職務。李煥已獲准辭職。

六月十七日　南美洲巴拉圭總統瓦斯莫抵台北訪問，與李登輝總統發表聯合聲明，宣稱將加強兩國間的雙邊關係。

六月廿一日　中華民國司法院大法官會議宣布，年邁的中央民意機構代表，必須在一九九一年十二月卅一日以前離職。

六月廿五日　中華民國政府宣布，大陸的新聞記者可以來台灣從事新聞採訪工作，中華民國的政府職員可以赴大陸探視患病的親屬或參加其葬禮。

七月四日　中華民國政府召開的國是會議，在對國會、中央及地方政府制度、憲法以及大陸政策等改革問題經過六天久的討論後，於今日宣告閉幕。

七月廿二日　中華民國政府宣布，與沙烏地阿拉伯王國斷絕外交關係，因為沙阿承認中共政權。

八月十日　中華民國政府宣布，支持聯合國要求世界各國對伊拉克實施制裁，因為伊拉克總統胡森軍隊侵略科威特。

八月卅一日　中華民國行政院長郝柏村在立法院答覆質詢時說，中華民國政府是在「一國兩區」的觀念下推行與大陸的關係。

九月一日　中華民國行政院郝柏村在立法院宣稱，政府的六年國家發展計劃的目標包括，對經濟、文化、教育及醫療等都有影響的公共建設計劃。

九月十七日　中華民國的運動員和教練約兩百人，前往大陸參加亞洲運動會的比賽，這是近二十多年來台灣的運動員首次參加在大陸舉行的比賽。

九月十九日　中華民國紅十字會與大陸紅十字會代表達成協議，訂定關於將非法進入大陸的分子遣回台灣的程序。

九月廿二日　第十一屆亞洲運動會在北京舉行開幕典禮，共有三十七個國家和地區的代表團參加。台灣的運動員首次參加在大陸舉行的運動比賽。

十月七日　中華民國政府設立「國家統一顧問委員會」，負責協助草擬國家統一政策的基本構架、及融合社會各階層對此問題的意見。

十月十一日　中華民國內政部發表聲明，重申釣魚台列島為中華民國領土。釣魚台列島包括八個無人居住的島嶼。

十月十八日　中華民國行政院設立「大陸事務委員會」負責擬訂與實施對大陸的政策。

十月廿七日　莫斯科市長波布夫抵達台北訪問，與中華民國官員討論加強蘇聯與中華民國之間的貿易關係。

十一月一日　中華民國總統李登輝，獲得其母校美國康乃爾大學頒給傑出國際校友獎狀。

十一月十五日　中華民國外交部宣布，中華民國與加拿大簽訂交換航空權協定，及中華民國將在加拿大主要城市設立經濟文化辦事處。

十一月二十日　中華民國與蘇聯的首次漁業合作會議在日本東京召開，商談有關交換技術及擴大漁區問題。

十一月廿一日　中華民國成立「海峽交流基金會」，負責處理台灣與大陸民間往來所發生的技術性事務。基金會係私人中介團體，獲得政府的財務支持。

十二月十九日　中共官方宣布，上海市證券交易所正式掛牌開業，這是中共准許大陸開辦的第一家證券交易所。

中華民國八十年（一九九一）

一月六日　中華民國與沙烏地阿拉伯兩國代表，簽署備忘錄規定在對方首都設立代表辦事處。

一月七日　法國工業部長法洛克斯來台北，參加中華民國與法國第七屆經濟合作會議。

一月卅一日　中華民國行政院會議通過大約三千零三十億美元的預算，作為六年國家發展計劃之需。

三月十四日　中華民國行政院會議通過「國家統一綱領」案，作為現今中華民國對大陸政策的最高指導原則。其遠程目標是建立一個民主、自由與平等繁榮的中國。

四月廿二日　中華民國第一屆國民大會第二次臨時會期的第六次大會，通過中華民國憲法「增添條款」，並通過廢止在「動員戡亂時期」的臨時條款。

四月三十日　中華民國總統李登輝發佈命令，宣布「動員戡亂時期」終止，自五月一日起生效。

五月九日　中華民國外交部發言人宣布，中華民國決定將蘇聯國民申請護照簽證的限制予以放寬，並且簽證申請的種類不再限於商務一項。

五月十五日　中共官方宣布，中共中央總書記江澤民應邀赴蘇聯訪問，與蘇聯總統戈巴奇夫會談。

五月廿四日　中華民國立法院會議通過，廢止「懲治共黨間諜條例」。

六月廿六日　中華民國財政部宣布，十九宗申請開辦私營銀行案中，有十五件已獲批准。

六月廿七日　中華民國新聞局長邵玉銘說，大陸新聞記者在辦理來台灣訪問申請時，不再需要宣布放棄其共產黨籍。

七月四日　中華民國與捷克斯拉夫達成協議，相互設立代表辦事處。

七月八日　中華民國與非洲的中非共和國，協議恢復兩國間的外交關係。

八月五日　中華民國總統李登輝與斐濟共和國總理麥拉宣布，兩國將於八月六日簽訂技術合作協定。

八月十二日　中國大陸的兩名新聞記

者抵達台北，這是大陸新聞界人士近四十年來首次來台灣採訪新聞。

八月十八日　中華民國副總統李元簇啟程赴中美洲三國訪問，及參加世界自由民主聯盟在哥斯達黎加首都聖荷西舉行的第廿三屆大會。他並預定訪問尼加拉瓜與宏都拉斯兩國。

九月廿五日　中華民國行政院大陸事務委員會宣布，決定設立工作小組負責打擊海峽兩岸的罪惡分子。

十月十日　中華民國雙十國慶紀念日，各地有例行慶祝活動。

十月十一日　中華民國的中華航空公司，開始飛行台北與澳洲雪梨間的直達客機航線。

十一月六日　中華民國與北歐的萊托維亞共和國，簽訂經濟合作和互設商務代表處的備忘錄。

十一月十三日　中華民國宣布參加「亞洲太平洋經濟合作組織（APEC），中國及香港亦參考此一組織。

十一月十五日　中華民國總統李登輝與南非聯邦總統柯立客，簽署聯合聲名宣稱將加強兩國間的關係。

十二月廿一日　中華民國第二屆國民大會代表舉行選舉的結果，中國國民黨候選人在總數三百廿五名代表的席次中獲得兩百五十四席。

十二月廿二日　中國大陸的民主運動人士方勵之，自美國抵達台北訪問，受到各界的歡迎。

十二月卅一日　中華民國在大陸時代選出的第一屆國民大會代表、第一屆立法院立法委員及第一屆監察院監察委員中的年邁者全部完成辦理退休。

中華民國八十一年（一九九二）

一月一日　中華民國開國紀念日，全國人民歡度假期。

一月二十日　法國對外貿易部長吉尼奈抵達台北訪問，討論法國參與中華民國六年國家發展計劃，及加強兩國經濟合作問題。

一月廿九日　中華民國與北歐的萊托維亞共同宣布，雙方協議建立總領事館級的關係。

二月四日　中華民國的公平貿易法開始生效。行政院已設立公平貿

易委員會。

二月十八日　美國總統的出口貿易委員會代表團抵達台北，與中華民國官員討論促進兩國貿易問題。

二月廿八日　中華民國與菲律賓簽訂投資保障協定，旨在保護中華民國企業界在菲國的投資。

二月廿八日　是日為一九四七年發生的「二二八」事變紀念日，台省籍的政界人士有私人紀念活動。

三月七日　尼加拉瓜總統查莫洛與李登輝總統在台北發表聯合聲明，宣稱決加強兩國的雙邊關係。

三月廿七日　中華民國與保加利亞獲致協議，實施兩國間的直接貿易業務。

四月十七日　中華民國立法院會議通過國民就業條例，將是外籍人士在中華民國就業的依據。

四月十九日　荷蘭的對外貿易部長洛歐抵達台北訪問，商討促進中、荷兩國的貿易事務。

五月十日　瑞典的交通部長奧得爾抵達台北訪問，與中華民國官員商討加強雙方合作事宜。

五月十七日　中華民國中央研究院院長吳大猷前往北京及天津參加學術會議。

五月三十日　中華民國憲法增添條款自第十一條到第十八條開始生效。

五月卅一日　中華民國大陸事務委員會決定，准許大陸居民來台灣照顧其年老或患病的親屬。

六月十日　中華民國的著作權法修正案開始生效，其中明確規定對智慧財產權的合法保護，及對侵害版權者加重處罰。

六月十九日　中華民國宣布與非洲奈及爾國恢復邦交。

七月三日　中華民國立法院會議通過民間團體組織法修正案，其中規定內政部將成立一個政黨評審委員會。

七月九日　南美洲的阿根廷共和國在台北設立商務與文化辦事處。

七月十六日　中華民國立法院會議，通過台灣地區居民與大陸地區居民關係條例。

七月十九日　美國總統布希批准，中華民國自美國租借三艘諾克斯級的炮艦，為期五年。

八月一日　中華民國行政院國家統一

委員會將「一個中國」意義定
為「一國兩區受到兩個政治實
體分別統治」。

八月一日 中華民國的台灣警備總司
令奉令撤消，另在國防部下設
立海岸巡防司令部。

八月廿三日 中華民國宣布與大韓民
國斷絕外交關係，因為南韓承
認中共政權。

八月廿五日 非洲奈及爾國總理奇方
抵台北訪問。

八月三十日 英國前首相撒切爾女士
抵達台北訪問。她發表談話表
示支持中華民國參加關稅總同
盟組織。

九月二日 加拿大國際貿易部長威爾
遜抵台北訪問，與中華民國官
員商討加強兩國貿易關係事
宜。中華民國的入出境管理處
宣布，中國大陸的「人民政治
協商會議」委員，可以申請來
台灣從事文化與學術交流活
動。

九月六日 中華民國與越南兩國間的
直達民航客機業務，在十三個
月內第二次恢復。

九月十三日 北歐的萊托維亞總理戈
德曼抵達台北訪問，預定與中

華民國簽訂投資保證協定。

九月廿一日 美國國防部宣布，美國
決定將十二架 SH-F 空降直昇
飛機售給中華民國。

九月廿九日 關稅總同盟會議通過中
華民國以觀察員地位加入關稅
總同盟，以及同意以「台灣、
澎湖、金門和馬祖特別關稅
區」名義申請加入關稅總同
盟。

十月十日 中華民國雙十國慶紀念
日，全國各地人民歡度假期。

十月十一日 中華民國總統李登輝與
巴拿馬總統安德拉簽署聯合聲
明，宣稱擴大雙邊合作事宜。

十月十二日 中華民國行政院長郝柏
村，與奧地利經濟部長舒賽爾
會談兩國經濟合作事宜。

十月廿七日 澳大利觀光部長格利菲
斯抵達台北，與中華民國官員
商談促進雙邊貿易關係事宜。

十一月七日 中華民國政府宣布金
門、馬祖、東沙與南沙地區安
全條例生效，金門與馬祖實施
三十年久的軍事管制予以解
除。

十一月九日 聖他露西亞總理康普頓
抵達中華民國訪問。聖他露西

西島位於加勒比海，原為英國殖民地，於一九六七年獨立建國。

十一月十二日　中華民國與美國國防部代表簽署協議，中華民國自美國購買 F-16A 和 F-16B 型噴射式戰鬥機一百五十架。

十一月十八日　德國副總理莫立曼與中華民國經濟部次長蕭萬長簽署協定，建立兩國間的直接民航客機業務及貿易關係。

十一月三十日　美國政府貿易代表卡爾拉抵達台北，與中華民國官員商談有關貿易問題。

十二月十九日　中華民國舉行第二屆立法委員選舉結果，中國國民黨獲得選票總數的百分之五十三點零二，民主進步黨獲得選票總額的百分之三十一點零三。

中華民國八十二年（一九九三）

一月一日　中華民國開國紀念日，全國各界歡度假期。

一月十四日　中華民國立法院通過政府一百廿四億七千萬美元的預算，自美國購買一百五十架 F-16 型噴射戰鬥機，與自法國購買六十架幻象型戰鬥機。

一月十五日　中華民國與菲律賓官員在馬尼拉簽署協定，規定將蘇必克灣的前美國海軍基地設施改建為工業公園。

二月廿六日　中國大陸的兩個籃球代表隊抵達台北，將與本地球隊進行表演賽。這是近四十年來大陸運動員與台灣運動員首次在台灣舉行比賽。

二月廿七日　中華民國立法院投票同意李登輝總統提名台灣省政府主席連戰為行政院長，接替郝柏村的院長職務。

二月廿八日　台北「二二八」事變週年紀念日，台灣省籍的政治人士舉行私下紀念活動。

三月廿一日　太平洋的島國納魯的總統杜威約哥，抵達中華民國訪問。

三月廿六日　中華民國總統李登輝對美國有線電視公司（CNN）記者發表談話說，中華民國願意與亞洲太平洋地區國家組織區域安全組織。

三月廿九日　中華民國與英國的民航公司，今日起開辦客機直達飛行業務便利公眾。

紐西蘭的觀光部長麥克柯萊率領代表團抵達台北訪問。

四月廿二日　中華民國立法院會議批准一九八九年中華民國與美國簽訂的版權協定，並且通過版權法修正案。

太平洋的東加王國總理法亞抵達台北訪問。

四月廿九日　中華民國的海峽交流基金會與大陸的海峽關係協會的雙方代表，在新加坡舉行的歷史性會議中，簽署三項協定與一項共同協議，三項協定和一項共同協議都將自今年五月廿九日起正式生效。

五月一日　中華民國在以色列特拉維夫設立的經濟貿易辦事處，今日開始正式辦公。

五月八日　中華民國的一百八十六人體育代表隊，在上海參加東亞運動會的比賽。

六月十一日　中華民國總統李登輝接見到台灣訪問的菲律賓前總統艾奎諾。

六月廿一日　中華民國與美國官員，在華盛頓簽訂田地環境保護農業合作協定。

七月八日　中華民國與中美洲的尼加拉瓜共和國簽署聯合聲明，保證雙邊合作政策。

七月十日　越南共黨政權在台北設立經濟文化辦事處。

七月十二日　中華民國在莫斯科設立的兩國經濟文化委員會，今日正式開始辦公。

八月十日　中華民國國民黨的部分黨員宣布脫離國民黨，自行組織「新黨」。他們原屬立法院的國民黨籍立委組成的「新聯線同盟」。

八月十一日　中華民國新通過的「有線電視法」，今日開始生效。

八月十六日　中國國民黨第十四次全國代表大會，在台北市陽明山舉行開幕典禮，由國民黨主席李登輝主持儀式。

八月十七日　中華民國與澳大利國代表，簽署保護工業產權備忘錄及促進投資和技術合作備忘錄。

八月十八日　中國國民黨第十四次全國代表大會，在今天的會議中選舉李登輝連任國民黨主席，並選舉副總統李元簇、前行政院長郝柏村、司法院長林洋港及行政院長連戰四人為國民黨

副主席。

九月二日　中華民國行政院會議通過行政革新方案，旨在根除政府機關中的腐敗和無效積弊。

九月廿三日　中華民國與比利時代表簽訂三項投資合作協定，以強化雙方間的經濟和技術關係。

十月廿六日　中華民國與墨西哥簽訂協定，促進投資與技術交換。

十一月十九日　中華民國經濟計劃與發展委員會的主任委員蕭萬長，代表李登輝總統參加亞洲太平洋經濟合作協會在美國西雅圖舉行的會議。

十一月廿五日　大韓民國在台北設立「韓國協會」，取代在中華民國與韓國絕交前的原韓國大使館職務。

十一月三十日　中華民國與阿根廷簽訂投資保障協定。

十二月九日　中華民國行政院新聞局宣布取消成立廣播電台的限制，並且批准十三家廣播電台成立的執照。

十二月十五日　中華民國立法院會議通過「大學法修正案」，授權各大學有較大的權力允許學生參加與校務有關的會議。

中華民國八十三年（一九九四）

一月一日　中華民國開國紀念日，全國各界歡度新年。

一月十一日　中華民國的消費者保護法正式開始生效，製造商應對使消費者受害的產品負責。

一月十二日　中華民國政府宣布，與南非洲的賴索托王國斷絕外交關係。

一月十五日　中華民國總統李登輝發佈命令，任命諾貝爾獎得主李遠哲為中央研究院長，接替吳大猷的院長職務。

二月九日　中華民國總統李登輝啟程，前往菲律賓、印度尼西亞及泰國作為期八天的訪問。

三月廿三日　中華民國立法院會議通過決議，將每年給予大陸配偶的永久居民名額，自現行的三百人增加到六百人。

三月廿五日　中華民國的海峽交流基金會代表，與大陸的海峽關係協會代表在北京舉行會議，討論漁業爭執及遣返非法入境和劫機分子。

三月廿八日　中華民國與非洲的中非共和國簽署聯合聲明，保證進一步加強兩國的關係。

四月十二日　中華民國大陸事務委員會決定，在大陸有關當局對浙江千島湖事件未提出合理與令人滿意的解釋之前，暫時停止與大陸的文化與教育交流措施。千島湖慘案發生於三月卅一日，有廿四名台灣旅客在船難事件中喪生。

五月四日　中華民國總統李登輝啟程。前往尼加拉瓜、哥斯達黎加、南非聯邦及史瓦濟蘭四國，從事為期十三天的正式訪問。

六月六日　中華民國行政院長連戰啟程赴墨西哥訪問。他是中、墨斷交廿三年來第一個中華民國高級政府官員赴墨國訪問。

七月七日　中華民國立法院會議通過省縣自治法，其中明確規定省長由人民直接選舉產生。立法院並且通過特別市（院轄市）法。台北市與高雄市為兩個特別市。

七月十三日　中美洲七國的外交部長和代表抵達台北，參加第三屆中華民國與中美洲國家聯合委員會大會，會議發表聯合聲明支持中華民國要求加入聯合國組織。

七月三十日　中華民國的海峽交流基金會與大陸的海峽關係協會雙方的代表，在台北市舉行會談。這是自今年三月卅一日發生浙江千島湖事件以來，這兩個中介組織的首次高階層會議。

八月八日　海峽交流基金會與海峽關係協會發表聯合聲明，證實兩會第二回合會談的結果。

八月九日　美國政府宣布，依據「皮萊修正案」規定對中華民國實施商務制裁措施，自一九九四年八月十九日起禁止台灣的野生物產品輸入美國。

九月七日　美國助理國務卿勞德正式通知中華民國駐美國代表丁懋時說，克林頓總統政府對台灣政策討論的結果是，美國同意將中華民國在美國的代表辦事處更名為「台北經濟文化代表辦事處」，及中華民國官員可以為公事訪問美國各政府機關辦公室，但白宮與國務院除外。

九月十九日　中華民國駐美國代表丁懋時與美國在台協會理事會主

席白樂奇，簽訂兩國貿易及投
資協定。

九月廿二日　聯合國大會總務委員會
決定，將有關中華民國進入聯
合國的建議案自大會議程中刪
除，因為總務委員會在九十分
鐘的辯論中，七票支持此案，
但有二十票加以反對。

十月十日　中華民國雙十國慶紀念
日，全國放假慶祝。

十月廿七日　中華民國立法院通過野
生物保護法。

十二月三日　中華民國舉行地方公職
人員選舉，國民黨的宋楚瑜當
選為第一任台灣省省長，民主
進步黨的陳水扁當選為台北市
長，及國民黨的吳敦義當選為
高雄市長。

十二月四日　美國交通部長皮納抵達
台北訪問，他是美國對中華民
國新政策下第一位來訪的美國
內閣級高級官員。

十二月十二日　中華民國行政院長連
戰的內閣實施改組，新閣人員
定十五日宣誓就職。

十二月廿九日　中華民國人員自行製
造的「經國式」戰鬥機的第一
個中隊，正式編入空軍服役。

中華民國八十四年（一九九五）

一月一日　中華民國開國紀念日，全
國人民歡度元旦。

一月五日　中華民國行政院通過計
劃，將使台灣發展成為亞洲太
平洋區域合作中心。

一月三十日　中國共產黨中央總書記
及國家主席江澤民在講演中提
出八點建議，促使台灣與大陸
舉行談判，以正式終結雙方間
的敵對情勢，係以鄧小平的
「一國兩制」為基礎。

二月十五日　根據中國官方統計，中
國大陸人口總數已達十二億之
眾。

二月廿八日　中華民國在台北市新公
園內建立「二二八事件紀念
碑」，李登輝總統發表談話，
對發生於一九四七年二月廿八
日的不幸事件中受難者家屬表
示歉意。這是政府當局首次對
「二二八事件」的公開紀念活
動。

三月一日　中華民國的全民健康保險
計劃正式開始實施。

三月六日　中華民國行政院的經濟計
劃與發展委員會成立亞太合作
中心的協調與服務處。

三月十一日　美國商務部長甘托爾與中國商務部長吳儀，在北京簽訂保護智慧財產權協定。

三月廿三日　中華民國立法院會議，通過「一九四七年二月廿八日意外事件受害者賠償條例」，其中規定將設立基金供處理有關事務之需，並且訂明「二二八事件」為國定紀念日。

奧林匹克各亞洲會員國的秘書長在台灣高雄舉行會議，正式成立奧林匹克亞洲會員國委員會。中國大陸為會員國之一。

四月一日　中華民國總統李登輝啟程，前往中東訪問阿拉伯聯合大公國及約旦王國。

四月八日　國家統一委員會舉行會議，李登輝總統在會中提出六點建議，作為中華民國與大陸關係的基本原則。

四月十九日　非洲馬拉威總統莫洛濟抵達台灣訪問。

五月七日　中國國家主席江澤民抵達莫斯科，參加俄國舉行的二次世界大戰德國無條件投降五十週年紀念慶祝活動，並與俄羅斯總理葉爾欽舉行會談。

五月十九日　中華民國立法院通過暫行福利條例，規定對老年農民每月發給新台幣三千元。

六月七日　中華民國總統李登輝抵達紐約，訪問其母校康乃爾大學。

六月十五日　中華民國行政院長連戰啟程赴歐洲，前往訪問奧地利、匈牙利與捷克斯拉夫三國。他是自中華民國政府於一九四九年移駐台北以來，第一位赴歐洲訪問的最高級政府官員。

六月三十日　美國政府宣布，決定取消對台灣野生物產品不准入口的「皮利修正案」禁令。

七月一日　中華民國立法院會議，通過中華民國總統與副總統選舉法，其中規定於一九九六年三月廿三日舉行總統與副總統普選投票（選民直接選舉）。

七月廿一日　中國大陸政府宣布，即日起開始對東海水域實施為期八天的地面對地面飛彈發射試驗，試射區在台灣以北約一百四十公里。

七月廿六日　美國國會議員在國會舉行盛大酒會，款待蔣夫人宋美齡女士，表揚她於第二次世界

大戰期間對同盟國所作的重大貢獻。蔣夫人在美國已居住多年。

八月十五日　中國大陸政府宣布，開始對東海水域實施為期十一天的戰術導向飛彈試射，實彈落於台灣島北方大約一百三十六公里海面。

八月十七日　中華民國監察院長陳履安宣布參加總統競選。（他於次日宣布放棄其四十二年久的國民黨籍。）

八月十九日　中華民國外交部發表聲明說，「聯合國大會一九七一年通過的第二七五八號決議案，今天應加以重新檢討」。聲明中強調，將中華民國排擠出聯合國組織的第二七五八號決議案，已經不合時宜與不公正的，應加以重新檢討。

八月廿二日　中國國民黨第十四次全國代表大會在台北市陽明山舉行開幕典禮，國民黨主席李登輝對大會宣布爭取國民黨提名參加總統競選。國民黨副主席林洋港宣布，他將以獨立候選人身分參加總統選舉。

八月卅一日　中國國民黨第十四次全國代表大會通過提名李登輝總統競選連任。他決定由行政院長連戰為副總統候選人。

九月三日　北京市舉行對日本抗戰勝利五十週年大會，中共總書記江澤民對大會發表演說。
台灣少數本省籍政界人士，受日本宣傳影響，將抗戰勝利與日本無條件投降妄稱為「終戰」。

九月七日　中華民國與新加坡簽訂協定，將合作推展人造衛星電訊合作計劃。

九月十七日　台北的故宮博物院舉行山水畫展覽，展出的七十一幅中國歷代山水畫珍貴作品，係借自巴黎羅浮宮（法國故宮）博物館的珍藏品。此項展覽將持續到明年一月十五日為止。

九月廿五日　台灣的民主進步黨在經過辦理十五週的初選投票後，通過提名前台灣大學政治學教授與長期流亡的「台獨」主張者彭明敏為民主進步黨的總統候選人。彭明敏稍後宣布立法委員謝長廷為副總統候選人。中美洲哥斯達黎加共和國副總統歐瑞莫諾抵達台北訪問。

十月十七日　中華民國與澳門當局簽訂為期五年並可延期的航空合約，規定中華民國的長榮航空公司及澳門的澳門航空公司開闢台灣與澳門間的民航客機服務。

十月廿一日　中華民國的獨立總統候選人陳履安宣布，現任監察委員王清峰為其副總統候選人。

十月廿四日　中國國家主席江澤民，在紐約參加聯合國成立五十週年慶典期間，與美國總統克林頓舉行自一九九三年以來兩人間第三次高層會談。

十一月十五日　中華民國的獨立總統候選人林洋港宣布，前行政院長郝柏村為其副總統候選人。

十一月十七日　中華民國總統李登輝派辜振甫代表他赴日本大阪市，參加亞洲太平洋經濟合作論壇會議。

十一月廿一日　中華民國與澳大利國簽署備忘錄，規定若干種貨物的免稅入口，以增加雙方間的貿易業務。

十一月廿五日　中華民國與波蘭簽訂加強經濟關係協定，以避免投資人雙重納稅及逃稅行為。

十二月二日　中華民國舉行第三屆立法院立法委員選舉投票，選出新立法委員一百六十四人。立法委員任期為四年。

中華民國八十五年（一九九六）

一月一日　中華民國開國紀念日，全國人民歡度元旦。

一月三日　中華民國宣布，中華民國與非洲塞內加爾恢復外交關係，使與中華民國有正式邦交的國家數字增加到三十一個。

一月十一日　中華民國副總統李元簇啟程赴中美洲，參加瓜地馬拉共和國新總統艾瑞哥延的就職大典。他搭機飛經美國洛杉磯轉往瓜國。

一月十六日　中華民國立法院會議通過三種電訊法律。

一月廿三日　中華民國教育部決定，選取故宮博物院的珍藏藝術品四百五十二件運往美國，在數大都市舉行為期十三個月的巡迴展覽。

二月十二日　中華民國行政院鑑於中共舉行軍事演習的威脅，特在行政院下設立臨時性的決策小組，負責密切注意情勢的發

展，並從事協調各單位的行動
適應各種情勢。

三月八日　中共軍方宣布，大陸軍隊
自本日開始，在接近台灣東北
部與西南部重要港口的水域，
舉行為期八天的地面對地面的
飛彈試射。

三月十二日　中共軍方宣布，大陸軍
隊自本日開始，在距中華民國
的金門島僅五十三公里及距澎
湖列島僅七十公里的台灣海峽
水域，舉行為期九天的海空軍
大演習。

三月十二日　美國政府宣布，美國軍
方為因應中國共產黨軍隊在台
灣海峽舉行大規模軍事演習，
駐泊於距台灣東海岸大約三百
公里海域的第七艦隊的航空母
艦「獨立」號，派出飛機從事
美國支持中華民國的揚威行
動。

三月十八日　中共軍方宣布，大陸軍
隊自本日開始，在距台灣本島
西北部僅約八十五公里的太平
洋水域，舉行為期八天的陸海
空三軍聯合大演習。

三月二十日　美國與中華民國政府官
員在華盛頓舉行軍事會議，討

論有關防衛台灣事務，美國同
意出售「斯丁格」式防空飛彈
等軍事裝備給中華民國。

三月廿三日　中華民國史上舉行首次
總統直接民選，共有四組總統
副總統候選人競爭，選民投票
的結果，中國國民黨候選人李
登輝與連戰分別當選為總統與
副總統。同時，中華民國第三
屆國民大會代表普選的結果，
選出新國民大會代表三百三十
四人。

三月廿八日　中華民國台北大眾捷運
系統木柵線高架鐵路工程，在
歷時八年久的建造後，終於全
部告成，並舉行盛大通車典
禮。

四月四日　中國大陸陝西省黃陵縣舉
行軒轅黃帝紀念大會，參加慶
典的民眾達五萬人，為空前盛
事。

四月廿九日　是日為辜振甫與汪道涵
會談三週年紀念日，中華民國
海峽交流基金會理事長辜振甫
發表談話，期盼大陸當局勿延
遲第二次辜汪會談的召開，以
使雙方能夠恢復謀求統一的商
討。

中華民國經濟部宣布，自今年七月一日開始，准許另一批共一千六百零九種的大陸工業日常用品輸入台灣。這是中華民國政府對大陸產品入口限制的一次最大幅度放寬。

五月十五日　美國政府宣布，美國決定對中華人民共和國採取多項報復性的措施，因為中國被指控侵犯美國的智慧財產權。

五月二十日　李登輝與連戰先後在總統府舉行就任中華民國總統與副總統宣誓典禮。

李登輝在就任宣誓演講中說，採取所謂「台灣獨立路線，是不必要的，也是不可能的。」他表示希望雙方以和平與寬恕來消除仇恨，並進而致力於終止海峽兩岸的敵對。他並且表示，他願意前往中國大陸作「和平之旅」。他說，為了達成兩邊交流與合作的新時代，他願意與大陸高層領導直接交換意見。

六月五日　李登輝總統任命副總統連戰兼任中華民國行政院長職務。

六月八日　中華民國立法院會議通過兼任行政院長連戰的新內閣人選。

連戰在首次記者招待會上說，中華民國並未勾消兩岸高級官員相互訪問的可能性。

六月廿八日　中華民國與白俄羅斯政府簽訂協議，相互在對方設立經濟與商務辦事處。白俄羅斯及俄羅斯等均係蘇聯解體之後成立的「獨立國家國協」的會員國。俄羅斯已與中華民國簽訂相同的協定。

六月三十日　南非聯邦外交部長尼索抵台北訪問三天。

七月四日　中華民國新選出的第三屆國民大會在台北市中山堂舉行首次會議，前外交部長錢復當選為國民大會議長。

七月十一日　南美洲巴拉圭總統瓦斯莫抵達台北訪問。

七月十五日　中美洲宏都拉斯總統瑞納抵達台北訪問。

七月十八日　北京外交部發言人發表談話，斥責日本侵略中國領土釣魚台列島，因為日本人在該列島中的一島上建造設施。

歐洲議會組織通過決議，表示支持中華民國參加國際組織的

努力。

七月廿四日　中華民國外交部向日本政府提出強烈抗議，因為日本決定將釣魚台列島包括於日本劃定的兩百海里經濟特區的範圍內。

七月廿九日　中共外交部發言人發表談話，嚴詞批評日本首相不顧抗議赴「靖國神社」參拜。

八月十二日　中華民國副總統兼行政院長連戰啟程赴中美洲，參加多明尼加共和國總統費南德茲的就任典禮。

八月十九日　中華民國副總統兼行政院長連戰，啟程赴歐洲訪問烏克蘭共和國。

八月廿四日　中華民國的代表隊，在美國賓州威廉斯堡參加世界少棒同盟的比賽中榮獲一九九六年的冠軍。

八月廿八日　中美洲薩爾瓦多共和國總統蘇爾抵台北訪問。

九月一日　中共政府宣布，新建成的全長二千五百五十二公里的北京與九龍間的鐵路，自九月一日開始正式營運。這是一條和北京與廣州間的京廣鐵路相平行的鐵路線。

九月十一日　美國宣布，將中華民國從野生物監視國家名單內刪除，這表示中華民國在保護受危害的野生物計劃上獲有進步。

九月十二日　中華民國宣布，對於有關釣魚台列島嶼日本爭執問題，中華民國採取四點立場：中華民國對釣魚台有絕對的主權、採取合理的態度、不與北京合作、及保護台灣的漁權。

十月十日　中華民國雙十國慶紀念，全國歡度國慶假期。

十月十八日　北京天文台報告說，他們在銀河以外發現一個新的「超級星」。

十一月二十日　非洲甘比亞總統查密吉抵達台北訪問。

十一月廿七日　南非共和國宣布，自一九九八年一月一日起承認中華人民共和國政府。

十二月十日　中華民國行政院成立台灣原住民事務委員會。

十二月十二日　台灣民主進步黨部分黨員，宣布退出民主進步黨另組織新政黨「台灣獨立黨」。中國香港特別行政區政府籌備委員會，認可選舉董建華為第

一任特區行政長官。

十二月十三日　中國二十世紀的著名戲劇作家曹禺（原名萬家寶）因病在北京逝世，享年八十六歲。

十二月十六日　中共政府國務院宣布，批准任命董建華為香港特別行政區第一任行政長官。

十二月十九日　中華民國政府決定，將外資投資於台灣股票市場的最高限額，自美金四億元提高到美金六億元。

十二月廿三日　中華民國行政院召開國家發展研究會，會期預定為五天。

十二月廿六日　中共政府國務院總理李鵬抵達俄羅斯京城莫斯科訪問。

十二月卅一日　中華民國台灣省政府主席宋楚瑜，向行政院長連戰提出辭職書。

中華民國八十六年（一九九七）

一月一日　中華民國開國紀念日，全國人民歡度新年。

一月七日　中華民國副總統兼行政院長連戰啟程赴中美洲，參加一月十日尼加拉瓜總統阿立曼的就職典禮。

一月十四日　中華民國副總統連戰在梵諦岡，與羅馬天主教若望保祿二世舉行會談，表示中國人民追求和平與人道的觀念。

一月十六日　中華民國副總統連戰抵達愛爾蘭，從事學術考察訪問。

二月五日　大陸新疆伊寧發生嚴重的騷亂，許多維烏爾人搗毀漢人的商店，並高呼維烏爾人「獨立」口號，地方治安當局採取鎮壓行動，造成流血事件。

二月十九日　中國共產黨元老鄧小平在北京病逝，享年九十三歲。鄧小平於一九〇四年出生於四川省公安縣，曾留學法國，一九二四年參加共產黨。

二月廿二日　中華民國立法院會議，通過「二二八事件處理與賠償條例」修正案，並規定「二二八」為「和平紀念日」國定假期。

三月十七日　蔣宋美齡女士在美國紐約慶祝一百歲華誕，許多親友從台灣前往參加祝壽活動。美國前參謀首長聯席會議主席（參謀總長）鮑威爾抵達中華

民國訪問。

三月廿二日　流亡印度的西藏精神領袖達賴喇嘛，抵達台灣訪問六天，受到熱烈的歡迎。

四月二日　美國國會眾議院議長金瑞奇抵台北訪問，與李登輝總統晤談，稱讚中華民國的政治進步與經濟成就。

李登輝總統命令公布，中華民國「與香港及澳門關係條例」，其中對香港將於今年七月一日起生效，及對澳門將於一九九九年生效。

四月廿二日　中共官方宣布，中共總書記與國家主席江澤民抵達莫斯科訪問六天。

五月五日　中華民國第三屆國民代表大會第二次會議在台北開幕，開始討論修訂憲法議案。重要議案是精簡地方政府體制、總統及國民大會代表選舉程序，以及總統與行政院長及立法院長關係的釐清等。

五月十五日　法國總統吉拉克抵達北京訪問四天。

五月十八日　中華民國外交部宣布，中華民國與巴哈瑪斷絕外交關係，因巴國承認中華人民共和國。

五月卅一日　中華民國立法院會議通過「公共電視台條例」，規定公共電視台於一九九八年開始映播節目。

六月廿一日　大陸的海峽關係協會，邀請台灣的海峽基金會理事長辜振甫赴香港，參加定六月三十日舉行的香港回歸中國的慶典。

七月一日　中華民國行政院的大陸事務委員會宣布設立香港事務局，負責處理在香港於七月一日回歸中國後中華民國與香港間的事務。

七月一日　一九九七年七月一日子夜零時開始，香港特別行政區正式成立，中國恢復對香港行使主權，英國的一百五十年的殖民統治告終，全國各地歡樂慶祝。

七月廿七日　中華民國外交部宣布，將駐高棉金邊的台北經濟文化辦事處關閉。

八月一日　中華民國司法院大法官會議裁定，當立法院會議期間有暴戾行為的立法委員，將不得享受逮捕與起訴的豁免權。

八月六日　中美洲尼加拉瓜總統萊加宇抵台北訪問五天。

八月十日　中華民國與中美洲哥斯達黎加共和國簽訂傳播合作協定。

八月十二日　中華民國與非洲的查德宣布恢復外交關係。

八月廿一日　中華民國副總統兼行政院長連戰，向李登輝總統請辭行政院長兼職。李登輝提名立法委員蕭萬長繼任行政院長職務。

八月廿六日　中國國民黨第十五次全國代表大會在台北市陽明山開幕，由黨主席李登輝主持。出席大會的黨代表兩千三百餘人。大會舉行投票結果，李登輝獲得百分之九十三的多數票，當選連任國民黨主席。大會在選出第十五屆中央委員後宣告閉幕。

八月廿八日　中國國民黨第十五屆中央委員第一次全體會議在台北市陽明山召開，全會選出中央常務委員十七人，另由黨主席李登輝指定常委十六人，共計三十三人。

九月一日　中華民國新任行政院長蕭萬長宣誓就職。他對首次記者招待會說，新內閣將致力於改善社會秩序，進一步發展經濟及使兩岸關係正常化等。

九月四日　中華民國總統李登輝啟程赴中美洲，前往參加「巴拿馬運河與巴拿馬市慶大會」，並訪問巴拿馬、尼加拉瓜及宏都拉斯三友邦。

九月十八日　中國共產黨第十五屆全國代表大會在北京開幕，通過修訂黨章案，將馬克思列寧毛澤東思想和鄧小平理論列為黨的行動方針。

九月十九日　中國共產黨第十五屆中央委員第一次全體會議，選舉江澤民為總書記及中央政治局常務委員。

十月三日　非洲史瓦濟蘭王國國王莫斯華特三世，抵達台灣訪問三天。

十月五日　中華民國副總統連戰啟程赴歐洲，前往訪問奧地利及冰島兩國，旨在加強中華民國與兩國的實質關係。

十月十五日　中華民國中央研究院院士朱棣文，榮獲一九九七年諾貝爾物理學獎。

十月廿六日　中國國家主席江澤民抵達華盛頓，從事為期兩週的訪問。他是近十二年來第一位訪問美國的中華人民共和國國家主席。

非洲查德共和國總統德貝抵台灣訪問五天。

十一月五日　非洲賴比瑞亞總統甘克偕夫人，抵達台灣訪問七天。

十一月九日　俄羅斯總統葉爾欽抵達北京訪問三天，與中國國家主席江澤民發表聯合公報，宣布兩國西部邊界的劃清與測量已告完成。

十一月十六日　中共外交部發言人宣布，大陸異議人士魏京生獲得釋放，並立即赴美國就醫。

十一月廿二日　中華民國與匈牙利簽署兩國海關合作同意書。

十一月廿五日　台灣的海峽基金會理事長辜振甫，代表中華民國總統李登輝，赴加拿大溫哥華參加亞洲太平洋經濟合作論壇會議。

十一月廿九日　台灣省舉行縣市長選舉投票結果，中國國民黨候選人在廿三個縣市中的八縣市獲勝，民主進步黨候選人獲得大捷，從上次選舉中的六個縣市增加一倍達到十二個縣市獲勝。無黨籍候選人在其餘的三個縣市告捷。

十二月一日　美國華爾街日報亞洲版，在台北市設立印刷廠生產報紙，為第一家國際大報的創舉。

十二月卅一日　中華民國政府宣布，與南非共和國斷絕外交關係。兩國於一九七六年建交。

中華民國八十七年（一九九八）

一月一日　中華民國開國紀念日，全國休假慶祝新年。中華民國副總統連戰偕夫人赴新加坡訪問，與新國高層官員討論亞洲金融風暴等問題。

一月十二日　中華民國行政院長蕭萬長抵達馬尼拉從事私人訪問。

一月二十日　中華民國行政院長蕭萬長抵達雅加達，與印尼總統蘇哈托討論可能建立亞洲太平洋經濟合作機構建議。

一月廿四日　中華民國舉行縣市議員及鄉鎮長選舉投票結果，中國國民黨候選人獲得大捷。

一月廿九日　中華民國政府宣布，與

中非共和國斷絕外交關係。

二月五日　中華民國政府實施局部改組，行政院有八個部會首長易人，其中包括內政部長及教育部長等。

二月十一日　馬來西亞副總理伊布拉漢抵達台灣訪問，與中華民國官員商談區域經濟不安問題。

二月十四日　中華民國外交部長胡志強啟程赴非洲，從事為期十二天的旅行計劃，將訪問塞內加爾、甘比亞、賴比瑞亞等七國。

三月四日　中華民國副總統連戰，於訪問約旦等中東國家後返國途中，抵達吉隆坡停留，與馬來西亞總理莫罕默德等高級官員商談亞太金融風暴問題。

三月十六日　中國新聞社（新華社）報導說，江澤民當選中華人民共和國國家主席，李鵬當選全國人民代表大會常務委員會委員長，及胡錦濤當選國家副主席。

三月十七日　中國國家主席江澤民宣布，任命朱鎔基為國務院總理，接替李鵬的職務。

三月卅一日　中國國務院總理朱鎔基

抵達倫敦，從事對英國的六天訪問。然後，他將轉往法國訪問三天。

四月三日　中華民國外交部發言人說，李登輝總統已獲提名為一九九八年諾貝爾和平獎得主。這是他在三年內第二次獲得和平獎得主提名。

四月廿一日　中美洲海地共和國總統普立發抵台北訪問四天。

四月廿二日　中華民國的海峽交流基金會代表抵達北京，與大陸的海峽關係協會代表舉行會議，安排召開第二次辜振甫與汪道涵會談事宜。兩岸的會談在一九九五年李登輝訪問美國康乃爾大學後中斷迄今。

四月廿四日　中華民國與斯洛法克共和國簽訂海關合作備忘錄。捷克斯洛法克共和國，於一九九三年分裂為捷克共和國與斯洛法克共和國。捷克仍以普拉格為首都，斯洛法克以布拉蒂斯拉為首都。

四月廿五日　中華民國行政院長蕭萬長，赴吉隆坡訪問三天，與馬來西亞官員商討加強雙邊關係及亞洲太平洋金融風暴問題。

中華民國中央銀行總裁彭淮南，赴日內瓦參加亞洲開發銀行第三十一屆董事會會議。

五月五日　中華民國副總統連戰啟程赴中美洲，參加哥斯達黎加總統羅楚圭茲的就任典禮。他的行程中並包括前往格倫納達訪問三天，也將與加勒比海地區其他數個與中華民國有邦交的島嶼國家官員會晤。

五月十一日　中華民國的三軍部隊在台灣東海岸的花蓮與台東地區，舉行本年度的陸海空軍聯合大演習。演習代號為「漢光十四號」，主旨在檢討國軍的戰備情勢與確保國家安全的能力等。

五月廿二日　南美洲的島國納魯總統克勞度瑪訪問台灣。

五月卅一日　匈牙利的商務代表尤萊克抵達台北，設立辦事處。匈牙利是繼捷克和波蘭之後，第三個在台灣成立貿易處的中歐國家。

六月十五日．非洲的紹度密島國總統曲福達抵台灣訪問。

六月廿五日　美國總統克林頓抵達北京，開始對中華人民共和國作為期九天的訪問。

六月廿七日　美國總統克林頓與中國國家主席江澤民舉行會談，會後舉行記者招待會發表談話。

六月三十日　美國總統克林頓在訪問上海時發表美國對台灣政策三大原則：「不支持台灣獨立、或兩個中國，或一個中國一個台灣」。他並且表示他不相信台灣應該成為「任何以國家為要件的組織的會員」。

七月二日　中華民國行政院長蕭萬長前往太平洋地區訪問與中華民國有雙邊關係的各國。

七月三日　中國、俄羅斯、哈薩克斯坦、塔基克斯坦和吉爾吉斯坦五國代表，在中亞的阿拉木圖舉行高階會談並發表聯合聲明。

十月九日　中華民國立法院通過重要法案，將台灣省政府降格為一個「非自治單位」，亦即一般所說的「廢省」政策，使台灣省只留虛名。

十月十日　中華民國雙十國慶節，全國休假慶祝。

十月十三日　中華民國中央研究院院士崔琦博士，榮獲一九九八年

諾貝爾物理學獎。

十月十四日　中華民國海峽交流基金會董事長辜振甫啟程赴上海，與大陸的海峽關係協會會長汪道涵舉行會談。辜氏說，五年前兩會在新加坡簽訂協議的諧和精神將獲得恢復。他在上海與汪道涵會談中當面邀請汪氏前往台灣訪問。

十月十八日　台灣海峽交流基金會董事長辜振甫，在北京拜會中共總書記江澤民。

十一月九日　美國能源部長李察遜抵達台北，參加第廿二屆經濟合作委員會會議。

中華民國與東加王國斷絕外交關係。

十一月十六日　中華民國經濟計劃與發展委員會主任委員江丙坤赴馬來西亞，代表李登輝總統出席亞洲太平洋經濟合作論壇高層會議。

十一月二十日　中華民國與太平洋的馬紹爾群島共和國發表聯合聲明，宣布兩國建立外交關係。

十一月廿二日　中國國家主席與中共總書記江澤民抵達莫斯科，開始為期四天的俄羅斯訪問計

劃。

十一月廿三日　中國國家主席江澤民，在莫斯科的醫院內與俄羅斯總統葉爾欽會談兩國有關的各項問題。

十一月廿五日　中國國家主席江澤民抵達東京，從事對日本的六天訪問。他是歷史上第一位到日本訪問的中國元首。

十二月五日　中華民國舉行第四屆立法院立法委員選舉投票的結果，中國國民黨候選人獲得大捷，贏得全部立法委員二二五席中的一二三席，民主進步黨獲得七十席，其餘的是無黨派等人士。同時，國民黨在台北市長及市議員選舉中的獲勝，但在高雄市長選舉中受挫，僅在市議員選舉中得勝。

中華民國副總統連戰率領各界人士代表團啟程赴中美洲，對遭受嚴重颶風災害的尼加拉瓜、宏都拉斯、薩爾瓦多和瓜地馬拉等友邦作慰問訪問。

十二月十七日　中國國家副主席胡錦濤抵達越南訪問。

十二月廿一日　中華民國政府開始實施重整台灣省政府機構措施，

為行政史上的一次重大改變，實際上將使台灣省名存實亡。

中華民國八十八年（一九九九）

一月一日　中華民國開國紀念日，全國休假慶祝元旦。

歐洲聯盟會員國自元旦開始使用共同貨幣「歐元」（EURO）。中國政府宣布，自一月一日起接受歐洲聯盟的新貨幣「歐元」。

一月九日　中華民國行政院長蕭萬長啟程赴中美洲，前往訪問加勒比海地區的多明尼加、海地和比利齊等友好國家。

一月十二日　中華民國立法院會議，通過廢除「出版法」，實施出版自由。

一月廿七日　中華民國與馬其頓共和國共同宣布建立外交關係。馬其頓原係南斯拉夫的一省，於一九九一年宣布獨立建國。

二月五日　馬紹爾共和國總統卡布亞抵台灣訪問一週。

二月廿八日　中國著名女作家冰心（謝婉瑩）在北京病逝，享年九十八歲。

三月七日　歐洲馬其頓共和國國會議長克立莫斯基，抵達台灣訪問六天。

三月十五日　中華人民共和國第九屆中國人民政治協商會議第二次大會，通過三項重大修訂中國憲法的決議案，決定將「鄧小平理論」納入憲法內。

三月十七日　中華民國原子能委員會決定，頒發許可證給台灣電力公司，准其興建中華民國的第四個核子發電廠。

三月廿二日　中美洲哥斯達黎加總統羅楚圭茲抵達台灣訪問六天。

三月廿九日　美國前總統卡特應私人機構之邀抵達台北訪問。因其決定承認中共政權一舉受到部分中華民國人士的批評。

四月六日　中共政府總理朱鎔基抵達華盛頓訪問八天。

四月廿四日　中華民國外交部長胡志強，抵達太平洋的馬紹爾共和國訪問三天。

四月廿五日　「法輪功」組織會員一萬多人，在北京政要區中南海外面舉行示威運動，強烈抗議政府當局的壓制行動。

四月廿八日　歐洲馬其頓共和國駐中華民國大使館正式開館辦公，

首任外交官是莫達努。

五月八日　中華人民共和國政府發表措辭強硬的聲明，抗議北大西洋公約組織飛機轟炸中國駐伯爾格萊德大使館址，表示極端的憤怒與嚴厲譴責此種野蠻行為。

五月十二日　德國總理施洛德抵達北京訪問。

五月廿七日　中華民國行政院長蕭萬長啟程赴中美洲，前往參加薩爾瓦多總統佛洛瑞的就任典禮，並將與巴拿馬及尼加拉瓜兩國總統會談。

六月一日　上海中國辭書出版社，印行「大英百科全書」國際版全套二十冊。

六月四日　北京天安門廣場民主運動屠殺事件十週年紀念會度過，未發生重大事件，但香港發生約有七萬人之眾的悼念悲劇的示威行動。

中華民國立法院會議，通過菸酒管理法，取代實行已久的菸酒專賣稅制度。

六月六日　歐洲馬其頓總統喬吉維斯抵達台灣訪問。

六月七日　中華民國總統李登輝對國際記者招待會說，中華民國將以三億美元的巴爾幹半島救濟計劃，援助科索伏的戰爭難民。

六月廿三日　中華民國與巴拿馬簽署新聞合作協議。

六月廿四日　中華民國的防止家庭暴力行為法開始生效。

七月九日　中華民國總統李登輝在對德國廣播公司記者的訪問談話中，首次宣稱中華民國與中國大陸間是一種「特殊的國與國的關係」。

中華民國與泰國簽訂交換航空權協定及避免雙重納稅協定。

七月二十日　中華民國總統李登輝發表談話，對其最近所說的海峽兩岸間是一種「特殊的國與國的關係」加以進一步的說明。他說，他的談話並非謀求「台灣獨立」，而只是重述兩岸是分別統治的。

七月廿二日　中國共產黨中央委員會及中國政府宣布說，法輪功是一個「非法組織」。

八月一日　中華民國行政院長蕭萬長率領經濟代表團，赴歐洲訪問新近建交的馬其頓共和國。

八月三十日　中華民國行政院長蕭萬長啟程中美洲，前往參加巴拿馬總統莫蘇柯的就任典禮。

九月四日　中華民國第三屆國民大會在台北市中山堂舉行會議，通過中華民國憲法修正案，將現任國民大會代表的任期自二〇〇〇年五月延長至二〇〇二年六月，並且規定第四屆國民大會代表全數一律按照政黨比例分配由總統加以任命以取代民選方式產生。

九月七日　第二屆中華民國與中美洲高階層會議在台北市召開。中華民國總統李登輝，與參加會議的七個中美洲國家領袖簽署聯合聲明，宣稱將加強合作關係。

九月九日　中華民國經濟計劃與發展委員會主任委員江丙坤，代表李登輝總統赴紐西蘭參加亞洲太平洋經濟合作論壇高階層會議。

九月廿一日　台灣遭到六十年來最大的地震災害。地震強度達芮氏地震儀的七點三級，全省各地已知有兩千多人不幸喪生，另有八千多人受到不同程度的體傷，財物損失的確實數字尚在調查中。

九月廿二日　中國共產黨中央委員會宣布，任命胡錦濤為中央軍事委員會副主席。

九月廿五日　中華民國總統李登輝發佈緊急命令，要求加速進行最近台灣大地震後的重建工作，緊急命令的效期為六個月。

十月一日　北京舉行大規模的軍事、經濟和文化展示的遊行，慶祝中華人民共和國建國五十週年國慶日。

十月十日　中華民國雙十國慶節，全國人民休假慶祝。

十月廿六日　中華民國的對外貿易委員會，在印度的孟買市設立辦事處，以促進中、印之間的商業關係。

十一月六日　台灣省雲林縣縣長補選投票結果，無黨派候選人張榮味擊敗國民黨候選人及民主進步黨候選人獲得勝利。

十一月十六日　中國國務院新聞出版總署宣布，根據中國共產黨中央委員會與國務院的授權，下令禁止政府和共黨機構發行新報紙，並且禁止現有的報紙獲

得公款的補助，這將使許多報
紙受影響。

十一月十七日　中國國民黨中央常務
委員會會議，批准中央紀律委
員會的建議，開除以獨立候選
人身份參加總統選舉的前台灣
省長宋楚瑜的中國國民黨黨
籍。

十一月二十日　太平洋納魯共和國總
統哈魯斯偕夫人抵達台灣訪
問。

十二月一日　非洲馬拉威共和國總統
莫魯齊抵台灣訪問。

十二月九日　俄羅斯總統葉爾欽抵達
北京訪問四天。這是他以俄羅
斯總統身分對中共的最後一次
訪問。

十二月十日　中華民國的主要反對派
民主進步黨的總統候選人陳水
扁宣布說，他已決定由桃園縣
長呂秀蓮擔任其副總統候選
人。總統選舉預定於二○○○
年三月舉行。

十二月二十日　中華民國總統李登
輝，接見來台灣訪問的美國國
會眾議員南茜・波洛西。

中國國家主席江澤民，在慶祝
澳門結束葡萄牙四百餘年的統

治及回歸中國的集會席間宣
稱，中國決心統一台灣並實施
「一國兩制」。同時，何厚燁
宣誓就任中國澳門特別行政區
首任行政長官。

十二月廿八日　中華民國外交部發言
人宣布，將駐澳門代表辦事處
更名為「台北經濟文化中
心」。

十二月三十日　中華民國政府宣布，
中華民國與太平洋島國帛琉建
立外交關係。帛琉原為德國殖
民地，第一次世界大戰後歸日
本統治，第二次世界大戰期間
被美軍攻佔，於一九九四年獨
立建國。

中華民國八十九年（二○○○）

一月一日　中華民國開國紀念日，全
國同胞歡度新年。

一月廿六日　中共外交部長唐家璇發
表談話，要求日本政府制止日
人企圖掩飾日本過去侵略行為
的歷史，特別是日本對一九三
七年「南京屠殺事件」的責
任。

二月廿三日　中華民國與非洲賴比瑞
亞共和國，簽署加強雙邊合作

關係的公報。

二月廿八日　是日為一九四七年台灣「二二八事件」週年紀念日，台灣省籍政界人士舉行紀念活動。

三月十八日　中華民國舉行第十任總統選舉，投票結果民主進步黨候選人陳水扁與呂秀蓮分別當選為總統和副總統，使中國國民黨失去在台灣五十年久的執政。

參加大選的三組總統與副總統候選人，民主進步黨的陳水扁、呂秀蓮獲得將近五百萬票，獨立候選人宋楚瑜和張昭雄獲得四百七十萬票，中國國民黨候選人連戰和蕭萬長獲得三百餘萬票。

三月二十日　中國國家主席江澤民發表談話，對台灣民主進步黨陳水扁當選中華民國總統一事評論說：「不論什麼人在台灣執政，我們都歡迎他來大陸，而且我們可以前往台灣。但是，對話與談判需要基礎，此即必須承認一個中國原則。在此前題下，任何事情都能夠討論。」

三月廿一日　中國國民黨主席李登輝因為國民黨在總統大選中失敗受到嚴厲批評，宣布辭職，國民黨主席職務由副主席連戰代理。

三月廿二日　美國政府代表漢彌爾頓，與中華民國總統當選人陳水扁舉行會談，就未來的雙方相關問題交換意見。

三月廿七日　維拉狄密爾・普亭當選俄羅斯總統，中國主席江澤民在電話中表示祝賀。

三月卅一日　曾以獨立候選人參加中華民國總統選舉失利的前台灣省長宋楚瑜，正式宣布組織新政黨並定名為「親民黨」，宋氏親自擔任黨主席，即由台灣籍聞人張昭雄擔任黨副主席職務。

四月十三日　大批「法輪功」會員在北京天安門廣場舉行示威，抗議共黨當局的迫害，警察加以鎮壓，有兩百多人被逮捕。

四月廿四日　中華民國第三屆國民代表大會在台北市中山堂舉行會議通過重大決議，將國民大會的職權加以削減，例如，國民大會將不再是一個常設的機

構，而只有當立法院提出彈劾
案、修憲案和國家領土改變案
時才召開國大會議。此即一般
所說的「任務性」國民大會。

五月二十日　中華民國第十任總統陳
水扁與副總統呂秀蓮，今日上
午在總統府舉行就任宣誓典
禮，由司法院大法官會議主席
翁岳生擔任監督。陳水扁和呂
秀蓮宣讀誓詞後，即由立法院
長王金平授與陳水扁「中華民
國之璽」、「榮典之璽」、
「總統之印暨總統之章」。
陳水扁總統在就職演說中宣
示，只要中國不對台灣動武，
他在四年的總統任期內，將不
會宣布台灣獨立、不更改國
號、不會推動兩國論入憲、不
會以公民投票推動統獨、也沒
有廢除國家統一綱領或國家統
一委員會的問題。此即一般所
說的「四不一沒有」的政策。
北京新華通訊社針對陳水扁總
統的就職演說，發佈中國共產
黨中央台辦和國務院台辦對當
前兩岸關係問題的聲明，全文
約兩千字。聲明指陳的宣示
「沒有誠意」。

陳水扁總統宣布任命出身空軍
的唐飛為行政院長，田弘茂為
外交部長，蔡英文為大陸事務
委員會主任委員等重要閣員人
選。新內閣當天宣誓就職。

六月九日　亞洲太平洋文化高階會議
在台北開幕，會期三天，來自
廿六個城市的市長及其他官員
參加會議。台北市政府文化局
為主辦機構。

六月十八日　五十八名偷渡的中國大
陸人，藏匿於自比利時齊布魯
港駛往英國多維爾港的冷藏貨
櫃輪船內，因為空氣調節器關
閉，全部被窒息死亡，造成一
大悲劇。

六月廿七日　中華民國新總統陳水扁
對美國一個代表團說，他接受
「一個中國」的原則，但要按
照一九九二年雙方的協議「各
自表述」。
台灣高雄市長謝長廷當選為民
主進步黨的主席。

六月三十日　大陸廣東省江門縣一家
炮竹工廠發生爆炸事件，造成
三十六人喪生和一百六十餘人
受傷的慘劇。

七月一日　中美洲巴拿馬總統莫斯柯

蘇抵達台灣訪問。

七月廿一日　中共政府宣布，決定將大陸的十家民用航空公司加以合併，改組為三個大的民航集團：中國國際航空公司、中國東方航空公司和中國南方航空公司。

八月十三日　中華民國新總統陳水扁啟程赴中美洲，前往訪問多明尼加、尼加拉瓜和哥斯達黎加三國，然後將赴非洲訪問甘比亞和查德等國。

九月一日　中華民國外交部發言人宣布，中華民國決定將駐非洲安哥拉、剛果和馬達加斯加三國的代表辦事處加以關閉。

九月廿二日　中華民國副總統呂秀蓮啟程赴中美洲，前往宏都拉斯、薩爾瓦多及瓜地馬拉訪問。

九月廿三日　新加坡政界元老李光耀抵達台北訪問四天。

十月三日　中華民國行政院長唐飛宣布辭職，陳水扁總統任命張俊雄繼任行政院長。唐飛擔任行政院長不滿半年。

十月十五日　中華民國前總統李登輝赴捷克首都普拉格，前往參加「公元兩千年論壇」會議。

十月廿七日　中華民國行政院長張俊雄宣布，行政院命令取消已建造一部分的第四核子動力發電廠計劃。

十一月十五日　中華民國中央銀行總裁彭淮南赴婆羅乃，代表陳水扁總統出席亞洲太平洋經濟合作論壇高階層會議。

十二月九日　中華民國總統陳水扁與中美洲薩爾瓦多總統皮瑞斯，在台北市簽署聯合聲明，宣稱將加強雙邊關係。

中華民國九十年（二○○一）

一月一日　中華民國開國九十年紀念，全國歡樂慶祝新年。中華民國的金門及馬祖島與大陸的廈門及福州港之間的「小三通」計劃，自元旦開始實施以便利雙方人民往來。所謂三通係指「通郵、通航、通商」。

一月八日　非洲甘比亞總統查密抵台灣訪問六天。

一月十五日　中華民國司法院大法官會議裁定，行政決定停止已建造一部分的第四核子動力發電廠一舉，有「程序上的錯

誤」。

二月六日　中華民國總統陳水扁，接見榮獲公元二〇〇〇年諾貝爾文學獎的作家高行健。

二月十四日　中華民國行政院長張俊雄宣布，行政院決定恢復進行中途停工的第四核子動力發電廠的建造工程。

二月廿五日　台灣出生的電影導演李安，以其作品「臥虎藏龍」獲得英國電影藝術學院的四項大獎即，最佳導演、最佳外國語電影、最佳音響和最佳服裝設計。

二月廿八日　台灣一九四七年「二二八事件」紀念日。

三月廿四日　中美洲多明尼加總統密吉亞抵達台灣訪問。

三月廿六日　台灣出生的電影導演李安的作品「臥虎藏龍」，榮獲美國好萊塢電影藝術學院第七十三屆奧斯卡金像獎的四項獎即，最佳外國語影片、最佳藝術導演、最佳寬螢幕攝影及最佳錄音。

三月廿九日　非洲賴比瑞亞總統泰勒抵達台灣訪問一週。

三月卅一日　流亡印度的西藏精神領袖達賴喇嘛，應中華民國佛教協會邀請，抵達台灣作為期十天的訪問。

五月十五日　中華民國行政院經濟計劃與發展委員會主任委員陳博志，在北京參加亞洲太平洋經濟合作論壇高階層會議的人力資源小組會議中，與中國國家主席江澤民會晤。

五月十六日　中華民國總統接見訪問台灣的加勒比海島國總理岡薩爾維斯。

五月廿一日　中華民國總統陳水扁啟程赴中美洲，前往訪問與中華民國友好的五個國家。

六月廿八日　中華民國外交部宣布，中華民國與巴爾幹半島的馬其頓斷絕外交關係，因其承認北京政府。

七月二日　中華民國總統陳水扁頒贈勳章給非洲賽內加爾總統華德，以酬庸其努力加強兩國間的友好關係。

七月十五日　中美洲尼加拉瓜總統阿立曼抵台灣訪問。

八月十四日　五位諾貝爾和平獎得主及數個非政府團體的代表，到台北參加二〇〇一年環球和平

大會。

十一月六日　第三十四屆棒球世界盃比賽在台北開幕，由中華民國總統陳水扁主持典禮，共有來自世界各地十六個代表隊參加比賽。

十一月十四日　中華民國第一夫人吳淑珍，在巴黎代表陳水扁總統接受國際自由協會頒發的二〇〇一年「自由獎章」。

十二月一日　中華民國第五屆立法委員選舉投票結果，執政的民主進步黨在總數二二五席的立法委員中獲得八十七席，中國國民黨獲得六十八席，親民黨獲得四十六席，台灣團結聯盟獲得十三席，其餘席次歸於數小黨和獨立人士。同時，縣市長選舉結果，在全部廿三個縣市中，民進黨及國民黨各獲九席，新黨獲得一席，獨立人士獲得二席。

十二月九日　中華民國副總統呂秀蓮，獲得在台北舉行的世界和平會議頒給「世界和平獎章」，因其對促進婦女權益與人權、民主及世界和平有貢獻。

十二月十九日　中華民國副總統呂秀蓮啟程赴非洲，前往參加甘比亞總統查密的連任就職典禮。

中華民國九十一年（二〇〇二）

一月一日　中華民國開國紀念日，全國各地休假慶祝元旦。中華民國自一月一日起，成為世界貿易組織的第一四四個會員國。

一月六日　中華民國副總統呂秀蓮啟程赴中美洲，前往參加尼加拉瓜總統吉耶爾的就任典禮，然後她將前往南美洲訪問巴拉圭三天。

一月廿一日　中華民國總統陳水扁宣布政府改組，任命民主進步黨主席游錫堃為新行政院長，接替張俊雄的職務。

三月十八日　中華民國副總統呂秀蓮啟程赴歐洲，前往匈牙利首都布達佩斯參加國際自由協會」年會。

五月卅一日　中華民國行政院通過「二〇〇八國際發展方案」，旨在使台灣變為「綠色的矽谷島」。

六月三十日　中華民國總統陳水扁啟程赴非洲作為期十天的訪問旅

行，旨在加強中華民國與馬拉威、史瓦濟蘭等四個友邦的雙邊關係。

七月一日　中華民國行政院環境保護署宣布，將實施限制使用塑膠袋和塑膠布處理辦法新政策。

七月廿一日　民主進步黨召開第十屆全國代表大會，陳水扁總統宣布兼任民進黨主席職務。

八月十四日　中華民國副總統呂秀蓮赴印尼訪問五天，從事促使台灣企業家對東南亞各國的投資。

九月十九日　陳水扁總統夫人吳淑珍到美國訪問十一天，今日在美國參議院酒會席間發表演說。

十月十日　中華民國雙十國慶紀念日，全國休假慶祝。

十月十四日　中華民國代表隊在第十四屆亞洲運動會的十六天比賽中，共獲得金牌十個、銀牌十七個及銅牌二十五個。

十月廿六日　中華民國中央研究院長李遠哲博士，代表陳水扁總統參加在墨西哥舉行的亞洲太平洋經濟合作論壇高階層會議。

十二月七日　台北及高雄舉行市長選舉，國民黨員馬英九當選連任台北市長，民主進步黨謝長廷當選高雄市長。

中華民國九十二年（二〇〇三）

一月一日　中華民國開國紀念日，全國人民休假慶新年。

一月十三日　中華民國的兩個職業棒球隊實行合併，定名為「中華民國職業棒球隊」。

一月廿六日　中華航空公司一架客機在上海浦東機場降落，接運在大陸的台灣商人返台灣度春節，這是台海兩岸首次非直航包機飛行。

四月廿三日　台北市立和平醫院七名職員發現有「薩爾斯」病徵象，這是台灣首次報導有此種嚴重呼吸器官疾病例。

七月五日　世界衛生組織宣布，世界衛生組織已將台灣從受「薩爾斯」疾病影響地區的名單中刪除，這表示台灣已無此種呼吸器官的威脅。

七月十五日　中華民國總統陳水扁的夫人吳淑珍啟程赴德國訪問，主持故宮博物院名貴藝術品的展覽會，她並將赴羅馬天主教梵諦岡訪問。

八月七日　中華民國副總統呂秀蓮啟程赴拉丁美洲訪問，前往參加南美洲巴拉圭總統佛魯特的就任典禮，然後轉往巴拿馬訪問。

八月廿一日　第四屆中華民國與中美洲國家元首高階層會議在台北召開，加勒比海的多明尼加共和國亦參加會議。

中華民國與中美洲的巴拿馬共和國，簽訂歷史上的首次自由貿易協定。

九月一日　中華民國外交部宣布，自九月一日開始頒發的新版護照封面加印英文「台灣」字樣。

十月十日　中華民國雙十國慶紀念日，全國休假慶祝。

十月十二日　中華民國外交部宣布，與非洲賴比瑞亞斷絕外交關係，因其承認北京政府。

十月十八日　中華民國中央研究院長李遠哲博士抵達曼谷，代表陳水扁總統參加亞洲太平洋經濟合作論壇高層會議。

十月廿三日　中華民國故總統蔣介石的遺孀宋美齡女士，在紐約市病逝，享壽一〇六歲。多位親友特地從台北前往參加其葬禮。

十月卅一日　中華民國總統陳水扁啟程赴中美洲訪問巴拿馬。當其過境紐約期間，接受國際人權同盟頒發給獎狀，表揚其在台灣對促進人權的貢獻。

十一月七日　中華民國外交部宣布，與太平洋島國吉瑞巴迪建立外交關係。吉瑞巴迪原為英國殖民地，於一九七五年宣布建國。

十一月十四日　號稱世界最高的摩天樓，台北市的金融中心大廈正式對公眾開放，樓高五〇八公尺，通稱「台北一〇一大廈」。

十一月廿四日　中華民國行政院宣布，提出公共工程投資擴大計劃，撥款新台幣五千億元，預計在五年期間完成「新十項重大工程」。

十一月廿八日　中華民國立法院會議，通過公民投票法，為人民對全國或地方性重大問題舉行直接投票表決提供法律基礎。

十二月廿四日　中華民國太空計劃署宣布，首次順利完成太空探險發射計劃，將「探測火箭三號

發射進入地球次軌道作科學試
驗」。

中華民國九十三年（二〇〇四）

一月一日　中華民國開國紀念日，全
國各地休假度新年。

一月十一日　台灣島第二條南北高速
公路建造完工開放交通，此公
路全長五一八公里。

一月十四日　台灣花蓮縣的楚古部落
族，獲公認為第十二種台灣原
住民。

二月十四日　中國國民黨總統候選人
連戰與民主進步黨總統候選人
陳水扁舉行電視競選辯論，開
中華民國歷史上的創舉。

二月廿八日　是日為一九四七年台灣
「二二八事件」紀念日，台省
籍政界人士發動舉行「手牽手
保護台灣運動」，表示抗議中
共的軍事威脅，參加的號稱百
萬之眾。

三月一日　中華民國派駐孟加拉迪希
首都達卡的代表辦事處正式成
立。孟加拉迪希原為巴基斯坦
的一部分，因反對受西巴基斯
坦的統治，於一九七一年宣佈
獨立建國。

三月十八日　中華民國立法院會議通
過政治獻金法。

三月十九日　在中華民國總統選舉投
票的前一天，陳水扁總統與呂
秀蓮副總統在台南市從事競選
之際遭到槍擊受傷。此即台灣
一般人所說的「兩顆子彈事
件」，一直是個懸案。

三月二十日　中華民國第十一任總統
選舉投票的結果，民主進步黨
員陳水扁當選連任總統，呂秀
蓮當選連任副總統，中國國民
黨員總統候選人連戰和親民黨
員副總統候選人宋楚瑜敗選。

三月三十日　中華民國外交部宣佈，
與加勒比海的多明尼加共和國
斷絕外交關係。

五月二十日　陳水扁和呂秀蓮在總統
府舉行宣誓典禮，分別就任中
華民國第十一任總統及副總統
職務。
陳水扁總統宣佈，任命游錫堃
繼續擔任行政院長職務。

五月廿一日　中華民國太空計劃署在
美國加利福尼亞州范登堡空軍
基地，發射「台灣二號」太空
科學研究人造衛星成功。

五月廿八日　中華民國副總統呂秀蓮

啟程赴中美洲，前往訪問薩爾瓦多、哥斯達黎加及瓜地馬拉三個友邦，旅行全程預定十四天。她在過境美國舊金山停留當中，接受「人權組織」頒贈她對台灣人權貢獻獎狀。

六月十一日　中華民國立法院會議，通過中央行政機構基本組織條例。將現有的部會加以精簡為十三個部、四個委員會及五個獨立單位。立法院會議通過勞工退休金條例。

六月十五日　中華民國政界人士宣佈成立「無黨派團結聯盟」，成為台灣的第一〇六個政黨。

七月一日　中華民國行政院設立金融監督委員會，負責監督台灣的銀行業務。

八月十三日　太平洋民主協會第二屆年會在台北市開幕，由中華民國副總統呂秀蓮主持儀式，參加的七十多位代表分別來自二十三個國家。大會發表聲明，將成立「太平洋民主聯盟」。

八月二十日　中華民國的女子射箭選手，在希臘首都雅典舉行的二〇〇四年奧林匹克運動會比賽中，榮獲銀牌獎。

八月廿三日　中華民國立法院會議，通過修改憲法決議案，將國民大會制度廢除，把國大職權訂於憲法的公民投票權內，將立法院立法委員的席次總數減少到現行數字的一半，以及將未來的立法委員選舉修改為「一個選區兩張選票」制度。

八月三十日　中華民國總統陳水扁啟程，取道美國夏威夷及西雅圖前往巴拿馬及比利齊兩國訪問。

九月一日　中華民國與大韓民國簽訂協定，將兩國間的直通民航客機業務予以恢復，雙方間的此種業務自一九九二年中斷迄今。

九月廿八日　陳水扁總統夫人吳淑珍率領的中華民國代表隊，在希臘雅典舉行的殘障人士奧林匹克運動會比賽中，榮獲兩個金牌、兩個銀牌及兩個銅牌獎。

十月十日　中華民國雙十國慶紀念日，全國各地人民休假慶祝。

十一月二十日　中華民國中央研究院長李遠哲代表陳水扁總統，參加在南美洲智利首都聖地牙哥舉行的亞洲太平洋經濟合作論

壇高階層會議。

十二月十一日　中華民國立法院立法
委員選舉投票的結果，民主進
步黨獲得立法委員總數二二五
席中的八十九席、中國國民黨
獲得七十九席、親民黨獲得三
十四席、台灣團結聯盟獲得十
二席、無黨派聯盟獲得六席、
新黨獲得一席、及獨立人士獲
得四席。本屆選舉選民投票率
低，只有百分之五十九點一
六。

十二月十四日　中華民國自行製造的
太空科學研究人造衛星「探測
四號」火箭，自台灣南部屏東
的空軍基地發射升空。

中華民國九十四年（二〇〇五）

一月一日　中華民國開國紀念日，全
國人民休假慶新年。

一月三日　中華民國與大陸交往的中
介團體海峽交流基金會董事長
辜振甫，在台北市病逝，享年
八十九歲。

一月廿七日　中華民國外交部發言人
宣佈，與加勒比海的島國格利
納達斷絕外交關係，因該國承
認北京政府。

三月十六日　在中華人民共和國於三
月十四日通過「反分裂法」之
後，中華民國總統陳水扁今日
發表包括六點的聲明，指出中
國的反分裂法「是試圖片面的
改變台灣海峽的現狀」。北京
的反分裂法授權政府「使用非
和平方式」對付台灣。

四月七日　中華民國總統陳水扁啟程
赴羅馬，前往參加天主教宗若
望保祿二世的葬禮。

五月廿三日　第五十八屆世界衛生大
會會議，通過修正「國際衛生
規則」，採納台灣謀求的「普
遍適用」原則。

六月七日　中華民國國民大會的特別
會議，通過一項憲法修訂案，
主要內容是將國民大會制度予
以廢除、將立法院立法委員席
次總數自現行的二二五席減少
到一一三席，以及在未來的立
法委員選舉中，採行「單一選
區兩票」制度。政治學者認為
「單一選區兩票制度」，不利
於小的政黨組織。

七月一日　中華民國政府宣佈，自本
年七月一日開始實施新的退休
金辦法，其中包括「個人退休

金帳戶制度」。

九月十三日　由於中華人民共和國的阻撓，聯合國大會拒絕將有關中華民國謀求進入聯合國組織的兩項建議案列入大會的議程內。此等建議係中華民國的友邦代表提出的。

十月廿五日　中華民國外交部發言人宣佈，與西非洲的賽內加爾斷絕外交關係，因為該國政府承認北京政府。

十月廿六日　中華民國立法院會議通過「國家傳播委員會組織條例」。

十一月十八日　陳水扁總統派國策顧問林信義赴南韓釜山，參加亞洲太平洋經濟合作論壇會議。

十二月三日　中華民國首次舉行「三合一」的地方公職人員選舉制度，投票選舉市長、縣長、市議員、縣議員以及鄉鎮長。但此次選舉並不包括兩個院轄市（特別市）台北市和高雄市。

中華民國九十五年（二〇〇六）

一月一日　中華民國開國紀念日，全國人民休假過新年。

一月十九日　中華民國行政院院長謝長廷宣佈辭職，內閣實施改組。陳水扁總統任命前台北縣長蘇貞昌為新的行政院長。

二月五日　中華民國行政院公佈「防止性騷擾條例」。

二月廿二日　中華民國行政院的國家傳播委員會正式成立開始辦公。

二月廿七日　中華民國總統陳水扁公開宣佈，行政院的國家統一委員會將停止作業，及國家統一綱領將停止適用。此兩決定引起相當大的爭議。

三月六日　中華民國出生的電影導演李安的新片「斷背山」，獲得美國好萊塢奧斯卡最佳導演金像獎。

三月卅一日　中華民國農業特別委員會，拒絕台北市立動物圓申請自大陸輸入大熊貓案。

四月十二日　世界貿易組織發表統計，中華民國獲列為全世界第十六位的最大貿易國家。

五月四日　中華民國總統陳水扁啟程赴拉丁美洲，前往訪問哥斯達黎加和巴拉圭兩個友邦。

五月十六日　美國的企業投資環境危險情報協會提出的首次調查報

告中說，中華民國的投資環境危險性頗低。

五月二十日　中華民國政府發表有史以來的第一次國家安全報告書。

五月廿二日　世界衛生組織決定，拒絕將中華民國申請作為世界衛生大會的議程內。世界衛生大會為世界衛生組織的程序決定機構。

七月二十日　中華民國國防部在台灣東部宜蘭縣境內舉行「漢光二號」軍事演習。此次軍事演習規模之大和參與演習部隊人數之多，皆為過去歷次軍事演習所不及。

七月廿八日　中華民國政府召開長期經濟發展會議，討論政府的工作效率、海峽兩岸的經濟情勢及貿易關係等課題。

八月五日　中華民國外交部宣佈，中華民國與非洲的查德斷絕外交關係，因該國承認北京政府。

八月廿九日　中華民國國防部在二〇〇六年的國防報告中，首次證實自一九九六年以來，大陸的人民解放軍時常侵犯中華民國的領空與領水。

九月三日　中華民國總統陳水扁啟程赴太平洋的帛琉共和國，出席第一屆中華民國與太平洋友邦的高階層會議，與帛琉、馬紹爾群島、諾魯、所羅門群島等國的領袖會談。

九月六日　中華民國行政院會議通過決議，將位於桃園的中正國際機場改名為「台灣桃園國際機場」。

九月十二日　聯合國第六十一屆大會在紐約市開幕，中華民國的友邦向大會提出兩項建議，一項是關於區域和平案，另一項是關於中華民國進入聯合國案。但是，此兩項提案都未被列入聯大議程內。

九月十四日　一名老年男子赴廣東探親途中心臟病突發，由飛機運回台北醫治。這是大陸與台灣之間的首次醫護包機飛行。

十一月十五日　美國國會圖書館宣佈，中華民國中央研究院院士余英時，為二〇〇六年「約翰·克洛吉人文研究」終身成就獎獲獎人之一。

十一月十七日　台灣半導體公司董事長張忠謀，代表陳水扁總統出

席在越南河內市舉行的亞洲太平洋經濟合作論壇高階層會議。

十二月七日　中華民國的棒球代表隊，在東京的亞洲運動會比賽中擊敗日本的代表隊，榮獲金牌獎。

十二月九日　台北市與高雄市舉行市長及市議會議員選舉投票的結果，台北市方面國民黨候選人郝龍斌擊敗民主進步黨候選人謝長廷及親民黨候選人宋楚瑜，當選台北市長。高雄市方面，民主進步黨候選人陳菊擊敗國民黨候選人黃俊英，當選高雄市長。

十二月十三日　中華民國行政院長蘇貞昌啟程赴非洲，前往參加甘比亞總統查密的就任典禮。

十二月廿四日　中華民國交通部宣佈，批准台灣高速鐵路火車正式開始營運。高速鐵路北端起自板橋，南端以左營為終點。

中華民國九十六年（二〇〇七）

一月一日　中華民國開國紀念日，全國各地休假慶元旦。

三月三日　香港文匯報報導說，福建省已啟動台灣海峽海底隧道項目，並且進入前期準備階段。福建省長黃小晶邀請近百位專家學者，為海峽兩岸經濟區的發展建設建言獻策。報導說，台海隧道的建設方案也由兩岸專家經過多年研討論證，提出三條路線即，北線從平潭至台灣新竹，長約一二五公里；中線從蒲田至台灣中部，長約一三〇公里；南線從廈門經金門、澎湖至台灣嘉義，總長約一七〇公里。

四月二十日　中國國家主席胡錦濤與美國總統布希在華盛頓舉行會談後發表聲明，誓言合作減少兩國間貿易的差額及遏阻核子武力的擴散等，但並未宣佈任何協議。胡錦濤的華府訪問之行，因美國方面的禮儀誤失而留下小污點。

七月四日　中國大陸東北遼寧省一家卡拉歐克酒吧發生爆炸事件，顧客多為大學青年人，至少有二十五人不幸喪生。

七月三十日　北京新華通訊社說，大陸南方地區近數週內暴雨成災，已有大約六百五十人不幸

死亡。

八月一日　美國玩具製造商麥特爾公司宣佈，將多達九六七、○○○件中國大陸製造的兒童玩具自市場收回，因為它們含有鉛質的油漆。

九月二日　中國政府宣佈，中國將發表龐大的軍事預算資料，並且將恢復中國出售普通武器的資料送給聯合國組織。中國政府自一九九六年迄今一直停止將此資料提供給聯合國。

九月十六日　中國政府發表聲明，嚴詞斥責台灣人民舉行群眾大會，支持陳水扁總統要求台灣加入聯合國的政策。北京警告說，中國現在準備應付此種「嚴重情勢」。但聲明中並未說明什麼造成「嚴重情勢」。不過，中共長期以來一直威脅說，如果台灣宣佈「正式獨立或者無限期拖延與大陸的統一」，北京將對台灣採取軍事行動。

台灣各地約有十萬人舉行街頭示威，支持陳水扁總統要求舉行關於台灣進入聯合國的公民投票。

中國政府的聲明中，並未提及中國國民黨提名的總統候選人馬英九支持的另一項台灣人民的集會。國民黨人士舉行的民眾大會也要求台灣進入聯合國組織，所不同的是，陳水扁派的大會要求以「台灣」名義加入聯合國，而國民黨人士的大會則要求以「中華民國」名義重返聯合國組織。（按中華民國係於一九七二年十月廿六日宣佈退出聯合國，因聯合國大會通過准許中華人民共和國加入聯合國組織。）（根據美國美聯社記者克利斯多夫·包定自北京發出的電訊）

十月十二日　北京的官方新聞社報導說，中國當局對環境損害情勢表示關切，尤其是長江三峽大壩附近地區的坍方危險，已經草擬計劃準備將多達四百萬人的居民遷往其他地區安置。

十月廿四日　中國太空計劃當局宣佈，「嫦娥一號」人造衛星發射成功，進入環繞地球軌道，從事為期一年的月球科學研究探險。這是中國的首次月球探險計劃。

十一月廿一日　中國軍事官員說，中國海軍的軍艦「深圳」號駛往日本訪問，將參加日本海軍的一次典禮。這是自第二次世界大戰結束以來，中國海軍艦隻第一次訪問日本。

十二月廿九日　北京政府官員說，香港特區行政長官第一次普選將予延期到二〇一七年舉行。以前一般曾預料香港特首普選可能在二〇一二年舉行。

中華民國九十七年（二〇〇八）

一月一日　中華民國開國紀念日，全國休假慶祝新年。

一月二日　紐約市場原油價格飛升，漲到每桶一百美元，創下空前高的紀錄，各地汽油普遍漲價。

一月十二日　中華民國第七屆立法委員選舉及兩項公民投票案舉行投票的結果，國民黨派候選人在立法院總席次一百十三席中，共獲得八十一席，超過三分之二多數，取得立法院的主導權，贏得壓倒性的勝利。執政的民主進步黨僅獲得二十七席，遠低於選前預期的三十八

席立法委員。其他政黨方面，親民黨獲得一席，無黨聯盟獲三席，獨立人士獲得一席。關於兩項公民投票案即「反對貪污腐敗」和「討回國民黨黨產」，因為領票的選民人數未達到合格選民總人數的二分之一，均告失敗。

一月廿一日　中國大陸北部山西省境的一處已經關閉的煤礦場，當工人正在進行重開一個礦坑之際，突然發生爆炸事件，至少有二十名礦工不幸喪生。

二月一日　日本政府官員說，至少有一七五名日本人在吃了自中國大陸進口的水餃後生病，因為大陸水餃受到殺蟲劑的污染。

三月十日　印度有關當局在達姆沙拉市附近，阻止數百名西藏人的示威行動。他們發動為期六個月的「西藏行軍」，抗議中國主辦奧林匹克運動會。

三月十一日　中國政府宣佈改革政府機構方案，將成立若干個新部，負責監督環境保護、社會服務、房屋建造、工業及新聞等事務。

三月十八日　新聞報導說，在最近數

天內，西藏首府拉薩發生喇嘛示威活動，抗議中國政府在西藏的統治措施。當地居民與公安部隊發生衝突。

三月二十日　美國美聯社記者自北京報導說，中國警察在西藏境內的偏遠市鎮加強控制，以圖恢復對西藏的控制，因為藏人發動反對中國的統治措施。中共官方的新華通訊社首次報導說，藏人的抗議行動已蔓延到相鄰的甘肅及四川省境。

北京的奧林匹克委員會高級官員說，西藏的不安將不影響今夏奧林匹克運動火炬隊行進到北京的計劃，火炬隊行程中包括經過西藏境內。

新華社報導說，與上週拉薩暴亂有關的約一百七十人已向當局降服。在事件中共有三百廿五人受傷，北京說有十六人死亡，但是西藏流亡團體說，有八十人喪生。

雖然中國當局加強鎮壓，但西藏人民仍到街頭示威，要求西藏獨立與要求他們的精神領袖達賴喇嘛返回西藏。

許多國家的奧林匹克委員會發表聲明反對抵制奧運的行動，但是有些運動員則表示關切此種抵制活動。

三月廿二日　中華民國第十二任行憲總統、副總統選舉投票結果，中國國民黨提名的候選人馬英九與蕭萬長，以超過二二○萬票的壓倒性多數，擊敗民主進步黨候選人謝長廷與蘇貞昌，分別當選為第十二任總統及副總統。此次大選完成台灣的第二次政黨輪替，也使國民黨在野八年後，恢復執政黨地位，為國民黨與泛藍集團人士帶來歡欣與鼓勵。至於由民進黨及國民黨分別提出的「加入聯合國」和「重返聯合國」的公民投票案，因為得票比例都未達法定數字，兩案皆告失敗。

在一七三二萬合格選民中，有一千三百多萬人參加投票，投票率高達百分之七十六。截至台灣時間深夜為止，馬、蕭共獲得七百五十餘萬票，得票率為百分之五十八點六七；謝、蘇共獲得五百三十多萬票，得票率為百分之四十一點四七。美國總統布希發表聲明，祝賀

馬英九當選總統，並希望兩岸利用此機會，尋求對話、溝通與接觸。

總統選舉結果揭曉，民主進步黨失敗，黨內檢討之聲不絕於耳。民進黨立法委員李俊毅說，民進黨可能重回過去的抗爭路線，明年底的縣市長選舉可能是重新出發的契機。

北京中國官方對台灣選舉的結果，當天尚無任何表示。

（根據美國世界日報刊載的消息）

三月三十日　西藏精神領袖釋迦比丘十四世達賴喇嘛丹增嘉措，通過新聞界發表對世界華人的聲明，特別說明：「為了扭轉目前這一情勢繼續惡化的局勢，我已向中國領導人表達了為實現和平與穩定而共同配合的意願。」

四月六日　當北京奧林匹克運動火炬傳遞隊在英國倫敦停留之際，支持西藏的抗議人士因企圖搶奪或者撲滅火炬而與警察發生衝突，有數人受傷。

北京中國政府官方表示，願意與西藏的達賴喇嘛舉行西藏問題的新商談。

四月十日　中國國務院總理溫家寶，在北京接見國際奧林匹克委員會主席羅格特明確表示，奧運火炬是和平、友誼、進步和光明的象徵。他堅信屬於全人類的奧運火炬不會熄滅。

四月十三日　中國共產黨中央總書記胡錦濤，在海南島博鰲舉行的「亞洲博鰲論壇」會議中，接見中華民國新當選的副總統、海峽兩岸共同市場基金會董事長蕭萬長。蕭萬長當面提出兩岸直航、大陸遊客赴台灣、經貿關係正常化、恢復兩岸協商機制等「四個希望」。胡錦濤也以「四個繼續」作為善意回應。雙方各派出十三人出席會談，時間約二十分鐘。會後，胡錦濤並請蕭萬長代他問候馬英九、連戰和吳伯雄三位。

胡蕭會談後，由「兩岸共同市場基金會與中國國台辦」聯合發佈新聞稿，北京新華通訊社及中央電視台都加以報導。中國外交部發言人提到蕭萬長是以兩岸共同市場基金會董事長身份而非其「政治身份」與胡

錦濤舉行會談。

四月十四日　正在美國訪問的達賴喇嘛在西雅圖說，雖然北京繼續批評達賴喇嘛集團在幕後指使拉薩的西藏人騷亂活動，他的特使最近仍在北京與中國官員進行交涉。

四月二十日　少數中國示威人士，在法國駐北京大使館外面抗議法國支持西藏人要求獨立，及責斥法國人在巴黎試圖奪取一名殘障的中國女運動員的奧林匹克火炬。

在中國大陸其他數個城市，亦有數百名抗議分子，聚集在法國人經營的卡利夫超級市場外面，揮動著中國國旗要求人民抵制法國人的生意。

據洛杉磯市警方說，約有兩千多名華裔美國公民，二十日聚集在好萊塢的有線電視公司辦公處外面抗議，要求該公司開除其評論員傑克·卡菲特，因為卡菲特月初指稱中國貨物為「假貨爛貨」，及中國的領袖是一批「笨蛋、無賴」。

四月廿二日　中國大陸最新的重大建設「杭州灣跨海大橋」業已完工，並定於五月一日正式開放交通。跨海大橋全長三十六公里，全線為雙向六車道，時速一百公里。開放通車後，從江蘇省的上海到浙江省的寧波，不需再繞道杭州，將現在的全程三百公里縮短到一百八十公里，從南岸的寧波慈溪到北岸的乍浦，中途不停只需二十分鐘的時間，使兩者間的往來極為方便。

五月六日　在台灣貪污腐敗案件頻傳聲中，又傳出有政府基金三千萬美元「被盜竊」事件，導致中華民國外交部長黃志成下台。據報導，這筆基金是陳水扁總統政府原擬給予太平洋的島國巴布新幾內亞，換取該國與北京政府斷交而承認中華民國政府。

五月十二日　北京消息，大陸四川省汶川縣十二日下午二時廿八分發生強達七點九級的大地震（中國地震局發佈為七點八級，美國聯邦地質研究所測出為七點九級）。地震威力相當於四百個原子炸彈，使北京、上海、大陸十九個省市、香

港、澳門及台灣等地都感到不同程度的震動。

據中國民政部統計，截至北京時間十三日清晨為止，四川、甘肅、陝西、重慶、雲南等地已有七千多人喪生，房屋倒塌五十餘萬間，各種財物損失情形尚待清查。汶川大地震是自一九七六年河北唐山大地震以來大陸地區規模最大的一次震災。

五月十九日　為表達對四川大地震遇難同胞的深切哀悼，中國各地自十九日開始三天的全國哀悼日。北京奧林匹克委員會也宣佈，在地震哀悼期間，奧運聖火的傳遞暫停三天。

中國國務院宣佈，從五月十九日至廿一日為全國哀悼日，十九日下午二時廿八分，即汶川大地震發生整整一週之際，全國十三億人民一致默哀三分鐘。屆時汽車、火車、艦船鳴笛，防空警報長鳴致哀，全國各機關一律下半旗致哀。

同時，中國的救災工作正積極進行中。外國的援助物資也開始運抵四川。美國空軍的兩架巨型運輸機，載運的賑濟物資十八日已飛抵四川省會成都。中國國家地震局宣佈，將汶川大地震的強度從原本的七點八級修正為八級。

五月二十日　中華民國行憲第十二任總統馬英九與副總統蕭萬長在台北市總統府宣誓就任，美國舊金山的英文紀事報刊登台北的電訊報導說：「哈佛大學畢業生馬英九，今天宣誓就任台灣的總統，他承諾謀求與敵對的中國有較大的經濟合作，及終結將近六十年之久的緊張情勢。」

「現年五十七歲的馬英九就任總統，正式改變了陳水扁八年總統的情勢。陳水扁的對抗性的親獨立政策，時常導致與北京及台灣最重要的外國夥伴美國間的摩擦。現年六十九歲的副總統蕭萬長，在馬英九舉行宣誓後不久亦宣誓就任。」

五月廿八日　中國共產黨中央總書記胡錦濤與中國國民黨主席吳伯雄，在北京舉行「胡吳會」，雙方同意在「九二共識」下，盡速恢復台灣海峽交流基金會

與大陸海峽關係協會的會談。胡錦濤並且提到，「促進恢復兩岸協商後，討論台灣民眾關心的參與國際活動的問題，包括優先討論參與世界衛生組織活動，至於週末包機與大陸觀光客赴台灣，胡錦濤允諾「最短時間內辦成辦好」。

吳伯雄在會談中，首先提議舉辦國共「兩岸和平論壇」。在海基和海協兩會領導人互訪方面，吳伯雄當面提出邀請，希望大陸海峽協會會長在適當時機訪問台灣，胡錦濤也回應說，在雙方方便的時候，進行兩會領導人互訪。

在胡錦濤與吳伯雄達成盡速恢復兩岸協商共識後，北京當局立即採取具體行動，由中共新華社發佈消息說，大陸海峽關係協會已致電邀請台灣海峽基金會組團，於六月十一日前往北京，就兩岸週末包機、大陸居民赴台灣旅遊等事宜進行商談。

五月三十日　中國官方消息證實說，大陸四川省汶川大地震死亡人數為六萬八千五百人，另有一萬九千人失蹤或者已喪生。

八月廿七日　俄羅斯宣佈稱讚喬治亞共和國的兩個地區宣佈獨立，它們是親俄的南奧斯蒂亞與阿布加西亞。這與俄軍入侵喬治亞半月來的重大發展，受到國際的重視。

九月十五日　美國李曼兄弟投資銀行宣告破產的重大事件及美林證券公司被美國銀行購併行動，使全球股票市場受到嚴重影響，美國華爾街股市崩盤，全球震盪，道瓊斯指數大跌五〇四點，為「九一一」事件以來最大的單日跌幅。各國中央銀行聯手為市場挹注數百億美元資金，以防此次危機引發全球金融體系瓦解。

台灣方面也遭受嚴重打擊，台灣股市狂跌二九五‧八六點，正式跌破六〇〇〇點大關，新台幣對美金匯率貶到三十二元二角。

九月十八日　涉入洗錢案的前總統陳水扁赴台灣各地接受電台訪問，訴求遭受司法迫害。馬英九總統說，司法尚未定罪前，確實無法限制涉嫌人的相關言

行，但社會自有公道。這是五月二十日迄今，馬英九和陳水扁少見的交鋒。陳水扁在嘉義市的電台節目中，強力辯護沒有貪污、介入軍火買賣及拿人事紅包等。馬英九承認不少南部民眾質疑他一手主導偵辦洗錢案，甚至有「追殺、清算」的字眼。

九月二十日　美國聯邦政府宣佈數字達萬億元的大規模金融紓困方案，財政部長鮑森與聯邦儲備會主席柏南基共同努力挽救瀕臨崩潰的金融市場，重大措施中包括承接房屋貸款壞帳、收購不良資產、擔保貨幣基金等項目。布希總統在白宮發表針對經濟危機的演說，表達力挽狂瀾的決心。

北京新華通訊社報導說，中國共產黨中央總書記、國家主席胡錦濤在中共中央黨校專題研究班開班儀式中，痛斥官員對群眾的呼應和疾苦置若罔聞，對群眾的生命安全某重大問題麻木不仁。近來中國大陸先後發生堤壩潰決事件和有毒奶粉事件，造成人民傷亡，人心恐慌情勢，因此已導致山西省長和河北石家莊市長等官員下台的事件。胡錦濤警告說，對這些事件及其後果的嚴重性，政府當局必須加以充分的估計，對其中的慘痛教訓必須牢牢記取。他特別指出，中國的執政能力與新形勢、新任務的要求還不完全適應。

十月廿一日　中國大陸海峽關係協會副會長張銘清，首次到台灣參加學術研討會的日程中，於廿一日上午在台南市參觀孔廟之際，遭受民主進步黨籍台南市市議員王定宇及群眾圍堵、抗議，雙方拉扯中，張銘清被推倒，後腦挨重拳，眼鏡掉落，衣服沾滿泥土。在混亂中，張銘清被隨行人員護送上車，但抗議民眾仍包圍座車，有一人還跳上車頂猛踹，僵持數分鐘後，張的座車才脫離群眾駛去。

大陸方面，國台辦及海協會都表示感到非常驚訝，也關心張銘清的情況。

至於此事件是否會影響大陸海協會會長陳雲林將訪問台北的

計劃,台灣海峽基金會秘書長高孔廉表示,陳雲林來台計劃「不會受此事件的影響」。

台灣民主進步黨女主席蔡英文說,「若事件的責任是在民進黨」,她會感到遺憾,也會下令黨員,在處理群眾事件時,應該注意基本問題。

十一月三日　中國大陸海峽關係協會會長陳雲林,率領六十人的代表團,於三日搭乘專機自大陸直接飛抵台灣參加兩岸的會談。陳雲林一行搭乘大陸中國國際航空公司的專機,於上午十一時四十五分降落台灣桃園縣的中正國際機場,在十一時五十八分踏出機門。這是台灣與大陸分裂六十年來,大陸政府正式授權的最高級代表首次踏上台灣省的土地。很多很多六十年前從大陸到台灣的人,對這件事有很多很多的感觸。陳雲林一行在機場受到台灣海峽基金會秘書長高孔廉的歡迎。稍後,陳等搭乘轎車在四輛警車前導下駛往台北市圓山大飯店,台灣海峽基金會董事長江丙坤在場等候歡迎。江丙

坤代表海基會致詞歡迎大陸客人。陳雲林在致詞時強調,他此次會談不會涉及兩岸政治問題,更不會涉及台灣島內任何政治問題。

民主進步黨主席蔡英文談話說,政府強力壓制抗議活動,將升高發生衝突的可能性,「民進黨要警告馬政府,如果阻撓民眾抗議,造成民眾損傷,民進黨絕不袖手旁觀,一定要馬政府付出嚴重的代價。」

十一月四日　美國總統選舉投票結果,民主黨候選人歐巴馬擊敗共和黨候選人馬侃,當選美國第四十四任總統,白登當選副總統。現年四十七歲的歐巴馬,成為美利堅合眾國史上第一個非洲黑人裔的總統。

美國大選投票的非正式結果為,歐巴馬獲得三四九張選舉人票,馬侃獲得一六三張選舉人票。歐巴馬獲得選票總數的百分之五十二,馬侃獲得百分之四十七。

美國國會選舉結果,民主黨也獲得勝利,聯邦參議院一百席

議員中，民主黨佔五十五席，眾議院議員民主黨佔二六一席，共和黨佔一七四席，國會兩院都控制在民主黨手裡。

州長選舉結果，共和黨員當選廿七位州長，較前減少一名，民主黨員當選廿三位州長，較前增加一名。

十一月六日　台灣海峽兩岸首次高階層的會晤，於六日上午十一時在台北市的台北賓館舉行，歷時只有短短的十分鐘，事先一般人關心的所謂「頭銜稱謂」問題並未發生。在雙方的會晤中，中華民國總統馬英九稱中華人民共和國台灣海峽關係協會會長陳雲林為「陳會長」，陳雲林將一幅國畫駿馬圖贈給馬英九時說了句「送給您」。（台方原希望聽到「馬總統」三字，大感失望。）

馬、陳會晤原預定六日下午四時三十分舉行，但民主進步黨人們於五日夜間抗議陳雲林出席在晶華酒店舉行的晚宴，引起暴力衝突，馬英九六日上午突然宣佈陳、馬會提前於上午十一時舉行，此舉激起民進黨人的更大憤怒，民進黨女主席蔡英文立即宣佈抗議「圍城計劃」亦提前啟動。台北市警察局出動警員三千人，在台北賓館附近地區戒備。正午時分，民眾與警察開始有爭打衝突，而且緊張情勢不斷升高。示威群眾亂擲石塊，叫喊不絕於耳。在數小時久的警民對峙中，警察有多人受傷，民眾亦有多人受傷。其後，抗議人群隊伍向信義路方向進行，到下午四時過後市中心情形逐漸恢復常態。

十一月七日　中國大陸的海峽關係協會會長陳雲林夫婦在結束台灣的五天不平安訪問後，於七日上午十時，自桃園中正國際機場搭乘中華航空公司的包機直飛北京首都機場，在下午一時五十分抵達北京。

在啟程前，台灣海峽基金會董事長江丙坤，在圓山飯店為陳雲林舉行歡送儀式。江致詞說，過去四天雙方簽署四項協議，並且舉辦兩次有關兩岸未來關係的座談會。陳雲林與江丙坤互道「來日方長」，然後

大陸客人前往機場歸去。

北京新華社報導說，陳雲林返抵北京機場時說，這次到台灣確實有干擾，但兩岸在和平發展道路上不斷向前進行，將有惠於台灣人民，是歷史發展的必然，所以他堅信公道自在人心。

十一月十二日　美國紐約時報刊載該報駐上海記者大偉·巴保薩的電訊報導說：台灣的前總統與熱心主張台灣獨立的陳水扁，在檢察官對他提出貪污及洗錢控告案謀求正式逮捕後，於十二日晚間被警方拘禁。陳水扁做了兩屆的總統，在今年三月的選舉後下台。下午，他在台北地方法院，就其政府貪污醜聞案接受檢察官數小時久的偵訊後，被警察戴上手銬押往看守所。

陳水扁將雙手鎖著的臂膀高舉過頭頂，讓電視拍照並喊著「台灣萬歲」及「政治迫害」。陳水扁否認他有錯誤行為，並且指稱是其繼任者馬英九總統與國民黨政府的政治性攻擊。但是，國民黨官員堅稱，他們並未影響陳案中的檢察官。

陳水扁被拘禁，是台灣的國民黨與民主進步黨數年來一連串政治戲劇中最新的一章。他是台灣的最具爭議的政界人物，於二〇〇〇年當選總統並且連任一屆。

十二月十五日　在中國共產黨元老與中華人民共和國全國人民代表大會常務委員會委員長葉劍英，於一九八一年九月三十日向中華民國提出九條和平建議（其中第二條為共同努力實現所謂三通即通郵、通航、通商）經過廿七年後，中國大陸與台灣省之間的通郵、通商、通航計劃於二〇〇八年十二月十五日終於獲得實現。台灣的報紙說，國民黨籍總統馬英九選前曾說「一年內協商完成三通」。十五日開始的三通在台灣稱為「大三通」，因為金門與廈門之間業已有了「小三通」。

三通第一天的活動是：海運方面，台灣有六艘商輪分別自基隆、高雄、台中開往上海、天

津、廈門等地。大陸的中遠公司的商輪自天津開往高雄。空運方面，中國東方航空公司的客機自上海直飛桃園機場，台灣復興航空公司的客機自台北直飛上海浦東機場。通郵方面，台北到上海的郵件，自原需的五天到七天，現縮短至一天到兩天。

（註：葉劍英提出的九條和平建議原文如次：一、舉行國共兩黨對等談判，實行第三次合作，共同完成祖國統一。雙方可先派人接觸交換意見。

二、雙方共同為實現通郵、通商、通航、探親、旅遊以及開展學術、文化、體育交流提供方便達成協議。

三、國家實現統一後，台灣可作為特別行政區，享有高度的自治權，保留軍隊，中央政府不干涉台灣地方事務。

四、台灣現行社會、經濟制度不變，生活方式不變，私人權益受到保護，外國投資不受侵犯。

五、台灣當局和各界人士的代表可以擔任全國性政治機構的領導職務，參與國家管理。

六、台灣地方財政遇有困難時，可由中央政府酌情補助。

七、台灣各族人民、各界人士願回祖國大陸定居者，保證妥善安排，不受歧視，來去自由。

八、歡迎台灣工商界人士回祖國大陸投資、興辦各種經濟事業，並保證其合法權益和利潤。

九、統一祖國人人有責，熱誠歡迎台灣各族人民、各界人士、各民眾團體通過各種渠道，採取各種方式提供建議，共商國是。）

十二月卅一日　中國共產黨總書記與中國國家主席胡錦濤，於十二月卅一日上午在北京人民大會堂舉行的中共「告台灣同胞書」發表三十週年紀念會中，提出進一步發展台灣海峽兩岸關係的六項意見：

一、恪守一個中國、增進政治互信；

二、推進經濟合作、促進共同發展；

三、弘揚中華文化、加強精神

地帶；

四、加強人員往來、擴大各界交流；

五、維護國家主權、協商對外事務；

六、結束敵對狀態、達成和平協定。

胡錦濤說，自一九四九年以來，大陸和台灣儘管尚未統一，但不是中國領土和主權的分裂，而是上世紀四十年代中後期中國內戰遺留並延續的政治對立，但這沒有改變大陸和台灣同屬一個中國的事實。他認為，兩岸統一，不是主權和領土的再造，而是結束政治對立。

胡錦濤也再次對民主進步黨表示，盼望民進黨認清時勢，停止台灣獨立分裂活動，不要再與全民族的共同意願背道而馳，大陸方面願意做出正面的回應。

中華民國九十八年（二〇〇九）

一月一日　中華民國開國紀念，全國人民休假賀新年。

馬英九總統在元旦祝詞中說，

過去一年兩岸關係出現歷史性的轉折，不但海峽基金會與海峽關係協會恢復協商，也正式跨入經貿關係正常化階段。這是馬英九總統第一個元旦。

大陸中國國家主席胡錦濤在除夕夜發表題為「共同促進世界和平、穩定、繁榮」的新年賀詞中，表示新的一年中國將繼續奉行互利共贏開放的戰略，及加強兩岸交流合作。

美國迎新年的壓軸好戲仍然是紐約時報廣場的水晶球落地倒數計時。今年的水晶比過去大了一倍，重達一萬一千八百七十五磅。儘管天氣奇冷，並有時速高達四十四英里的勁風，但民眾熱情未減，國會參議員喜萊莉·柯林頓、前總統柯林頓和紐約市長彭博，於除夕深夜十一時五十九分按鈕讓「大蘋果」落地時，萬眾引頸翹盼，忘情的幫忙倒數計時，現場民眾歡聲雷動。

但是，聖地加薩地帶最近發生的以、巴流血衝突，印度孟買不久前的恐怖攻擊事件，特別是全球金融危機等等，都為各

地的新年慶祝活動蒙上陰影。二〇〇九年是中華人民共和國成立六十週年紀念，也是中華民國政府從大陸移駐台北辦公的六十週年紀念。

一月一日　羅馬天主教教宗本篤十六世，在梵帝岡發表新年與世界和平日文告，敦促世界各國領袖團結一致，對抗貧窮、暴力和仇恨，祈求全球和平。

一月一日是美利堅合眾國承認中華人民共和國政府三十週年紀念，兩國政界人士發表談話。

一月四日　數千名以色列部隊在坦克車和直升飛機支援下，先施以猛烈砲兵轟擊之後，即越過邊境攻入加薩走廊境內，將有居民大約四十萬眾的加薩城加以包圍。據以色列軍事首領說，在進攻中，巴勒斯坦極端頭子哈瑪斯的部屬受到重大的損失。聯合國安全理事會三日夜間已要求以、巴雙方立即停火。

一月五日　美國國內安全部公民與移民服務局在日前發出的備忘錄中說，美國的入籍證書及公民證書上，可以將「台灣」列為持證人過去的國籍及出生地。這是美國移民局的一項重要的改變措施。備忘錄的改變措施是指入籍申請表 N-400 與公民證書上的「前國籍及出生地」欄。

一月七日　台灣海峽交流基金會董事長江丙坤七日啟程赴大陸訪問四天，為解決大陸台籍商人經營困難等問題舉行座談會，聽取各方面的意見，並可能與大陸的海峽關係協會會長陳雲林再度晤談。

一月八日　美國舊金山市議會選舉新議長，華裔市議員邱信福當選議長。市議會選舉競爭激烈，經過七次投票，邱信福終於獲勝。他是舊金山史上第一位華裔市議長，為華裔大大增光。

一月十五日　美國航空公司一架雙引擎的空中巴士 320 型客機，下午自紐約拉瓜地亞機場起飛後不久，遭到飛鳥的撞擊，隨即在酷寒的天氣裡迫降在哈德遜河中。但由於機長的緊急處置得宜，機上的全體一百五十名乘客和機員全部安全無恙，為

民航史上的奇蹟，深獲各界人士讚揚。

一月二十日　美國第四十四任總統巴拉克·歐巴馬宣誓就任。他宣稱，「新責任時代來臨」。他是民主黨員，也是美國建國兩百三十二年來的第一位非洲黑人裔總統。副總統白登亦宣誓就任。

一月廿六日　據「美國之音」報導說，美國新政府的國務卿喜萊莉·克林頓曾於廿二日在國會作證時說，關於台灣問題，歐巴馬政府將繼續維持「一個中國」政策，遵守美國與中國的三個「聯合公報」及美國的「台灣關係法」。她並且表示，美國將繼續支持台灣拓展國際活動空間的努力，其中包括台灣成為世界衛生組織觀察員。

一月廿六日是陰曆元旦，也就是中國十二生肖的第二生肖牛年的新年。歐巴馬總統特發表聲明，向全球所有慶祝陰曆新年的人們祝賀新年。

中國陰曆元旦假期，台北市立動物園的一對大陸贈送的大熊貓首次與市民相見，萬人爭看熊貓真面目，一大早就有市民大排長龍爭看牠們。上午觀眾特別擁擠，動物管理人員實施限制，每人只能欣賞幾秒鐘，下午因人數較少，不再加以限制，尤其是小朋友們都要看個夠。據園方統計，元旦一天有一萬八千人看過「團團圓圓」。

一月三十日　美國亞利桑那州發生重大車禍，一部載有中國大陸觀光客的旅遊大巴士，在著名的胡佛水壩附近的公路上翻覆，初步消息說，至少有七人喪生，及十人受輕重傷。意外事件詳情正在亞利桑那州警方調查中。稍後的報導說，一位在醫院治療的大陸婦女說，她與其丈夫、父親及叔叔一家四人都來自上海觀光，不幸遇到意外事件。

二月二日　中國國務院總理溫家寶，在英國的著名學府劍橋大學發表演講，題目是「用發展的眼光看中國」。他演說之際，有一名白人青年將一隻鞋子扔向溫家寶，但並未擊中，英國

安全人員將鞋子從講台上撿走。

溫家寶在接受倫敦金融時報記者訪問時說，中國政府正在研究與準備採取更有力的措施刺激經濟情勢。他並且批評美國說，此次金融危機的原因是始作俑者美國等自身經濟嚴重失衡，長期赤字存在等所致。

二月十二日　美國大陸航空公司一架自新澤西州紐華克飛往水牛城的客機，因機件故障失事墜毀，機上乘客和機員四十八人及地面一人喪生。

二月十三日　中華民國總統馬英九，在對美國紐約時報記者發表的訪問談話中表示，他希望美國新政府在海峽兩岸問題上發揮積極作用，「美國可以在鼓勵兩岸維持現狀問題上，扮演積極角色」。他並且說，「美國務卿喜萊莉·柯林頓他們在未來訪問北京時不提台灣問題，我們沒有任何不滿。」

二月廿五日　美國新總統歐巴馬宣佈，提名曾任華盛頓州長的華裔駱家輝為新內閣的商務部長，使他成為美國新政府的第二位華裔部長。歐巴馬先前已宣佈提名華裔朱棣文為能源部長，這是美國建國以來政府中第一次同時將有兩位華裔擔任部長職位，旅美華人深以為榮。

二月廿八日　是日為一九四七年二月廿八日台北發生的警民衝突事件紀念日，也是馬英九總統上任後的第一個「二二八」紀念日。他於上午在高雄市參加紀念儀式，曾遭到數次責斥，下午回到台北市又參加紀念會，經過亦不順利。報紙上出現的有關「二二八」的文章、看法仍然紛紜。

三月二日　由於美元在國際外匯市場中的地位超強，亞洲各國貨幣除日圓外，其他各國貨幣紛紛貶值，新台幣更貶破三十五元大關，即美金一元相當於新台幣三十五元。這是自一九八九年新台幣完全解除管制以來最低匯價紀錄。三月二日新台幣對美元的匯率貶到三十五元一角四分兌一美元。

三月三日　中國全國人民政治協商會議第十一屆第二次會議，於三

日下午在北京人民大會堂開
幕，會期預定九天，為近年來
會期最短的一次會議。據會議
發言人趙啟正對記者說，經濟
問題是今年政協委員們最關切
的話題，討論最多的話題。

美國東部連續兩天的暴風雪、
冷雨，為廣大地區帶來嚴重的
損失，大部分地區降雪一英尺
左右，至少有六人死亡、一千
多架次民航班機被迫取消，數
十萬戶電力中斷，以及數百萬
名學生停課。此次大風雪天
氣，自一日開始，受影響的地
區包括東海岸各州、新英格蘭
各州等地。東部各地三日起晴
朗、極冷。

三月五日　中國政府國務院總理溫家
寶，在人民政協第十一屆第二
次會議上提出政府工作報告時
說，今年北京對台灣的施政方
針，內容是維持「胡六點」基
調，並且提出要全面加強海峽
兩岸的經濟合作，支持台灣企
業在大陸的發展，以及加強兩
岸雙向投資和產業合作，建立
具有兩岸特色的經濟機制等。

三月九日　據香港中共黨報文匯報報

導說，中國外交部副部長王光
亞透露，中國國家主席胡錦濤
已向美國新總統歐巴馬發出邀
請，歐巴馬在今年內赴北京訪
問的可能性很大，美方人士已
向中方表達這種想法。同時，
中國駐美國大使周文重在全國
政協會議的提案中警告說，因
美國陷入經濟困境，使美國國
內的「中國威脅論」可能再度
升高。他並且預料，美國也可
能進一步要求中國擴大農畜產
品進口，進一步開放航空、金
融、保險、電信等服務業。

中國第十一屆人民代表大會第
二次全代會議在北京舉行，人
大委員長吳邦國在報告中指
出，今年可能是中國經濟發展
最困難的一年。

三月十日　美國國防部九日發表消息
說，中國的五艘船隻八月在海
南島南方的國際海域，駛近一
艘美國無武裝的海軍海洋偵察
船「無懈號」。美國防部批評
中國船隻違反國際法。白宮發
言人也指出，希望中國遵守國
際海洋法規。美國駐北京大使
館也因此種「不當騷擾」，已

向中國外交部提出抗議。

美國防部發言人說，美船「無懈號」八日在海南島南方大約七十英里（約一百十二公里）的國際公海作例行操演時，遭到中國五艘船隻駛近跟隨。發言人說，兩艘中國船隻故意直接停在「無懈號」的前面，雙方險些相撞。

針對美國指控中國船隻在中國南海騷擾美國海軍船隻事件，中國駐華府大使館發表聲明說：中國多次通過外交渠道，要求美方停止在中國專屬經濟區從事非法活動。美方所謂在公海進行活動，是不符合事實的。中方不能接受美方的無理指責。中方要求「美國停止此類非法測量活動，多做有利中美關係穩定發展的事情。」

三月十三日　中國國務院總理溫家寶，在中國人民代表大會閉幕式記者招待會上說，雖然他今年已經六十七歲了，但他真心希望能有機會到台灣去走一走，看一看，如果有這種可能，走不動就是爬他也願意去。

溫家寶在談到台灣參與世界衛生組織大會問題時表示，對於涉及台灣同胞利益的一些國際組織，比如像世界衛生組織，中國會做出合情合理的安排。

三月十四日　關於中華民國參與世界衛生組織大會問題，兩岸已獲初步協議。據高層人士透露，中國當局初步同意台灣以「觀察員」身分參與世界衛生組織大會，而且原則採「逐年參與」方式，但是有關邀請方式、與會名稱、代表層級等仍待兩岸人員正式磋商決定。對於北京堅持台灣「逐年參與」的立場，等於未來仍須透過事前協商才具有觀察員資格，這與現有的天主教廷等六個觀察員有差別待遇。台北高層人士承認，北京的策略就是對台灣「逐年控管」。

三月十四日　三月十四日是中國政府制定「反分裂國家法」四週年紀念日，中華民國總統府發言人王郁琦對記者招待會發表聲明說，馬英九總統上任九個月以來，兩岸關係已由緊張走向緩和，反分裂國家法制定的時

空環境已有重大改變。因此呼籲大陸當局應慎重考量台灣人民的感受，「對該法做出適當的處理」。

三月十八日　美國在台協會理事會主席薄瑞光，對台北記者會指出，當前的美、台關係極好，美國對台海兩岸關係的現況也感到放心，兩岸持續對話有助於彼此穩定和避免誤解。

對於記者詢問關於大陸對台灣部署千餘個飛彈的看法，薄瑞光承認「那是個威脅，我們也希望它們撤走。」這是美國行政部門罕見的公開呼籲中國將飛彈撤除。薄瑞光理事長是自馬英九上任以來第一次來台灣訪問。

中美洲的薩爾瓦多國總統當選人毛瑞賽·傅尼斯說，他在六月就任後將考慮承認北京中國政府。

三月廿三日　據英國的金融時報報導說，今日世界的三家最大的銀行都是中國的銀行，它們是中國的工商銀行、建設銀行和中國銀行。十年前世界最大銀行中幾乎全是美國和英國的大銀行，今天世界的二十家大銀行中，美國只有四家，英國只有一家即老牌的匯豐銀行。

中華民國新聞局長蘇俊賓宣佈，新聞局派駐加拿大多倫多的新聞秘書郭冠英，因為「言行不當、蓄意欺瞞」，記大過兩次予以免職。郭冠英表示他對政府的處置無法心服。他說：「在中華民國，台灣人可以公然辱罵中國人，但中國人想要重申立場表示反擊都不行。」郭案起因於他被指控在電腦網路上以化名「范蘭欽」發表有關批評台灣人與外省人爭議問題的文章。

三月廿五日　美國國防部公佈中國軍力報告說，台灣兩岸關係過去一年雖然降低緊張，但解放軍對台灣的軍力部署並無明顯改變的跡象。國防部文件中首次證實，中國已經在海南島建造新海軍基地，為其配備彈道飛彈的艦隊服務，並且繼續對台灣部署更多的短程飛彈。

美國防部發言人說，中國官方說軍事預算數字已從二〇〇〇年的二七九億美元增至六〇一

億美元，但美國防部的估計中國的軍事預算，可能已高達一○五○億至一五○○億元之鉅。

三月廿七日　美國國內安全部發表的二○○八年永久居民證（綠卡）統計報告中說，共有一百十萬七千一百廿六人領有綠卡，及有一百零四萬六千五百三十九人宣誓入美國籍獲得公民證。國內安全部說，去年獲得綠卡數字最多的國家是墨西哥，計有十八萬九千九百八十九人，其次是中國計有八萬二千七百十人，第三名是印度計有六萬三千三百五十二人。新公民人數，也以墨西哥人居首位，計有二十三萬一千八百十五人，其次是印度人計有六萬五千九百七十一人。中國人歸化美國的計有四萬零十七人。

三月廿九日　台北市大安區舉行立法委員補選投票結果，國民黨候選人蔣乃辛獲勝，但國民黨得票率比去年的立法委員選舉及總統選舉都減少。國民黨主席吳伯雄表示，這是一項警訊，行政團隊和國民黨都必須徹底反省檢討，謙卑傾聽人民的意見，才對得起支持國民黨的選民。

馬英九總統的發言人王郁琦表示，這次選舉的投票率很低，國民黨候選人蔣乃辛與對手得票的差距縮得小，投票結果是對行政團隊的警訊，政府一定會深切檢討，加倍努力改進。

民主進步黨女主席蔡英文說，民進黨雖然失敗，但已威脅到國民黨在台北市的鐵票區，顯示「藍綠版圖並非無法動搖」。

此次補選結果，國民黨的蔣乃辛獲得四萬六千零六十五票，民進黨的周伯雅獲得三萬六千四百六十五票。大安區立法委員補選，是因為原任立委李慶安持有美國永久居留證案自行辭職。

三月廿九日　據美國紐約時報報導，加拿大多倫多大學研究中心人員說，全世界一○三個國家的至少一千二百九十五台政府和民間辦公室的電腦，曾遭到一項龐大的電子間諜作業滲透和

竊取文件。他們說，控制這個電子間諜系統的電腦幾乎全部都設在中國，但研究人員強調他們無法斷言中國政府介入其事。

中國駐紐約總領事館發言人發表談話，駁斥有關中國涉及這種間諜作業的說法，宣稱「中國政府反對和嚴格禁止任何網路罪行」。

四月一日　美國總統歐巴馬與中國國家主席胡錦濤，一日在英京倫敦會談後發表聲明說，決定雙方在所有層面上加強交流，並且建立新的「美中戰略及經濟對話」，誓言共同恢復全球經濟穩定成長，反對保護主義，並儘快恢復人權對話。聲明中提到歐巴馬總統已接受胡錦濤主席的邀請，將在今年下半年赴中國訪問。

歐巴馬總統在倫敦二十國集團金融高層會議二日舉行之前，一日先與胡錦濤舉行會談。

四月五日　美國紐約州賓漢頓市警察局發表，在三日發生於「公民協會」槍擊事件中死亡的十四人名單。這十四人分別來自八個不同的國家，其中有四人來自中國大陸，他們來美國學習英文，不幸遭到殺害。兇嫌與另一人來自越南。

美國維幾尼亞州菲爾法克縣警察局發表，亨頓鎮於二日清晨發生驚人血案，現年五十五歲來自台灣的移民陳和璧，將妻子刺殺後放火將房屋燒毀，然後自殺死亡。據死者的友人說，陳和璧是交通方面的工程師，曾經營公司，後因案服刑期兩年，但近年的工作情形不悉，可能是在家做股票失敗，為了避免妻子楊啟玲背負重債竟而出此下策造成家庭悲劇。楊啟玲在台灣曾擔任教師。他們於一九八七年移居於現址。友人們說，楊啟玲個性直爽，樂於助人，長期在社區擔任義工，人緣很好。陳和璧雖然木訥寡言，但對於子女課餘活動也熱心參與。死者夫婦有一子一女，兒子已就業，女兒仍在讀大學。悲劇傳出後陳家的親友都覺得難以置信。

四月七日　中華民國行政院會議提出「行政院組織法修正案」，將

現有的三十七個部會加以緊縮為二十九個部會。行政院原擬將僑務委員會併入外交部，並將新部易名為「外交僑務部」。但此項計劃受到海外各地僑胞的強烈反對，也受到中國國民黨海外組織系統的有力反對，迫使馬英九總統不得不順從數千萬僑胞的公意，最後行政院決定維持僑務委員會的現行組織，不受行政院精簡機構的影響。

中華民國外交部於四月六日深夜舉行緊急記者招待會宣佈，業已證實台灣高雄籍的漁船「穩發一六一號」遠洋漁船，於六日上午在印度洋塞席爾群島附近海域遭海盜劫持。

「穩發一六一號」為穩集漁業公司所有，負責人為謝龍隱，船上有船員三十名，船長顏順男與輪機長黃麟祥為台省籍，另有五名大陸船員、六名印尼船工、十七名菲律賓船工。台灣與該船船員已失去聯絡。船東及外交部都尚未接到海盜要求贖金或其他情況的進一步消息。

數百年前的「維京」近來成為廿一世紀的奇聞。太空時代的海盜不但不像賭城拉斯加表演的那般「好玩」，他們的新武器中有防空飛彈，能夠打落各國護航的武裝直升飛機。四月七日的新聞報導說，非洲東海角索馬利亞的海盜在多國軍艦鎮壓下依然十分猖獗，在短短四十八個小時內竟然劫持五艘商船，其中有台灣、英國、法國及德國的船隻。海盜匪徒目前至少控制著十七艘船隻和兩百五十多名人質，造成航海事業意外的威脅。

索馬利亞海盜活動雖然是近來世界注意的事件，但實際上已不是新聞。據航海界人士說，去年一年內索國海盜曾發動一百三十多次的攻擊，劫持的船隻達五十艘。航界人士說，海盜使用勒索得來的黑錢購買各種武器、大型母船、高速快艇、自動步槍、榴彈發射器、無線電通訊器材、海事衛星電話及海面搜索雷達等現代化裝備。現在共有十個國家派出海軍艦艇在亞丁灣索馬利亞水

域，執行武裝護航任務，但航行威脅仍然嚴重。

四月十八日　在海南島軍事基地博鰲召開的亞洲論壇會議，十八日舉行開幕式，中國國務院總理溫家寶表示，中國政府因應金融危機的經濟發展計劃，對增強信心發揮了重要作用，而且已初見成效。

中華民國前監察院長錢復代表政府出席會議，於十八日下午與中國國務院總理溫家寶會晤，課題中包括台灣對大陸的貢獻等。

大陸國務院台灣辦公室主任王毅，十七日晚在博鰲設宴款待台灣的代表錢復時說，大陸的海峽關係協會與台灣的海峽基金會人員的預備性商談，十八日在台北舉行，順利的話，四月最後一週兩岸兩會將在南京舉行第三次江丙坤與陳雲林會談。第三次會談的主要課題包括兩岸航空定期航班、啟動金融合作、共同打擊犯罪及司法協助等。

同時，在台北舉行的預備會談已獲協議，第三次江陳會談定

四月廿五日在南京舉行。

四月廿三日　中華人民共和國海軍為慶祝建軍六十週年，在山東青島舉行首次多國海軍檢閱活動。中國海軍派出潛水艇四艘、水面艦艇二十五艘及飛機三十一架接受檢閱，最受外界注意的是中國自行建造的兩艘核子動力潛水艇。中國國家主席胡錦濤和多國海軍高級將領共同搭乘軍艦舉行海軍檢閱典禮。

四月廿六日　中華民國的海峽基金會與中華人民共和國的海峽關係協會的負責人江丙坤與陳雲林，在大陸南京市舉行第三次兩會會談，於廿六日下午三時簽訂兩岸航空定期航班、金融合作、共同打擊犯罪等三項協議。大陸海峽關係協會會長陳雲林致詞表示，兩會同意於下半年在台北舉行第四次會談，未來的商談課題包括漁業合作、避免雙重課稅及農產品檢驗檢疫等項目。

關於兩岸定期航空班機一項，雙方協議增加南線和第二條北線雙向直航航路，航空班機每

週自一〇八班增加到二七〇班，兩岸定期航點也將增加。

四月廿七日　由於豬流感疫症已經在墨西哥各地造成多達一五二人死亡的嚴重情勢，除北美洲傳出有多起病例外，其他國家廿七日也傳出疑似豬流感的病例，迫使世界衛生組織宣佈將對豬流感的警報級提高到第四級，這顯示爆發疫疾的危險性明顯的升高，並且可能經由人際傳染散播病毒。

世界衛生組織流感警報系統共分五級，第五級是指病毒經由人際傳染散播到同一地區至少兩個國家，那即顯示爆發疫疾流行。

目前已向世界衛生組織報備豬流感病例和疑似病例的國家包括：墨西哥死亡一五二人，及疑似或確認的一九九五人。美國確認的有四十八人。加拿大確認的有六人。哥斯達黎加疑似的有十七人。秘魯有疑似的一人。巴西有疑似的一人。以色列有疑似的二人。法國有疑似的四人。瑞士有疑似的五人。捷克有疑似的二人。紐西蘭有疑似的十三人。

四月廿九日　中華民國參與國際活動空間，今年獲得突破。世界衛生組織秘書長富珍，致函行政院衛生署長葉金川，邀請葉金川率同，以「中華台北」名義，使用觀察員身份出席今年五月十八日至廿七日的世界衛生組織在瑞士日內瓦舉行的世界衛生組織大會。

五月三日　世界衛生組織發表聲明說，雖然 A 型（豬流感）確診病例還有增加，但跡象顯示疫情未向北美以外地區持續擴散。墨西哥的疫情似已趨於緩和，不過提醒各界仍不可掉以輕心。

五月九日　中華民國前總統陳水扁於七日還押後開始絕食，八日晚身體出現明顯不適，台北看守所九日晨將他送至衛生科檢查後，發現他心臟狀況也不佳，決定將他送入台北縣立醫院作詳細檢查。

馬英九總統在海峽交流基金會說，兩岸交流頻繁，「也許可考慮雙方在某些項目上互設機構」。行政院大陸事務委員會

發言人劉德勳說，可朝設立「綜合性辦事機構方向進行」，時機接近成熟。

五月十二日　中國大陸紀念汶川大地震一週年的活動，於十二日下午在四川省汶川縣映秀鎮舉行。中國國家主席胡錦濤在紀念儀式中，向在大地震災害中不幸罹難的同胞表達深切的思念。北京新華通訊社報導說，截至四月三十日為止，共收到國內外汶川大地震捐款人民幣六五九億九六〇〇萬元，及捐贈物資折合人民幣一〇七億一六〇〇萬元。

五月十五日　一九八九年北京天安門廣場「六四」屠殺事件二十週年紀念前夕，已故中國共產黨中央總書記趙紫陽的關於「六四」錄音回憶錄中英文版於五月中旬分別在香港及美國出版。據趙紫陽在書中披露說，二十年前武力鎮壓學生完全是鄧小平一人的決定，這一說法與過去外傳在五位政治局委員投票不能決定的情況下，由退休的政治老人一起決定的說法明顯不同。趙紫陽回憶錄中文版書名為「改革歷程」，全書三百八十四頁，英文版書名為「國家的囚徒：趙紫陽的秘密日誌」。

五月十七日　台灣民主進步黨於五月十七日夜間發動的反對總統馬英九的大遊行，中途發生意外事件，台北市警察局的一部巡邏車撞上參加遊行的男子張忠雄及徐仁山兩人，兩名受傷者都送入台大醫院急救。據新聞報導說，張忠雄的傷勢嚴重，有生命危險。肇事的兩名警員林建智和廖乾智被依傷害罪嫌移送檢方偵辦。此意外事件給予民進黨攻擊馬英九的藉口，也無疑會增加「馬英九下台」口號的聲音。

五月十八日　世界衛生組織第六十二屆年度大會，上午在瑞士日內瓦的聯合國辦事處大樓舉行開幕典禮，來自台灣的中華民國行政院衛生署長葉金川前來參加，坐於「中華台北」的觀察員席位上。這是在經過三十八年之久後，中華民國代表重返世界衛生組織大會，但並非「中華民國」重返世界衛生組

織，而只是「中華台北」（Chinese Taipei）觀察員出席衛生組織大會。這與中華民國以「中華台北」名義參加國際奧林匹克委員會的情形相同。

五月十九日　是日是馬英九總統就任一週年紀念前夕，他在就任一週年記者招待會上說，金融危機對台灣的傷害很大，政府提出各種振興經濟方案，到目前為止，已出現一些止跌現象，雖然回升還需一些時間，但曙光已經在望。他說，一年來兩岸交流，多數民意認同，民進黨卻上街頭反對。他說「如果要我們回到執政前八年的情況，我真的做不到，那並不是一個很值得我們繼續走的路線。」

五月二十日　馬英九總統在就任滿週年的國際記者招待會上，對外籍記者有關兩岸關係和台灣前途的詢問答覆說，兩岸目前談的是經濟問題不需要舉行公民投票，涉及統一或獨立的問題可能需要公民投票，但不論在他第一或第二任期，兩岸絕不會就統一問題做任何討論或協商，兩岸關係的未來，應由子孫這一代來決定。

五月廿二日　台灣對外貿易協會董事長王志剛說，該會已收到上海世界博覽會邀請，以「台灣館」名義參加二〇一〇年五月舉行的上海世界博覽會。

台灣高雄市的民主進步黨員市長陳菊到大陸訪問，在北京與中共中央委員及北京市長郭金龍會面中，在談到金融危機時說，今年台灣經濟成長率至今仍為負數，「我們中央政府的馬英九總統，感受到很大的壓力，他務必要改善台灣的經濟」。他是台灣地方官員首次公開提到馬英九的官銜。

五月廿五日　正當南韓陷入前總統盧武鉉跳崖自殺的驚駭之際，北韓共黨突然於廿五日上午先舉行地下核子試驗，不久又舉行發射一個短程飛彈，引起全球注意。大韓民國總統李博明下令軍隊動員，聯合國安全理事會召開緊急會議討論情勢，美國總統歐巴馬責北韓威脅世界和平。

五月廿六日　中共中央總書記胡錦濤，下午在北京人民大會堂會晤中國國民黨主席吳伯雄率領的代表團人員時，引用一首古詩句「欲窮千里目，更上一層樓」來比喻海峽兩岸的關係。吳伯雄對政協主席賈慶林說，希望大陸多和台灣各黨派人士接觸。

六月三日　台北市的美國商會發表馬英九政府上台後的首次年度白皮書，雖然肯定馬政府的兩岸開放政策，但批評政府缺乏效率，指出沒有效率是台灣競爭力落後的根本原因。美國商會特別點名國家博播委員會、健保局及立法院三大單位是有問題的政府機構。

六月四日　六月四日是一九八九年北京天安門廣場學生民主運動遭中共武力鎮壓流血事件的二十週年紀念日，在國外各地都有紀念活動，台灣及香港亦如此。但是美國華盛頓郵報記者自北京發出的電訊中報導說，北京於天安門廣場鎮壓二十週年紀念日「仍然平靜，只有香港數萬人舉行抗議活動。」報

導中說：「首都實際上被鎖閉，異議人士遭軟禁，警察控制著廣闊的天安門廣場，新聞記者不能進入。」

美國國會眾議院於二日夜間，以三九六票對一票的壓倒性多數表決通過紀念「六四」事件的決議案，要求對事件的真相舉行獨立的調查。

做了總統的馬英九，一改過去的「六四不平反，統一不能談」的說法，變成「不能用六四當時的尺度看今日的大陸。」剛結束台灣訪問之行返美的大陸學生運動領袖王丹，批評馬英九對「六四」事件的立場「始終不如一」。其他政論家也有類似的看法。

六月十日　中國國民黨主席吳伯雄和馬英九總統舉行記者招待會，宣佈馬英九決定參選國民黨主席。馬英九對記者會說，他是「基於行政、立法事權統一，提升行政效能，才決定參選下任黨主席。」但很多政論家並不認同馬英九的說法。

六月十三日　中國國防部對美國海軍神盾級驅逐艦「馬侃號」十一

日在菲律賓近海航行時，其拖曳聲納陣列被中國潛水艇撞毀的報導不願加以評論。美國國防部對路透社記者證實此一消息，並承認美艦的聲納系統受損，但拒絕透露碰撞的原因。不過中國的專家指出，碰撞的原因是「馬侃號」當時未發現尾隨的中國潛水艇。日本的新聞報導說，「馬侃號」當時正在利用聲納陣列搜尋中國潛水艇的位置和聲紋。

六月二十日　北京電訊報導說，湖北省石首市十九日晚間發生大規模警民流血衝突事件。起因於一名年輕廚師日前離奇陳屍於任職的酒店外，警方指廚師是跳樓自殺，並急於將屍體火化。但家人拒絕接受警方的死因調查，阻止警方搬屍，最多時有數萬人聚集在這家有政府背景的旅館外面，協助家屬護屍，與上千的警察發生連番的衝突，有兩百多民眾受傷，多輛警車及消防車被民眾砸毀。衝突持續到二十日晨才告平息。

六月廿一日　親民黨主席宋楚瑜廿一日下午前往翠山莊拜會前總統李登輝，兩人會談兩個多小時之久，引發政壇高度關注。親李人士說，過去雙方有些「誤會」，當面說一說，聊一聊也很好。另有人士說，宋系人馬已被國民黨收編，李登輝也想從藍綠陣營中找尋出路，李、宋算是困境中的「異業結盟」。

六月廿二日　美國在台協會在台北市內湖興建的新會址廿二日舉行動工儀式，預定三年內完成。這表示美國在台協會至少會持續三年。新會址基地六點五公頃，比去年完成的美國駐北京大使館基地還大。建造費達一億七千萬美元，辦公大樓一棟面積計一萬四千平方公尺，另有停車場等附屬建築物。美國如此重視一個所謂「非官方機構」的房屋，不會沒有特別的理由吧？

六月廿七日　中華民國前總統李登輝說，他不反對「台灣與中國深化交流」，在世界貿易組織的架構下，「三通、四通、五通都不要緊」，但同時務必推展

「和中、親美日」政策，並以國家的身分繼續保有超然的地位。他並說，目前的「中台關係」應該是「你是你，我是我，但你我是朋友」。李登輝批評馬英九政府假造所謂「九二共識」，欺騙台灣人民。

六月廿九日　中華民國總統馬英九啟程赴中美洲巴拿馬、宏都拉斯等國訪問，但宏國突然發生政變，總統塞拉雅被逐下台。因此，馬英九被迫縮減行程。

美國軍隊自伊拉克克城巴格達撤離，伊國人民狂歡慶祝，伊政府宣布三十日為「國家主權日」。

七月三日　中華民國總統馬英九於中美洲巴拿馬訪問之際，在越洋記者訪問中，對北京政府國務院台灣事務辦公室主任王毅提出台灣開放「海峽中線」的建議加以拒絕。他說，海峽中線是空軍的訓練場所，實在無法開放。馬英九說：三次陳雲林與江丙坤會談之前，中共方面也有類似建議，但「我們也非常明確的告訴他，海峽中線是空軍演訓場所，實在無法開放。不是我們不願意或故意刁難，而是與安全有關。」

對於開放海峽中線問題的出現，在台灣引起深刻的重視。評論界有明顯的反響。台北聯合報的「觀察站」文中說：北京接連拋出開放海峽中線問題，多少有測試台灣談判的底線的意味。這也意味著兩岸爭奪談判主控權，當北京持續測試、近逼，馬政府就得防守、全力阻擋。後續兩岸磋商議題只會更棘手，才讓馬政府急於畫出底線。」同時其他政論人士並提到，與海峽兩岸關係極有關的美國的態度也很值得注意。

七月五日　北京官方消息說，新疆首府迪化（烏魯木齊）五日發生近三十年來最嚴重的少數民族動亂，數千的維吾爾族人在街頭舉行示威，攻擊路人及縱火焚燒車輛，與趕來鎮壓的武裝警察發生嚴重衝突。中國官方說，到目前為止，至少有一百四十人喪生，八百廿八人受傷，及傷亡人數可能在增加中。官方指稱，這是以「熱比

亞為首的世界維吾爾代表大會」指揮煽動的「境外指揮、境內鬧事」的事件。新聞報導說，熱比亞上週在美國表示，「維吾爾族人在種族歧視和不公平政策下，受苦多年。」

七月七日　是日為一九三七年日軍侵華的蘆溝橋事變紀念日，台灣沒有任何紀念活動，這顯然與日本的邪惡宣傳有關。

七月九日　由中國國民黨榮譽主席連戰領導的「國共論壇」（國共平台），數年來對兩岸關係的改進，有莫大的貢獻，其性質類似大陸時代的國共兩黨談判。馬英九現決定將名稱改為多黨型的「兩岸論壇」，顯然是受了中共在國台辦下成立「多政黨小組」決定的影響。連戰可能不再參與會談。

七月廿六日　中國國民黨第十八屆全國代表大會在台北市陽明山中山樓召開黨主席選舉會議，只有黨員馬英九一名候選人參選。國民黨黨魁紛爭事在台北鬧了數月之久，涉及的是吳伯雄和馬英九。台北的聯合報上月曾報導說，「外界批評馬英九硬搶黨主席」。

全會代表舉行投票的結果，馬英九當選國民黨主席，這是他第二次當選國民黨主席，並預定於十月黨大會中正式就任黨主席職位，接替吳伯雄的職務。

八月八日　莫拉克颱風帶來超量的豪雨，在台灣南部引發極嚴重的土石流災情，高雄縣甲仙鄉的小林全村房屋在大風災中完全消失。各地詳細災情正在繼續報告中。

八月十二日　據莫拉克颱風災後應變中心統計，截至十二日中午為止，已有六十七人喪生，六十一人失蹤，及四十五人受傷。共有一萬一千六百十七人獲撤離和救援。台灣空勤總隊的直昇飛機，十一日在進行搜救任務之際，不幸墜毀於屏東縣的伊拉山谷，機上三名人員無一生還。

馬英九總統在屏東視察災情時說，他暫不考慮發佈緊急命令。但立法院的國民黨和民主進步黨的黨團，皆主張應發佈緊急命令應付災情。

八月十三日　據第一批進入高雄縣小林村的救災人員說：「全村都埋在泥土裡，只剩下兩間民房。」該村生還村民說，可能有五百至六百人遭活埋。截至十三日為止，全台各地已有一百十一人喪生，及五三六人失蹤，災情較「九二一大地震更為嚴重」。

馬英九總統在台南視察災情時說，外傳政府拒絕外國協助救災之說「絕無此事」。

八月二十日　台灣南部地區受到五十年來最嚴重的颱風水災，由於馬英九總統對緊急情勢應變的無能，更推諉責任，激起災區居民及全島人民的憤慨，近日紛紛要求馬英九「下台」及改組內閣等呼籲。報章、電視等評論亦嚴辭責斥馬英九政府，使天然災害變為政治危機。

八月卅一日　北京中共當局對於西藏宗教領袖達賴喇嘛到台灣訪問一舉表示堅決反對。國務院台灣辦公室發言人說：「民進黨策動長期從事分裂活動的達賴赴台灣是別有用心的。達賴赴台灣勢必對兩岸關係造成不利影響。」台灣南部災區六個民主進步黨當權的縣市，邀請達賴到台灣「安慰災民」。但一般認為是民進黨借口當此水災嚴重之際，給馬英九總統增加難題。達賴於卅一日抵台，預定九月四日離台。

九月八日　以「清高」與「博士內閣」自矜及假想「連任」自詡的總統馬英九，終於台灣八月八日風水災恰滿一整月的九月八日，向災民的哭聲和全島的斥責聲屈膝，宣布徹底改組他的政府。馬英九宣布行政院長劉兆玄已獲准辭職，接著宣布由中國國民黨副主席兼秘書長吳敦義出任行政院長及桃園縣長朱立倫出任行政院副院長。

九月十日　吳敦義的新內閣於九月十日宣誓就職。這是馬英九政府的第二屆內閣，以劉兆玄為行政院長的第一屆內閣只維持十五個月之久。

九月十一日　中華民國前總統陳水扁與家人舞弊案，台北地方法院十一日宣布判決，全案被告共十四人，其中陳水扁被判無期徒刑，褫奪公權終身。陳妻吳

淑珍被判無期徒刑，褫奪公權
終身，其他被告被判不同刑
期。陳水扁辦事處表示一定上
訴。

十月一日　「中華人民共和國」成立
六十週年紀念，大陸各地舉行
種種慶祝活動。

十二月七日　中華民國政府自大陸遷
至台北辦公六十週年紀念。六
十年前政府宣布自成都遷到台
北市。

中華民國九十九年（二〇一〇）

一月一日　中華民國開國九十九年元
旦慶典。

十月十日　中華民國慶祝雙十國慶
節。

中華民國一百年（二〇一一）

一月一日　中華民國開國一百年元旦
慶典。

十月十日　中華民國百年雙十國慶慶
典。

KMT'S 60-YEAR IN TAIWAN

Major events before 1949

1931

Sept. 18 JAPANESE TROOPS OCCUPY SHENYANG (MUKDEN)

1937

Jul. 7 JAPANESE FORCES ATTACK WANPING (MARCO POLO BRIDGE INCIDENT)

1943

Nov. 23-26 GENERALISSIMO CHIANG KAI-SHEK, PRESIDENT ROOSEVELT AND PRIME MINISTER CHURCHILL CONFER IN CAIRO, EGYPT

Dec. 3 THE JOINT DECLARATION OF CAIRO CONFERENCE IS ISSUED IN CHUNGKING, WASHINGTON AND LONDON

1945

Aug. 14 JAPAN SURRENDERS UNCONDITIONALLY TO THE ALLIES

28 MAO TSE-TUNG ARRIVES IN CHUNGKING TO MEET WITH CHIANG KAI-SHEK

Sept. 9 GEN. HO YING-CHIN ACCEPTS THE SURRENDER OF JAPAN'S FORCES IN CHINA FROM GEN. OKAMURO IN NANKING

Oct. 25 TAIWAN PROVINCE IS RETROCEDED TO CHINA

1947

Feb. 28 RIOTING BREAKS OUT IN TAIPEI FOLLOWING AN INCIDENT BETWEEN POLICE AND A WOMAN-PEDDLER VIOLATING THE TOBACCO MONOPOLY

1949

Jan. 1 President Chiang, in a New Year's Day message to the nation, expresses wishes for a peaceful settlement of the government-Communist dispute.

5 General Chen Cheng is sworn in as governor of Taiwan.

15 Tientsin falls.

21 President Chiang announces his retirement from the presidency and leaves for Hangchow. Vice President Li Tsung-jen is empowered to exercise

presidential powers temporarily.

Mar. 26 The Communists announces peace negotiations will open on April 1 in Peiping.

Apr. 1 A government peace delegation flies to Peiping.

12 The 37.5 Per Cent Farm Rental Reduction Program goes into effect in Taiwan.

15 The Communists demands government acceptance of their eight-point proposal by April 20.

19 The government rejects the Communists demand.

21 The Communists resumes their all-out offensive and crossed the Yangtze River.

23 Government forces evacuated Nanking.

27 President Chiang, arriving in Shanghai, reiterates his determination to suppress the Communist rebellion.

May 8 Acting President Li Tsung-jen arrives in Canton from Nanking.

15 Government forces evacuate Hankow and Wuchang.

20 Sian is evacuated.

27 Shanghai is evacuated.

Jun. 15 Taiwan adopts a new currency.

Jul. 10 At the invitation of Philippine President Elpidio Quirino, President Chiang flies to Baguio to discuss formation of a Far Eastern Anti-Communist Alliance.

Aug. 1 The Office of *Tsung Tsai* (director general) of the Kuomintang is established in Taipei.

3 At the invitation of Korean President Syngman Rhee, President Chiang flies to Chinhae, Korea, to discuss formation of a Pacific alliance.

15 A Southeast China Governor's Office is established in Taipei with General Chen Cheng as governor.

Sept. 27 China files a complaint with the UN General Assembly against the Soviet Union's aid to the Chinese Communists and violation of the Sino-Soviet Treaty of 1945 and the UN Charter.

Oct. 1 The Communists set up a puppet regime in Peiping with Mao Tse-tung as "chair-man," which is recognized by the Soviet Union next day.

3 China severs diplomatic relations with the U.S.S.R.

The U.S. State Department reaffirms U.S. recognition of the National Government as the only legal government of China.

9 President Chiang's Double Tenth message condemns Soviet aggression in China and reiterates determination to fight Communism to the bitter end.

12 The government moves its seat from Canton to Chung-king.

13 Government troops evacuate Canton.

17 Amoy is evacuated.

25 Government troops win a resounding victory at Kinmen (Quemoy).

Nov. 30 Chungking falls.

Dec. 5 Acting President Li Tsung-jen leaves Hong Kong for the United States.

7 The government moves its seat to Taipei.

10 President Chiang flies from Chengtu to Taipei.

27 Government troops evacuated Chengtu.

1950

Jan. 11 The UN Security Council rejects a Soviet proposal for the immediate expulsion of the Chinese delegation. The Russian delegation walks out.

28 The Foreign Ministry declares that China will not be bound by any agreement signed between the Chinese Communist regime and the Soviet Union.

Feb. 9 The government proclaims that, as of zero hour Feb. 12, 1950, in addition to the continental ports already declared closed, the portion of the continental coast including the ports of Chankiang

(Kwangchowwan) and Pakhoi are closed until further notice.

Mar. 1 President Chiang resumes office in Taipei.

2 President Chiang nominates General Chen Cheng as president of the Executive Yuan.

Apr. 5 The Executive Yuan grants Taiwan authority to carry out self-government by popular election in counties and cities within two months.

11 China lodges a complaint with the United Nations against Soviet aid to the Chinese Communists, the Soviet invasion of China and Soviet violation of the UN Charter.

23 Government troops evacuates Haikow.

May 2 Hainan Island is evacuated.

16 Government troops evacuate the Choushan Islands.

Jun. 25 (North Korean Communist invades the Republic of Korea, starting the Korean War.)

27 U.S. President Truman orders the U.S. Seventh Fleet to prevent a Communist attack on Taiwan and asks the Chinese government to cease air and sea operations against the mainland.

28 Foreign Minister George K.G. Yeh declares the Republic of China has in principle accepted American government's

proposal to cease operations against the mainland and the necessary orders have been given to the navy and air force.

Jul. 2 A popular election for county council at Hualien is held, marking the beginning of self-government in Taiwan.

31 General Douglas MacArthur arrives in Taipei to confer with President Chiang.

Aug. 5 A Kuomintang Central Reform Committee is set up in Taipei.

10 U.S. Minister Karl L. Rankin arrives in Taipei as charge d'affaires of the U.S. embassy.

16 Taiwan, formerly consisting of 8 counties and 9 cities, is redivided into 16 counties and 5 cities.

Oct. 7 Communist troops entered Tibet.

22 Popular elections of magistrates are held at Hualien and Taitung.

Nov. 1 The Chinese Communists announces aid to the Korean Communists in the fight against the UN forces in Korea.

13 President Chiang in a broadcast to the mainland people, urges the people to oppose the Communists and not to fight against the UN forces in Korea.

1951

Feb. 1 The UN General Assembly condemns the Chinese Communists as aggressors in Korea.

May 1 U.S. Major General William C. Chase arrives in Taipei as the first chief of the Military Assistance Advisory Group (MAAG) in Taiwan.

18 The UN General Assembly approves a global embargo on shipments of arms and war materials to the Chinese and North Korean Communists.

25 The Legislative Yuan adopts the 37.5 Per Cent Farm Rental Reduction Act.

30 The government announces plans to sell arable public land to tenant farmers on easy payment terms.

Sept. 3 The government declares that the peace treaty with Japan to be concluded in San Francisco will not be binding on China.

8 (The peace treaty with Japan is signed in San Francisco.)

Nov. 5 The fifth session of the UN General Assembly rejects by 20 to 11, a Soviet proposal to discuss the "Question of China's Representation" in its sixth session.

Dec. 11 The Taiwan Provisional Provincial Assembly is established.

1952

Jan. 11 The Control Yuan impeaches Vice President Li Tsung-jen *in absentia*, for violating the laws of the nation and other dereliction of duty.

Feb. 1 The UN General Assembly founds the Soviet Union guilty of violating the 1945 Sino-Soviet Treaty of Friendship and Alliance.

Apr. 28 The Treaty of Peace between the Republic of China and Japan is signed in Taipei.

Jul. 31 The Legislative Yuan ratifies the Sino-Japanese Peace Treaty.

Aug. 7 The Legislative Yuan approves the designation of July 1, instead of January 1, as the beginning of the fiscal year.

Oct. 22 The first world-wide Overseas Chinese Conference is opened in Taipei.

31 The China Youth Corps organized.

1953

Jan. 20 The Legislative Yuan adopts the Land-to-the-Tiller Act.

25 President Chiang announces abrogation of the Sino-Soviet Treaty of Friendship and Alliance of 1945 and its related documents.

Apr. 2 Karl L. Rankin becomes American ambassador to China.

12 Owing to difficulties in the way of elections, the Legislative Yuan passes a bill submitted by President Chiang, extending the term of office of legislators for another year, i.e., to May 7, 1954.

May 5 The second plenary session of the Seventh Central Committee of the Kuomintang is opened in Taipei and adopt two important resolutions: (1) to unite all anti-Communist forces both in Taiwan and abroad; and (2) to convene the second session of the First National Assembly in 1954.

Jul. 2 The last contingent of nearly 30,000 interned Chinese soldiers of General Huang Chieh's First Army Group, including dependents, arrives in Taiwan from Indo-China.

17 Guerrillas on Kinmen conducts a successful raid against the Communist-held Tungshan Island off the south Fukien coast.

Sept. 16 The eighth session of the UN General Assembly rejects a Soviet proposal to seat the Chinese Communists in the United Nations.

27 President Chiang recommends the extension of the term of office of the delegates to the First National Assembly, elected

in 1947, until such time as the Second National Assembly meets.

Oct. 31 China's Permanent Representative to the United Nations, Tingfu F. Tsiang, announces that an agreement has been reached by China, the United States and Thailand for evacuation of 2,000 guerrillas and dependents from the Burma-Yunnan border area to Taiwan.

Nov. 24 The Government protests to the United States against the proposed American transfer to Japan of the Amami Oshima Islands.

27 Korean President Syngman Rhee arrives in Taipei for a visit.

Dec. 29 The Legislative Yuan revises the quorum for the National Assembly from the original one-half (1,523) to one-third (1,015) of the total number of members.

1954

Jan. 23 More than 14,000 Chinese Communist POWs in Korea, who have refused to return to the Chinese mainland, arrives in Taiwan.

Feb. 19 The second session of the First National Assembly opens in Taipei.

Mar. 10 Li Tsung-jen is recalled from office as Vice President of the

Republic of China.

11 The second session of the First National Assembly approves indefinite extension of the Temporary Provisions During the Period of Communist Rebellion.

22 Chiang Kai-shek is re-elected president for a second six-year term.

24 Chen Cheng is elected Vice President.

Apr. 2 The Legislative Yuan passes the Extradition Law.

May 20 President Chiang and Vice President Chen are sworn in President Chiang nominates O. K. Yui president of the Executive Yuan.

Jun. 4 President Chiang appoints C. K. Yen governor of Taiwan.

Jul. 6 The Legislative Yuan adopts the Statute for Investment by Foreign Nationals.

16 The Planning Commission for the Recovery of the Mainland is created with Vice President Chen Cheng as head.

31 The China Chapter of the Asian People's Anti-Communist League is established in Taipei.

Sept. 9 U.S. Secretary of State John Foster Dulles arrives in Taipei to confer with President Chiang.

21 The ninth session of the UN General Assembly rejects, by 43

to 11, a Soviet proposal to oust the Republic of China and seat the Chinese Communists in the United Nations.

Dec. 3 The Sino-American Mutual Defense Treaty is signed in Washington.

1955

Jan. 14 The Legislative Yuan ratifies the Sino-American Mutual Defense Traeaty.

20 Ikiangshan, northernmost islet of the Tachen Islands, falls after 720 gallant defenders died to the last man.

26 The U.S. House of Representatives approves, by 409 to 3, a resolution authorizing President Eisenhower to employ American armed forces to defend Taiwan, the Pescadores and "related positions and territories."

29 American President Eisenhower signs the Taiwan defense resolution.

Feb. 7 Government troops begin to evacuate the Tachen Islands.

Mar. 3 Foreign Minister George K.C. Yeh and U.S. Secretary of State John Foster Dulles exchange instruments of ratification of the Sino-American Mutual Defense Treaty in Taipei.

13 U.S. Secretary of State Dulles said "if Communist Attack against Kinmen and Matsu is deemed part of an attack against Taiwan, the United States will move, under the Sino-American Mutual Defense Treaty, to protect the islands and no longer have reason to restrain the Republic of China from retaliating."

Apr. 23 The Government Information Office declares that the Chinese government will not recognize the validity of the treaty reportedly signed between the Indonesian government and the puppet regime in Peiping relating to the nationality of Chinese in Indonesia.

Jul. 7 Vice President Chen Cheng breaks ground near Taoyuan for the construction of the multipurpose Shihmen Dam.

24 Foreign Minister George K.C. Yeh declares that the Republic of China will reject any proposal to sit at the same conference table with representatives of the Peiping regime in or outside the United Nations.

26 The United States assures China that American negotiations with the Peiping regime in Geneva does not imply "any degree of diplomatic recognition of the

Chinese Communists" and will not "involve the claims rights or essential interests of the government of the Republic of China."

Aug. 5 U.S. President Eisenhower declares that the United States has no intention of recognizing the Peiping regime and will not discuss problems relating to Taiwan without the presence of representatives of the Republic of China.

Sept. 20 The 10th session of the UN General Assembly rejects by 42 to 12, a Soviet proposal to oust the Republic of China from the United Nations.

Oct. 15 A single Chinese Air Force Saber jet shoots down one MIG in a dogfight with 12 Chinese Communist MIGs north of Matsu.

21 The government announces termination of the state of war with Germany as of Oct. 20, 1955.

Nov. 8 The Legislative Yuan adopts the Statute for Investment by Overseas Chinese.

Dec. 13 In UN Security Council China veto admission of Outer Mongolia into the United Nations.

1956

Jan. 12 The Taiwan Provincial Government promulgates Rules for the Enforcement of the Statute on Urban Land Reform.

Mar. 16 U.S. Secretary of State John Foster Dulles arrives in Taiwan to confer with President Chiang.

Apr. 19 R.O.C. recognizes Morocco and Tunisia.

25 R.O.C. establishes diplomatic relations with Haiti.

May 17 R.O.C. severs diplomatic ties with Egypt following Egypt's recognition of the Communist regime in Peiping.

22 The Ministry of the Interior declare that China has indisputable territorial rights over the Nansha (or Spratley) Islands in the South China Sea.

28 Foreign Minister George K.C. Yeh informs Philippine Ambassador Narciso Ramos that the Republic of China has full sovereignty over the Nansha Islands.

Jun. 2 The Foreign Ministry denounces the Vietnamese government's claims of "territorial sovereignty" over the Paracels and Nansha Islands.

22 The Chinese Air Force shot down four Chinese Communist MIG-17s and damage two others over Matsu.

Oct. 1 The government implements regulations governing distribution of land to retired servicemen.

Nov. 16 The 11th session of the UN General Assembly rejects, by 47 to 24, an Indian proposal to seat the Peiping regime in the United Nations.

1957

Jan. 2 The Chinese Air Force discloses the biggest airdrop since 1949 over the Communist held mainland, penetrating to the outskirts of Peiping, 1,700 miles north of Taiwan.

9 The Foreign Ministry reiterates that an independent government should be set up in the Ryukyus.

May 3 The Council of Grand Justices of the Judicial Yuan rules that the nation's three top representative organs – the Legislative Yuan, the Control Yuan and the National Assembly – will collectively represent the Chinese parliament in all international parliamentary organizations.

8 Vice Admiral Stuart H. Ingersoll, commander of the U.S. Taiwan Defense Command announces that a U.S. guided missile Matador unit has been assigned to Taiwan.

24 A mob protesting against the acquittal of U.S. M/Sgt. Reynolds in the alleged manslaughter of Chinese, Liu Tze-jan, ransacks the U.S. Embassy and the U.S. Information Service in Taipei and injures several Americans. In Washington, Ambassador Hollington K. Tong calls at the U.S. State Department to deliver government's apology for the incident.

28 Foreign Minister George K.C. Yeh declares that the May 24 incident is not an "expression of any general anti-American sentiment in Taiwan but a spontaneous protest against what is widely regarded as miscarriage of justice in the acquittal by a U.S. court martial of M/Sgt. Reynolds."

Jun. 2 Japanese Prime Minister Nobusuke Kishi arrives in Taipei to confer with President Chiang.

Jul. 27 R.O.C. recognizes Tunisia.

Aug. 5 R.O.C. established diplomatic relations with Liberia.

8 General Chow Chih-jou is appointed governor of Taiwan, succeeding C.K. Yen. R.O.C. established diplomatic relations with Jordan.

Sept. 16 Presidential Secretary General

Chang Chun goes to Tokyo as a special envoy of president Chiang.

26 The first council meeting of the Asian Peoples' Anit-Communist League opens in Taipei.

Oct. 20 President Chiang is re-elected *Tsung Tsai* (director general) of the Kuomintang.

23 Vice President Chen Cheng is elected deputy director general of the Kuomintang.

24 The 12th session of the UN General Assembly rejects by 47 to 27 with 7 abstentions, an Indian proposal to seat the Peiping regime in the United Nations.

31 Yang Chen-nine and Lee Tsung-dao become the first Chinese to win Nobel Prizes.

Nov. 5 The R.O.C. Navy sink six Communist warships off Matsu.

26 The R.O.C. Navy sink three Communist warship north of Kinmen.

1958

Feb. 19 The R.O.C. Navy sink three Chinese Communist warships and damaged three others in a battle off the Min River estuary.

Mar. 9 Peking Opera performer Chen Yanqiu dies.

10 The Presidential Commission on Administrative Reform is inaugurated.

14 U.S. Secretary of State John Foster Dulles arrives in Taipei for talks with President Chiang.

Apr. 28 Turkish Prime Minister Adman Menders arrives in Taipei for a three-day state visit.

29 The Sputnik Federated Cooperative, Red China's first people's commune, is established in Henan Province.

May 14 Mohammed Reza Pahlevi, the Shah of Iran, arrives in Taipei for a five-day state visit.

30 President Chiang accepts the resignation of Premier O.K. Yui.

Jul. 1 Vice President Chen Cheng is appointed to the concurrent post of president of the Executive Yuan (premier).

31 August 3, Nikita Khrushchev, First Secretary of the Communist Party of the Soviet Union, visits Red China. On the last day he and Mao Tse-tung issue a joint communiqué expressing unanimity on all matters, but making no mention of Taiwan.

Aug. 1 The insurance program for 180,000 government employees for maternity, illness, injury, disability or death is put into effect.

14 The R.O.C. Air Force shot down three Communist MIG-17s over

Matsu.

23 The battle of the Taiwan Straits begins with the Chinese Communists firing 41,000 rounds on the Kinmen Islands in two hours.

Sept. 2 The R.O.C. Navy sink 11 Communist warships.

8 The R.O.C. Air Force shot down seven Communist MIG-17s and damaged two others off the mainland coast.

18 The R.O.C. Air Force shot down five Communist MIG-17s and the Chinese Navy sank three Communist torpedo boats

23 The 13th session of the UN General Assembly votes 44 to 28, With 9 abstentions, a draft proposal to shelve discussion of the so-called Chinese representation issue.

24 The R.O.C. Air Force shot down 10 Communist MIG-17s and probably damaged six others off the mainland coast.

Oct. 10 The R.O.C. Air Force shot down five Communist MIG-17s and damage two others off the mainland coast but lost one Saber jet in the battle.

23 President Chiang and U.S. Secretary of State John Foster Dulles issue a joint communiqué reaffirming solidarity between the two countries and stating that the Kinmen and Matsu Islands are "closely related" to the defense of Taiwan and Penghu under present conditions.

Nov. 3 The Chinese Communists fire 36,000 rounds at Kinmen.

1959

Jan. 7 The Chinese Communists fire 33,000 rounds at Kinmen.

Mar. 6 The Faith (36,000 tons), first super-tanker built in the Republic of China, is launched at Keelung.

9 King Hussein of Jordan arrives in Taipei for an eight-day state visit.

10 Armed rebellion begins against the Chinese government in Lhasa, Tibet. By March 23, the revolt is suppressed in Lhasa, and on March 31, the Dalai Lama flees Tibet and enters India.

23 Some 300,000 Tibetans revolt against the Communists.

26 President Chiang, in a special message to the Tibetan people, pledges that "the government will assist the Tibetan people to realize their own aspirations in accordance with the principle of self-determination."

Apr. 1 (The Dalai Lama arrives in India from Tiber.)

27 Liu Shao-chi succeeds Mao Tse-

tung as "chairman" of the Peiping regime.

May 11 R.O.C. establish diplomatic relations with Libya.

Jul. 5 The R.O.C. Air Force shot down five Chinese Communist MIG-17s south of Matsu.

21 The Legislative Yuan revises the Conscription Law drafting 19-year-olds for two years service in the Army or three years in the Navy or Air Force.

Aug. 7 The worst floods in more than 60 years hit central and south Taiwan.

15 The R.O.C. Army received Nike-Hercules ground-to-air guided missiles from the United States under the military aid program.

Sept. 1 The Law of Compensation for Wrongful Detentions and Convictions, designed to compensate people in cases of miscarriages of justice, goes into effect.

22 The 14th session of the UN General Assembly votes 44 to 29, with 9 abstentions, for the U.S. draft resolution to shelve for another year the so-called question of Chinese representation.

Oct. 12 The UN General Assembly votes for a full-scale debate on Chinese Communist bloodshed

in Tibet.

Dec. 8 The Legislative Yuan amends Article 12 of the Organic Law of the National Assembly, to enable the President to appoint an acting secretary general of the National Assembly when it is not in session.

The Legislative Yuan amends the Statute for Investment by Foreign Nationals.

10 President Chiang appoint Ku Cheng-kang acting secretary general of the National Assembly.

18 An agreement on the deportee issue is signed at Manila by Chinese Ambassador Tuan Mau-lan and Philippine Foreign Secretary Felixberto Serrano.

25 The Philippine government lifts the six-week ban on the entry of Chinese nationals.

1960

Jan. 12 A defecting Chinese Communist MIG-15 jet fighter crash-lands and burns near Ilan.

Feb. 12 The Council of Grand Justices of the Judicial Yuan announces the total membership of the Natinal Assembly, under the present period of national emergency, shall be 1,576.

20 The third plenary session of the First National Assembly opens

in Taipei.

23 R.O.C. establishes diplomatic relations with Cameroun.

Mar. 11 The third session of the First National Assembly adopts an amendment to the temporary provisions of the Constitution. This stipulates that during the period of Communist rebellion, the President and the Vice President may be re-elected without being subject to the two term restriction prescribed in Article 47 of the Constitution.

19 The third session of the First National Assembly decides to set up a committee to study the exercise of initiative and referendum by the National Assembly.

21 Chiang Kai-shek is re-elected to a third term as President.

22 Chen Cheng was re-elected to a second term as Vice President.

May 2 Philippine President and Mrs. Carlos P. Garcia arrives in Taipei for a six-day state visit.

8 R.O.C. established diplomatic relations with Togo.

9 The east-west cross-island highway is opened to traffic.

20 President Chiang and Vice President Chen were sworn in.

Jun. 17 The Chinese Communists dumped 85,965 shells on Kinmen on the eve of U.S.

President Eisenhower's visit to the Republic of China.

18 U.S. President Eisenhower arrives in Taipei for a state visit.

19 President Chiang and U.S. President Eisenhower issue a joint communiqué pledging that their governments will "continue to stand solidly behind the Sino-U.S. Mutual Defense Treaty in meeting the challenge posed by the Chinese Communists in this area."

The Chinese Communists hit Kinmen with 88,798 shells. Ordered to retaliate, R.O.C artillery destroy eight Communist coastal guns, seven Communist fortifications and four communist ammunition depots.

26 R.O.C. establishes diplomatic relations with the Malagasy Republic.

Aug. 2 R.O.C. recognizes Dahomey, Nigeria and Upper Volta.

11 R.O.C. recognizes the Ivory Coast and Chad.

13 R.O.C. recognizes the Central African Republic.

15 The Council of Grand Justices of the Judicial Yuan rules that, according to Article 77 of the Constitution, courts of all levels shall be placed under the jurisdiction of the Judicial Yuan.

R.O.C. recognizes the Congo (Brazzaville).

16 R.O.C. recognizes Gabon.

25 R.O.C. Olympic Team carries a large sign "Under Protest" in the opening procession of the Olympic Games in Rome to protest against the International Olympic Committee's ruling to compel the Chinese athletes to compete under the name of "Taiwan" instead of "the Republic of China."

31 The Legislative Yuan passes the Statute for Encouragement of Investment.

Sept. 3 R.O.C. severs diplomatic relations with the Castro government of Cuba.

6 R.O.C. establishes diplomatic relations with Cyprus.

23 R.O.C. recognizes Senegal and Mali.

Oct. 1 R.O.C. recognizes Nigeria.

9 R.O.C. establishes diplomatic relations with the Congo (Leopoldville).

21 R.O.C. severs diplomatic relations with Mali.

Nov. 1 The R.O.C. government announces that, beginning Nov. 1 all foreign tourists from friendly nations may stop over for 82 hours in Taiwan without visas.

28 R.O.C. recognizes Mauritania.

Dec. 1 Philippine Vice President and Mrs. Diosado Macapagal arrive in Taipei for a six-day visit.

3 The Ministry of Education conferrers first Chinese Doctorate of Law on Chow Tao-chi, associate professor of the National Chengichi University.

10 R.O.C. establishes diplomatic relations with Gabon.

1961

Jan. 10 The Legislative Yuan passes the Statute of Commercial Arbitration, applicable to both domestic and international trade disputes.

19 The foreign ministers of R.O.C., the Philippines, Korea and Vietnam, after a two-day conference, declare in a communiqué that friendly consultations have strengthened the friendship and cooperation among them.

30 President Chiang declares that the government is ready to give 10,000 tons of rice for emergency famine relief on the Chinese mainland.

Mar. 13 A total of 253 items of Chinese art treasures, selected from the collections of the National Palace Museum and the National Central Museum, arrive in Washington for exhibition at the National Art Gallery in May.

20 R.O.C. and Liberia sign an agreement on agricultural, fishery and industrial cooperation.

23 The first group of anti-Communist escapees form the Burma-Laos-Thailand border arrive in Taiwan.

Apr. 13 The Republic of China's first nuclear reactor is installed at the Institute of Nuclear Science of the National Tsinghua University at Hsinchu.

May 14 U.S. Vice President and Mrs. Lyndon B. Johnson visit R.O.C.

15 President Chiang and Vice President Johnson issue a joint communiqué reaffirming Sino-American unity.

22 Peruvian President Manuel Prado y Ugarteche paid a state visit to China.

Jul. 1 Vice President and Premier Chen Cheng opens the first phase of the Yangmingshan Forum to discuss the nation's financial and economic problems. A total of 84 business leaders from home and abroad attended.

29 Vice President and Premier Chen Cheng, accompanied by Mme. Chen, leave for Washington for an official visit.

Aug. 1 Former Japanese Prime Minister Nobusuke Kishi arrives in Taipei for a six-day visit.

25 The second phase of the Yangmingshan Forum opens to study the nation's educational and cultural problems.

31 President Chiang Kia-shek tells 70 visiting American newsmen that Kinmen and Matsu "are as important as West Berlin".

Sept. 1 R.O.C. and Dahomey sign in Taipei an agreement on agricultural and technical cooperation.

Oct. 7 Two defected Chinese Communist pilots, Shao His-yen and Kao Yu-tsung, arrive from South Korea.

13 R.O.C. and Liberia sign in Monrovia a technical cooperation agreement.

27 The 16th UN General Assembly votes for the admission of Outer Mongolia. R.O.C. abstains.

Nov. 21 Fifteen Chinese farmers leave for Liberia on a two-year mission to help Liberian farmers grow more rice.

Dec. 1 The first nuclear reactor in free China, installed by Chinese scientists at the National Tsinghua University campus at Hsinchu, is put into operation.

15 The 16th UN General Assembly adopts, by 61 to 34, with 7

abstentions, a five-nation draft resolution providing that the so-called issue of the Chinese representation will be considered an important question within the meaning of Article 18 of the UN Charter. Immediately thereafter, the Assembly rejects, by 48 to 36, with 2- abstentions, a Soviet proposal to seat the Peiping regime.

18 China establishes diplomatic ties with Upper Volta.

1962

Jan. 15 China establishes diplomatic ties with Chad.

20 China establishes diplomatic ties with Dahomey.

Feb. 9 The Taiwan Stock Exchange, the first in free China, is opened.

24 Hu Shih, president of the Academia Sinica, dies of a heart attack.

Mar. 3 Liu Cheng-szu, Chinese Communist air force second lieutenant, defects in an improved MIG-15 and lands safely at Taoyuan air base, 16 miles southwest of Taipei.

13 Foreign Minister Shen Chang-huan declares China does not recognize Japan's so-called "residual sovereignty" over the Ryukyu Islands.

Apr. 3 President and Mme. Philibert Tsiranana of the Malagasy Republic arrive for a six-day state visit.

20 Twenty-five farm technicians from 11 newly independent African nations begin six months of agricultural training in Taiwan.

May 16 China establishes diplomatic ties with Laos.

17 The Hongkong government declares that between May 1 and 16 a total of 25,999 refugees are deported.

18 The Free China Relief Association appeals to the UN refugees organization to help Chinese fleeing the mainland and to stop the Hongkong authorities from sending them back.

20 China and Dahomey sign an agreement on agricultural and technical cooperation.

21 Vice President and Premier Chen Cheng declares that the government will accept Chinese refugees reaching Hongkong who wish to come to Taiwan.

22 The total number of Chinese refugees who reach Hongkong in the recent influx pass 70,000.

29 Tingfu F. Tsiang, China's chief delegate to the United Nations, appeals to UN members to help

the Chinese refugees in Hongkong.

31 China establishes diplomatic ties with the Central African Republic.

Jun. 27 A group of 62 Chinese refugees who recently fled the mainland to Hongkong arrives in Taiwan for resettlement.

Jul. 5 China recognizes Algeria.

6 The Foreign Ministry declares that the Republic of China will consider any move by a free nation to recognize the Peiping regime a "most unfriendly act."

14 The Legislative Yuan amends the Maritime Law promulgated in 1929.

28 A collection of 253 art objects is returned to Taiwan after successful exhibition in five cities in the United States.

29 Liu Chieh, Chinese ambassador to Canada, is appointed permanent representative to the United Nations, succeeding Tingfu F. Tsiang.

Aug. 23 The Chinese Olympic Committee issues a statement urging the expulsion of Indonesia from the Asian Games Federation and all other international sports bodies for obstructing R.O.C. participation in the Fourth Asian Games.

31 China recognizes Trinidad.

Sept. 7 The government orders withdrawal of R.O.C. embassy personnel from Vientiane after breaking off diplomatic relations with Laos.

8 R.O.C. opens an embassy in Kingston, capital of Jamaica.

9 Chinese Air Force headquarters reports one of its U2 high-altitude reconnaissance planes, bought from the Lockheed Aircraft Corporation of the United States in 1960, is missing on a routine mission over the Chinese mainland.

22 R.O.C. and the Ivory Coast sign in Taipei an agricultural and technical cooperation agreement.

29 R.O.C. and Cameroun sign agreements for commercial, cultural and economic cooperation.

Oct. 1 Expansion of Hualien harbor in eastern Taiwan is completed to accommodate 10,000-ton ships.

10 The first commercial television station in China goes into operation.

13 The Government Information Office sponsors the first Chinese film festival.

30 The 17th UN General Assembly rejects, by 56 to 42, with 12 abstentions, a Soviet proposal to seat the Peiping regime.

The government rejects the

McMahon Line as the boundary between China and India.

Nov. 10 China and Niger sign in Taipei an economic and technical cooperation agreement.

22 General Huang Chieh is appointed governor of Taiwan, succeeding General Chow Chi-jou.

Dec. 27 The Foreign Ministry declares the border treaty signed between the Peiping regime and Outer Mongolia invalid.

28 The Foreign Ministry declares boder agreements signed between the Peiping regime and Outer Mongolia and Pakistan illegal and not binding on China.

1963

Jan. 8 The Ministry of National Defense confirms that the government had sent many groups of guerrillas to the mainland.

19 R.O.C. and Gabon sign an agreement in Taipei for agricultural cooperation.

Feb. 14 R.O.C. and Dahomey sign a technical cooperation pact in Porto Novo.

15 The second seminar for African agricultural technicians is opened.

Mar. 1 The Foreign Ministry declares that the Republic of China does not recognize the border agreement signed between Peiping and Karachi.

4 Vice President and Premier Chen Cheng leaves for Saigon for a five-day state visit.

20 Vice President and Premier Chen Cheng leaves for Manila for a three-day state visit.

23 China and the Congo (Brazzaville) sign an agricultural and technical cooperation agreement.

Apr. 6 The Executive Yuan proclaims December 25 "Constitution Day" and a national boliday.

28 C.K. Yang breaks the world decathlon record by scoring 9,121 points at Mt. San Antonio College stadium near Los Angeles.

May 20 R.O.C. recognizes Togo.

Jul. 1 The Executive Yuan announces abolition of the National Defense Special Assessment.

21 R.O.C. and the Ivory Coast establishes diplomatic ties.

25 R.O.C. and Niger establishes diplomatic relations.

Aug. 4 The Foreign Ministry declare R.O.C. would not recognize the border treaty signed between the Peiping regime and Afghanistan.

23 Ambassador to the United States Tingfu F. Tsiang signs the nuclear test ban treaty for R.O.C.

Sept. 1 The Council for International Economic Cooperation and Development is inaugurated to replace the Council for U.S. Aid. Hualien, eastern Taiwan city facing the Pacific, is opened as an international port.

11 Typhoon Gloria lashes northern Taiwan, claiming more than 200 lives.

27 The government announces a protest against the Putaguese government's ban on anti Communist activities in Macao.

Oct. 7 Dahomey President and Mme. Hubert Maga arrive for a six-day state visit.

21 The 18th U.N. General Assembly rejects, by 57 to 41, with 12 abstentions, an Albanian proposal to seat the Peiping regime.

30 Upper Volta Ambassador Henri Ouattara, first African envoy accredited to the Republic of China, presents his credentials to President Chiang.

Nov. 8 R.O.C. and the Dominican Republic sign a technical cooperation agreement in Taipei.

12 The ninth National Congress of the Kuomintang opens in Taipei.

21 The ninth National Congress of the Kuomintang elects Chiang Kai-shek director general and Chen Cheng deputy director general.

22 R.O.C. and Kuwait establishes diplomatic relations.

Dec. 4 President Chiang approves the resignation of Vice President Chen Cheng from his concurrent post as Premier.

16 New Premier Yen Chia-kan assumes office.

1964

Jan. 18 A strong earthquake, with its epicenter in Chiayi in southern Taiwan, killed 109 persons, injured about 500 and destroyed 900 houses.

Feb. 10 The Ministry of Education announces that 1,818 persons from 14 Afro-Asian countries have received third-country technical training in the Republic of China during the last 10 years

11 R.O.C. severs diplomatic relations with France.

Mar. 18 The fourth seminar for African agriculturalists is opened in Taipei.

20 R.O.C. and Sierra Leone sign an agricultural cooperation agreement in Freetown.

Apr. 7 R.O.C. and Chad sign an agricultural cooperation agreement in Taipei.

17 R.O.C. severs diplomatic relations with the Congo

(Brazzaville).

27 A second six-member Chinese medical team leaves for a two-year stay in Libya.

May 8 R.O.C. and Chile sign a trade agreement in Santiago.

25 R.O.C. and Upper Volta sign an agricultural cooperation agreement in Ouagadougou.

Jun. 3 R.O.C. and the United States sign a US$18 million farm surplus agreement.

8 R.O.C. and Peru sign a trade agreement in Lima.

14 The NT$3,200 million multipurpose Shihmen Dam dedicated.

15 The 11th Asian Film Festival open in Taipei with participants from seven Asian nations and Hongkong.

17 R.O.C. and Ecuador sign a trade agreement in Quito.

20 R.O.C. and Colombia sign a trade agreement in Bogota.

Chinese Anti-Communist National Salvation Army commandos raid Lufeng county, Kwangung province.

A C-46 passenger plane of the Civil Air Transport crashes in central Taiwan, killing all 57 aboard.

29 R.O.C. and Guatemala sign a trade agreement in Guatemala City.

30 The Legislative Yuan revises the Copyright Law.

Jul. 6 R.O.C. recognizes Malawi.

10 R.O.C. and Colombia sign in Bogota a treaty of amity and cultural relations.

Taiwan province enforces the program for equalization of urban land rights.

16 The Executive Yuan lifts the ban on import of Japanese goods by government establishments and public enterprises.

Aug. 12 General Chang Chun, secretary general to President Chiang, leaves for Tokyo for a 10-day goodwill visit.

R.O.C. and Togo sign in Lome an agricultural technical cooperation agreement.

17 A 40-member Chinese cultural goodwill mission leave for Africa for a three-month performance.

General Chang Chun arrives in Seoul from Tokyo for a week's goodwill visit.

25 R.O.C. and the Philippines sign in Manila a land reform and agricultural technical cooperation agreement.

Sept. 14 A six-member economic goodwill mission led by P.Y. Hsu, governor of the Central Bank of China, leave for Central America.

25 R.O.C. and Mexico sign a trade agreement in Mexico City.

Oct. 6 R.O.C. and Uruguay sign a treaty of amity in Taipei.

7 A 15-man Chinese military advisory mission leaves for Saigon.

11 R.O.C. and the Dominican Republic sign a trade agreement in Santo Domingo.

13 R.O.C. and the Congo (Leopoldville) sign an agricultural technical cooperation agreement in Taipei.

23 R.O.C. and El Salvador sign a trade agreement in San Salvador.

26 R.O.C. and Panama sign a trade agreement in Panama City.

30 R.O.C. and Nicaragua sign a trade agreement in Managua.

Nov. 4 R.O.C. and Costa Rica sign a trade agreement in San Jose.

5 R.O.C. severs diplomatic relations with the Central African Republic.
R.O.C. and Honduras sign a trade agreement in Tegucigalpa.

8 R.O.C. severs diplomatic relations with Senegal.
China and Guatemala sign a trade agreement in Guatemala City.

10 Yu Yu-jen, president of the Control Yuan, dies at 86.

23 The 10th Conference of the Asian Peoples' Anti-Communist League opens in Taipei.

26 R.O.C. opens a consulate in Kuala Lumpur, Malaysia.

27 R.O.C. and Korea sign a treaty of amity in Seoul.

Dec. 1 Premier Yen Chia-kan leaves for Seoul for a four-day official visit.

22 The Legislative Yuan revises the Statute for Encouragement of Investment.

31 R.O.C. and the United States sign two agreements in Taipei for the purchase of US$66,364,000 worth of American farm products.

1965

Jan. 5 Prime Minister S. Ramgoolam of Mauritius arrives for a nine-day visit.

27 Taiwan's first eye bank is set up in the southern port city of Kaohsiung.

29 R.O.C. and the U.N. Special Fund sign an agreement to provide US$880,200 to help Taiwan develop animal husbandry.

Feb. 5 China expresses opposition to French President de Gaulle's proposal for a five-nation conference, including the Peiping regime, to discuss matters concerning the United Nations.

8 Tainan and Monterey, California, U.S.A. are united as sister cities.

11 Soviet Prime Minister Aleksei Kosygin meets Mao Zedong and Liu Shaoqi when he visits Beijing on his return trip from Hanoi to Moscow.

24 The fifth agricultural seminar for African technicians is opened in Taipei with 49 students from 17 countries.

Mar. 5 Vice President Chen Cheng dies of liver cancer at 67.

13 The Education Ministry authorizes National Taiwan University and National Chengchi University to confer honorary doctorates on foreign nationals.

27 R.O.C. and Gabon sign an agricultural technical cooperation agreement in Taipei.

29 The Foreign Ministry closes its Commissioner's Office in Macao.

Apr. 1 The Academia Sinica establishes Institutes of Ethnology, Modern History and Chemistry.

2 The government declares "protocols" signed recently by the Peiping regime with Afghanistan and Pakistan illegal and not binding on R.O.C.

President Chiang appoints General Hsueh Yuehh as acting chairman of the Planning Committee for Recovery of the Mainland.

8 R.O.C. severs diplomatic relations with Dahomey.

9 R.O.C. and the United States conclude in Taipei an accord to establish a Sino-American fund for economic and social development in Taiwan.

12 R.O.C. and the United Nations sign in Taipei an accord to establish the National Maritime Development Institute in Taiwan.

18 The Taiwan Provincial Government announces revised regulations governing the entry and exit of civilian vessels and aircraft of countries having no diplomatic ties with R.O.C.

The Legislative Yuan revises the law governing demarcation of national, provincial and county revenues.

24 Liberian Vice President William R. Tolbert arrives for a six-day visit.

26 R.O.C. and Japan sign in Taipei a US$150 million loan for economic development of Taiwan.

28 The World Bank and R.O.C. sign in the United States a US$20 million loan agreement under which China will

modernize its railway system.

May 1 A R.O.C. Navy patrol craft sinks four Chinese Communist gunboats and damages two others near Matsu.

14 Thomas Wen-yi Liao returns from Tokyo after renouncing his "Taiwan independence movement."

15 R.O.C. and Korea sign a cultural agreement in Taipei.

22 The Foreign Ministry announces China and Honduras have agreed to elevate their legations to embassy status from May 20.

25 R.O.C. and the United States sign in Taipei an inventory of atomic equipment and materials to be reported to the International Atomic Energy Agency.

26 R.O.C. and Rwanda sign a handicraft technical cooperation agreement in Kigali.

Jun. 4 The Communications Ministry says R.O.C. has joined the Provisional Committee on the Communication Satellite.

25 R.O.C. and El Salvador exchange in Taipei ratifications of a trade agreement signed in San Salvador in October, 1964.

The Legislative Yuan approvers a bill to sanction expansion of the number of seats on the UN Security Council and the Economic and Social Council.

26 R.O.C. and Chad issue a joint communiqué in Taipei, announcing a US$3 million Chinese grant to Chad for economic and social development.

Jul. 1 Five research centers (mathematics, chemistry, chemistry, biology, physics and engineering) are inaugurated in Taipei, Hsinchu and Tainan.

The United States phases out economic aid to R.O.C.

2 R.O.C. and the Philippines sign a three-year technical cooperation agreement in Manila.

26 The Sino-African agricultural technical cooperation workshop is opened in Abidjan, Ivory Coast.

R.O.C. and Sierra Leone sign an agreement on technical cooperation in Taipei.

Aug. 1 The government enforces the revised exit and entry regulations for foreign visitors with the abolition of the 72-hour visa-free ruling which have been in effect for three years.

3 R.O.C. and Upper Volta sign a technical cooperation agreement in Taipei.

6 Two R.O.C. Navy gunboats sink five Communist ships and

damage two others south of Kinmen.

11 R.O.C. recognizes Singapore.

14 Lee Shih-tsung is elected president of the Control Yuan.

15 Premier Nguyen Cao Ky of South Vietnam arrives for a five-day visit.

21 The Sixth agricultural seminar for African technicians is opened in Taipei.

22 Madame Chiang Kai-shek leaves for the United States on a private visit.

23 The Kinmen County Government announces 134 Kinmen inhabitants have been killed and 426 others wounded by Communist gunfire since 1958.

31 R.O.C. and the United States sign in Taipei an agreement on the status of U.S. forces in R.O.C.

Sept. 3 *Red Flag* publishes Lin Biao's article Long Live the Victory of the People's War to commemorate the twentieth anniversary of the War of Resistance against Japan.

6 The Foreign Ministry announce R.O.C. has recognized the provisional government of the Dominican Republic.

10 The Foreign Ministry announces the Chinese legation in Haiti has

been elevated to the status of an embassy.

11 R.O.C. severs diplomatic relations with Mauritania.

13 Phan Huy Quat, former Premier of South Vietnam, arrives for a week's visit.

16 R.O.C. and the UN Food and Agriculture Organization sign a forestry development agreement in Taipei.

18 The first windmill power plan in the Far East begins operations in Penghu.

19 Defense Minister Chiang Ching-kuo leaves for the United States for a 10-day visit.

26 The fifth Asian Soft Tennis Tournament is opened in Taipei.

Oct. 4 The ninth Executive Council meeting of the Far Eastern Regional Organization for Public Administration and the Seminar of Administration of Land Reform for Rural Development is opened in Taipei.

8 The Asian Christian Anti-Communist Conference is opened in Taipei.

15 The third Sino-Vietnam Economic Cooperation Conference is opened in Taipei.

16 R.O.C. and South Korea exchange notes on the revised Sino-Korean air agreement in

Seoul.

20 R.O.C. and South Vietnam Sign an electric power technical contract in Taipei.

Nov. 5 The first International Conference of Chinese Buddhists is opened in Taipei.

10 In the Shanghai newspaper *Wenhui bao*, Yao Wenyuan denounces Wu Han's drama *Hai Rui's Dismissal* as an anti-Party poisonous weed. The article leads on to fierce denunciations in the press of this and other literary works in the following months.

11 Three Chinese Communist airmen defect to Taiwan in a Russian-made IL-28 jet bomber.
National Chengchi University confers China's first honorary doctorate on Paul M.A. Linebarger, professor of political science at Johns Hopkins University.

12 The nation observes the birthday centennial of Dr. Sun Yat-sen, Founding Father of the Chinese Republic.
Malagasy President Tsiranana arrives for a four-day unofficial visit.

13 The R.O.C. Navy sink four Chinese Communist gunboats off the Wuchiu Islands near the Chinese mainland.

16 The World Health Organization declares Taiwan has eradicated malaria.

17 The UN General Assembly rejects a draft resolution to seat the Chinese Communists.

23 U.S. warships return to China 102 cases of rare books that were sent to the United States for safekeeping during World War II.

Dec. 9 The United States turns over F-5A Freedom Fighter jet planes to R.O.C.

22 President Chiang issues a decree convoking an extraordinary session of the National Assembly in Taipei on Feb. 1, 1966.

27 The Defense Ministry announces the Chinese Communists fired 9,430 shells against Kinmen and Matsu in 1965.

28 The Foreign Ministry announces R.O.C. had donated 60 tons of relief rice to the Philippines for victims of the Taal volcano eruption Sept. 28.

1966

Jan. 1 U.S. Vice President Hubert H. Humphrey arrives for a one-day visit.

2 Two former Chinese Communist airmen, Li Hsien-

ping and Li Tsai-wang, renounce their membership of the Chinese Communist Party and are enlisted in the R.O.C. Air Force.

4 The sixth agricultural seminar for African technicians is concluded.

9 A Chinese Communist LCM (Landing Craft, Mechanized) defects from Foochow to Matsu. President Chiang issues a decree convoking the National Assembly on February 1.

11 The Legislative Yuan approves the agreement on the status of U.S. forces in Taiwan.

20 A seven-man Chinese delegation leaves for New Delhi to attend the 15th convention of the Pacific Area Travel Association.

27 Forty-two Chinese medical personnel leave for Libya to help set up a health education center and promote health education in schools.

Feb. 1 The extraordinary session of the National Assembly is opened in Taipei.

5 The seventh agricultural seminar for African technicians opens in Taipei.

15 Korean President Park Chung Hee arrives for a four-day state visit.

R.O.C. is designated by the U.S. Agency for International Development to supply goods to Vietnam, Laos and Korea under AID financed emergency procurement.

19 R.O.C. and Iran exchange in Taipei the ratification instruments of cultural convention signed on November 11, 1957.
R.O.C. and Ecuador sign a technical cooperation agreement in Quito.

20 The fourth plenary session of the National Assembly is opened in Taipei.

24 The Executive Yuan approves the revision of the Sino-Malawi technical cooperation agreement.

Mar. 1 Monsignor Giuseppe Caprio, Vatican Minister to R.O.C. announces that Bishop Stanislaus Lo Kuang of Tainan has succeeded Thomas Cardinal Tien as archbishop of Taipei.

4 The Foreign Ministry announces R.O.C.'s opposition to admission of East Germany to the United Nations.

5 The Foreign Ministry announces R.O.C. has extended support to the new Ghanaian government.

10 The Kuomintang nominates Chiang Kai-shek and Yen Chia-kan as candidates for President

and Vice President.

12 The Foreign Ministry protests against French seizure of the Paris premises of the R.O.C.'s mission to the U.N. Educational, Scientific and Cultural Organization.

14 R.O.C. and Japan sign in Tokyo an agreement for sale of 150,000 tons of rice to Japan.

17 The Executive Yuan approves floating of NT$2.3 billion in short-term public bonds and NT$500 million in patriotic bonds in fiscal 1967.

19 R.O.C. and Argentina sign a cultural agreement in Taipei.

20 The first Postal Museum of R.O.C. is inaugurated at Hsintien near Taipei.

21 The national Assembly elects President Chiang Kai-shek to a fourth term as President of the Republic.

22 The National Assembly elects Premier C.K. Yen as the fourth Vice President of the Republic.

25 "Sino-Philippine Friendship Year" is opened.

26 The Foreign Ministry announces China's opposition to U.S. recognition of Outer Mongolia.

30 R.O.C. and Japan revise the Sino-Japanese Air Transport Agreement.

31 The Executive Yuan approves

the Sino-Gabonese Agricultural Cooperation Agreement.

The China Open Golf Tournament opens in Tamsui with 103 golfers from 11 nations participating.

Apr. 7 The Foreign Ministry announces R.O.C. has recognized the new government of Ecuador.

12 Chen Wan-fu, former chairman of the "Taiwan Democratic Party" and a leader of the "Taiwan independence movement" in Tokyo, returns after 20 years of self-exile in Japan.

13 The Sino-U.S. agreement on the status of U.S. armed forces in Taiwan come into effect.

15 A large-scale anti-Chinese demonstration take place at the Chinese Embassy in Jakarta, with demonstrators ransacking the building.

21 The Foreign Ministry announces R.O.C. and Dahomey resumed diplomatic relations.

24 Defense Minister Chiang Ching-kuo leaves for Seoul for a six-day visit.

26 A nine-member Chinese farm demonstration team returns from Sierra Leone after two years of service.

27 A Chinese agricultural tea leaves for Africa for a month's

survey tour.

The Taiwan Garrison Command conducts an island-wide air-raid exercise.

May 1 The two-week anti-TB seminar sponsored by the World Health Organization's West Pacific Region is opened in Taipei.

The 71-kilometer Northern Cross-Island Highway is opened to traffic.

2 Philippine Vice President and Mrs. Fernando Lopez arrive for a six-day visit.

10 Admiral U.S. Grant Sharp, commander-in-chief of U.S. Forces Pacific, arrives for a two-day visit.

16 The Chinese Communist Politburo announces its decision to set up the Cultural Revolution Group, and calls for attacks on all representatives of the bourgeoisie.

17 Three hundred and sixty-four members of the Legislative Yuan call on the U.S. Congress to avoid appeasement of the Chinese Communist regime.

20 Chiang Kai-shek and Yen Chia-kan are sworn in as the fourth President and fourth Vice President of the Republic.

21 Vice President Yen Chia-kan is named to served concurrently as president of the Executive Yuan (premier).

27 Korean Deputy Premier Chang Key Young arrives to attend the second Sino-Korean Economic Cooperation Conference in Taipei.

President Chiang appoints five new cabinet members: Vice Premier Huang Shao-ku, Interior Minister Hsu Ching-Chung, Foreign Minister Wei Tao-ming and Ministers Without Portfolio Hsu Peh-yuan and Lien Cheng-tung.

28 R.O.C. and Rwanda sign a technical cooperation agreement in Taipei.

31 The Legislative Yuan approves the floating of NT$2,800 million (US$70 million) worth of public bonds in fiscal 1967.

Jun. 1 A 17- member Chinese farm demonstration team leaves for the Ivory Coast for two years of service.

3 The Foreign Ministry announces R.O.C. has sent 129 technicians to South Vietnam to help fight Communist aggression.

The Foreign Ministry voices opposition to France's intended nuclear test in the Tuamotu archipelago of the Pacific.

12 Foreign Minister Wei Tao-ming leaves for Seoul to attend the Asian and Pacific Ministerial

Conference.

14 R.O.C. and Upper Volta sign an agricultural cooperation agreement in Taipei.

15 The conference on Sino-American Cooperation in the Humanities and Social Sciences opens in Taipei.

18 The Asian Agricultural Development Seminar opens in Taipei.

21 Thirteen Chinese farmers leave for the Ivory Coast to help increase farm production.

23 The seventh African Seminar on Agricultural Techniques is concluded in Taipei.

29 President Chiang Kai-shek appoints Cha Liang-chien as president of the Supreme Court.

Jul. 1 R.O.C. and Venezuela agree to elevate their legations to the embassy level.

3 U.S. Secretary of State Dean Rusk arrives for a brief visit.
Eleven Chinese medical personnel leaves for Libya to help promote public health.

5 The Foreign Ministry announces R.O.C. recognizes the new government of Argentina.

6 The Legislative Yuan approves the Sino-Haiti treaty of amity signed in Port-au-Price on February 15, 1966.

7 R.O.C. establishes diplomatic relations with the Maldives.

11 R.O.C. establishes diplomatic relations with Malawi.

20 Kim Chung Yul, president of the Council of the Asian Peoples' Anti-Communist League, arrives from Seoul for a week's visit.

28 The Executive Yuan appoints Liu Chieh chief delegate to the 21st U.N. General Assembly.

29 R.O.C. and Bolivia sign a treaty of friendship at La Paz.

Aug. 6 The Foreign Ministry announces R.O.C. has donated US$10,000 to the United Nations for relief of Palestine refugees.

11 The Control Yuan concurs in President Chiang Kai-shek's appointment of 19 members of the Examination Yuan.

12 The Legislative Yuan ratifies the Charter of the Asian Development Bank.
R.O.C. and Gambia sign a technical cooperation agreement in Bathurst.

19 R.O.C. and South Vietnam sign a provisional air transport agreement in Taipei.

24 The Sino-Korean-Vietnamese Central Bank Governors' Conference is opened in Taipei.

Sept. 1 Sun Fo is sworn in as president of the Examination Yuan.

16 South Korea sign an agreement

in Taipei to buy 30,000 metric tons of Taiwan rice.

A Central News Agency dispatch from Hongkong says some 2,000 fishermen of Kwangtung Province have fled to the British colony in 10 days.

R.O.C.'s first school of the air, a commercial course at the high school level, opens in Taipei.

23 Vice President-Premier C.K. Yen says government agents are active in 27 provinces and major cities on the Communist-held mainland.

29 The R.O.C. chapter of the International Chamber of Commerce is inaugurated in Taipei.

30 The Planning Commission for Mainland Recovery holds its 24th meeting in Taipei.

Oct. 10 A three-day Armed Forces Athletic Meet opens in Taipei as the Republic celebrated its 55th National Day.

12 The fifth Far East Boy Scouts Conference opens in Taipei.

19 The annual military exercise "Operation Nanchang" is held in northern Taiwan.

21 The council meeting of the Asia Broadcasting Union opens in Taipei.

26 Madame Chiang Kai-shek returns after a 14-month visit to the United States.

27 The three-day 11th plenary session of the Committee for the Promotion of Sino-Japanese Cooperation opens in Taipei.

28 The Legislative Yuan approves the Sino-Argentine cultural convention signed in Taipei in March and the Sino-Haiti treaty of amity signed in Port-au-Prince in February.

Wu Chen-nan, former leader of the "Taiwan Independence Revolutionary Council" in Japan, returns to Taiwan.

30 A six-member Chinese delegation leaves for Seoul to attend the 12th conference of the Asian Peoples' Anti-Communist League.

31 The nation celebrates President Chiang's 80th (79th by Western reckoning) birthday.

Nov. 2 China Air Lines and Air Vietnam sign an agreement to open Taipei-Saigon flight service.

3 Liu Yueh-sheng, assistant managing editor and city editor of the *Wen Wei Pao*, one of the two leading Chinese Communist papers in Hongkong, defects and arrived in Taiwan.

The R.O.C. government decides to offer 1,500 tons of rice to the U.N. World Food Program as gifts to developing countries.

7 The three-day Fifth Asian Advertising Congress opens in Taipei.

10 The Executive Yuan approves a draft plan submitted by the Ministry of Communications for establishing a ground communication satellite station in Taiwan.

11 The Legislative Yuan today passes a resolution restricting legislators from practicing law or serving as chartered accountants.

12 President Chiang dedicates the newly completed Chinese Cultural Hall of the Chung Shan Building at Yangmingshan at the 101st anniversary of the birth of Dr. Sun Yat-sen and designates November 12 "Chinese Culture Renaissance Day".

14 Foreign Minister Wei Tao-ming leaves for New York to head the Chinese delegation at the U.N. General Assembly.

16 The Republic of China becomes the 54th member of the International Chamber of Commerce.

18 Lt. Gen. Abdullah Al-Mutlag, chief of the general staff of the Saudi Arabian armed forces, arrives for a four-day visit.

21 Leabua Jonathan, prime minister of the Kingdom of Lesotho, arrives for a week's visit.

The fourth Congress of Overseas Chinese Traders opens in Bangkok.

22 Frank B. Cooper, newly appointed Australian ambassador to the Republic of China, arrives in Taipei.

23 The Republic of China and Thailand sign a trade agreement in Bangkok.

29 The U.N. General Assembly votes by substantial majority to bar the Peiping regime from the United Nations for the 16th time.

Dec. 3 Chao Ying-hun, chief of the Chinese Communist-operated Hongkong Film Studio, defects and arrives in Taiwan.

The Kaohsiung Export Processing Zone is inaugurated.

6 The preparatory meeting for the third Sino-Korean ministerial conference on economic cooperation opens in Taipei.

7 U.S. Secretary of State Dean Rusk arrives in Taipei for a visit. A 110-member Chinese athletic team leaves for Bangkok and the fifth Asian Games.

12 Takeshi Watanabe, president of the Asian Development Bank, arrives in Taipei for a visit.

14 Wu Ah-ming of the Republic of

China wins the decathlon at the Asian Games.

16 A general census is carried out in Taiwan, Penghu and the offshore islands of Kinmen and Matsu.

23 The R.O.C. government lodge a strong protest with the Portuguese government against its sending of seven free Chinese sailors to the Peiping regime.

26 The Ninth Central Committee of the Kuomintan holds its four-day fourth plenary session at Yangmingshan in suburban Taipei.

30 R.O.C. and Botswana, a newly independent African country, establishes diplomatic relations.

1967

Jan. 1 Taipei becomes a special municipality by incorporating several outlaying and bordering districts and areas.

24 The Republic of China's first cardinal, Thomas Tien, dies of pneumonia at 78.

3 The Executive Yuan decides to extend the period of compulsory education from six to nine years beginning in 1968.

1968

Jan. 11 The Taiwan University Hospital

announces success of the first kidney transplant performed May 27.

Sept. 1 The Chinese government starts today the implementation of a nine-year free education system, thereby extending the constitutionally provided mandatory education by three years. The move is designed to upgrade the quality of the nation's manpower.

Nov. 10 The Republic of China's first "eye bank" is inaugurated in Taipei.

1969

Aug. 21 The cabinet announces that the new port, the fourth in Taiwan will be built at Wuchi near Taichung.

24 Jubilation sweeps over Taiwan as news dispatches from the United States reporting that the Taichung Golden Dragons win the 23rd Little League World Series by defeating Santa Clara, California 5-0.

Nov. 15 The first popular elections for members of the Taipei Municipal Council are held today. Out of 77 candidates, 48 are elected councilors of Greater Taipei whose status as special municipality was acquired more than two years ago.

Dec. 28 The earth station for commercial satellite communications located atop Yangingshan in suburban Taipei begins operation.

1970

Feb. 2 China Airlines inaugurates its trans-Pacific flight.

Jul. 6 Vice President-Premier C.K. Yen leaves for Tokyo on a week-long visit to open the China Day celebration in Expo 70 in Osaka.

1971

Mar. 2 Henry Ford II, board chairman of Ford Motor Company, arrives on a 24-hour visit to study the possibility of Ford's participation in economic development here.

Apr. 26 China Airlines inaugurates its second trans-Pacific route by a flight to Los Angeles via Tokyo and Honolulu. Its first route was to San Francisco on Feb. 2, 1970.

May 17 King Faisal Ibn Aziz al Saud of Saudi Arabia arrived today for a four-day state visit at the invitation of President Chiang Kai-shek who greeted him at the airport.

26 The Chinese delegation walks out of the United Nations General Assembly immediately before the Assembly votes 76-35 with 17 abstentions for an Albanian resolution to seat Peiping and expel the Republic of China.

18 The Bank of China, the oldest of the four state banks in the Republic of China, is converted into a private commercial bank named "China International Commercial Bank."

1972

Mar. 21 President Chiang Kai-shek is reelected to an unprecedented 5th term with near unanimity. All but eight of the 1316 ballots cast go to the President.

22 Vice President C.K. Yen wins reelection as 1095 of the 1307 votes cast go to him.

May 2 The Legislative Yuan elects Nieh Wen-ya as its president and Liu Kuo-tsai as its vice president in the first ballot.

26 The Legislative Yuan gives almost unanimous consent to President Chiang Kai-shek's nomination of Chiang Ching-kuo as premier.

30 The Chiang Ching-kuo cabinet sworn in. The lineup is as follows Premier – Chiang Ching-kuo; Vice Premier – Hsu Ching-chung; Interior Minister – Lin Chin-sheng; Foreign Minister – Shen Chang-huan;

Defense Minister – Gen. Chen Ta-ching; Finance Minister – K.T. Li; Education Minister – Tsiang Yien-si; Economic Affairs Minister – Y.S. Sun; Justice Minister – Wang Jen-yuan; Communications Minister – Henry Kao.

Jun. 20 The R.O.C. Mei Ho baseball team wins the Senior League world title.

27 The Taipei Little League baseball team wins the world title.

Sept. 21 Ford Motor Co. concludes an agreement to purchase controlling interest in the Lio Ho Automobile Industrial Corporation headquartered in Taiwan.

28 The Republic of China severs diplomatic relations with Japan.

Oct. 16 President Dawda Kairba Jawara of Gambia arrives for an eight-day visit.

Nov. 12 The Republic of China wins the World Cup Golf Championship in Melbourne.

Dec. 2 Forty-five business and industrial leaders of Taiwan organize a "East Asia Relations Association" to handle economic and cultural exchange between the Republic of China and Japan after the severance of their diplomatic relations Sept.

29.

23 An election of additional members to the National Assembly. Legislative Yuan, the Taiwan Provincial Assembly, and of new mayors and county magistrates is held in Taiwan, Kinmen, and Matsu.

26 The East Asia Relations Association sign an agreement with Japan's Interchange Association to insure coordination of Sino-Japanese relations on a non-governmental level.

1973

Jan. 23 Taiwan Provincial Governor Shieh Tung-min announced an anti-poverty program named "operation Well-To-Do" to help some 390,000 destitute citizens in this island to stand on their own feet.

Feb. 15 Finance Minister K.T. Li announces a 5 percent upward revaluation of the New Taiwan Dollar.

Mar. 1 The Cabinet approves the draft of a revised aviation law calling for death penalty to hijackers.

6 Premier Chiang Ching-kuo outlines a nine-point measures to fight inflation which is touched off by a combination of Taiwan's large trade surplus and

internal monetary chaos. The rate of inflation was 4.7 per cent in 1972. Trade surplus in 1972 reached US$545,000,000.

Apr. 2 The Central News Agency, founded by the Kuomintang in 1924, is reorganized as a limited company to facilitate its overseas operations.

May 9 The Republic of China and Saudi Arabia reach agreement under which more Chinese experts will go to Saudi Arabia for technical cooperation projects.

Jun. 7 The R.O.C. threatens "strong measures" including the interception of Japanese commercial aircraft, if Japan should alter the Sino-Japanese air agreement in exchange for an air treaty.

Jul. 8 An official Indian mission arrives here to investigate the mysterious disappearance of Shri Subhas Chandra Bose an Indian independence leader in 1945.

23 U.S. Secretary of Commerce Frederick B. Dent announces today the plans to open a U.S. trade center in Taipei next year. He says the center will be opened in the spring of 1974 with an exhibition of U.S. industrial and scientific

instruments by approximately 15 American firms.

Aug. 2 The Cabinet approves a US$444,700,000 budget for the construction of the first two stages of the North-South Freeway.

Sept. 1 The United States has begun to withdraw air force transport units that comprise almost 60 per cent of American military forces on Taiwan, official Chinese military sources disclosed.

13 Dr. Sun Fo, president of Examination Yuan and only son of Dr. Sun Yat-sen, the founding father of the Republic of China, dies of a heart attack today at the age of 82.

18 Provincial Governor Shieh Tung-min announces construction of the Projected Taichung harbor, Taiwan's fourth international seaport, will begin in November.

Oct. 17 The Asian Vegetable Research and Development Center, located at Shanhua, north of Tainan city, is officially dedicated today.

30 Tsengwen Dam and Reservoir, the largest in Taiwan, is completed.

Nov. 8 Premier Chiang Ching-kuo has ordered the lifting of curfew in

Keelung, making the north Taiwan port open 24 hours a day. The Premier instructed Communications Minister Henry Kao to put that order into effect as soon as practicable.

14 A contract is signed today between the China Shipbuilding Corporation (CSC) and Gatx Oswego Corporation of the United States under which Taiwan will build four 450,000-ton giant oil tankers.

22 The Cabinet today orders a 25 per cent cut in energy consumption by all its agencies, including 13 government enterprises.

Dec. 3 The Chinese government decides to invest NT$7.3 billion (US$1921 million) for the extension of Keelung and Kaohsiung in the next five years. Both have serious port congestion problem.

10 The Taiwan Provincial Government announces that construction of the Suao-Hualien railroad will start Christmas Day (Dec. 25) on schedule despite the shortage of building materials. The 80-kilometer railroad will cost roughly NT$2.777 billion (US$73 million).

25 Construction of the Suao-

Hualien railroad is launched.

1974

Jan. 1 Premier Chiang Ching-kuo tells the New York Times that the Republic of China will never negotiate with the Chinese Communists. "To do so would be suicide, and we would not be so stupid as that," he said.

12 The Chinese government decides to float government bonds worth NT$10 billion (US$263 million) to help finance nine key development projects here i.e. Taiwan Area Freeway, Taichung Harbor, Taoyuan International Airport, Suao-Hualien Reilway, Suao Port, an integrated steel mill, a giant shipyard, electrification of the west coast trunk railway and the development of petrochemical industry.

18 The Ministry of Foreign Affairs reaffirms the Republic of China's sovereignty over the Nan Sha (the Spratley Island) and Hsi Sha (the Paracel Island) archipelagoes.

26 Premier Chiang Ching-kuo announces an across-the-board price adjustment to help stabilize the economy.

27 The Cabinet announces an economic stabilization program

calling for an across-the-board price adjustment designed to help stabilize the economy against the impact of a worldwide inflationary spiral.

Feb. 1 The Ministry of National Defense confirms today that the Republic of China has stationed a garrison force on the Spratleys.

15 President Richard Nixon today nominates Leonard Unger, who has been U.S. ambassador to Thailand since 1967, as ambassador to the Republic of China. He will replace Amb. Walter P. McConaughy who will return to the United States for retirement. Unger's appointment is hailed in Taipei as a sign of continued U.S. commitment to the R.O.C.

Apr. 19 The Chinese government today cut the air link between Taiwan and Japan, served by their flag-carriers China Airlines and Japan Air Lines, in protest of Japanese Foreign Minister Ohira's insulting remarks on the national flag of the Republic of China. CAL's Korean service is also stopped on the same day. But its cross-Pacific flights are maintained via the Guam route.

May 14 Chen Te-nien, director of the Taiwan Railway Administration, and Peter Godwin, representing Lazard Brothers Co., sign an agreement under which a British consortium will loan £575 million to TRA's railway electrification.

28 The Third General Session of the Pacific Asian Congress of Municipalities (PACOM) opens in Taipei today. The meeting, attended by some 140 delegates from 20 countries, is the largest international gathering held in the Republic of China this year.

Jun. 6 The Republic of China and the Republic of Korea sign a three-year agreement today on exchange of science information.

Jul. 16 Foreign Minister Shen Chang-huan discloses today that the Republic of China and the United States are cooperating in the manufacture of modern jet fighters and helicopters in Taiwan.

29 The Sanchung-Chungli section of the North-South Freeway is opened to traffic.

Aug. 3 The Republic of China and Paraguay sign today a memorandum for broad economic cooperation in the future.

24 The Chinese team from Kaohsiung bests Red America West (Bluff, Calif.) to win the 1974, Little League World

Championship. It is the fourth straight year that a Republic of China team wins the annual tournament and the fifth time in six years.

26 Vice Admiral Edwin K. Snyder, newly appointed commander of the United States Taiwan Defense Command, arrives here today to assume his new post. He replaces Vice Admiral Phillip A. Beshany, who is retiring after 40 years of service with the U.S. Navy.

Sept. 3 Economic Affairs Minister Y.S. Sun discloses today that the Republic of China will invest US$130 million for the construction of an oil refinery and a fertilizer plant in Saudi Arabia in cooperation with the Saudi Arabian government.

6 China Airlines, the flag-carrier of the Republic of China, has decided to withdraw from the International Air Transport Association (IATA) for financial reasons. The withdrawal will become effective as of Sept. 17.

Oct. 2 Economic Minister Y.S. Sun confirms today large amount of national gas deposits are found off the coast of Kaohsiung. Beginning last year, the state-owned Chinese Petroleum Corporation and six American oil companies are engaged in oil prospecting work in the Taiwan Straits.

6 Techi Dam, the second tallest dam in the Far East which is located in Central Taiwan, is dedicated today after five years of construction. The multi-purpose dam system has power generation capacity of 244,000 kilowatts. One of the biggest development projects in the Republic of China. Techi Dam has also irrigation capabilities.

11 The Ministry of National Defense announces the Sino-US joint manufacturing of the supersonic F-5E Freedom Fighter in Taiwan.

12 Finance Minister K.T. Li reveals that the U.S. Export-Import Bank has agreed to lend US$934,890,000 to the Republic of China to finance the construction of ten basic development projects in Taiwan.

30 The first F5E Freedom jet fighter made in the Republic of China rolls off the assembly line.

Nov. 3 A high-powered economic and trade mission from the Republic of China, led by Economic Minister Y.S. Sun, leaves for South America today to promote trade.

14 Charles Smith, UPI Hongkong manager, reports that a major American California-based firm will soon sell to the Republic of China "an extensive air defense system" with the blessing of the U.S. State Department and Defense Department.

The Chinese government announces today a 14-point anti-slump program to help business and industry fight their current woes. The program covers the fields of finance, taxation, economic activities and production. Prominent among the anti-slump measures is the lifting of the ban on the construction of tall buildings early last year.

24 The ruling Kuomintang marks its 80th founding anniversary with a rally which is attended by 2800 party leaders at all levels. The only foreign delegate present at the meeting is Yoshio Kikuchi, a former member of Japanese Diet who joined the KMT only last year. The occasion also serves as the opening ceremony of the Fifth Anniversary Meeting of the 10th KMT Central Committee.

Dec. 1 The Free China Relief Association appeals to the British authorities in Hongkong not to turn the so-called "illegal immigrants" over to the Chinese Communists. The FCRA made the statement as the Hongkong government handed over five mainland escapees to the Communists at a border point on Nov. 30.

2 Foreign Minister Shen Chang-huan reveals, that overseas Chinese holding passports issued by the Peiping regime may get the passports of the Republic of China only if they surrender the Communist passports and admit their mistakes in holding Peiping-issued passports in the first place.

10 Toshio Urab, former Japanese ambassador to the Philippines, arrives in Taipei today as the new head of the Taipei Office of the Interchange Association of Japan. With his arrival, the director of the Taipei Office of the Interchange Association is elevated in rank from minister to ambassador.

21 Official information reports that per capita income in the Republic of China will hit US$700 this year compared with US$470 in 1973.

27 The Japanese army straggler, found on Morotai Island in the

Malku Group of Indonesia yesterday, is identified as Li Kuang-hui, a 55-year-old Ami tribesman in Taitung County. He was drafted by the Japanese in 1942, and was last reported missing in action on March 5, 1945. His Japanese name is Teruo Nakamura, a private first class of the Japanese Army.

1975

Feb. 3 The Republic of China and Jordan sign an air cooperation agreement today enabling China Airlines to fly to Amman and ALIA, the Jordanian flag-carrier, to fly to Taipei.

25 The executive committee of the International Press Institute (IPI) decides to reinstate the membership of the Republic of China national committee after a suspension in 1972 in the wake of Yuyitung brother case. The Yuyitungs were the publisher and editor of a Chinese newspaper in Manila. They were deported to Taiwan by the Philippine government in 1971. The brothers were subsequently tried and convicted here on the charge of doing propaganda for the Chinese Communists. They were released after serving a one-year and two-year

reformation detention respectively.

5 The Cabinet reports economic growth rate of the Republic of China in 1974 nosedived to 0.6 per cent due to world wide recession compared with over 10 per cent in the previous years.

17 The China Steel Corp., the Continental Illinois National Bank, and the Trust Company of Chicago sign a US$200 million loan contract to help finance construction of a steel mill in Kaohsiung.

24 The Chinese government held a three-day National Economic Conference beginning today to chart the future course of the economic development of the nation. A total of 126 government leaders, business and industrial leaders, and top-flight economic experts took part in the meeting.

27 China Airlines requested the government approval for a special "Visit the Republic of China" fare for both Chinese and foreign travelers coming here from the West Coast of the United States. The special fare will be US$750 round-trip from the West Coast to Taipei compared with the regular fare of US$1,162. It will be further

reduced to US$650 if the traveler is with a group of 15 persons or more.

Apr. 5 President Chiang Kai-shek passes away at 11:50 p.m. today of a heart attack. He was 87. (1887-1975).

6 Yen Chia-kan, vice president of the Republic of China since 1966, takes the oath of office as the nation's second constitutional president.

16 Twenty foreign missions including the U.S. mission led by Vice President Nelson A. Rockefeller, and Senator Barry Goldwater and Japanese mission led by former Japanese Prime Ministers Nobusuke Kishi and Disaku Sato attend the national memorial service for the late President Chiang Kai-shek.

17 U.S. Vice President Nelson Rockefeller delivers a message from President Gerald Ford to Premier Chiang Ching-kuo reaffirming American support to the Republic of China after the passing of President Chiang Kai-shek.

26 Former South Vietnamese President Nguyen Van Thieu arrived in Taipei just before the fall of Saigon to the advancing North Vietnamese forces. He is forced to resign by his opposition. Mrs. Thieu will go to Taiwan on May 1 from Bangkok to join her husband in exile.

28 President Chiang Ching-kuo is elected to newly created post of chairman of the Kuomintang Central committee at its extraordinary session of the Kuomintang. The election has made him the leader of the government and the ruling party.

May 3 The Chinese government sets up a refugee reception center in Kaohsiung to provide temporary shelter to overses Chinese refugees from South Vietnam. Navy ships have been sent to Vietnam to pick up Chinese refugees there before the fall of Saigon. Some 1400 chinese refugees are expected to arrive soon from Vietnam and Cambodia.

8 A group of 884 refugees from Vietnam, nearly all of them Chinese descendants, arrive in Kaohsiung today abroad Chinese naval vessels after the Communist conquest of South Vietnam.

26 The Embassy of the Republic of China in Saigon suspends operations.

30 The Ministry of Justice announces that 3600 convicted

prisoners will be released on July 14 when the Statue for the Commutation of Sentences will go into effect. Jail terms for 54,000 others will also be slashed. Premier Chiang Ching-kuo proposes the act of leniency in memory of President Chiang Kai-shek.

Jun. 9 The Republic of China terminates diplomatic relations with the Republic of the Philippines.

19 An agreement is signed today in Riyadh between the Republic of China and Saudi Arabia to further strengthen economic and technical cooperation between the two countries.

Jul. 1 The R.O.C. terminates diplomatic relations with Thailand.

9 The Republic of China and Japan sign a private aviation agreement that restores the Taiwan-Japan services of China Airlines and a Japanese airline.

11 Chang Yen-tien, chairman of East Asia Relations Association of the Republic of China, and Teizo Horikoshi, chairman of Japanese Interchange Association, sign an agreement today in Taipei for the resumption of direct air links between the Republic of China

and Japan after a 17-month suspension.

16 The second harbor entrance of Kaohsiung is dedicated today after nine years of construction at a cost of NT$1.4 billion. It can accommodate ships up to 75,000 tons.

Aug. 9 Premier Chiang Ching-kuo suggests the scrapping of the Four-Year Economic Plan in favor of a Six-Year Economic Plan after 1976. He explains that the Four-Year Plans are no longer adequate in view of the fact that the major construction projects going on in the country take more than four years to complete. A longer period will enable the government to make a more reasonable allocation of resources to broaden the infrastructure and upgrade the industrial development of Taiwan. The Republic of China is now in the third year of the Sixth Four-Year Economic Plan.

10 The air link between the Republic of China and Japan is resumed today after the Flight 002 of China Airlines left Taipei for Tokyo enroute to the United States in the afternoon.

26 The newly built southern porton of the Suao-Hualien railroad is opened to traffic.

30 The official Central Daily News reports today that the Chinese Airforce is scheduled to start production of an improved model of Sidewinder air-to-air missile in coming September. The report says through research and development, the CAF is now able to modify certain part of the American-supplied Sidewinder, and make it into a superior new air defense weapon. During the Battle of Kinmen in 1958, the Chinese Airforce defeated the Red Chinese airforce through the use of the U.S. supplied Sidewinders.

Sept. 22 President Alfredo Stroessner of Paraguay arrives in Taipei today to begin a four-day state visit at the invitation of President C. K. Yen of the Republic of China.

Oct. 6 Members of the Anti-Communist National Salvation Army (ANSA), a commando outfit in the Republic of China, has carried out 230 missions on the Chinese mainland, ANSA sources said today. About 70 per cent of missions were carried out "with complete success." The source described the missions as conducting raids on the mainland, giving support to anti-Communist elements behind the enemy lines and guerrilla bands, punishing Communist chieftains, and helping defecting Communist cadres and refugees fleeing to the free world.

10 The Republic of China today held a grand military parade in celebration of its national day. The last military parade was held in 1964.

Nov. 2 The 1975 Billy Graham Crusade in Taipei is ended today with a capacity attendance at the Taipei City Sports Stadium despite periodic rains. Among the listeners at the final meeting is Premier Chiang Ching-kuo.

3 The National Education Conference opens today to tackle the major educational problems of the nation. It is attended by over 300 educational experts.

9 Dr. F. A. von Hayek, 1974 winner of the Nobel Prize on economics, arrives here for a ten-day visit. Dr. Hayek speaks highly of the economic performance and stability in the Republic of China. He particularly praises the land reform in Taiwan which, he said, will contribute to the promotion of freedom of mankind.

17 The economic growth rate in the Republic of China has been

revised up from 6.5 per cent to 7.5 per cent a year when the Six-Year Plan begins in 1976, C. C. Chang, chairman of Economic Planning Council said today.

Dec. 3 A CNA report from Washington says that a House resolution calling on the U.S. government to do nothing to compromise the freedom of the Republic of China has won the support of a majority of members in the House of Representatives. The number of sponsors of the said resolution reaches 218. This represents a majority in the 435-seat House of Representatives.

9 U.S. Assistant Secretary of State for East Asian and Pacific Affairs Philip Habib arrives in Taipei and briefed Premier Chiang Ching-kuo on the results of U.S. President Gerald Ford's recent trip to the Chinese mainland. The meeting lasts 90 minutes. The American diplomat assures the Premier that the American policy of maintaining friendly relations with the Republic of China remains unchanged.

18 Philip Habib, the U.S. Assistant Secretary of State for East Asian and Pacific Affairs, during his testimony at the Congress yesterday, indicates the

"Japanese Formula" is not applicable to the R.O.C.-U.S. ties because the U.S. has certain treaty obligations toward the Republic of China. He says the Chinese Communists are "quite aware" that the United States has an obligation to come to Taiwan's defense if it is attacked.

26 The Legislative Yuan today passes the Radio and Television Act. Under the law, commercial ads on TV and radio should not exceed 15 per cent of the broadcast time, and at least 45 per cent of the time should be devoted to news, education, culture, public service and explaining government regulation.

1976

Jan. 9 Chou En-lai dies on Jan. 8. communist affairs experts in Taipei believe that Chou's death, which is long expected, is unlikely to produce great impact on Red China's succession problem and its foreign policy.

Feb. 8 Local mainland affairs experts says the naming of Hua Kuo-feng as the "acting premier" of Red China confirms the long-held view here that Mao Tse-tung is helping his wife's radical group to take over after he dies. Western experts are generally surprised by Hua's promotion because they have assumed that Teng Hsiao-ping will get the premiership as a matter of course.

19 The Cabinet today approves the First Six-Year Economic Plan which starts this year. Under the Plan, the economic growth rate in 1976 is set at 6.4 per cent, while the per capita income in this year is projected at US$779.

21 With full government backing, two airlines in the Republic of China, namely China Airlines and Far Eastern Transport Corp., will purchase from the United States seven aircraft worth about US$95 million.

CAL, the flag-carrier of the ROC, will buy five Boeings worth US$87 million. The FAT will spend US$8 million for two Boeing 737s.

27 Premier Chiang Ching-kuo today lashes at the theory of Taiwan independence in his administrative report to the Legislative Yuan. He charges that "people who want Taiwan independence in his administrative report to the Legislative Yuan. He charges that "people who want Taiwan

to go a separate way are destroying themselves." The Premier says advocacy of "Taiwan is Taiwan and China is China" is "either ignorant of history, geography ethnic ties, and tradition of China, or playing into the hands of the Chinese communists."

Mar. 8 A five-day economic and technical cooperation conference between the Republic of China and Kingdom of Saudi Arabia opens today in Taipei amid growing economic ties. Forecast for two-way trade this year is around US$450 million.

10 Chinese Finance Minister K. T. Li and Dr. Mahsou Bahjat Jalal, vice chairman and managing director of the Saudi Fund for Development who is visiting Taipei sign a loan agreement under which the Republic of China will receive US$50 million from Saudi Arabia to finance the construction of Taiwan Area Freeway.

26 Dr. Lin Yu-tang, 81, one of the best known Chinese writers in English, dies in Hong Kong.

Apr. 5 Local experts on Chinese Communist affairs believe the riot at the Tien An-men Square in Peiping today is organized by forces loyal to Teng Hsiao-ping and marks the beginning of the counter attack of the capitalist roaders against the radicals of the Chiang Ching camp.

26 The Fourth Asian Writers Conference opens today in Taipei. Some 80 delegates attend the meeting.

The Republic of China and Republic of South Africa today upgrade their official ties by elevating their mutual representation to embassy status.

Jun. 1 The state-owned Chinese Petroleum Corporation decides to tap a natural gas field outside the Kaohsiung coast whose daily yield is estimated at 50 million cubic meters, or ten times the total gas output on land in Taiwan. CPC says the gas deposits can be taped for 20 years.

Jul. 1 The Chinese government will spend roughly NT$1400 billion (US$36.8 billion) for the implementation of the Six-Year Economic Plan which starts this year, the Economic Planning council announces.

17 The Republic of China Olympic team today decides to withdraw from the Montreal Games to keep its national identity intact. It takes this painful decision because the International Olympic Committee's final ruling has suggested that the Chinese athletes compete at Montreal under the name of Taiwan instead of Republic of China.

30 Free China Relief Association today decides to render effective help to victims of the devastating earthquake which flattened industrial city of Tangshan of North China on July 28. Experts here estimate that the quake casualties may exceed one million.

Aug. 4 New York Times reports today that the United States will supply the Republic of China a sophisticated radar air defense system valued at US$34 million and 60 F-5 fighters in addition to 120 F-5s already promised to beef up the defense capability of the ROC. The State Department, when asked to comment, did not deny the report. Chinese sources here neither confirm nor deny the Washington report.

16 The Central Weather Bureau today pinpoints the epicenter of today's earthquake on the Chinese mainland at a spot in the vicinity of Chungwei of Ninghsia province with a magnitude of 7 at the Richter

scale. Subsequent foreign reports show that the strong earthquake hit the densely populated northern Szechwan province. The Chinese Communists have admitted the quake, but refused to reveal the extent of damages in the case of the devastating Tangshan case.

25 The American Chamber of Commerce in the Republic of China has completed a draft document calling on the United States Government to stop considering granting diplomatic recognition to the Chinese Communist regime. The document also calls for continued U.S. support to the ROC. This is an unprecedented action taken by the American business community in Taiwan amid growing States side reports of possible early recognition of Communist China before Mao Tse-tung dies.

Sept. 1 Government Information Office describes as "malicious fabrication" American press reports that the Republic of China has started secretly processing spent uranium fuel to make nuclear weapons.

9 News of Mao Tse-tung's death is greeted with jubilation throughout the Republic of China as it reaches here late this afternoon.

Firecrackers exploded in many parts of this island as people learn of the news from radio broadcasts, special bulletins or by word of mouth.

The 82-year-old Mao dies at 12:10 a.m. today (Peiping time).

Oct. 12 Taipei is surprised by press reports from Peiping that Chiang Ching, widow of Mao Tse-tung, and three other ultraleftist Chinese Communist Party Politburo members have been arrested by the authorities in Peiping on charges of plotting a coup.

The report was filed by Nigel Wade, Peiping correspondent of London Daily Telegraph, who quoting reliable sources said that the arrests were announced to political organizers at special weekend briefings. The other three politburo members arrested were Wang Hung-wen, second vice chairman of the Chinese Communist Party; Chang Chun-chiao, first vice premier; and Yao Wen-yuan, a leading ideologue and polemicist in Communist China.

The arrest of the "Shanghai clique" is the biggest political upheaval in Red China since the alleged coup attempt made by the former "Defense Minister" Lin Piao in 1971 when Mao was still in power.

21 The Cabinet approves today the Six-Year Economic Plan which starts this year to make the Republic of China a developed national by 1981. Total investment under this plan will amount to NT$1658 billion (US$43.63 billion).

31 China Airlines today starts its Taipei-Jeddah service to promote trade and friendly relations between the Republic of China and Saudi Arabia.

Taichung Port in west central Taiwan is formally opened.

Nov. 12 In his political report to the 11th National congress of Kuomintang on Nov. 12, Premier Chiang Ching-kuo warn the United States against using the Republic of China as a chip in its diplomatic gamble to play off the Chinese Communists against the Russians.

He also declared that Taipei will not accept any "good-will" or "guarantee" arrangements in exchange for a "breathing spell" or "temporary respite."

16 The ruling Kuomintang today elect Premier Chiang Ching-kuo chairman of the ruling party.

Before that, he was the chairman of the central committee of the KMT. His leadership of the party is thus reaffirmed.

Dec. 6 Government sources indicate that the Republic of China is expected to achieve an economic growth rate of 11.6 per cent this year far exceeding the originally targeted 6.4 per cent.

8 American business leaders friendly to the Republic of China set up today a United States- Republic of China Economic Council in Chicago to foster trade and investment relations between the two countries. Chinese Economic Minister Y.S. Sun has traveled to U.S. to personally extend his congratulations to that organization.

20 The Chinese government approves an average power rate hike of 20 per cent beginning today to maintain the continuous power development in the Republic of China. It is also designed partly to offset the impact of the increased world oil prices in the next year.

The Organization of Petroleum Exporting Countries (OPEC) announces it is raising prices of crude from 5 to 10 per cent from

Jan. 1, 1979.

But the government decides to freeze prices of its oil products until July 1, 1977. The main purpose of this decision is to maintain price stability in Taiwan.

1977

Jan. 18 The Legislative Yuan today passes a bill empowering the government to bring its 20-year-old urban land equalization program to all rural areas throughout Taiwan and the offshore islands. Under the revised Equalization of Land Rights Act, a land owner has to pay progressive land value increment tax for sale of land located in any nonurban areas. Currently, only sales of urban land are subject to tax.

Feb. 7 Kuwaiti tanker Borg, with 30,000 metric tons of crude oil worth US$2 million, hits a reef off Keelung today. Oil slicks invaded the northern Taiwan beaches, killing off the marine life along the coast. (The tanker defied the frantic efforts of the Chinese Navy and experts flown in from Europe, and sank after a week on Feb. 15.)

26 The inauguration of the ROC-USA Economic Council takes place today at the Mandarin Hotel with 184 of its 224 members present. Members of the organization is founded to bring about closer economic ties between the Republic of China and the United States. T. K. Chang, former economic minister and now chairman of Chung Hsing Bills Finance Corporation, is elected chairman of the Council.

Mar. 16 The Economic Planning Council today projects the economic growth rate of the nation at 8.5 per cent this year. The Per capita income will rise to NT$34,127 or US$898.

26 The Chinese research vessel Hai Kung returns to Keelung after a 115-day exploratory expedition to the Antarctic.

May 4 The Republic of China and United States today reach a preliminary agreement on export of Taiwan-made non-rubber footwear to the United States in the next four years. Under the agreement, the annual ceiling of export of locally made shoes to United States will be around 125 million pairs compared with the estimated 200 million pairs in 1976. Shoemakers here are urged by the authorities to turn out better shoes to beat the import quota.

18 China Airlines' new Boeing 747SP begins nonstop service between Taipei and the US West Coast.

Jun. 3 The 445,000-ton tanker Burmah Endeavor, built by the China Shipbuilding Corp, for US Gatx Oswego, is launched at Kaohsiung. It is the world's third largest vessel.

Jul. 7 Fan Yuan-yen, a squadron leader of the Chinese Communist airforce, pilots a MIG-19 and defects to free China today. His plane landed at Tainan at 2:12 p.m. The whole nation is electrified with his sensational news, and firecrackers are exploded everywhere. Premier Chiang Ching-kuo receives the defected MIG pilot on the same day, and praises him for his courage and patriotism.

9 President C. K. Yen leaves today for Saudi Arabia on a three-day state visit at the invitation of King Khalid. This is his first visit abroad after he became president on April 6, 1975 following the death of President Chiang Kai-shek.

Aug. 25 Strong typhoon Thelma hits Kaohsiung this morning with its devastating strong winds and heavy rain. The result is extensive damage to the power generating system, port facilities and industrial plants in Kaohsiung and South Taiwan. Unofficial but reliable estimate puts the typhoon loss at around NT$10 billion.

26 Richard C. Holbrooke, U.S. assistant secretary of state for East Asian and Pacific affairs, arrives here today to brief the Chinese government on Secretary of State Cyrus Vance's talks with the Chinese communists. His conversation with Premier Chiang Ching-kuo last for an hour and 50 minutes. Official sources are silent on the contents of the conversation. The Republic of China was shocked by Vance's speech on June 29 which clearly indicated the U.S. intention to recognize Communist China. But shortly before the American secretary of state made his mainland trip on Aug. 22, President Carter declared that Vance's Peiping trip was only "exploratory" in nature.

Oct. 1 The Republic of China receives two destroyers from the United States Navy to further strengthen her defensive capability. The two war vessels are purchased by the ROC with military sales credits extended by the U.S.

5 The Chinese government decides to go ahead with the implementation of four major transportation projects which will cost NT$22 billion. The four projects are the completion of a round-the-island railway system, construction of three new cross-island highways, widening the Pingtung-Oulanpi Highway into a four-land road, and completing the second and third phase construction of the Atichung Harbor.

28 Free China's first geothermal power plant starts under-going a test run today. The power plant located at Chingshui, Yilan, utilizes a geothermal will drilled by the Chinese Petroleum Corp. as its source of energy. It has approximately a power generating capacity of 200-300 kilowatts a year.

Nov. 5 The Taiwan Garrison Command today announces the cracking of subversive organization which called itself "People's Liberation Front" with the arrest of three suspects. As it is a case of great seriousness, the garrison command has given a reward of NT$1 million to an informant.

16 The Republic of China inaugurates its first nuclear generator and starts power production today to usher the nation into the nuclear power era.

Dec. 1 The Cabinet today appoints Minister without Portfolio S. K. Chow as the Chinese ambassador to the Vatican to replace Amb. Chen Chih-mai who will be reassigned.

20 The government announces today that economic growth rate this year is 8.1 per cent in real terms. The 1976 growth rate is 11.5 per cent. The lower growth rate is attributed to smaller capital investment and slower growth in exports of products and services this year.

28 The Central Standing Committee of Kuomintang decides today to hold on Feb. 14-15, 1978 the second plenary meeting of the 11th Central Committee to nominated the party's candidates for the president and the vice president. The National Assembly, which is the electoral college of the Republic of China, is scheduled to meet for 35 days beginning Feb. 19. One of its principal tasks is to elect the sixth constitutional president and vice

president of the Republic.

1978

Jan. 7 The Central Standing Committee of the Kuomintang today accept President C. K. Yen's recommendation to name Premier Chiang Ching-kuo as the ruling party's presidential candidate this year.

9 President C. K. Yen today issues an order for the convocation of the Sixth Congress of the National Assembly for the election of the nation's sixth constitutional president and vice president. The congress will be convened from Feb. 19 to March 25.

Feb. 15 The ruling Kuomintang nominates Premier Chiang Ching-kuo and Provincial Governor Shieh tung-min as the party's presidential and vice presidential candidates.

Mar. 21 Premier Chiang Ching-kuo is elected the sixth constitutional president of the Republic of China today by a nearly unanimous vote at the National Assembly.

22 Taiwan Provincial governor Shieh Tung-min is elected today the vice president of the nation by the National Assembly.

28 The Second Joint Conference of

the ROC-USA Economic Council and the USA-ROC Economic Council opens today at the Grand Hotel with more than 700 Chinese and American business leaders participating.

30 The first generator of Taiwan's first nuclear power plant begins its full capacity operation of 636,000 kilowatts.

May 6 The International Communications Agency (ICA), Embassy of the United States, announces today that because of budget reductions, its branch post in Taichung and its reading room in Tainan will discontinue operations as of July 15. Diplomatic observers here believe that the measure is connected with the U.S. policy of "normalizing" relations with the Chinese communists.

20 President Chiang Ching-kuo and Vice President Shieh tung-min begin their six-year term this morning after they are sworn in at a brief and solemn ceremony at the Sun Yat-sen Memorial Hall.

Some 2600 government leaders, resident diplomats, visiting dignitaries and representatives of overseas Chinese communities and civic groups witness the ceremony which last less than 25 minutes.

26 The Legislative Yuan today overwhelmingly endorses President Chiang Ching-kuo's appointment of former Economic Minister Y.S. Sun as the new premier.

The vote are 329 to 12. A simple majority would be sufficient.

29 The ruling Kuomintang today approves Premier Y.S. Sun's appointment of Lin Yang-kang, who is formerly the mayor of Taipei, as governor of Taiwan Provincial government, and that of Li Teng-hui, who is formerly a minister without portfolio, as mayor of Taipei.

Jun. 20 The Republic of China is listed as the 25th largest trading country in the world by the International Monetary Fund.

29 The Chinese government approves a commercial agreement signed between the Republic of China's flagcarrier China Airlines and Cargo Lux and Lux Air of Luxemburg which will enable planes of the two countries to extend their flight services to each other's territories. Observers see this move as the first step for CAL to extend its passenger service to Europe once landing rights have been obtained in a leading Western European city.

Jul. 10 The Central Bank of China announces this afternoon that the Chinese government decides to raise the value of New Taiwan Dollar by about 5.26 per cent and revise the exchange rate from NT$38 to NT$36 for on U.S. dollar. The Bank also says that from now on the government will announce further readjustment of the exchange rate from time to time as the situation may demand.

25 The U.S. Senate today approves 94-0 an amendment warning President Carter to consult with it before making any changes in the 24-year-old mutual defense treaty with the Republic of China in Taiwan.

The vote comes in a "sense of the Senate" amendment proposed by Senator Robert Dole (R-Kan.), with 11 other Republicans and four Democrats as co-sponsor.

29 President Chiang Ching-kuo today reaffirms the Republic of China's basic policy of "never establishing contact with any Communist regimes," saying the dissemination of such abusive words as "Taipei-Peiping negotiation" or "Taipei-Moscow axis" is designed by those

having hidden purposes to jeopardize free China's national interest.

Aug. 16 The only Chinese cardinal, Archbishop Paul Yupin, dies suddenly today in Vatican City.

Yupin, 77, the Archbishop of Nanking, but in fact a resident in Taiwan, falls ill at the religious hospital where he is staying and dies two hours later of a heart attack, church sources say.

He fainted last Saturday during the funeral for Pope Paul. The U.S. Embassy here nearly confirmed press reports that the U.S. government is seeking to withdraw from the Joint Commission of Rural Reconstruction by terminating the 30-year-old agreement with the Chinese government upon which the JCRR was founded.

Sept. 27 The U.S. Embassy in Taipei predicts that the Republic of China's real economic growth this year, buttresses by a surge in exports, will probably reach 13 per cent. The embassy forecast is higher than the recent prediction of 12 per cent GNP growth in real terms by Premier Y.S. Sun and well above the government target of 8.5 per cent of the whole year.

Oct. 10 President Chiang Ching-kuo

reviews the parade of the 12,000 crack troops held to mark the Double Tenth National Day. The main attraction of the 1978 military parade is the home-made Hsiung Feng Six guided missiles.

31 The Taiwan Area Freeway, with a total length of 377 km, is opened to traffic.

Nov. 9 The Cabinet decides today to make Kaohsiung a special municipality in July 1979.

16 The government approves the revision of economic growth rate from the original 7.5 percent to 8.5 percent for the second half of the Six-Year Economic Development Plan (from 1979 to 1981) due to the rapid economic growth in the last three years. The rate of economic growth in 1978 is around 13 percent.

30 Athletes in the Republic of China today declares their categorical refusal to accept Chinese Communist invitation to join the forthcoming Asian Games as part of the Peiping delegation. In a declaration signed by more than 432,000 athletes in Taiwan, they also announce, their refusal to take part in any mainland tryout.

Dec. 8 The Legislative Yuan passes the

revised *Foreign Exchange Management Regulations* under which the New Taiwan dollar is no longer pegged to the US dollar.

16 U.S. President Jimmy Carter announces Friday night (U.S. time) the United States will establish full diplomatic relations with communist China on Jan. 1, 1979 and end official relations with the Republic of China on that date.

In a message handed to President Chiang Ching-kuo by U.S. Ambassador to China Leonard Unger, Carter says the U.S. government will send a high-ranking official to Taipei shortly to discuss with the Chinese government on the readjustment of Sino-American relations following the severance of diplomatic ties.

The U.S. will continue to sell arms to the Republic of China but Taipei's shopping list will be approved on "selective basis." The U.S. will also officially notify the Republic of China on Jan. 1, 1979 of its intention to discontinue the Sino-U.S. Mutual Defense Treaty signed in 1954. The treaty calls for one-year advance notice if one party wishes to terminate it. The other treaties and agreements signed between Taipei and Washington will remain unchanged before satisfactory substitutes are found. President Chiang Ching-kuo strongly condemns the US decision to sever diplomatic relations with the Republic of China in favor of the Peking regime.

27 A six-member U.S. delegation, headed by Deputy Secretary of State Warren Christopher, arrives here today for a two-day meeting with the Chinese government on the readjustment of their relations after the U.S. recognizes communist China on Jan. 1, 1979. (The Christopher mission left Taipei on Dec. 29 as scheduled without reaching agreement between the two governments. However, they agreed that discussions will continue in Taipei and Washington in the coming months.

1979

Jan. 7 The Chinese government appoints Vice Foreign Minister H. K. Yang to represent the Chinese government in the second round of negotiation with the U.S. government in

Washington on post-derecognition arrangements.

Feb. 23 Taipei and Washington agree that by March 1, the Republic of China will be represented in Washington by the Coordination Council for North American Affairs. The United States will maintain an unofficial entity in Taipei called American Institute in Taiwan.

Mar. 1 The US embassy in Taipei formaliy closes, to be succeeded by the American Institute in Taiwan.

The Washington Office of the Coordination Council for North American Affairs of the Republic of China opens.

13 Taipei is consoled by the news from Washington that the U.S. House of Representatives and Senate give approval today to a new American relationship with the ROC under which an attack from Communist China against Taiwan will be considered of "grave concern" to the United States.

20 President Chiang Ching-kuo announces today that the government will buy 18 F-5E Freedom jet fighters with the Self-reliance and National Salvation Funds which has amounted to NT$3 billion and is still increasing.

Apr. 8 The Republic of China Olympic Committee has no objection to the recent International Olympic Committee ruling, says Shen Chia-ming, president of the ROCOC today.

The International Olympic Committee meeting in Montevideo, Uruguay decides to maintain recognition of the Republic of China Olympic Committee and at the same time recognize the "Chinese Olympic Committee" located in Peiping.

10 U.S. President Jimmy Carter today signs legislation permitting continued commercial and cultural relations between the U.S. government and the ROC in the wake of break of diplomatic ties.

16 The military tribunal of the Taiwan Garrison Command today sentences Wu Chun-fa to death and his associates to prison terms ranging from eight years to life on charge of attempting to overthrow the government with violence.

The same court also sentences Yu Teng-fa former magistrate of Kaohsiung, to eight years for failure to inform against Wu and for spreading Chinese Communist propaganda.

May 19 The R.O.C. government today announces that Konsin Shah, former Chinese ambassador to New Zealand, is appointed as the chief of all U.S. field offices of the Coordination Council for North American Affairs.

Jul. 1 The Chinese government today elevates Kaohsiung as the second special city in Taiwan. Taipei is the first special city operating under the direct jurisdiction of the central government.

17 The Legislative Yuan today passes a new law authorizing the establishment of a special industrial park at Hsinchu to attract investment in technology intensive industries.

19 The Republic of China will turn out its first locally designed combat jet, designated as XA-3, before the end of the next year, according to Lt.-Gen. Chiang Sheng-lin, director of Department of Materiel, Ministry of National Defense. The jet is designed primarily for giving close support to ground forces as well as a fighter.

Sept. 6 The Chinese government today announces the decision to establish an economic zone of 200 miles around Taiwan and extend the nation's territorial waters from three miles to 12 miles.

10 A team of doctors in the National Taiwan University Hospital successfully separates Siamese twins sharing the same ischium. It is the world's second successful operation of its kind. The operation is the most extensively covered single event in the nation's journalistic history.

15 Premier Y. S. Sun departs today for a three-day official visit of Saudi Arabia. This is the first foreign trip since he took over the rein of the government 15 months ago.

Oct. 19 Lord Killanin, chairman of International Olympic Committee, accompanied by Mrs. Killanin and an entourage of three, arrives in Taipei today for a three-day visit. The purpose of his visit is to meet with Chinese Olympic officials in an effort to resolve the China representation problem in the IOC.

Nov. 2 Premier Y. S. Sun arrives in Seoul today to represent the Republic of China government at a state funeral on Nov. 3 for the late Korean President Park Chung Hee who was murdered on Oct. 27 in a political plot.

16 The Republic of China and the United States conclude their 40-day talks on the revision of their air transportation agreement. In the ad referendum initiated by the two parties, the ROC will be able to expand its civil air services to the U.S. by obtaining four new points of service, namely Guam, Seattle, New York and Dallas-Fort Worth. In return, more American airlines will extend their services to Taiwan after the formal signing of the new air accord.

23 The Republic of China Olympic Committee has filed a suit against the International Olympic Committee charging that the IOC Executive Board rulings on the ROCOC are illegal. The suit was filed with a Lausanne court, Switzerland on Nov. 15. The IOC has its headquarters in Lausanne.

26 The International Olympic Committee votes today 62-17 to require the Republic of China to change its name within the IOC if it wants to continue taking part in the Olympic Games. The Republic of China Olympic Committee lodges a strong protest against the IOC over the postal balloting on the China representation issue, calling it a violation of the Olympic spirit and legal procedures. The ROCOC has been forced to seek redress through the court of law now that the IOC has acted in contravention with its own rules, it said in a written statement.

Dec. 10 The "Formosa" magazine organized a riot at Kaohsiung today in which 183 security personnel and a taxi driver are injured by the mob. All the ring leaders of the riot except one are arrested a few days later. They will be tried by an open military court.

25 The Chinese government today announces sharp price, increase for gasoline, diesel fuel, fuel oil, in the wake of rising international oil price. The average rate of increase is about 37 percent. Electricity rates will be increased by 18 percent, effective Jan. 1, 1980.

1980

Jan. 1 The US government informs the ROC government that it will resume arms sales to the ROC after a one-year suspension.

Feb. 12 Premier Y. S. Sun reports today the government has allocated a special fund of NT$25 billion for the current fiscal year to finance weapons purchase and defense related research and development projects. The special appropriation is allocated in addition to the NT$7 billion ordinance development fund created in the wake of break of Sino-U.S. diplomatic ties.

20 The military prosecution of Taiwan Garrison Command today brings sedition charges against eight ringleaders of the Kaohsiung riot case and referred 37 other detainees to the civilian courts for prosecution.

21 The Cabinet today approves the issuance of NT$500 and NT$1,000 New Taiwan Dollar bills beginning February 25.

27 The Civil Aeronautics Administration and the China Airlines have set up a board of inquiry to look into the cause of the crash of a CAL's Boeing 707 jetliner at the Manila International Airport. All 135 persons aboard the jetliner survived the crash, but three of them are still unaccounted for.

Mar. 6 The Cabinet today approves a ten-year economic development plan stressing a stable economic growth between 1980 and 1989. under the plan, the nation's economy will register an annual growth of 7.9 percent, and per capita income will hit US$6,107 by the end of 1989.

9 Premier and Mrs. Y. S. Sun leave today for a visit to four African countries at the invitation of their government. The four countries are South Africa, Malawi, Lesotho and Swaziland. He and his party will return to Taipei March 23.

18 Sedition trial opens today for the eight ringleaders of Kaohsiung riot case at a military court.

Apr. 4 The Chung Cheng Memorial Hall, named after the late President Chiang Kai-shek, is dedicated today along with the 25-hectare park in which it is situated.

17 The Republic of China today loses its membership in the International Monetary Fund when Communist China was voted into the Fund at an IMF meeting in Washington.

18 The military tribunal of Taiwan Garrison Command hands down its verdict on the ringleaders of Kaohsiung riot case. Legislator Huang Hsin-chieh, publisher of Formosa Magazine, received 14 years. Shih Ming-the, general manager of Formosa Magazine and mastermind of the Kaohsiung riot, is sentenced to life imprisonment.

Other ringleaders of the riot, including Yao Chia-wen, Chang Chun-hung, Lin Yi-hsiung, Lin Hung-hsuan, Lu Hsiu-lien and Chen Chu, each receives a prison term of 12 years.

May 6 The Legislative Yuan today sets the stage for resumption of the suspended parliamentary elections later this year by enacting into law the Statute Governing the Election and Recall of Public Office- Holders.

Jun. 11 The Kuomintang Central Standing Cimmittee and the National Security Council today decide the quota for the forthcoming parliamentary election. The quota is 205, 81 more than 124 that were to be elected at the aborted Dec. 23, 1978 election which were called off due to the U.S. recognition of the Chinese communist regime.

Jul. 4 The Central Election committee today picks Dec. 6 as the day for casting ballots to elect members of Legislative Yuan and National Assembly. It, however, yet to decide the date for electing members of the Control Yuan. A total of 205 seats in three parliamentary branches are up for grabs in the upcoming elections.

Aug. 29 Premier and Mrs. Y. S. Sun today departs for Central America on a 15-day three-nation tour. The three Latin American countries to be visited are Costa Rica, Panama and the Dominican Republic.

Oct. 2 The Coordination Council for North American Affairs and American Institute in Taiwan, the two private institutions that handle the U.S.-ROC relations today sign an agreement in Washington granting "privileges and immunities" to representatives of the two countries. The agreement means that the representatives will be entitled to almost all of the benefits ordinary diplomats receive even though their mission is technically unofficial.

13 Prime Minister Pieter W. Botha of South Africa and Madame Botha arrive in Taipei today on a state visit to the Republic of China at the invitation of Premier Y. S. Sun. Accompanying them during the Taiwan visit is a large group of key ministers of South Africa.

Nov. 8 The Banque de Paris et des Pays-Bas (Paribas) and other three European banks decide to extend a huge loan for China Airlines (CAL) to buy three airbuses. Delivery of the first airbus will be made in June, 1982, and the other two planes will be delivered within 1983.

Dec. 6 The biggest election, also the first parliamentary election held in Taiwan since Dec. 20, 1975, is held today in an orderly way. The balloting goes on without incident.

The ruling Kuomintang captures most of the seats at stake in the National Assembly and the Legislative Yuan. Of 70 seats at stake in the 316-member Legislative Yuan, the KMT captures 56. Of 76 seats at stake in the 1,142-seat National Assembly, the ruling party wins 63. The voters turnout is around 68 per cent.

20 The Dutch parliament in The Hague votes to sell two submarines to the Republic of China despite the threat of reprisal from the Chinese Communists. The deal between the ROC and Holland, including two submarines and other nuclear power generation equipment will eventually top US$1 billion instead of US$500 million as previously reported.

28 A general census is taken today all over the Republic of China, including the Tungsha (Pratas) and Nansha (Spratlys) islands. The first since 1965, the census taking this year is the most important because a great deal has changed curing the past 14 years as a result of rapid economic progress. The changes include those of population, family patterns, living condition and social conditions.

The 1980 general census on housing and population ends at a.m. this morning without incident. All information of the general census will be passed to the government for policy reference. The government will use findings from the census as reference in making policies on manpower utilization, public housing and planning of various reconstruction projects.

29 Twenty-two supplementary members are elected to the Control Yuan from among 54 candidates by members of the Taiwan Provincial Assembly, the Taipei City Council, and the Kaohsiung City Council.

1981

Jan. 5 The Central Bank of China today lifts the ceiling on bank deposit interest rates from 12.5 to 15 percent and also raised the lending interest rates for various lending accommodations. The move is designed to attract more savings from the private sector.

9 Holland sets up the Taipei office of The Netherland Council for Trade Promotion today.

10 China Airlines, the flag-carrier of the Republic of China, acquires the aviation rights to fly to Turkey last week.

Feb. 26 The Dutch government today removes the last stumbling block to the sale of two submarines to the Republic of China when a majority of the parliament refuses to raise a new challenge. On Feb. 28, communist China immediately recalls its ambassador from The Hague and asked for the recall of Dutch Ambassador Jan Kneppelhout from Peiping.

Mar. 29 The 12th National Congress of ruling Kuomintang opens today at Yangmingshan. Chairman Chiang Ching-kuo, who presides at the meeting, declares that "The 70's of the Republic of China is the era of victory of the Three Principles of the People and the recovery of the mainland."

Apr. 2 President Chiang Ching-kuo is reelected chairman of the Kuomintang by acclamation at the 12th National Congress in Taipei.

23 Tsai Wei-ping, newly appointed representative of the Coordination Council for North American Affairs (CCNAA) Office in the United States, is scheduled to leave Taipei for Washington D.C. to assume his office. The former vice foreign minister replaces Konsin Shah who will be reassigned.

May 4 The first European Products Exhibition opens today for a one-week at the Taipei World Trade Center with 293 companies from 123 European countries participating. The two-way trade between the Republic of China and Western Europe in 1980 reached roughly US$5 billion, and is still increasing.

Jun. 17 The nation's annual economic growth rate will be set at 8 percent in the next four years beginning 1982, according to a plan drafted by the Council for Economic Planning and Development. The growth rate in this year will be less than 6 percent due to recession.

The ruling Kuomintang today named Yang Chin-tsung, vice president of the state-owned Taiwan Power Company, mayor of Kaohsiung, replacing Wang Yu-yun, who will be given a new post. Yang, 58, a native of Hualien, is formerly director of reconstruction of the Taiwan Provincial Government. Kaohsiung and Taipei, with population well over one million, are the two special cities in Taiwan under the direct jurisdiction of the Executive Yuan.

18 Gen. Cheng Wei-yuan, former minister of national defense, is sworn in today as the chairman of the Vocational Assistance Commission for Retired Servicemen to succeed the late T. Y. Chao, who dies of cancer in the United States earlier this month.

Jul. 1 The National Tort Claims Law goes into effect today.

4 The Ministry of Finance is working on a proposal to raise its ceiling of foreign loan guaranty from the present US$6.5 billion to US$10 billion.

Aug. 12 The exchange rate between the U.S. dollar and the New Taiwan dollar is readjusted today from 1 to 36 to 1 to 38. The devaluation is less than 5 percent.

23 The government decides to set up a board of inquiry to look into the cause of the Worst air disaster that killed 110 persons aboard the Far Eastern air

Transport (FAT) Boeing 737 over Miaoli yesterday morning.

26 Some 140 Chinese and overseas historians attend the conference on the History of the Republic of China. The meeting will last for three days.

Sept. 3 Unprecedented rainfall in Central and South Taiwan results in a flood disaster which claims 23 lives and property damage amounting to over NT$2.3 billion. Agriculture and fisheries suffer the most severe loss. The Taiwan Provincial Government appropriated NT$5 billion as a special fund for flood relief.

13 The Central Bank of China reveals today that the nation's foreign exchange reserve rose sharply to near US$8 billion, a record high in the history of the Republic of China.

Nov. 14 Over 10 million eligible voters in the Republic of China go to polls today to elect county and city officials and representatives. The result is: The ruling Kuomintang captures 15 of the 19 mayors and county chiefs' office. In the battle for Provincial Assembly, where 77 seats are up for contest, the KMT captures 60. The independents get 17 seats.

Of the 51 seats in the Taipei City Council, the ruling Kuomintang takes 38 seats. The ruling party also captures 32 of the 42 seats in the Kaohsiung City Council, while the independents 10 seats.

17 The Legislative Yuan today approves the organic law of Environmental Protection Bureau.

25 The Central Standing Committee of Kuomintang today announces a major shakeup of the Sun Yun-suan cabinet and the change of mayors of Taipei and Kaohsiung.

26 President Chiang Ching-kuo orderes a major reshuffle of the nation's top military posts Gen, Hau Pei-tsun, commander-in-chief of the Army, is named chief of the General staff to succeed Adm. Soong Chang-chilh, who has been appointed minister of national defense in the cabinet shakeup.

Dec. 8 Premier Sun Yun-suan, accompanied by a group of ranking officials and military officers makes a five-day "unofficial" visit to Indonesia. Economic and trade cooperation is main topic of discussion between Sun and Indonesian leaders.

Foreign news agency reports indicate that ROC supply of military hardware to Indonesia, including missiles, is also included in the discussion.

1982

Jan. 1 The Council for Economic Planning and Development declares that the government has decided to focus on five strategic industries, including machinery, transportation, machine tools, electric machinery and electronics and information, for the development in the coming four years, starting in 1982.

8 More than 50 top badminton players from all over the world meet at Taipei to compete in the 1982 Masters Invitational Badminton Championship, which will last for one week in Taipei Municipal Stadium.

15 The Legislative Yuan passes the Commodity Labeling Law of 18 articles, providing penalties ranging from a fine of NT$5000 to revocation of business license.

16 The ruling Kuomintang captures 682 out of 799 seats contested in the election for 19 city and country councils held across Taiwan.

Feb. 13 The Board of Foreign Trade ban

the import of 1500 items of Japanese products and placed a one-year moratorium on the import of Japanese trucks and buses of over seven tons and chassis, as a warning to the Japanese government for neglecting to deal with the widening of trade gap between the Republic of China and Japan.

18 Premier Sun Yun-suan tells the 69th session of the Legislative Yuan that the ROC is making preparations to manufacture tanks, ships and other sophisticated weapons and military equipment. Many of these items are close to the production stage. He also said the ROC has made considerable progress in the development of its own defense industry.

Jun. 14 The Bank of Communications, the nation's development bank, floats US$20 million worth of floating rate certificates of deposit (FRCDs) in Hongkong.

20 The Directorate General of Telecommunications (DGT) opens the first public data switching service in the ROC.

Jul. 2 The 5th World Women's Softball Championship takes place from July 2 to 11 in Taipei.

30 Vice Minister Li Mo said that the ROC government has

expressed its concern over the proposed revision by the Japanese government of history textbooks for high schools.

Aug. 21 Economics Minister William Y. T. Chao announces the partial lift of an import ban on 842 categories of Japanese consumer goods.

Sept. 18 Chou Ling-fei, the grandson of Lu Hsun, a moder Chinesee writer most admired by the Chinese Communists, defects to the ROC from Tokyo, Japan, in order to marry his girlfriend, Chang Chun-hua, resident of Taipei, ROC.

Oct. 5 The Taiwan Garrison Command announces that two Chinese businessmen, Tu Shao-hsi, 42, and Chang Jung-yi, 39, have been arrested for conspiring to help Red China develop its electronics industry with ROC machinery and technical know-how.

16 Aleksandr I. Solzhenitsyn, 1970 Nobel Literature Prize winner, arrives in Taiwan from Tokyo at the invitation of Wu San-lien Literary Foundation of the ROC.

22 The Grand Alliance for China's Reunification Under the Three Principles of the People's inauguration ceremony takes place at the Chung Shan

Building on Yangminshar.

31 Wu Jung-ken, a 25-year-old MIG-19 pilot of the Red Chinese air force who flew to a U.S. military base outside Seoul on Oct. 16, arrives in Taipei at 12:50 p.m. Oct. 31 to choose freedom.

Nov. 21 The Coordination Council for North American Affair today appoints Dr. Fredrick F. Chien its representative to Washington, D.C. one day after he is relieved of his job as vice foreign minister.

Chien succeeds Dr. Tsai Wei-ping, who is getting an ambassadorial assignment after his return to Taipei from Washington.

22 The R.O.C. government today decides to lift import ban on 689 Japanese consumer products to show its sincerity to improve its trade relations with Japan.

Dec. 12 The Republic of China high proportion of medals including four gold medals and 16 others and a special prize at the 31st World Fair for Inventions held on Dec. 4-12 in Brussels.

23 The R.O.C. government announces today the selection of Japan's largest auto maker, Toyota, as the ROC's partner in a US$540 million joint venture to produce compact cars in Taiwan. The projected gigantic auto plant will produce 300,000 cars annually within eight years from the start of production.

1983

Jan. 14 The Legislative Yuan passes the revision of the Trade mark Law in third reading. The revised law imposes prison term of up to five years for infringement of trademarks already registered by another person or company, and up to three years for infringement of foreign trademarks not registered in Taiwan. The move is to prevent counterfeiting of foreign trademarks and to protect the good image of the Republic of China as reliable and worthy exporter.

Feb. 16 The Dutch airline Martinair inaugurates its light service to Taiwan, marking the opening of air service between the Netherlands and the Republic of China.

Mar. 20 China Airlines (CAL) inaugurates its two weekly flights to New York today. The flight between Taipei and New York takes 15 hours and will stop over in Anchorage, Alaska, for refueling.

24 The Republic of China and Solomon Islands set up diplomatic relations. Located in South Pacific, Solomon Islands consists of a group of volcanic islands totaling 560 square kilometers.

Apr. 12 China Airlines inaugurates its regular flight service to Amsterdam today as the first step toward establishing a world-girdling commercial air service.

May 10 The Republic of China and the Commonwealth of Dominica formally set up diplomatic ties today. Dominica became independent on Nov. 3, 1978. It has a population of 81,000 and a land area of 289.5 square kilometers.

Jun. 2 The Executive Yuan approves at its regular meeting a revision to raise by ten folds the compensation for "wrongful detentions and executions."

7 The Legislative Yuan approves the Firearms Control Law in the third reading today, putting manufacture, possession and use of firearms and other weapons under a stricter control.

Jul. 12 A groundbreaking ceremony is held this morning to mark the start of Taipei's underground railway project. The project will bury 2.8-kilometer section of railtracks between Linsen North Road and Kwangchow Street underground. The whole project is scheduled to completed by 1991 at an estimated cost of NT$17.2 billion.

Aug. 22 China Airlines has suspended its CI811 flight to Manila this morning, owing to the order of the Philippine civil aviation authority. Manila has warned international airlines not to allow opposition leader Benigno Aquino to board their planes for return to the Philippines on the ground he did not have legal travel papers. Aquino was gunned down after soldiers escorted him off a China Airlines flight from Taipei upon his return to Manila after three years of self-exile in the United States.

24 Chinese Communist pilot Lt.-Col. Sun Tien-chin, who flew a MIG-21 to South Korea from China mainland on Aug. 7, arrives in Taiwan.

Sept. 3 The Republic of China bans Philippine Airlines from flying to Taipei.

14 The Philippine Civil Aeronautics Board has lifted the ban on China Airlines flights and the Civil Aeronautics

Administration of the Republic of China also lifts the ban on Philippine Airlines flights to Taipei on the same day.

16 Dr. Chien Shih-liang, president off Academia Sinica, dies of heart failure at the Taiwan University Hospital.

Oct. 31 Taipei's Kuantu Bridge, the first iron arch bridge in East Asia, opens to traffic today. The bridge, 809 meters long, took three years and cost NT$700 million to complete.

Nov. 1 Dr. Wu Ta-you takes over the presidency of Academia Sinica at the Tsai Yuan-pei Hall in its Nankang compound. He succeeds Dr. Chien Shih-liang.

14 Another Chinese Communist pilot flies his MIG-17 to the Chiang Kai-shek International Airport this morning to start a new life in the Republic of China. The pilot, identified as Wang Hsueh-cheng, 28, from Honan, lands at the airport at 10:15 a.m.

Dec. 3 The ruling Kuomintang wins a big landslide in the supplementary parliamentary election held today. Out of the 71 contested seats in the Legislative Yuan, the KMT captures 62 seats. The opposition wins six seats, while the independents three. The biggest upset in the election is that Kang Ning-hsiang, the opposition leader, loss his seat which he has held for 14 ears.

1984

Jan. 4 The Government Information Office announces it will allow import of four Japanese films on a one-year trial basis this year, thus lifting the government ban on the Japanese films imposed in 1973.

5 The cross harbor tunnel in the port city of Kaohsiung is completed, two years and seven months after construction began. The tunnel, which cost over NT$3 billion to build, will open to traffic in May after the finishing touches are completed.

7 A Fishermen's Broadcasting Station is inaugurated on Penghu to serve the nation's 600,000 fishing population. To be heard on 738 and 1143 KH, the station's broadcasts will be on the air from 6:00 a.m. to midnight daily.

Feb. 15 The Second Plenary Session of the Kuomintang Central Committee nominates President Chiang Ching-kuo and Governor Lee Teng-hui as the party's presidential and vice presidential candidates and elects a new Central Standing Committee.

Mar. 1 The Republic of China's first home-developed jet trainer AT-3 rolls off the assembly line. The twin-seat trainer is developed by the Aeronautical Industry Development Center. Chungshan Institute of Science and Technology. It is fitted with two Garrett TFE 731-2-2L engines each with a thrust of 1590 kilograms.

21 President Chiang Ching-kuo is re-elected for a second six-year term, winning all but eight of the 1020 ballots cast by members of the National Assembly, the electorate of the Republic of China.

22 Governor Lee Teng-hui is elected the seventh term vice president of the Republic of China, polling 873 of 999 ballots cast by members of the National Assembly. He needs only a simple majority to get elected.

A Hongkong Chinese Liang Wei-chiang hijacks a Peking-bound British Airways 747 jetliner with 355 people aboard and forces the pilot to fly to Taiwan. Liang is taken into custody when the plane lands at Taipei's Chiang Kai-shek International Airport. The other 337 passengers and 17 crew members are released along with the plane which returns to Hongkong six hours after the drama began.

Apr. 12 A China Airlines Boeing jet takes off at the Chiang Kai-shek International Airport today to start the air carrier's historical round-the-world service. The flight CI-012 heads for New York by way of Anchorage, and then proceeds to Amsterdam. In Amsterdam, passengers heading for the Far East may book CAL's weekly flight to Taipei.

May 20 President Chiang Ching-kuo is sworn in for his second six-year term at the Chungshan Building on Yangmingshan at 9:00 a.m. Vice President Lee Teng-hui takes the oath of office after president Chiang. It is Lee's first term as vice president of the Republic. They are sworn in by Huang Shao-ku, president of the Judicial Yuan.

President Chiang Ching-kuo names Yu Kuo-hwa, chairman of the Council for Economic Planning and Development and governor of the Central Bank as the next premier.

25 President Chiang Ching-kuo

formally appoints Yu Kuo-hwa as premier after the Legisiative Yuan confirms his nomination.

31 The Yu Kuo-hwa Cabinet is sworn in a ceremony presided over by President Chiang Ching-kuo.

Jun. 29 The Legislative Yuan passes the Eugenics and Health Law, allowing pregnant women with justifiable reasons to undergo abortion. The new law will go into force as of New Year's Day 1985 after promulgation by the President.

Jul. 9 The last part of a transoceanic telecommunication cable system, which will link Taiwan, Hong Kong, and Singapore, is hauled ashore in Toucheng, Ilan.

19 The Ministry of National Defense announces that a domestically developed surface-to- air missile named "Sky Bow" made a successful debut in a test firing.

20 The legislative Yuan passes the Basic Labor Standards Law. The newly passed Legislation not only considers the overall interests between labor and management but also takes into account the nation's situation in the present stage of development.

Aug. 3 The six Chinese freedom-seekers freed by the Korean government arrive in Taipei. The six – Cho Chang-jen, Chiang Hung-chun, Wang Yen-ta, Wu Yun-fei, An Chien-wei and Miss Kao Tung-ping – hijacked a Chinese Communist Trident from Shenyang, Manchuria to Seoul, Korea on May 5, 1983.

Sept. 20 After the initialing of an agreement on Hongkong to Red China and Britain, Premier Yu Kuo-hwa says the government and people of free China extend to the colony's residents their deepest concern. He also pledges eleven points of assistance for the Chinese residents of Hongkong.

29 ROC decathlon athletes Ku Chin-shui and Li Fu-en win a gold and silver medal respectively in the sixth Asian Track and Field Championships in Jakarta, Indonesia.

Oct. 1 The first of four giant hydroelectric generators in the Minghu Pumped Storage Project hooks up with the power distribution system in Taiwan. The Minghu project will cost NT$31,169 million. It will have four generators of 250 megawatts each. Construction began in September 1981 and will be completed by the beginning of 1986.

Nov. 12 The government mounts an unprecedented crackdown on organized crime by rounding up the key members of the nation's crime syndicates. More than 50 underground figures are arrested the firstday.

1985

Jan. 1 The total population in Taiwan and the island of Pengh has reached the 19 million mark, the Interior Ministry Population Administration Department announces.

8 The Hong Kong Affairs Task Force under the Executive Yuan decides to simplify exit and entry application procedures, relax controls on foreign exchange, and adopt incentive measures to encourage large enterprises and monetary institutions in Hong Kong to move to Taiwan.

Feb. 18 Secretary General of Kuomintang Central Committee Mah Soo-lay formally takes over his post from his predecessor Tsiang Yien-si this morning.

Mar. 13 The Kuomintang Standing Committee approves the nomination of Ta-hai Lee as minister of economic affairs at

its regular meeting. The KMT moves quickly to fill up the post vacated by the resignation of Hsu Li-the, who quits in the face of mounting criticism over his handling of the Tenth Credit Cooperative affair while he was finance minister from 1980 to 1984.

Apr. 16 The first test tube baby in the Republic of China is born at Veterans General Hospital in Taipei.

22 The Industrial Technology Research Institute successfully develops an amorphous-silicon solar battery of high commercial value.

May 2 The Economic Renovation Committee is inaugurated, a week after Premier Yu Kuo-hwa proposed it. It is a tripartite organization, made up of government officials, economists and industrialists. The committee is to chart a new course for the economy and is to finish the job within six months.

7 The Republic of China has successfully developed its first ground-to-air missile and is in the process of developing two other types of missiles. Liu Shu-hsi, deputy director of the Chungshan Institute of Science, says a successful testfiring of

the "Sky Arrow No. 1" was conducted last March 20. It is designed to bring down enemy planes flying at medium and low attitudes and the "Sky Arrow No. 2," designed to knock down high-attitude aircraft, is scheduled to undergo test-firing in December 1988. Liu says the institute is also developing an air-to-air missile with the target date set in December 1986.

Jun. 9 Honduran Foreign Minister Edgardo Paz Barnica officiates at an opening ceremony of the Honduran Embassy in Taipei. In his opening speech, Minister Paz says that he is instructed by Honduran President Roberto Suazo Cordova to open the Honduran Embassy here, indicating that Honduras has placed high value on ROC-Honduran relations.

28 The Legishative Yuan completes its third and last reading of the Revised Copyright Bill, which will become law upon signing by the President. The new legislation, intended to fight the rampant practice of piracy, extends the scope of copyright protection while stiffens penalty for violators. However, aliens will have to register their works with the Chinese government before they are entitled to copyright protection in the Republic of China.

Jul. 5 The government reaffirms its policy of not to engage in direct trade with the Communist-controlled Chinese mainland. Dr. Chang King-yuh, director general of the Government Information Office, says exporters and importers in the country are forbidden to make any form of contact or enter into business transactions with Red China or its trade agencies and officials stationed in other countries.

11 The Foreign Ministry issues a statement, protesting the establishment of diplomatic relations between Bolivia and the Chinese Communists, and announcing the immediate severance of the nation's formal ties with Bolivia.

Aug. 21 The Central Standing Committee of the ruling Kuomintang nominates Robert Chun Chien, deputy governor of the Central Bank, as minister of finance. Chien, 56 succeeds J. K. Loh, who has resigned to assume administrative responsibility for the Taipei Tenth Credit Cooperative scandal.

Sept. 4 Vice President and Mrs. Lee Teng-hui starts a 21-day official visit to three Latin American nations including Costa Rica, Panama and Guatemala.

5 The Supreme Court upholds the life sentences meted out to two gangsters by the Taiwan High Court for the slaying of Chinese American writer Henry Liu at his home in Daly City, California, last October. Chen Chi-li, 42, and Wu Tun, 35, both leaders of the Bamboo Union gang, are transferred to the Taipei Penitentiary today to begin their life terms. They will be eligible for parole after 10 years if they behave well in prison. Another man involved in the same case is Vice Admiral Wong His-ling, former director of the Military Intelligence Bureau, who instructed Chen to "teach Liu a lesson," is separately tried by a military tribunal and is also sentenced to life. Wong's two aides are sentenced to lighter terms. They have been serving their terms since last April.

15 The Minghu Pumped Storage Project, the largest hydraulic power project in Taiwan, is inaugurated today, six years after construction began. The NT$27 billion-plus project, which is built by the Ret-Ser Engineering Agency, will generate an average of 1769 million kwh of electricity a year by the most conservative estimate.

20 Hsiao Tien-jun, the 35-year-old pilot of the Chinese Communist H-5 torpedo attack bomber, who flew his plane to South Korea last Aug. 24, arrives in Taipei today.

Nov. 10 The Chinese government is ready to accept school teachers in Hongkong and Kowloon who are loyal to the cause of the Republic of China for resettlement in Taiwan in case of emergency. The nature of emergency is not specified, but apparently it refers to 1997 when the Chinese Communists are slated to take over control of Hongkong and Kowloon. The Executive Yuan has prepared a set of regulations that will apply to resettlement of school teachers from Hongkong and Kowloon. They will be implemented at an appropriate time.

16 Fourteen million eligible voters in the Republic of China go to the polls today for four local

elections. They will choose 21 new mayors and magistrates from among 54 candidates, 77 members of the Taiwan Provincial Assembly from among 158 contestants, 51 members of the Taipei City Council out of 74 aspirants and 42 members of the Kaohsiung City Council from 71 contenders.

19 The Legislative Yuan approves the revision of the Trademark Law. The revision permits foreign corporate bodies or organizations to file suit against Chinese nationals for violation of their trademarks even though they are not registered with the competent Chinese authorities.

Dec. 7 The Ministry of Foreign Affairs announces the decision to suspend diplomatic relations with the Republic of Nicaragua. The Chinese government takes the action after Nicaragua has decided to establish diplomatic relations with the Peking regime.

12 "Cousin Lee," created by Ranan R. Lurie, the famed American cartoonist, is unveiled before some 1000 guests who have been holding their breath for the first glimpse. It also flashes across TV screen for people in Taiwan who have been waiting for their "Cousin" impatiently.

Lurie hopes that Cousin Lee will be representative of present-day Chinese as Taro-san is of the Japanese.

25 President Chiang Ching-kuo reaffirms his pledge that he will not have one of his family members to succeed him. Addressing the National Assembly on the occasion of the 38th anniversary of the Republic of China's constitutional government, the President also assures the nation that there will be no military rule in this country.

1986

Apr. 23 National Taiwan University Hospital separates a pair of 14-day-old Siamese twins, saving one of the baby girls' life and setting a world record for separating the youngest Siamese twins.

24 ROC Minister of Foreign Affairs Chu Fu-sung and Paraguayan Foreign Minister Carlos Augusto Saldivar sign an extradition treaty in Taipei on behalf of their respective governments.

May 18 The Ministry of National Defense announces that an air-to-air "Sky Sword" missile has been successfully tested by shooting down a Hawk missile.

Aug. 3 Construction of the Synchronous Radiation Research Center is started at the Hsinchu Science-Based Industrial Park.

Sept. 25 The Republic of China, after withdrawing 13 year ago, is readmitted to the Olympic Council of Asia (OCA).

Oct. 6 The Ministry of Economic Affairs decides to invest NT$1.2 billion in developing anti-pollution technology over the next three years.

15 Lee Yuan-tseh, a member of the Academia Sinica, wins the 1986 Nobel Prize in chemistry.

Nov. 6 The Democratic Progressive Party (DPP) holds its first Representative Assembly and releases a draft of its charter and platform.

1987

Jun. 23 The Legislative Yuan passes the *National Security Law during the Period of National Mobilization for Suppression of the Communist Rebellion*. After the law becomes effective, the *Emergency Decree* in Taiwan and the Pescadores (Penghu) will be lifted.

Jul. 15 The *Emergency Decree* is lifted in the Taiwan area, the *National*

Security Law is promulgated, and foreign exchange controls are relaxed.

Aug. 1 The Council of Labor Affairs is formally established under the Executive Yuan.

Nov. 2 The ROC Red Cross Society begins accepting applications from local residents wishing to visit relatives in mainland China.

10 ROC-US talks on intellectual property rights begin in Taipei.

1988

Jan. 1 Registrations for new newspapers are opened, and restrictions on the number of pages per issue are relaxed.

11 The Legislative Yuan passes the *Law on Assembly and Parades during the Period off National Mobilization for Suppression of the Communist Rebellion*; which outlines three fundamental principles and specifies areas that will be off-limits to demonstrators.

13 President Chiang Ching-kuo passes away of heart failure and hemorrhage at 3:50 p.m.
Vice President Lee Teng-hui is sworn in as president of the Republic of China to complete the late President Chiang's second six-year term, which runs from 1984 to 1990.

Mar. 3 The Council for Economic Pianning and Development approves the establishment of an US$11 billion International Economic Cooperation and Development Fund to assist developing countries.

24 The Government Information Office and the Ministry of National Defense reiterate that the ROC has never engaged in the development of nuclear weapons. This is confirmed by the US government.

Apr. 18 The ROC Red Cross Society begins forwarding mail from Taiwan residents to mainland China.

28 An ROC delegation attends the annual convention of the Asian Development Bank (ADB) in Manila.

Jul. 8 Acting Chairman Lee Teng-hui is elected chairman of the Kuomintang at the ruling party's 13th National Congress.

28 The Executive Yuan approves regulations governing the import of publications, films, and radio and television programs from communist-controlled areas.

Aug. 18 The Mainland Affairs Task Force is established under the Executive Yuan.

30 ROC-US talks on finance and banking open in Washington.

The ROC negotiators agree to open the Taiwan market to credit card companies and to expand credit for foreign banks.

Sept. 5 The Executive Yuan announces that the long-range Hsiung Feng II missile has been successfully developed and will soon be added to the ROC arsenal.

Oct. 25 A comprehensive farmer health insurance is initiated.

Nov. 3 The Mainland Affairs Task Force revises regulations to allow mainland compatriots to visit sick relatives or attend their funerals in Taiwan.

17 The Executive Yuan approves the private installation of small satellite dish antennas, which will allow viewers to tune into the KU-band and receive television programming from Japan's NHK station.

Dec. 1 The Executive Yuan announces guidelines governing unofficial participation in international academic conferences and cultural and athletic activities held on the mainland, as well as regulations governing visits to Taiwan by overseas mainland scholars and students.

1989

Jan. 10 The ROC and the Commonwealth of the Bahamas

establish diplomatic relations.

20 The Legislative Yuan passes the *Law on Civic Organizations*.

26 The Legislative Yuan passes the *Law on the Voluntary Retirement of Senior Parliamentarians*.

Mar. 6 President and Madam Lee Teng-hui arrive in Singapore for a four-day visit.

27 The Central Bank of China announces the cancellation of limits on the daily fluctuation of the NT dollar against the US greenback, to be effective April 3.

Apr. 7 The Chinese Taipei Olympic Committee announces the ROC athletic teams and organizations will participate in international sports events held on the mainland under the name "Chinese Taipei".

17 The Mainland Affairs Task Force passes the proposal to allow teachers and staff of public schools to travel to the Chinese mainland for family visits. On the 18th, the council decides to permit newsgathering and filmmaking on the mainland.

22 Official mourning is held in central Beijing for Hu Yaobang. Many thousands of students demonstrate in Tiananmen Square to mourn him, and also

to demand his rehabilitation as will as democratic reforms.

27 An enormous demonstration, with well over 100,000 student and other participants, takes place in Beijing in direct defiance of a government ban.

30 Finance Minister Shirley Kuo leads an ROC delegation to the 22nd annual Asian Development Bank meeting in Peking.

May 1 Another enormouse demonstration takes place in Beijing, with much smaller ones in several other cities, in commemoration of the May Fourth Movement of 1919 (China's first modern large-scale student movement).

13 A large-scale rally for democracy and freedom converges on Tiananmen Square in the heart of Beijing. Students declare they will remain in occupation of the square until their pro-democracy demands are met, and about 1000 students begin a hunger strike.

19 Early in the morning Zhao Ziyang appears in Tiananmen Square to express sympathy with hunger-striking demonstrators, his last public appearance before the Beijing massacre of June 3-4.

20 The State Council declares

martial law in parts of Beijing to take effect from 10 a.m. the same day. Mass demonstrations continue in Beijing, with opposition to the imposition of martial law and demands for the overthrow of Li Peng being central issues. The crowds, while people erect barricades to prevent its advance towards Tiananmen Square.

25 A pro-democracy demonstration of some 100,000 workers and intellectuals takes place in Beijing demanding the resignation of the premier, Li Peng.

28 Ching Kuo, the first ROC-developed and manufactured indigenous defense fighter, successfully completes its first test flight.

31 One million students participate in a Hand in Hand, Heart to Heart rally in support of the mainland democracy movement.

Jun. 1 Lee Huan is sworn in as premier of the ROC.

3 Crowds of people, especially students again prevent mainly unarmed soldiers from entering Tiananmen Square by erecting barricades and other means. According to the government, leaders of the student movement incite the mobs to kill soldiers;

this together with other actions, marks the beginning of a counter-revolutionary rebellion.

3-4 The Beijing massacre. Troops of the 27th Army of the PLA and the People's Armed Police move along the Chang'an Boulevard in Beijing to Tiananmen Square to clear the square of demonstrators. Violence erupts at about 10 p.m. on June 3 and continues at intervals throughout the night and following morning. Troops force their way through barricades set up by ordinary people, many casualties resulting. By midday on June 4, troops have sealed off Tiananmen Square.

4 President Lee Teng-hui issues a statement condemning the Tiananmen Massacre.

5 The CCPCC and the State Council claim initial victory against a counter-revolutionary riot instigated by a handful of people aimed at 'negating the leadership of the CCP, destroying the socialist system and overthrowing the People's Republic'.

6 In Shanghai, eight people are killed when an express train runs into a human barricade trying to prevent soldiers from entering the city. About 30

others sustain fatal injuries.

9 Dent Xiaoping, Yang Shangkun, Li Peng, Qiao Shi, Wan Li, Yao Yilin, Wang Zhen, Peng Zhen and other leaders appear at a televised meeting in central Beijing to praise the military action of June 3-4. Deng Xiaoping's speech commends the troops for suppressing counter-revolutionaries trying to overthrow the CCP' and for putting down the counter-revolutionary rebellion'.

10 Direct telephone links are opened between the two sides of the Taiwan Straits.

19 The Hong Kong and Macau Affairs Task Force announces the government's plan to simplify procedures for the relocation of Hong Kong and Macao compatriots in Taiwan and to provide assistance for their emigration to a third country.

24 The Fourth Plenum of the Thirteenth CCPCC dismisses Zhao Ziyang from all leading posts in the Party and elects Jiang Zemin to replace him as general secretary.

Sept. 4 Guatemalan President Marco Vincicio Cerezo Arevalo and President Lee Teng-hui sign a joint communiqué in Taipei calling for closer bilateral relations.

15 Prime Minister Mary Eugenia Charles of the Commonwealth of Dominica arrives in Taipei for a six-day visit.

26 The executive Yuan permits pro-democracy supporters from the mainland to settle in Taiwan.

Oct. 2 The ROC and Liberia re-establish diplomatic relations. Peking severs formal ties with Liberia in protest.

12 The ROC and Belize announce the establishment of diplomatic relations.

Dec. 2 Elections for the Legislative Yuan, Taiwan Provincial Assembly, Taipei and Kaohsiung city councils, county magistrates, and provincial-level city mayors are held.

1990

Jan. 14 President Lee Teng-hui and President Prosper Avril of Haiti sign a joint communiqué calling for stronger bilateral cooperation.

16 Low-ranking government employees are permitted to visit relatives across the Straits, and native Taiwanese who moved to the mainland before 1949 are allowed to visit relatives in Taiwan.

Feb. 13 The Mainland Affairs Task Force permits Taiwan's performing artists to stage commercial performances on the mainland and to participate in activities sponsored by the Chinese communists.

26 President Lee Teng-hui and El Salvadoran President Alfredo Felix Cristiani Burkard sign a joint communiqué for closer bilateral cooperation.

Mar. 1 The Executive Yuan approves direct trade between the ROC and the Soviet Union and Albania.

17 Thousands of university students stage a sit-down protest at the Chiang Kai-shek Memorial Hall Plaza to express opposition to the National Assembly's attempt to expand its authority.

21 Lee Teng-hui is elected vice president of the ROC.

27 The eighth plenum of the National Assembly approves a motion to force members who failed to attend the plenary session to retire by the end of July 1990.

Apr. 5 The ROC reestablishes diplomatic relations with the Kingdom of Lesotho. Peking severs ties with Lesotho two days later.

8 Economics Minister Chen Li-an and Singaporean Minister of Trade and Industries, Lee Hsien Loong, preside over the first ministerial-level conference between the two countries on economic cooperation.

30 Elected officials of all levels are permitted to make private visits to the mainland during recesses. Veterans who were stranded on the mainland after the national government moved to Taiwan in 1949 are allowed to apply for resettlement in Taiwan.

May 16 The KMT Central Standing Committee accepts the resignation of Premier Lee Huan and His Cabinet ministers.

20 Lee Teng-hui and Li Yuan-zu are inaugurated as president and vice president of the ROC.
President Lee Teng-hui announces a special amnesty, which includes the pardoning of dissidents Hsu Hsin-liang and Shih Ming-teh.

29 Premier nominee Hau Pei-Tsun is approved by the Legislative Yuan, and is immediately appointed premier by President Lee Teng-hui.

Jun. 17 President Andres Rodriguez of Paraguay arrives in Taipei to sign a joint communiqué calling for closer bilateral relations with the ROC.

21 The Council of Grand Justices announces that senior parliamentarians should terminate their responsibilities by December 31, 1991.

25 Reporters from the mainland are permitted to visit Taiwan for newsgathering purposes, and government employees from Taiwan are allowed to visit sick relatives or attend funerals on the mainland.

Jul. 4 The National Affairs Conference concludes in Taipei, after six days of discussions on parliamentary reforms, the central and local government system, the Constitution, and mainland policy.

22 The ROC government declares its support of a United Nations call for world sanctions against Iraq over its invasion of Kuwait.

Aug. 10 The ROC government declares its support of a United Nations call for world sanctions against Iraq over its invasion of Kuwait.

31 Premier hau Pei-tsun advises the Legislative Yuan that ROC relations with the mainland will operate under the concept of "one country, two areas."

Sept. 1 Premier Hau Pei-tsun announces the objectives of the Six-Year National Development Plan, which includes public construction projects affecting economics, culture, education, and medicine.

17 A team of 200 athletes and coaches flies to the Chinese mainland for the ROC's first attendance of the Asian Games in 20 years.

19 The Red Cross societies of the ROC and the mainland reach agreement on procedures for the repatriation of illegal mainland entrants to Taiwan.

Oct. 7 The National Unification Council is established under the Office of the President to help plan the policy framework for national unification, and to integrate various opinions about the issue at all levels of society.

11 The Ministry of the Interior reiterates that the Tiaoyutai island group belongs to the ROC. The chain of eight uninhabited islets, located in the East China Sea, also is claimed by Japan and communist China.

18 The Mainland Affairs Council is established under the Executive Yuan to formulate and implement mainland policy.

27 Moscow City Mayor Gavriil H. Popov arrives for a formal visit to the ROC to discuss the strengthening of ROC-Soviet

trade relations.

Nov. 1 President Lee Teng-hui receives an Outstanding International Alumnus Citation from Cornell University.

15 The Ministry of Foreign Affairs announces the ROC-Canadian agreement to exchange aviation rights and establish Taipei economic and cultural offices in major Canadian cities.

21 The Straits Exchange Foundation, a private intermediary organization financially supported by the government, is established to handle technical affairs arising from people-to-people contacts between Taiwan and the mainland.

1991

Jan. 6 A memorandum is signed between the ROC and Saudi Arabia for the mutual establishment of representative offices in their capital cities.

7 French Minister of Industry and Territorial Development Roger Fauroux participates in the seventh ROC-France Economic Cooperation Conference in Taipei.

31 The Executive Yuan approves a budget of about US$303 billion for the Six-Year National Development Plan.

Mar. 14 The Executive Yuan passes the *Guidelines for national Unification*, which are now the highest directives governing ROC mainland policy. Its long-term goal is to establish a democratic, free, and equitably prosperous China.

Apr. 22 The second extraordinary session of the First National Assembly passes, at its sixth plenary meeting, the *Additional articles of the Constitution of the ROC* and approves the abolishment of the *Temporary Provisions Effective During the Period of Communist Rebellion*.

30 President Lee Teng-hui declares the termination of the Period of National Mobilization for Suppression of the Communist Rebellion, effective on May 1. He abolishes the *Temporary Provisions* and promulgates the *Additional Articles of the Constitution*, also effective on May 1.

May 9 Visa application restrictions for USSR nationals are relaxed, and visa applications for purposes other than business are permitted.

24 The Legislative Yuan approves the abolishment of the *Statutes for the Purging of Communist*

Agents.

Jun. 26 Approval is given to 15 of the 19 applications to set up private commercial bank.

27 Government Spokesman Shaw Yu-ming announces that mainland journalists will no longer have to renounce their membership in the Chinese Communist Party when applying to visit Taiwan.

Jul. 4 The ROC and Czechoslovakia agree to exchange representative offices.

Aug. 5 President Lee Teng-hui receives Fijian Prime Minister Ratu Sir Kamises Mara; an ROC-Fiji technological cooperation agreement is signed on August 6.

12 Two mainland journalists arrive in Taipei, marking the first-ever visit by the mainland Chinese press.

18 Vice President Li Yuan-zu leaves for a state visit to Costa Rica, Nicaragua, and Honduras.

Sept. 25 The Mainland Affairs Council announces the establishment of a task force to combat crime across the Taiwan Straits.

Oct. 11 Direct air service begins between Australia and the ROC.

Nov. 6 The ROC and Latvia sign memoranda for economic cooperation and the exchange of trade offices.

13 The ROC joins the Asia-Pacific Economic Cooperation (APEC) along with Hong Kong and mainland China.

15 South African President Frederik Willem de Klerk signs a joint communiqué with President Lee Teng-hui for closer relations between the two countries.

Dec. 21 The ruling Kuomintang wins 71 percent of the vote and 254 of the 325 seats in the election for the Second National Assembly.

22 Dissident mainland Chinese astrophysicist Fang Li-chih visits Taipei.

31 All senior delegates to the First National Assembly, Control Yuan, and Legislative Yuan retire from office.

1992

Jan. 20 The French Secretary of State for Foreign Trade Jean-Noël Jeanneney visits Taipei to discuss participation in the Six-Year National Development Plan and further economic cooperation between the ROC and France.

27 The Fair Trade Commission is established under the Executive Yuan.

29 The ROC and Latvia announce the establishment of relations at

the consulate-general level.

Feb. 4 The *Fair Trade Law* goes into effect.

18 A delegation from the US President's Export Council arrives to promote ROC-US trade.

28 The ROC and the Philippines sign an official investment guarantee agreement to protect investments by Taiwan businessmen.

Mar. 7 Nicaraguan President Violeta Barrios de Chamorro and President Lee Teng-hui sign a joint communiqué in Taipei for stronger bilateral relations.

23 The first-ever meeting convenes in Peking between the SEF and the mainland's Association for Relations Across the Taiwan Straits, to discuss issues related to document verification and indirect registered mail services.

27 The ROC and Bulgaria agree to establish direct air links between Taipei and Sofia.

Apr. 17 Legislative proceedings are completed for the *National Employment Act*, which will serve as the basis for the employment of foreign nationals in the ROC.

19 Minister of Foreign Trade Yvonne C.M.T. van Rooy of the Netherlands visits Taipei to seek stronger bilateral relations.

May 10 Swedish Minister of Transport and Communications, Mats Odell, visits Taipei to discuss with the ROC officials.

17 Wu Ta-you, president of Academia Sinica, attends academic conferences in Peking and Tientsin.

30 The *Additional Articles* 11 through 18 of the Constitution go into effect.

31 The Mainland Affairs Council allows Chinese mainlanders to come Taiwan and care for their old or sick relatives.

Jun. 10 A revised *Copyright Law* goes into effect, providing explicit legal protection for intellectual property rights and imposing heavier penalties for infringement of copyright.

14 Ronald Freeman, Vice President of the European Bank for Reconstruction and Development, visits the ROC to discuss Sino-European trade and financial relations.

The Legislative Yuan approves the *Law on Foreign Futures Contracts*, which will take effect in January 1993.

Jul. 3 The Legislative Yuan passes a revision of the *Law on Civic Organizations*, which calls for a Political Party Review

Committee be formed under the Ministry of the Interior.

7 The Legislative Yuan passes a revision of the *National Security Law*, which would reduce the number of black-listed persona non grata from 282 to five.

9 The Argentine Trade and Cultural Office is opened in Taipei after a 20-year break in diplomatic relations.

16 The Legislative Yuan passes the *Statute Governing Relations Between People of the Taiwan Area and the Mainland Area.*

19 The ROC's five-year lease of three Knox-class frigates from the United States is approved by US President George Bush.

Aug. 1 The National Unification Council defines "one China" as "one country and two areas separately ruled by two political entities."

Taiwan Garrison General Headquarters, the ROC's highes security institution in the Taiwan area, is disbanded; and the Coastal Patrol General Headquarters is established under the Ministry of National Defense.

18 The Department of Anti-Corruption is established under the Ministry of Justice.

23 The ROC severs diplomatic relations with South Korea.

25 Niger's Prime Minister Amadou Cheiffou arrives in Taipei to advance mutual understanding between the two countries.

30 Former British Prime Minister Margaret Thatcher expresses support for the ROC's entry into the GATT during her visit to Taipei.

Sept. 2 President Lee Teng-hui and Guatemalan President Jorge Antonio Serrano sign a joint communiqué calling for closer bilateral cooperation in Taipei.

Canadian International Trade Minister Michael Wilson visits Taipei to boost ROC-Canada trade ties.

The Bureau of Entry and Exit announces that members of the Chinese People's Political Consultative Conference in mainland China may apply to visit Taiwan for cultural and academic exchanges.

6 Direct air service between the ROC and Vietnam resumes for the second time in 13 months.

13 Latvian Prime Minister Ivars Godmanis visits Taipei to seek mutually beneficial cooperation; an ROC-Latvia investment guarantee agreement is signed on September 17.

21 The US Department of Defense

decides to sell 12 SH-2F light airborn multipurpose system helicopters to the ROC.

22 Political Vice Foreign Minister John Chang and Oleg Lobov, Chairman of the Export Council to the Russian President Boris Yeltsin, sign two diplomatic memoranda and a document of state protocol pledging the promotion of trade, tourism, investment, cultural, and scientific and technological exchanges.

24 Foreign Minister Fredrick Chien and his Vanuatu counterpart Serge Vohor sign a joint communiqué pledging reciprocal recognition.

29 The ROC is granted observer status in the GATT, which also resolves to accept the ROC's application into GATT under the name, the "Separate Customs Territory of Taiwan, Penghu, Kinmen and Matsu".

Oct. 11 President Lee Teng-hui and Panamanian President Guillermo Endara sign a joint communiqué to expand bilateral cooperation.

12 Premier Hau Pei-tsun receives Austrian Minister for Economic Affairs Wolfgang Schüssel.

22 Belgian Foreign Trade Minister Robert Urbain visits Taipei to relay a message of welcome to Taiwan businessmen intending to invest in Belgium.

27 Australian Tourism and Resources Minister Alan Griffiths visits Taipei to promote closer bilateral trade relations.

Nov. 3 Indonesian Minister of Research and Technology Bacharuddin Habibie leads a 30-member delegation to Taiwan.

4 Vice Minister of Economic Affairs Chiang Pin-kung heads an observer delegation to the Geneva meeting of GATT Council of Representatives after the ROC's absence of 21 years.

7 After more than three decades of military administration, Quemoy (Kinmen) and Matsu revert to civilian rule as the *Statute Governing the Security and Guidance of the Kinmen, Tungsha, and Nansha Areas* goes into effect.

12 ROC and US defense representatives sign a letter of offer and acceptance for the ROC's purchase of 150 F-16A and F-16B jet fighters from the United States.

18 German Vice Chancellor Jürgen Möllemann and Economics Minister Vincent C. Siew reach an agreement on the

establishment of direct air links and channels of communication on trade between the ROC and Germany.

19 The Council of Agriculture bans all import, export, and trade of rhino-horn products.

Dec. 19 The Kuomintang wins 53.02 percent and the Democratic Progressive Party 31.03 percent of the popular vote in the election for the Second Legislative Yuan.

1993

Jan. 14 The legislative Yuan approves a US$12.47 billion budget for the purchase of 150 F-16 jet fighters from the United States and 60 Mirage 2000-5s from France.

15 ROC and Philippine officials sign an agreement in Manila, setting the guidelines for transforming the former US naval facility at Subic Bay into an industrial complex.

Feb. 22 Taiwan-made film *The Wedding Banquet* wins a Golden Bear Award for Best Picture at the 43rd annual Berlin International Film Festival.

26 Two China mainland basketball teams arrive in Taiwan to play exhibition matches against local teams; this marks the first time in four decades that athletes from Taiwan and the mainland will compete in Taiwan.

27 Taiwan Provincial Governor Lien Chan succeeds Hau Pei-tsun as premier of the ROC following his confirmation by the Legislative Yuan.

Mar. 21 Republic of Nauru President Bernard Dowiyogo visits Taipei.

26 In an interview with the US Cable News Network, President Lee Teng-hui stresses the ROC's willingness to form a regional collective security system with Asia-Pacific countries.

29 Direct air service between the ROC and the United Kingdom begins.

New Zealand's Minister of Customs and Associate Minister of Tourism, Murray McCully leads a nine-member delegation to Taipei.

Apr. 22 The Legislative Yuan ratifies the 1989 ROC-US copyright agreement and passes amendments to the *Copyright Law*, which go into effect on April 26.

Tonga's Prime Minister Vaea and Madame Vaea visit the ROC.

29 Representatives of the Straits Exchange Foundation and its mainland counterpart, the

Association for Relations Across the Taiwan Straits, sign three agreements and a joint accord at a historic meeting in Singapore; the agreements and accord go into effect on May 29.

May 1 The Taipei Economic and Trade Office in Tel Aviv begins operation.

7 The first ROC-made PFG-2 missile frigate, the Cheng-kung, goes into service.

8 A 186-member team from the ROC participates in the first East Asian Games in Shanghai.

Jun. 11 President Lee Teng-hui receives former Philippine President Corazon Aquino.

21 An ROC-US agreement for technical cooperation in the field of environmental protection is signed in Washington, D.C.

29 President Lee Teng-hui receives former US Vice President Dan Quayle.

30 The Executive Yuan approves an Economic Stimulus Package to accelerate industrial upgrading and to develop Taiwan into an Asia-Pacific Regional Operations Center.

Jul. 2 The *Public Functionary Assets Disclosure Law* goes into effect.

10 Vietnam's Economic and Cultural Office in Taipei opens.

12 The Taipei-Moscow Economic and Cultural Coordination Commission begins operation in Moscow.

Aug. 10 The New KMT Alliance breaks with the ruling Kuomintang and forms the New Party.

11 The *Cable Television Law* goes into effect.

16 The 14th National Congress of the KMT opens. President Lee Teng-hui is reelected chairman of the KMT; while Vice President Li Yuan-zu, former Premier Hau Pei-tsun, Judicial Yuan President Lin Yang-kang, and Premier Lien Chan are elected vice chairmen on August 18.

17 The ROC and Australia sign two memoranda on the protection of industrial property rights and on investment promotion and technical cooperation.

Sept. 2 The Executive Yuan passes an administrative reform package to eradicate corruption and inefficiency in the government.

23 The ROC and Belgium sign three investment cooperation agreements to boost economic and technological ties.

Oct. 26 The ROC and Mexico sign a pact to promote investment and technology transfer.

Nov. 19 Vincent C. Siew, chairman of the Council for Economic

Planning and Development, represents President Lee Teng-hui at the APEC leaders economic conference in Seattle.

25 South Korea opens its Korean Mission in Taipei to replace the embassy closed after South Korea and the ROC broke off diplomatic relations.

Dec. 9 The Government Information Office lifts the ban on radio stations and approves the applications of 13 broadcasting companies for operation licenses.

15 The Legislative Yuan approves a revision of the *University Law*, which gives more autonomy to colleges and allows students to participate in meetings related to school affairs.

1994

Jan. 11 The *Consumer Protection Law* goes into effect; manufacturers are held responsible for harming consumers even when negligence or intent to do harm are not found to be factors.

5 Lee Yuan-tesh succeeds Wu Ta-you as president of Academia Sinica.

Feb. 9 President Lee leaves for the Philippines, Indonesia, and Thailand on an eight-day visit.

Mar. 2 The ROC and Belize sign a joint communiqué pledging bilateral

cooperation.

23 The Legislative Yuan increases the annual number of permanent residency permits for mainland spouses from 300 to 600.

25 The SEF and the ARATS holds talks in Peking on fishery disputes and the repatriation of illegal entrants and hijackers.

Apr. 12 The Mainland Affairs Council decides to suspend all cultural and educational exchanges with the mainland before the Chinese communists provide reasonable and satisfactory explanations of the Qiandao Lake tragedy on Mar. 31 in which 24 Taiwan tourists are killed.

May 2 The ROC and Grenada sign a joint communiqué pledging bilateral cooperation.

4 President Lee Teng-hui leaves for Nicaragua, Costa Rica, South Africa, and Swaziland on a 13-day official visit.

Jun. 6 Premier Lien Chan pays the first visit of a high-ranking ROC official to Mexico in 23 years after the two severed diplomatic ties.

Jul. 7 The Legislative Yuan passes the *Self-governance Law for Provinces and Counties*, explicitly stipulating that provincial governors be chosen by direct election. The *Self-*

governance Law for Special Municipalities is passed the next day.

13 Seven foreign ministers and representatives from Central American countries come to Taiwan to participate in the Third Mixed Commission Conference of Central American Nations, and sign a joint declaration with the ROC supporting the ROC's bid for UN participation.

30 The SEF and the ARATS start talks in Taipei. This is the first high-level dialogue between the two organizations since the Qiandao Lake incident on Mar. 31, 1994.

Aug. 8 The SEF and the ARATS sign and make public a joint press release confirming the results of the second round of Chiao-Tang talks.

9 The US government announces trade sanctions against the ROC under the Pelly Amendment, placing a ban on imports of Taiwan wildlife products effective from August 19, 1994.

Sept. 7 US Assistant Secretary of State Winston Lord formally notifies the ROC representative in Washington, Ding Mou-shih, of the result from the Clinton administration's policy discussions about Taiwan: The US agrees to the ROC representative office changing its name to the Taipei Economic and Cultural Representative Office in the United States, and to ROC officials visiting all US government offices except the White House and the Department of State on official business.

19 On behalf of their respective governments, the ROC representative in Washington, Ding Mou-shih, and the chairman of the American Institute in Taiwan, Natale Bellocchi, sign a *Trade and Investment Framework Agreement*.

22 The chairman of the UN General Committee drops the proposal on the ROC's UN membership from the agenda after a 90-minute debate in which seven nations support the ROC and 20 oppose the proposal.

Oct. 27 The Legislative Yuan passes revisions to the *Wildlife Conservation Law*, greatly toughening penalties against violators and stipulating that the breeding in captivity of endangered animals must cease within three years.

Dec. 3 The first popular elections for the governor of Taiwan Province and mayors of Taipei and Kaohsiung municipalities are held. James C.Y. Soong is elected governor of Taiwan. Chen Shui-bian and Wu Den-yih win the mayor seats of Taipei and Kaohsiung, respectively.

4 US Secretary of Transportation Federico Pena visits the ROC, becoming the first US cabinet member to carry out the new US policy governing high-ranking official visits to Taipei.

12 The Lien cabinet is re-organized and new cabinet members are sworn in on December 15.

29 The first squadron of Ching-kuo indigenous defense fighters is officially commissioned, upgrading the combat ability of the ROC Air Force and demonstrating initial results of research and development.

1995

Jan. 5 The Executive Yuan Council approves the plan for developing Taiwan into an Asia-Pacific Regional Operations Center.

30 Mainland Chinese President Jiang Zemin offers an eight-point proposal, urging Taiwan to hold talks with the mainland to officially end the hostile standoff between the two sides.

Feb. 28 President Lee expresses an apology to families of the victims of the Feb. 28, 1947. Incident at the Taipei New Park, where a monument commemorating the tragedy was built with government sponsorship.

Mar. 1 The National Health Insurance program is formally inaugurated.

6 A Coordination and Service Office for the Asia-Pacific Regional Operations Center (also known as the APROC Window) is established in the Council for Economic Planning and Development to ensure that the Asia-Pacific Regional Operations Center plan is faithfully implemented.

23 *Regulations Governing the Management and Compensation for Victims of the Feb. 28, 1947 Incident* passes the Legislative Yuan. According to the regulations, a foundation will be established to manage affairs concerned, and Feb. 28 will be designated a national commemoration day.

The two-day convention of secretaries-general of the Olympic Council of Asia member nations opens in Kaohsiung. Following international practice, the convention hoists the flags of all OCA members – including the five-star flag of mainland China.

Apr. 1 President Lee starts his four-day visit to the United Arab Emirates and Jordan.

8 At the meeting of the National Unification Council, President Lee offers a six-point proposal for Taiwan-mainland relations.

May 19 The Legislative Yuan approves the temporary statute on welfare payments for elderly farmers, granting them a monthly stipend of NT$3,000.

22 The ROC and Papua New Guinea sign a joint communiqué in Taipei and establish mutual recognition in order to improve cooperation on the basis of reciprocal benefits.

Jun. 7 President Lee arrives in the United States for a reunion at his alma mater, Cornell University.

15 Premier Lien Chan launches a six-day visit to three European countries: Austria, Hungary, and Czechoslovakia. He is the highest ROC official to visit Europe since the ROC government moved to Taipei in 1949.

30 The US government officially announces cancellation of the sanctions against Taiwan issued under the Pelly Amendment.

Jul. 1 The ROC resumes full diplomatic relations with Gambia after a 21-year hiatus.

9 The Legislature approves the *Presidential and Vice Presidential Election and Recall Law*, setting ground rules for the March 23, 1996, popular election of the ROC president and vice president.

21 The Chinese mainland begins eight days of firing surface-to-surface missiles into the East China Sea about 140 kilometers north of Taiwan.

26 The US Congress honors Madame Chiang Kai-shek at a Capitol Hill reception in recognition of her contribution to Allied efforts during World War II.

Aug. 15 The Chinese mainland begins eleven days of firing tactical guided missiles and live artillery shells into the sea 136 kilometers north of Taiwan.

17 Control Yuan President Chen Li-an announces his candidacy for president and, on the following day, renounces his 42-year KMT membership.

19 The Foreign Ministry issues a position paper entitled "Why the UN Resolution No. 2758 Adopted in 1971 Should Be

Reexamined Today." The paper stressed that UN Resolution 2758, which excluded the ROC from the UN system and its activities, is obsolete and unjust and ought to be reexamined.

22 The KMT convenes its 14th National Congress and Lee Teng-hui, party chairman, announces he will seek the party's presidential nomination. Lin Yang-kang, a KMT vice chairman, declares his intention not to seek the nomination but to run as an independent.

31 The KMT nominates incumbent President Lee as its presidential candidate; the next day President Lee names Premier Lien as his running mate.

Sept. 7 The ROC and Singapore initial an agreement to cooperate on a project to launch a telecommunications satellite.

17 An exhibition of 71 landscape paintings from the collection of the Louvre in Paris opens at the National Palace Museum in Taipei. The exhibition runs through Jan. 15.

21 Economics Minister Chiang Pin-kung leads a delegation to the 19th Joint Conference of ROC-USA and USA-ROC Economic Councils in Anchorage, Alaska.

25 The DPP nominates Peng Ming-min, a former political science professor and a long-time dissident in exile, as its presidential candidate after a 15-week primary; Peng later names Legislator Frank Hsieh as his running mate.

27 Jeffrey Koo, chairman of the Chinese National Association of Industry and Commerce, leads a delegation to the Pacific Economic Cooperation Council meeting in Peking.

Oct. 3 Manuel Saturnino da Costa, prime minister of Guinea-Bissau, arrives in Taipei for a six-day visit.

17 The ROC and Macau establish a five-year renewable air pact allowing Eva Airways, Transasia Airways, and Air Macau to fly routes between Taiwan and Macau.

21 Independent presidential candidate Chen Li-an names Wang Ching-feng, a Control Yuan member, as his running mate.

Nov. 15 Independent presidential hopeful Lin Yang-kang names former Premier Hau Pei-tsun as his running mate.

17 Koo Chen-fu, a senior adviser to the ROC president, arrives in Osaka, Japan, to attend the Asia-Pacific Economic Cooperation

forum summit in place of President Lee.

21 The ROC and Australia sign a memorandum of understanding to permit temporary duty-free entry of certain goods as a means of increasing two-way trade.

25 The ROC and Poland, to boost economic ties, initial an agreement to avoid double taxation and prevent tax evasion by investors.

Dec. 2 The Republic of China elects 164 lawmakers to the Third Legislative Yuan.

1996

Jan. 3 The ROC and the Republic of Senegal resume full diplomatic relations, increasing to 31 the number of nations with which the ROC maintains such relations.

11 Vice President Li Yuan-zu leaves for the Republic of Guatemala to attend the inaugural ceremony of President Alvaro Enrique Arzu Irigoyen, traveling via Los Angeles, USA.

23 An ROC Ministry of Education ad hoc committee decides that 452 works of art from the National Palace Museum in Taipei will be allowed to go on a 13-monthh exhibition trip to

the United States. This is one of the largest bodies of national treasures ever to tour overseas.

Feb. 12 Faced with threatening military maneuvers undertaken by Peking, the Executive Yuan sets up a temporary policy-making task force to closely follow developments and coordinate the actions of various agencies to respond to the situation.

Mar. 8 The Chinese mainland begins eight days of test-firing surface-to-surface missiles in waters close to major ports in northeastern and southwestern Taiwan.

12 The Chinese mainland commences nine days of naval and air military exercises in an area of the Taiwan Straits only 53 kilometers from Kinmen and 70 kilometers from the Penghu Islands.

18 The Chinese mainland begins eight days of war games involving ground, air, and naval forces in an area of sea 85 kilometers northwest of Taiwan proper.

23 Four pairs of candidates compete in the first-ever direct election of the ROC president and vice president. The Lee-Lien ticket wins, garnering 54 percent of the vote. At the same

time, 334 members of the Third National Assembly are also elected.

28 After eight years of construction, the Mucha Line of the Taipei Mass Rapid Transit Systems officially commences operations.

Apr. 28 The Ministry of Economic Affairs announces that starting July 1, 1996, imports of another 1,609 categories of industrial commodities will be allowed from the Chinese mainland, marking the ROC government's largest-scale relaxation of restriction on mainland imports.

29 On the third anniversary of the Koo-Wang talks, Koo Chen-fu, chairman of the ROC's Straits Exchange Foundation, appeals to the Chinese mainland not to postpone the second Koo-Wang talks so that both sides can resume their pursuit of reunification.

May 20 Lee Teng-hui and Lien Chan are sworn in as ROC president and vice president, respectively.

In his inaugural address, President Lee emphasizes that it is neither necessary nor possible to adopt a so-called "Taiwan independence" line. He expresses his hope that the two sides will counter animosity with peace and forgiveness and turn to the important task of ending the enmity across the Straits. President Lee also indicates his willingness to make a "journey of peace" to the Chinese mainland. He says that in order to bring forth a new era of communication and cooperation between the two sides, he is willing to meet and directly exchange opinions with the top mainland leadership.

Jun. 5 President Lee Teng-hui appoints Vice President Lien Chan to serve concurrently as ROC premier. A cabinet reshuffle is passed three days later.

7 At his first press conference as Vice President/Premier, Lien Chan indicates that the ROC has not ruled out the possibility of the two sides exchanging visits by high-ranking officials. He also emphasizes the need to reopen channels for cross-strait talks.

28 The ROC exchanges economic and trade representative office with the Republic of Belarus. Belarus is the second (Russia being the first) member of the Commonwealth of Independent States to establish such a level of relations with the ROC.

30 South African Foreign Minister Alfred Nzo arrives for a three-

day visit.

Jul. 4 The National Assembly convenes and subsequently elects Fredrick Chien speaker and Shieh Lung-sheng deputy speaker.

18 The European Parliament passes a resolution supporting ROC efforts to be represented in international organizations.

24 The Foreign Ministry protests Japan's decision to include the Tiaoyutai Islets in its 200-nautical-mile exclusive economic zone.

30 Chen Jing wins a silver medal in women's table tennis singles at the Olympics in Atlanta.

Aug. 12 Vice President and Premier Lien Chan departs for the Dominican Republic to attend the Aug. 16 inauguration of President Leonel Fernandez.

19 Vice President and Premier Lien Chan visits Ukraine.

24 The ROC wins the 1996 Little League World Series in the US city of Williamsport, Pennsylvania.

Sept. 11 The US removes the ROC from an wildlife conservation watchlist in recognition of its progress in protecting endangered species.

12 The ROC states a four-point position in the Tiaoyutai Islets

dispute with Japan: the ROC's absolute sovereignty, a rational attitude, no cooperation with Peking, and the protection of Taiwan's fishing rights.

Nov. 20 Gembian President Yahya Jammeh visits the ROC.

27 South Africa says it will switch full diplomatic recognition from Taipei to Peking on Jan. 1, 1998.

Dec. 2 Foreign Minister John Chang departs for South Africa.

6 The Legislature revises the *Labor Standards Law* so that employees in nearly all industries will be covered by the end of 1998.

10 The Cabinet-level Council of Aboriginal Affairs is established. The Taiwan Independence Party (TAIP), a DPP splinter group, is established.

19 The ceiling on foreign institutional investments in the stock market is raised from US$400 million to US$600 million.

23 The five-day National Development Conference begins. Discussion focuses on three major topics: enhancing constitutional system of government and multiparty politics; economic development; and cross-strait relations.

31 Taiwan Provincial Governor

James Soong submits his resignation to Premier Lien Chan.

1997

Jan. 7 Vice President and Premier Lin Chan departs for Nicaragua to attend the Jan. 10 inauguration of President Arnoldo Aleman.

14 Vice President and Premier Lien Chan meets with Pope John Paul II and shares with him views on world peace and humanitarian pursuits.

Feb. 23 The Legislative Yuan passes the amendment to the fourth article of the *February 28 Incident Disposition and Compensation Act*, stipulating that February 28, also named "Peace Memorial Day," be a national holiday.

Mar. 1 Taipei and Kaohsiung cities officially launch a system that prohibits physicians from directly dispensing medicines.

17 Madame Chiang Kai-shek celebrates her centennial birthday.
Former Chairman of the US Joint Chiefs of Staff General Colin L. Powell visits the ROC.

22 Tibetan spiritual leader Dalai Lama pays a six-day visit to the ROC.

Apr. 2 US House of Representatives Speaker Newt Gingrich meets with President Lee Teng-hui during his four-hour visit to the ROC, praising Taiwan's political progress and economic achievement.

May 5 The second session of the Third National Assembly begins to amend the *Constitution*. The focus of the session is to streamline the local government; reform the election process for the president and members of the National Assembly; and clarify the president's relations with the Executive Yuan and the Legislature.

6 The ROC establishes formal diplomatic relations with the Democratic Republic of Sao Tome and Principe in western Africa.

31 The Legislative Yuan passes the third reading of the *Public Television Bill*, which will enable the public television station to begin broadcasting in 1998.

Jun. 14 Vice President and Premier Lien Cha announces that the government will establish a Ministry of Culture.

21 Koo Chen-fu, chairman of the Straits Exchange Foundation, is invited by mainland's Association for Relations Across the Taiwan Straits to

attend the ceremony marking the transfer of Hong Kong's sovereignty to the Chinese mainland on June 30.

Jul. 1 The Mainland Affairs Council sets up the Hong Kong Affairs Bureau to handle ties between Taipei and Hong Kong after Hong Kong is reverted to the Chinese mainland.

Aug. 1 The Council of Grand Justice rules that legislators who engage in violence during legislative sessions will no longer be immune from arrest and prosecution.

12 The Republic of Chad resumes official ties with the ROC after a 25-year hiatus.

21 Vice President and Premier Lien Chan heads the cabinet and tenders resignation to the president. Legislator Vincent C. Siew will succeed him to be the new premier of the ROC.

26 President Lee Teng-hui is re-elected chairman of the ruling Kuomintang with 93 percent of the votes cast by over 2,000 party representatives of KMT's 15th National Congress.

28 KMT's 15th Central Committee elects 17 members to the enlarged Central Standing Committee, along with 16 appointed by the chairman,

immediately following conclusion of National Congress.

Sept. 1 The ROC swears in a new cabinet with Vincent C. Siew as the premier. At a press conference after his inauguration, Premier Siew vows to improve law and order, further develop the economy, raise people's quality of life, and normalize cross-strait relations.

4 President Lee Teng-hui leaves for Latin America via the US to attend the World congress on the Panama Canal in Panama City, where he will meet with heads of state of ROC allies including Panama, Nicaragua and Honduras.

19 The ROC's *Tobacco Hazard Control and Prevention Law* goes into effect.

Oct. 3 Swaziland King Mswati III visits the ROC through Oct. 5.

5 Vice President Lien Chan embarks on a 12-day visit to Iceland and Austria to strengthen ROC's substantive ties with the two nations.

9 Taiwan film "Such a Life" wins the Best Picture Award at the 42nd Asia-Pacific Film Festival.

15 Steven Chu, member of the ROC Academia Sinica, wins the 1997 Nobel Prize for physics.

Nov. 5 Liberian President Charles

Ghankay Taylor, accompanied by his wife and a 43-member delegation, arrives in Taipei for a 7-day state visit.

22 The ROC signs a letter of intent with Hungary on cooperation in customs affairs.

26 Stricter regulations on firearms go into effect as part of the ROC government's efforts to strengthen and stabilize social order.

29 In the election for county magistrates and city mayors, the ruling KMT takes eight seats out of the 23 seats at stake. The Democratic Progressive Party doubles its number of seats from six of the last election to 12. The remaining three seats go to the hands of independents.

Dec. 2 The *Asian Wall Street Journal*, the first multinational newspaper to set up a printing site in Taipei, launches printing operations.

31 The ROC severs its official ties with South Africa.

1998

Jan. 1 Vice President Lien Chan and his wife start a four-day private visit to Singapore, Discussions over financial turmoil in the Asia-Pacific with high-ranking officials of the host nation stand high on his agenda.

20 Premier Vincent C. Siew arrives in Jakarta, where he is scheduled to meet with Indonesian President Suharto to discuss the possibility of establishing a financial cooperative mechanism in the Asia-Pacific region.

21 Bishop Shan Kuo-hsi of the Catholic diocese in Kaohsiung is formally appointed one of only three cardinals representing the world's Chinese communities by Pope John Paul II.

24 The Republic of China elects local-level county and city councilmen, and rural and urban township chiefs. The ruling KMT wins a landslide victory.

Feb. 5 A partial reshuffling of the cabinet results in eight position assignments including interior and education ministers.

11 Malaysian Deputy Prime Minister Anwar Ibrahim pays a visit to the ROC as part of his government's drive to seek cooperative measures to stabilize the region's troubled financial sector.

14 Foreign Minister Jason C. Hu launches a 12-day visit to ROC allies in Africa including Senegal, Gambia, Liberia, Burkina Faso, Chad and Sao

Tome and Principe to cement ties with these nations.

24 Jordan University confers an honorary doctorate upon Vice President Lien Chan. During his trip to Jordan.

Mar. 4 On his way back to Taiwan from a trip to Jordan, Bahrain and the United Arab Emirates, Vice President Lien Chan arrives in Kuala Lumpur for a four-day private visit.

Apr. 3 The Ministry of Foreign Affairs announces that President Lee Teng-hui has been nominated for the 1998 Nobel Peace Prize. It is the second time in three years that President Lee has been nominated for the honor.

21 Haitian President René Garcia Preval arrives in Taipei for a four-day state visit.

22 A delegation sent by the Straits Exchange Foundation with its deputy secretary-general, Jan Jyh-horng, at the head arrives in Peking. Jan is scheduled to meet with his ARATS counterpart and set agendas for the second round of Koo-Wang Talks slated to be held in autumn. The visit marks the restoration of cross-strait consultation and negotiation, which were unilaterally broken off by Peking since 1995 following

ROC President Lee Teng-hui's journey to the US to visit his alms mater, Cornell University in June of the same year.

24 The ROC signs a memorandum of understanding on customs cooperation with the Slovak Republic.

25 Premier Vincent C. Siew Starts his three-day visit to Kuala Lumpur to meet with high-ranking officials of the host nation. How to further bolster bilateral ties and deal with the Asian financial turmoil stand as the centerpiece of the meeting.
The president of the Central Bank of China, Perng Fai-nan, leads a delegation to attend the 31st board director meeting of the Asian Development Bank in Geneva.

May 5 Vice President Lien Chan, sent by President Lee as a special envoy, leaves for Costa Rica to attend the inauguration of President-elect Miguel Angel Rodriguez slated for May 8.

11 The ROC armed forces conduct their annual routine joint military exercise in the eastern Taiwan counties of Hualien and Taitung. The drill, code-named "Han Kuang No.14" will serve as a revies of the military's combat readiness and ability to

ensure national security.

22 ROC President Lee Teng-hui and Nauru President Kinza Clodumar sign a joint communiqué to reinforce bilateral cooperation. The head of the Republic off Nauru and his entourage pay a four-day visit to the ROC.

31 Gyorgy Ujlaky, Hungary's newly appointed representative to the ROC, arrives in Taipei to set up a trade office in Taipei to promote bilateral exchanges.

Jun. 1 Premier Vincent C. Siew presides over the opening ceremony of the newly established Southern Taiwan Service Center in Kaohsiung City.

15 Democratic Republic of Sao Tme and Principe President Miguel A.C.L. Trovoada and his wife arrive in Taipei for a five-day state visit.

Jul. 2 Premier Vincent Siew embarks on a 9-day Pacific trip to consolidate bilateral relation with ROC diplomatic partners in the region.

21 The opening of the Taiwan International Mercantile Exchange is a milestone for Taiwan's financial sector.

Oct. 9 The Legislative Yuan passes the statute to streamline the Taiwan

Provincial Government, making the TPG a nonautonomous body under the central government.

13 Daniel C. Tsui, member of the ROC's Academia Sinica, wins the 1997 Nobel Prize for physics.

14 Straits Exchange Foundation Chairman Koo Chen-fu arrives in Shanghai to meet with his ARATS counterpart Wang Daohan. During his trip, Mr. Koo states that the conciliatory spirit of agreements signed between the two sides in Singapore five years ago will be restored.

Nov. 3 President Lee Teng-hui meets with former German Chancellor Helmut Schmidt to exchange views on world economic development.

9 US Secretary of Energy Bill Richardson arrives in Taiwan to attend the 22nd annual USA-ROC Economic Council.

16 P. K. Chiang, chairman of the Council for Economic Planning and Development, heads for Malaysia to attend the APEC annual conference on behalf of President Lee Teng-hui.

Dec. 5 Vice President Lien Chan leads a humanitarian delegation of government officials and representatives from chairity and religious organizations on an 11-day visit to hurricane-stricken allies including Nicaragua, Honduras, El Salvador, and Guatemala.

In the election for the Fourth Legislative Yuan the ruling KMT secures 123 of the 225 seats and the DPP garners 70 seats while the rest goes to the NP and other minority parties. The KMT also triumphs in elections for Taipei mayor and councilmen of Taipei and Kaohsiung cities, but it loses the mayoral election in Kaohsiung City.

21 Operation begin to streamline the provincial government, a vital part of the efficiency-oriented master plan to restructure the government in Taiwan.

1999

Jan. 9 Premier Vincent Siew heads for the Dominican Republic, Haiti, and Belize to consolidate relations in the Caribbean.

12 The Legislative Yuan unanimously abolishes the Publication Law.

26 The ROC launches ROCSAT-1, its first wholly-owned and operated satellite, into orbit from Cape Canaveral, Florida, USA, marking the ROC's entry into the era of advanced space technology.

27 The ROC and the Republic of Macedonia sign a joint communiqué to establish formal relations. Macedonia thus becomes ROC's second diplomatic ally in Europe, after Holy See.

Mar. 5 Foreign Minister Jason Hu signs a memorandum with his Macedonian counterpart, Aleksandra Dimitrov, in Skopje to promote bilateral economic cooperation.

17 The Atomic Energy Council issues a permit for Taiwan Power Company to construct the ROC's fourth nuclear power plant.

Apr. 28 The Embassy of the Republic of Macedonia commences operation with Verka Modanu as Macedonia's first resident envoy to the ROC.

30 Foreign Minister Jason C. Hu arrives in the Marshall Islands for a three-day official visit to strengthen bilateral ties in such areas as tourism, fisheries, and investment.

May 27 Premier Vincent Siew heads to the Central Caribbean to attend the inauguration of El Salvador President Francisco flores.

Jun. 4 The Legislative Yuan passes the

third reading of the Cigarette and Wine Management Law, revoking the decades-old monopoly tax system.

6 Macedonian President Ljubco Georgievski, head of a 59-member delegation, arrives Taipei for a six-day official visit. During his visit to the ROC, he signs agreements on economic cooperation, investment guarantees, and prevention of the double taxation of investors to strengthen relations with the ROC government.

7 In an international press conference, President Lee Teng-hui announces that the ROC will provide the Balkan a US$300 million aid package to ease the plight of Kosovo war refugees.

16 The Legislature passes the third reading of the amendments to the public lottery act, ensuring the right of lottery issuance by the central government.

23 The ROC signs a press cooperation agreement with Panama.

24 The Domestic Violence Prevention Law goes into effect.

Jul. 9 In an interview with the German Broadcasting company Deutsche Welle, President Lee Teng-hui first announces the concept that Taiwan and the Chinese mainland have a "special state-to-state relationship."

To enhance bilateral economic and trade ties, the ROC and Thailand sign pacts on aviation exchanges and avoidance of double taxation.

20 President Lee Teng-hui further elaborates his recent remarks of the "special state-to-state relationship" between the two sides of the Taiwan Strait by saying that he did not put forth the statement to seek Taiwan independence but simply to reiterate the afct that both sides are separately governed.

Aug. 30 Premier Vincent Siew departs for Panama to attend the Sept. 1 inauguration of Panamanian President-elect Mireya Moscoso.

Sept. 4 The Third National Assembly passes a constitutional amendment which extends the current terms of the deputies form May 2000 to June 2002, and includes the appointment of all deputies on the basis of party proportional representation in the fourth Assembly.

20 President Lee Teng-hui and Paraguayan President Luis Angel Conzalez Macchi sign a joint communiqué reaffirming the two countries' commitment to stronger cooperative relations.

21 Taiwan is hit by its deadest earthquake in more than 60 years. The 7.3 magnitude quake claims more than 2,000 lives and injures over 8,000 more.

25 President Lee issues an emergency decree to cut through red tape and expedite reconstruction in areas hit by the earthquake. The decree, which supersedes certain existing laws is effective for six months.

Oct. 1 The Civil Aeronautics Administration announces the indefinite suspension of direct flights between Taipei and Manila after a breakdown in negotiations in weekly passenger quotas.

26 The Taipei-based China External Trade Development Council (CETRA, not known as TAITRA) opens a branch office in Bombay, India to promote bilateral trade.

Nov. 7 *Darkness and Light*, a film by Taiwan director Chang Tso-chi, wins the aware for best picture at the 12th Tokyo International Film Festival.

13 Tokyo Governor Shintaro Ishihara arrives for a three-day visit, making him the highest-profile Japanese official to visit Taiwan since the two countries cut diplomatic relations in 1972.

20 President Lee greets visiting Nauru President Rene Harris and his wife in Taipei.

Dec. 1 President Lee presides over a welcoming ceremony for Malawi President Bakil Muluzi in Taipei.

16 The ROC is named a permanent observer of the Central American Parliament Speakers Forum (CAPSF) at the ninth meeting of the CAPSF in Panama.

28 Taiwan renames its representative office in Macau the Taipei Economic and Cultural Center.

30 Diplomatic relations with Palau are formed.

2000

Jan. 24 Chen Wu-hsiung, vice chairman of the Council of Agriculture, is elected vice chairman of the Asian-African Rural Reconstruction Organization – one of the few international organizations in which the ROC participates in an official capacity.

Feb. 5 In central Beijing, police break up a Falungong demonstration gathered to mark the Chinese New Year and the Year of the Dragon, beating and detaining some demonstrators.

21 A State Council policy white paper declares that China would be forced to use drastic measures, including military force should Taiwan indefinitely delay negotiations aimed at reunification with the mainland.

Mar. 2 A CCP Central Committee and State Council document announces China's intention to limit population growth to 1.5 per cent annually, declaring the next decade a vital period for sustaining a low birth rate.

18 DPP candidate Chen Shui-bian and his running mate Lu Hsiu-lien are elected president and vice president, respectively, ending the KMT's more than 50-year hold on the presidency in Taiwan.

20 Commenting on Chen Shui-bian's victory in the Taiwan elections, Jiang Zemin states: 'No matter who is in power in Taiwan we shall welcome him to the mainland, and we may go to Taiwan. But dialogue and negotiations need a basis, which is that he must acknowledge (*chengren*) the principle of on China. On this precondition, anything can be discussed.'

23 US envoy Lee Hamilton meets with President-elect Chen Shui-bian to exchange views on future bilateral relations.

31 James Soong, after losing his independent presidential bid, formally establishes the People First Party (PFP) with himself as its chairman.

Apr. 13 Police suppress a Falungong protest in Tiananmen Square, Beijing detaining some 200 members.

24 The Third National Assembly approves a landmark amendment to drastically reduce its powers and functions, such as relinquishing its state as standing body and agreeing to convene only when proposals of impeachment, constitutional amendment, and national boundary changes are initiated by the Legislature.

25 Police suppress a series of coordinated protests in Tiananmen Square by the Falungong, marking the anniversary of the major demonstrations outside Zhongnanhai in 1999 which marked the beginning of such activities of this body.

May 19 Red China and the European Union sign an agreement for China to join the WTO.

20 Chen Shui-bian and Lu hsiu-lien are sworn in as president and vice president respectively, and

Tang Fei takes office as the new premier.

In his speech at the ceremony inaugurating him as president of Taiwan, Chen Shui-bian pledge not to declare the independence of Taiwan during his term in office 'as long as the CCP regime has no intention to use military force against Taiwan', and affirms his belief that the leaders on both sides of the Taiwan Strait 'possess enough wisdom and creativity to jointly deal with the question of a future "one China"'.

21 Taiwanese director Edward Yang wins a Golden Palm Award for best director at the Cannes Film Festival for *A One and a Two*.

Jun. 9 The 2000 Asia-Pacific Cultural Summit, sponsored by the Taipei City Government's Bureau of Cultural Affairs, begins a three-day conference in Taipei.

25 The DPP elects Kaohsiung Mayor Frank Chang-ting Hsieh as its new chairman.

Jul. 1 Panamanian President Mireya Elisa Moscoso Rodriguez arrives in Taipei for a five-day state visit.

18 In Beijing, Russian President Vladimir Putin and Jiang Zemim

issue a joint statement, which includes strengthening security relations and opposition to the United States proposal for a National Missile Defence (NMD) system.

21 China announces that it will merge ten of its airlines into its three largest groups: Air China, China Eastern and China Southern.

Aug. 4 In response to a move by Senegal for Taiwan's representation in the United Nations, Chinese UN representative Wang Yingfan writes to UN Secretary-General Kofi Annan reaffirming China's view that there is but one China, that Taiwan is part of its territory.

Sept. 1 The Ministry of Foreign Affairs announces the closure of the representative offices in the Congo, Angola, and Madagascar.

18 Weightlifter Li Feng-ying wins the silver medal in the woman's 53-kilogram category at the 2000 Olympic Games in Sydney, Australia.

23 Singapore's Senior Minister Lee Kuan Yew arrives for a four-day private visit.

Oct. 3 Premier Tang Fei resigns and is succeeded by Vice Premier Chang Chun-hsiung.

15 Former President Lee Teng-hui attends the Forum 2000 conference in Prague.

27 Premier Chang Chun-hsiung announces that the Executive Yuan is canceling the partly built Fourth Nuclear Power Plant.

Dec. 9 President Chen signs a joint communiqué in Taipei with his El Salvadorian counterpart, Francisco Guillermo Flores Perez.

10 Taiwan director Chang Chih-yung wins the best director award at the 2000 Asia Pacific Film Festival for his film *Lament of the Sand River.*

2001

Jun. 1 The "Mini-Three-Links" (direct trade, postal, and transportation) between the islands of Kinmen and Matsu and China's Xiamen and Fuzhou harbors are opened.

15 The Councii of Grand Justices rules that the Cabinet's controversial decision to halt work on the Fourth Nuclear Power Plant has "procedural errors."

Feb. 6 President Chen meets Chinese-born Nobel literature laureate Gao Xingjian in Taipei.

14 Premier Chang Chun-hsiung makes an official announcement

to resume the construction of the Fourth Nuclear Power Plant.

18 *Betelnut Beauty,* a film by Taiwan director Lin Cheng-sheng, wins a Silver Bear Award at the 51st Berlin Film Festival.

25 *Crouching Tiger, Hidden Dragon,* directed by Taiwan-born director Ang Lee, wins four British Academy Awards for best director, best foreign-language picture, best soundtrack and best costumes.

Mar. 15 Burkina Faso President Blaise Compaore arrives in Taipei for a six-day visit.

26 The film *Crouching Tiger, Hidden Dragon* wins four Oscars at the 73rd Annual Academy Awards for best foreign-language film, best art direction, best cinematography, and best original score.

31 Tibetan spiritual leader Dalai Lama arrives for a ten-day visit at the invitation of the Buddhist Association of the ROC.

May 15 Council for Economic Planning and Development Chairman Chen Po-chih meets PRC President Jiang Zemin during a ministerial meeting on human resources at the APEC forum in Beijing.

16 President Chen Shui-bian receives St. Vincent and the

Grenadines Prime Minister Ralph Gonsalves.

Jun. 18 Diplomatic relations with Macedonia are severed.

Jul. 2 President Chen Shui-bian decorates visiting Senegal President Abdoulaye Wade with the Order of Brilliant Jade in recognition of his efforts to strengthen relations between the two countries.

Aug. 14 Five winners of the Nobel Peace Prize and representatives from several nongovernmental organizations gather in Taipei for the 2001 Global Peace Assembly.

Nov. 6 President Chen opens the 34th Baseball World Cup in Taipei, with 16 participating teams from around the world.

11 The World Trade Organization (WTO) approves Taiwan's entry at its fourth ministerial meeting in Doha, Qatar.

14 On behalf of President Chen Shui-bian, First Lady Wu Shu-jen receives the "2001 Prize for Freedom" in France from the London-based Liberal International.

Dec. 1 In the election for the Fifth Legislative Yuan, the DPP wins 87 seats of the 225 seats available, the KMT 68 seats, the PFP 46 seats, and the Taiwan

Solidarity Union (TSU) 13 seats, while the rest go to minority parties and independents. In the election for county magistrates and city mayors, the DPP and the KMT each takes nine seats out of the 23 seats available, the PFP wins two seats, the NP wins one seat, and the remaining two seats go to independents.

9 Vice President Lu receives the World Peace Prize in Taipei for her work in promoting women's and human rights, democracy, and world peace.

2002

Jan. 1 Taiwan formally becomes the 144th member of the WTO.

6 Vice President Lu leaves for Nicaragua to attend the inauguration of President Enrique Bolanos Geyer,.

21 President Chen Shui-bian announces Yu Shyi-kun as the new premier.

Mar. 18 Vice President Lu leaves for Budapest to attend the annual conference of liberal International held during March 21-23.

29 The Executive Yuan decides to liberalize the policy relating to investment in silicon wafer plants in China.

May 31 The Executive Yuan approves

the Challenge 2008 National Development Plan, aiming to transform Taiwan into a "green silicon island."

Jul. 1 The Environmental Protection Administration implements the policy of restricted use of plastic bags and disposable plastic tableware.

21 President Chen assumes chairmanship of the DPP at the party's tenth National Congress.

Aug. 14 Vice President Lu takes a five-day trip to Indonesia in an effort to encourage Taiwanese businessmen to invest in Southeast Asian countries.

Oct. 14 Taiwan wins 10 gold, 17 silver, and 25 bronze medals in the 14th Busan Asian Games during the 16-day competition.

Dec. 7 KMT incumbent Ma Ying-chiu and DPP incumbent Frank Chang-ting Hsieh win the mayor seats of Taipei and Kaohsiung, respectively.

2003

Jan. 13 Taiwan's two professional baseball leagues merge under the name "Chinese Professional Baseball League."

26 Sent to pick up Taiwanese businessmen coming home for Chinese New Year, a passenger plane of Taiwan's national flag

carrier China Airlines makes a historic landing at Shanghai's Pudong International Airport for an indirect chartered flight across the Taiwan Strait.

Apr. 23 Taiwan's first mass infection of severe acute respiratory syndrome (SARS) is reported after seven staff members at Taipei Municipal Hoping Hospital showed symptoms of the disease.

24 The Shihsanhang Museum of Archaeology, northern Taiwan's sole prehistoric archeological museum, is inaugurated in Bali Township, Taipei County.

Jul. 1 Taiwan launches the world's first all-Hakka television station, Hakka TV, to promote Hakka culture and language.

5 The World Health Organization removes Taiwan from the list of SARS-affected areas.

15 First Lady Wu Shu-jen departs for Germany, where a National Palace Museum collection is being exhibited.

26 Tsao Chin-hui, the first Taiwanese player to pitch in the US for Major League Baseball, wins his debut game for the Colorado Rockies.

Aug. 7 Vice President Lu Hsiu-lien leaves for Paraguay to attend the inauguration of President

Nicanor Duarte Frutos.

21 The Fourth Summit of the Heads of State and Governments of the ROC, Central America and the Dominican Republic is held in Taipei.

Sept. 1 New ROC passports with "Taiwan" in Roman script on the cover are formally issued.

Oct. 12 Diplomatic relations with Liberia are terminated.

18 Academia Sinica President Lee Yuan-tseh arrives in Bangkok as Taiwan's emissary at the 11the APEC Economic Leaders' Meeting.

23 Soong Mayling, the Widow of former President Chiang Kai-shek, passes away in New York at the age of 106.

31 President Chen Shui-bian leaves for a six-day diplomatic tour to Panama.

Nov. 7 Diplomatic relations with the Republic of Kiribati are established.

14 Taipei Financial Center (Taipei 101), the world's tallest skyscraper at a height of 508 meters, opens its doors to the public.

24 The executive Yuan formally proposes the Public Works Expansion Investment Plan and allocates NT$500 billion over five years for the Ten New Major Construction Projects.

28 The Legislative Yuan passes the *Referendum Act*, providing the legal basis for the people of Taiwan to vote directly on issues of national or local importance.

Dec. 24 The National Space Program Office (NSPO) successfully launches Taiwan's first space-probe, Sounder Rocket No. 3 (SR-3), to perform sub-orbital science experiments.

2004

Jan. 11 The entire length of Taiwan's 518-km second north-south freeway, later named Formosa Freeway, opens.

14 The Truku tribe of Hualien County is officially recognized as Taiwan's 12th indigenous group.

Feb. 14 The first-ever televised presidential debate in Taiwan's history features DPP candidate Chen Shui-bian and KMT candidate Lien Chan.

28 A human-chain several hundred kilometers long (dubbed "Hand in Hand to Protect Taiwan" campaign) spans Taiwan, with over two million people expressing their displeasure at China's military threats.

Mar. 1 Taiwan's second representative

office in South Asia, the Taipei Representative Office in Dhaka, Bangladesh, begins operation.

18 The *Political Contribution Act* is passed.

19 One day before the presidential election, president Chen Shui-bian and Vice President Lu Hsiu-lien are shot and injured while campaigning in Tainan City.

20 With a 80.28-percent turnout rate, incumbent President Chen Shui-bian and Vice President Lu Hsiu-lien win the 2004 presidential election by a narrow margin.

May 20 Chen Shui-bian and Lu Hsiu-lien are sworn in as the 11th-term president and vice president of the Republic of China. Yu Shyi-kun is reappointed premier.

21 FORMOSAT-2, Taiwan's second satellite, is launched from Vandenberg Air Force Base in California, enabling Taiwan to become an exporter of satellite images and a leader in the field of upper-atmospheric lightning research.

28 Vice President Lu Hsiu-lien embarks on a 14-day state visit to El Salvador, Costa Rica, and Guatemala.

Jun. 11 The Legislative Yuan passes the

Basic Organic Act of Central Administrative Agencies to streamline the central government into 13 ministries, four commissions, and five independent agencies.

The Legislative Yuan passes the *Labor Pension Act*, requiring businesses to set up individual portable retirement accounts for the ROC citizens they employ.

14 Kaohsiung City wins the bid to host the 2009 World Games under the International World Games Association.

15 The Non-Partisan Solidarity Union (NPSU) is established as Taiwan's 106th political party.

Jul. 1 Taiwan's five terrestrial television stations begin test-broadcasting 14 digital TV channels, thereby revolutionizing Taiwan's media infrastructure.

The cabinet-level Financial Supervisory Commission is established to oversee Taiwan's banking sector.

Aug. 13 Presided over by Vice President Lu Hsiu-lien, the second annual Democratic Pacific Assembly is held in Taipei. Over 70 distinguished guests from 23 countries sign a Pacific Declaration to establish the Democratic Pacific Union in

2005.

20 The women's archery team earns Taiwan a bronze medal at the 2004 Olympic Games in Athens, Greece.

21 The men's archery team wins Taiwan a silver medal at the 2004 Olympic Games.

23 The Legislative Yuan passes a resolution for constitutional amendments to abolish the National Assembly, codify the right to referendum in the Constitution, halve the number of seats in the Legislature, and adopt the "single-constituency, two-ballot system" for future legislative elections.

26 Men's taekwondo champion Chu Mu-yen and women's taekwondo champion Chen Shih-hsin earn Taiwan its first two Olympic gold medals.

27 Men's taekwondo champion Huang Chih-hsiung wins a silver medal at the 2004 Olympic Games.

Sept. 1 Taiwan and South Korea sign an agreement to resume bilateral air traffic routes, which were terminated in 1992.

28 Headed by First Lady Wu Shu-jen, Taiwan's delegation to the 2004 Paralympic Games in Athens wins two gold, two silver, and two bronze medals,

its best record to date.

Oct. 1 Taiwan's first free trade port area begins operation in Keelung Port.

Nov. 20 Academia Sinica President Lee Yuan-tseh attends the 2004 APEC Economic Leaders' Meeting at Santiago, Chile, on behalf of President Chen Shui-bian.

Dec. 11 With the lowest voter turnout rate ever for a parliamentary election at 59.16 percent the DPP wins 89 of the 225 seats, KMT 79 seats, People First Party 34 seats, Taiwan Solidarity Union 12 seats, NPSU six seats, New Party on seat, and independents four seats.

14 Sounder Rocket No. 4, the first completely Taiwan-made rocket and scientific payload, lifts off from an air base in Pingtung County.

2005

Jan. 3 Straits Exchange Foundation Chairman Koo Cheng-fu passes away in Taipei at the age of 89.

Feb. 19 *The Wayward Cloud* by director Tsai Ming-liang receives the Silver Bear Award at the 2005 Berlin International Film Festival.

Mar. 16 Following China's enactment of an anti-separation law (so-called anti-secession law) on March 14, authorizing the use of non-peacful means against Taiwan, President Chen Shui-bian issues a six-point statement, indicating that China's enactment of the law is an attempt to unilaterally change the status quo in the Taiwan Strait.

31 The Directorate-General of Budget, Accounting and Statistics announces that Taiwan's total fertility rate for 2005 was 1.1, which was lower than the average for both developed countries and neighboring nations.

Apr. 7 President Chen Shui-bian departs for Vatican City to attend the funeral mass for His Holiness Pope John Paul II.

May 1 Wang Chien-ming makes his debut for the New York Yankees, becoming the second player from Taiwan to play as a starting pitcher in US Major League Baseball.

23 The 58th World Health Assembly (WHA) adopts the revised International Health Regulations (IHR). The accompanying WHA resolution accepts the "universal application" principle that Taiwan had sought to include in the IHR.

Jun. 7 The ad-hoc National Assembly ratifies a constitutional amendment package, abolishing itself, halving the number of seats in the Legislature from 225 to 113, and adopting a "single-constituency, two-ballot" system for future legislative elections.

Jul. 1 A new pension system consisting of portable individual retirement accounts goes into effect.

Aug. 5 The Ministry of Foreign Affairs announces that Taiwan has severed diplomatic relations with the Republic of Chad.

29 The Ministry of National Defense publishes the *2006 National Defense Report*, which confirms for the first time that the People's Liberation Army has frequently violated Taiwan's airspace and waters since 1996.

Sept. 3 President Chen Shui-bian departs for Palau to attend the first Taiwan-Pacific Allies Summit.

6 The Executive Yuan passes a resolution to change the name of the Chiang Kai-shek International Airport to Taiwan Taoyuan International Airport.

12 The 61st session of the United Nations General Assembly opens. Two proposals, one regarding regional peace and

one Taiwan's UN participation,
are submitted by Taiwan's allies.
However, both proposals are
excluded from the assembly's
agenda.

13 Due to Beijing's obstruction, the
two proposals submitted to the
United Nations by Taiwan's
diplomatic allies fail to be
included on the agenda of the
UN General Assembly.

14 The first medical charter flight
between Taiwan and China
brings back to Taiwan for
treatment an elderly man who
has suffered a stroke on his way
to visit relatives in Guangdong.

Nov. 15 The US Library of Congress
announces that Yu Ying-shih,
arenowned historian and
member of Taiwan's Academia
Sinica, is among the winners of
the 2006 John W. Kluge Prize
for lifetime achievement in the
study of humanities.

17 Morris Chang, Chairman of
Taiwan Semiconductor
Manufacturing Corporation, is
appointed President Chen Shui-
bian's special envoy to the 2006
APEC Economic Leaders'
Meeting in Hanoi, Vietnam.

Dec. 3 Taiwan holds an unprecedented
"three-in-one" election for city
mayors, and county magistrates;
city and county council

members, and township chiefs.

7 Taiwan's baseball team defeats
its Japanese opponent and
clinches the nation's first-ever
gold medal in baseball at the
Asian Games.

9 Elections for the mayor and city
councilors of Taipei and
Kaohsiung cities are held. In
Taipei, Kuomintang (KMT)
mayoral candidate Hau Lung-
bin defeats opponents Frank
Chang-ting Hsieh of the
Democratic Progressive Party
(DPP) and James Soong of the
People first Party. In Kaohsiung,
DPP candidate Chen Chu wins
the mayorship by just 1,114
votes over the KMT's Huang
Chun-ying.

24 The Ministry of Transportation
and Communications approves
the operation of the high-speed
railway on the stretch
connecting Panchio in the north
to Tsuying in the south.

2006

Jan. 19 Premier Frank Chang-ting Hsieh
resigns and the cabinet is
reshuffled. President Chen Shui-
bian names Su Tseng-chang as
premier.

Feb. 1 Super marathoner Kevin Lin
wins the 4 Deserts Race.

5 The *Sexual Harassment*

Prevention Act is promulgated.

22 The National Communications Commission begins operations.

27 President Chen Shui-bian announces that the National Unification Council will cease to function and the *Guidelines for National Unification* will cease to apply.

Mar. 6 Taiwan-born director Ang Lee wins Best Director at the Academy Awards for *Brokeback Mountain*.

10 The World Health Organization (WHO) clarifies that Taiwan is not affected by the H5N1 virus. The body had previously included Taiwan as a part of China in its map of affected areas.

31 A special review committee of the Council of Agriculture rejects an application to import giant pandas from China submitted by the Taipei Zoo and a zoo affiliated with a private foundation, stating that neither applicant was fully prepared to care for the animals in terms of necessary breeding equipment and training of medical and nursing staff.

Apr. 12 The World Trade Organization lists Taiwan as the world's 16th largest economy.

15 A constellation of six micro-satellites is launched as Taiwan's third satellite project, FORMOSAT-3, comes to a successful conclusion. The satellites are to monitor atmospheric conditions and conduct climate research.

May 4 President Chen Shui-bian visits Paraguay and Costa Rica.

18 The European Parliament requests that the WHO immediately include Taiwan's Centers for Disease Control as an official participant in its Global Outbreak and Alert Response Network to ensure the rapid exchange of relevant information on a regional and global basis.

20 Taiwan publishes its first-ever national security report.

22 Taiwan's bid to participate in the WHO as an observer is excluded from the agenda of the body's rulemaking World Health Assembly.

Jun. 16 After nearly 15 years of construction, the Hsuehshan Tunnel, the fifth-longest highway tunnel in the world, opens to traffic.

Jul. 20 The "Han Kuang 22" military exercises are held in Yilan County. These are the largest, in scope and number of personnel, exercises ever to be held in

Taiwan.

28 The Conference on Sustaining Taiwan's Economic Development concludes. Participants on the conference's panels discussed government efficiency, cross-strait economic and trade relations, and fiscal and financial reform.

2007

Apr. 20 Chinese President Hu Jintao and President Bush vow to cooperate on reducing the trade deficit between the two countries and on stemming nuclear proliferation, but no deals are announced. Hu's visit is marred by U.S. gaffes in protocol.

Jul. 4 In Liaoning province, China, a karaoke bar full of university students is destroyed by an explosion; there are at least 25 fatalities.

10 Zheng, Xiaoyu, former head of China's food and drug regulatory agency, is executed.

30 China's Xinhua News Agency reports that unusually bad flooding from rain over the past few weeks has left some 650 people dead, including 17 in the past two days.

Aug. 1 The American toy maker Mattel recalls 967,000 Chinese-manufactured toys that contain lead-based paint.

2 China's official news agency, Xinhua, says that sandstorms are reducing to piles of dirt more than 50.5 km (37mi) of the Great Wall in Gansu province.

Sept. 2 China declares its intention to release information about its burgeoning military budget and to resume submitting date to UN on its trade in conventional weapons; it has stopped sending such information in 1996.

16 China's government condemns a huge rally organized by Taiwan's President Chen Shui-pien calling for the island's membership in the United Nations, warning that Beijing is now preparing for a "serious situation." The statement does not say what constitute a serious situation, although China has long threatened to take military action against Taiwan if it declares formal independence or indefinitely delays unifying with China.

More than 100,000 people go to the streets to back planned referendum on U.N. membership, in support of Chen's pro-independence policies and defying previous Chinese threats.

Beijing's statement does not

mention another rally in favor of U.N. membership staged by Nationalist Party presidential candidate Ma Ying-chiu, considered to be China's favorite to win next year's election.

While Chen's rally pushes for U.N. re-entry under the name Taiwan, Ma's advocates using the island's official name, the Republic of China.

Oct. 12 The official state media in China report that concerns over environmental damage, including the danger of landslides in the area around the Three Gorges Dam have led to plans to relocate as many as four million people.

24 China launches the satellite Chang'e-1, which is expected to orbit the moon for a year, returning images; it is China's first lunar probe and follows one launched by Japan in September.

Nov. 7 The U.S. Consumer Product Safety Commission orders the recall of the Chinese-made toy Aqua Dots; the toy consists of plastic beads that when wetted stick together to form toys but when ingested release a poisonous chemical related to the date rap drug GHB.

21 The warship Shenzhen sails from China for the first port visit by the Chinese navy to Japan since World War II; the destroyer is to take part in military ceremonies with the Japanese navy.

Dec. 22 China's new National Center for the performing Arts in Beijing, designed by French architect Paul Andreau, holds its first public concert; the building, a glass dome over a shallow lake, is entered via a passageway under the lake.

29 Chinese government officials announce that the first election in which Hong Kong voters may directly elect their leader will not take place until at least 2017; previously it had been thought that the elections in 2012 might be held democratically.

2008

Jan. 2 The price of barrel of light crude sweet oil for the first time reaches US$100 on the New York Mercantile Exchange.

12 Legislative election in Taiwan, are won by the Nationalist Party, which takes 81 of the 113 seats; President Chen Shui-pien resigns as head of the ruling Democratic Progress Party.

21 In Shanxi province, northern China, as miners attempt to

reopen a shaft in a closed mine, an explosion takes place that kills at least 20 pelple.

29 In Guizhou province, China, which is among those areas suffering prolonged severe winter storms, a bus goes off an ice coated road; at least 25 passengers perish.

Feb. 1 Government officials in Japan say that at least 175 people have become ill after eating dumplings imported from China that were tainted with insecticide.

Mar. 5 The U.S. Food and Drug Administration reports that heparin associated with bad reactions, including 19 death, was produced with ingredients made in China and contained contaminant that effectively mimicked the active ingredient in genuine heparin.

10 Indian authorities block of hundreds Tibetan protesters near Dhamshala at the beginning of a six-month march to Tibet to protest China's hosting of Olympic Games.

11 Chinese government announces planned reorganization of its government that will create ministries to oversee environmental protection, social service, housing and construction, and industry and information.

12 CHENGDU, China (AP) Police with rifles and machine guns guard checkpoints at every entrance to the Tibetan quarter in this city of 10 million people. Inside, police cars are parked every few yards, their lights flashing as dozens of troops march by monks and other shoppers.

The heightened security Wednesday in this part of Sichuan's provincial capital, a popular gateway to Tibet, reflects Beijing's efforts to crush unrest in Tibetan communities this month, 50 years after a failed uprising against Chinese rule in Tibet and a year after violent demonstrations across a quarter of the country.

Paramilitary forces, a constant presence in Tibet and surrounding provinces since last year's anti-Chinese protests, have poured into the area in larger numbers, resulting in a kind of martial law.

13 It is reported that hundreds of monks in Tibet have been protesting China's rule over the province for the past few days.

14 It is reported that violence breaks out in Lhasa, the capital

of Tibet, between residents and the Chinese security forces.

22 Ma Ying-chiu of Nationalist Party is elected president of the Republic of China. Ma campaigns on a platform of seeking closer economic ties with China.

25 The Chinese government expresses its new willingness to meet with envoys of the Dalai Lama for discussions on Tibet.

26 In Xinjiang province, China, as authorities attempt to destroy illegal fireworks outside the city of Turpan, an unplanned explosion occurs; 22 people are reported killed.

Apr. 6 At the Olympic torch relay in London, pro-Tibet protesters attempting to seize or extinguish the torch to express their opposition to Chinese human rights abuses are engaged a series of scuffles with police and prevented from achieving their goal.

13 BEIJING (Los Angeles Times) China's president met with the incoming vice president of Taiwan on Saturday, signaling a possible thaw in a frosty relationship between the rival governments that has lasted almost six decades.

Beijing played down the brief exchange between President Hu Jintao and Vice President-elect Vincent Siew on the sidelines of an economics forum in southern China's Hainan province, but observers suggested it broke new ground.

"Certainly this is a very significant step forward in terms of thawing the ice from the two sides," said Andrew Yang, secretary-general of the Chinese Council of Advanced Policy Studies, an independent research tank in Taipei, Taiwan's capital.

On Saturday, the Chinese Foreign Ministry was careful to refer to Siew not in his political capacity but as the chairman of the Cross-Strait Common Market Foundation, a private group that seeks to build economic cooperation between China and Taiwan.

For the most part, the two leaders tried to frame Saturday's conversation in terms of economics. "On this occasion, I am happy to exchage opinions on the cross-strait economy with Siew," Hu said. Siew said, "Reality proves that cross-strait economic development is the common wish of people on both sides."

May 6 In Taiwan, in the midst of a

scandal in which US$30 million of government money (intended to be given to Papua New Guinea if it switched its diplomatic relations from China to Taiwan) seems to have been stolen, Foreign Minister James Huang and Vice-Premier Chiou I-chen resign.

12 A magnitude-7.9 earthquake with its epicenter in Wenchuan causes devastation in Sichuan province, China, as schools collapse, factories are destroyed, and whole villages are demolished; the initial death toll about 10,000.

15 The California Supreme Court rules that state laws that limit marriage to opposite-sex couples are same-sex couples also have the right to marry.

20 Harvard graduate Ma Ying-chiu takes office as president of the Republic of China, promising to seek greater economic cooperation with rival China and end nearly six decades of tension.
The inauguration of the 57-year-old Ma formally turns the corner on the eight-year presidency of Chen Shui-pien whose confrontational pro-independence policies often lead to friction with the Red China –

and with the United States, Taiwan's most important foreign partner. Vice president Vincent W.C. Siew, 69, is sworn in shortly after Ma.

28 The leader of Taiwan's new ruling party tells Chinese president Hu Jintao that the self-governed island needs to have an international presence, but acknowledges there will be no quick solution to long-standing disputes. The hour-long meeting between Hu and Wu Poh-hsiuang, Taiwan's Nationalist Party Chairman, is the political climax of a trip intended to boost business ties. It marks a symbolic closing of the ranks between the rivals, whose ties have strengthened since Nationalist Ma Ying-chiu was elected president of the Republic of China in March.

29 China's New China News Agency says that the torrential rains that kills 28 people in southern China are forecasted to continue for next three days. The news agency reports that more than 500,000 people in 17 cities and counties in Guizhou are affected.

30 The confirmed death toll in China Sichuan province earthquake is reported as 68,500

people, with a further 19,000 missing and person dead.

Jun. 1 Parents in several cities in Sichuan province, China protest the shoddy construction of schools that collapsed in the earthquake three weeks earlier, crushing many children.

12 China and Taiwan officials agree to establish offices in one another's capitals to facilitate discussions about closer relationships.

Nov. 4 TAIPEI, Taiwan (AP) Envoys from Taiwan and China approved a plan to hold periodic high-level talks today during a meeting on a trade agreement that could help ease the threat of war between the rivals.

The historic session came a day after Chen Yunlin – the highest-ranking Chinese official to visit Taiwan in six decades – was greeted on arrival by anti-China protesters waving signs, calling him a communist bandit and rallying outside the Legislature.

During the two-hour meeting, Chen and chief Taiwanese negotiator Chiang Pin Kung agreed to hold high-level talks every six months alternatively in Taipei and Beijing, Taiwanese official Kao Koong Lian said.

Kao said the next round will focus on financial cooperation. The two sides will aim to sign a memorandum of understanding allowing banks to set up branches on each side, he said.

The two envoys are expected to sign the trade pact later today; a deal would allow direct shipping links across the Taiwan Strait and would further expand the number of weekly passenger flights from 36 to 108. Cargo flights would be allowed for the first time, with 60 crossing the strait each month.

In a statement as the meeting opened, Chen said that the session meant "both sides have grasped a rare historic opportunity" and that future talks should deal with finance.

"We face a global economic slowdown and uncertainties have increased in the environment. The financial turmoil is more severe than the 1997 Asian financial crisis," he said. "The conditions pose severe challenges to both sides and highlight the importance of financial and economic cooperation."

Chen was mostly insulated Monday from the noisy crowds of Taiwan independence supporters, who were blocked or dragged away by security forces. About 5,000 police were guarding the capital, Taipei, during his five-day trip.

Making sure that Chen's visit went smoothly was extremely important to Taiwanese President Ma Ying-chiu. He was elected last March, promising voters he would ease tensions with China and forge closer trade ties with the huge neighbor, just 100 miles across the Taiwan Strait.

It has taken such a high-ranking Chinese official six decades to visit this island because deeply rooted hostilities and suspicions have prevented such exchanges.

China and Taiwan have been ruled separately since the Communists won a bloody civil war in 1949 and took over the mainland.

Nov. 12 SHANGHAI (New York Times) Chen Shui-bian, the former president of Taiwan and an ardent advocate of continued independence for the island, was detained by the police there late Tuesday after prosecutors sought his formal arrest on corruption and money-laundering charges.

Chen, who served two terms as president but was voted out of office in March with his administration mired in a corruption scandal, was led to court in handcuffs on Tuesday afternoon after several hours of questioning by prosecutors in Taipei, Taiwan's capital.

The former president paused briefly before television cameras, raised his arms over his head and defiantly shouted, "Long live Taiwan" and "Political persecution."

Late Tuesday evening, However, Taipei television reported that the court hearing had been suspended and that Chen had been taken to a hospital complaining that he had been roughed up by the police.

Last year, Ma was indicted for misuse of funds while serving as mayor of Taipei, which forced him to step down. The Supreme Court later cleared him of the charges, paving the way for his presidential candidacy.

Chen, one of Taiwan's most controversial political figures, was first elected in 2000. A populist with a penchant for fiery rhetoric, he was known during his two terms for his strong opposition to Beijing and his insistence that Taiwan, which separated from China in

1949, was not a province of the mainland.

During his second term, prosecutors began investigating whether Chen, his senior aides and his family member, including his wife, were involved in embezzling millions of dollars in campaign funds. Chen's son, daughter and other relatives also have been questioned; some have been named as defendants.

Chen's approval ratings plummeted late in his second term, and there were huge protests in Taipei against his rule.

Ma, who took office in May, has pushed for closer ties with mainland China and opened the possibility of eventual reunification.

Last week officials from Beijing met in Taiwan with Ma and other high-ranking officials, in the highest-level exchange in 59 years, though the meeting drew strong protests from members of Chen's Democratic Progressive Party.

Chen has suggested that prosecutors are focusing on him to win favor from Beijing. In recent weeks, with his party under siege because of the corruption investigation, he has accused Ma of committing treason and selling out the island by moving closer to Beijing.

Chen, 57, has denied wrongdoing in the case and accused his successor, President Ma Ying-chiu, and the governing Kuomintang of a politically motivated attack. Officials of the Kuomintang, the Nationalist Party, insist that they have not influenced prosecutors in the case.

The detention is the latest chapter in a series of political dramas that have been unfolding in Taiwan for a few years as the island's two major parties, the Kuomintang and the Democratic Progressive Party, have bickered over relations with China and traded accusations of corruption.

Dec. 13 Prosecutors indict former president Chen Shui-pien on graft charges, a stunning blow for a man who rode to power 8 years ago on promises to reform the island's corrupt political culture. Prosecutor Lin Che-hui says the former leader could be given a life sentence if convicted on all charges.

Indicated together with Chen, 57, are his wife, Wu Shu-chen, his son and daughter-in-law, three of his former aides in presidential office, and eight other associated and family member.

Prosecution spokesman Chen Yuan-nan says Chen and his wife together embezzled NT$104 million (US$3.12 million) from a special presidential fund and received dollars worth US$9 million in connection with a government land procurement deal.

2009

Jan. 1 SAN FRANCISCO (S.F. Chronicle) Fireworks explode over the Sydney Harbor Bridge and the Opera House, left, as Australians celebrate the New Year today. In San Francisco, above, Colin Budd (right) and his siter, Brenna Budd, snap pictures of the festivities as New Year's Eve revelers gather on the Embarcadero. Earlier, in the Financial District, workers deserted buildings by 5 p.m., but not before tossing torn pages from 2008 calendars out skyscraper windows onto Battery Street.

5 GAZA CITY (Gaza Strip) (AP) Thousands of Israeli troops backed by tanks and helicopter gunships surrounded Gaza's largest city and fought militants at close range Sunday, the ground offensive in the coastal territory.

Israel said it has inflicted a heavy blow against Hamas as it expands a weeklong offensive meant to stop rocket fire on southern Israel. But spiraling civilian casualties among Palestinians fueled an international outcry, even as the United States blocked approval of a U.N. Security Council statement Saturday night calling for an immediate cease-fire.

Israel's ground forces moved in Saturday following hours of intense artillery shelling to clear ther way, and Hamas warned that its fighters wouldturn Gaza into an Israeli "graveyard."

20 WASHINGTON (S.F. Chronicle) For African Americans across the country, the plan was hatched on election night, if not weeks before. If Barack Obama won the presidency, they would a find a way to get to the nation's capital to see him sworn in.

"We said, 'If this happens, we have to be there,'" said Oscar Hall, a retired carpenter from Indianapolis, as he walked the Mall on Monday, searching for a spot to watch Obama take the oath of office. His wife, Mollette, added, "We wouldn't miss it."

The swearing-in of the country's first black president has sparked a mass pilgrimage of African Americans to Washington. They have come by plane, train and bus. They are crowding the region's hotels and crashing on friend's couches. They will pack the Mall today to witness a moment that many see as vindication after a centuries-long struggle for racial equality.

Mar. 12 WASHINGTON (AP) The United States and China agreed Wednesday on the need to reduce tensions and to avoid a repeat of a confrontation between American and Chinese vessels in the South China Sea, Secretary of State Hillary Rodham Clinton said.

"We both agreed that we should work to ensure that such incidents do not happen again," Clinton told reporters after meeting Chinese Foreign Minister Yang Jiechi at the State Department.

The two countries remained at odds over the exact circumstances.

"We have each stated our positions, but the important point of agreement coming out of my discussions with Minister Yang is that we must work hard in the future to avoid such incidents and to avoid this particular incident having consequences that are unforeseen," she said.

Clinton told reporters that Yang's visit was a "very positive" development and that she looked forward to continuing discussions that she stared with him during a trip to Beijing last month to build a "positive, cooperative and comprehensive relationship."

Before their private meeting, neither Clinton nor Yang mentioned the dispute, even as China's Foreign Ministry in Beijing responded for a second consecutive day to U.S. complaints that Chinese vessels harassed a U.S. Navy surveillance ship in international waters on Sunday.

Yang plans to meet today with President Obama and his national security adviser, James Jones. White House spokesman Robert Gibbs said he expects the dispute will be discussed but will not dominate the conversation.

Jun. 4 BEIJING (Washington Post) Mainland China remained quiet Thursday on the 20th anniversary of the bloody Tiananmen Square crackdown, while tens of thousands of people staged a protest in Hong Kong.

Beijing, the capital, was on virtual lockdown. Key foreign news Web sites were blocked, dissidents were placed under house arrest, and police blanketed the vast square where a still-undetermined number of pro-democracy activists were killed in a violent clash with the military June 4, 1989. Journalists were kept away from the scene.

Several foreign governments called on Beijing this week to revisit its policy of ignoring the crackdown. Secretary of State Hillary Rodham Clinton said in a statement Wednesday that China "should examine openly the darker events of its past and provide a public accounting of those killed, detained or missing, both to learn and to heal."

On Tuesday, Congress urged China to agree to a U.N.-backed inquiry into the crackdown, and House Speaker Nancy Pelosi, D-San Francisco, said she had directly petitioned President Hu Jintao to free the estimated 30 people still being held for participating in the protests.

Over the years, Beijing has taken a two-pronged approach to the massacre. Domestically, the incident is ignored in history books, and discussion about it is banned to the point that many young people know nothing of what happened. In arguments directed to the international community, Beijing has said the crackdown was necessary to ensure social stability, which it says was a condition for the market-driven changes that have since transformed China into the world's third-largest economy.

In the weeks before the anniversary, authorities erased most traces of the massacre from the capital. Twitter and other Internet services that people could have used to coordinate gathcrings were blocked, as were news Web sites such as CNN and the BBC. Foreign newspapers and magazines that had been covering commemorative protests in Hong Kong were delivered with pages ripped out. Writers, activists and even mothers of victims were put under surveillance or house arrest.

On Thursday, the only place on Chinese soil where a large-scale protest took place was Hong Kong, the former British colony that has maintained its own legal system since it reverted to Chinese rule in 1997.

Police estimated that 62,800 people, dressed either in white or funeral black, showed up for a vigil in downtown Victoria Park.

Aug. 31 Communist China denounces Taiwan President Ma Ying-chiu's decision to allow the Tibet's Dalai Lama to visit the self-ruled island, casting a shadow over rapidly improving relations between Peking and Taipei. Peking has long vilified the Dalai Lama for what they say are his attempts to fight for independence of Tibet. The visit invitation to the Tibetan spiritual leader is made by the officials of Taiwan's pro-independence opposition party, D.P.P.

Sept. 9 In his first major cabinet shuffle, Nationalist president Ma Ying-chiu of the Republic of China, dumps Dr. Liu Chao-hsuan, the President of Executive Yuan (Prime Minister) and replaces him with Wu Tun-yee, 51, the ruling KMT's Secretary-General. Ma's action is considered the result of heavy pressure by the island-wide reforming demands following the heaviest Typhoon Morakot storm floods in five decades last month.

11 Chen Shui-pien, 57, former president of the Republic of China, is sentenced to life prison by the Taipei District Court after convicting him on graft in the greatest corruptions case in Taiwan's history. Chen's wife, Wu Shu-chen, gets life prison too. They and their son and daughter are among a total of 14 defendants in this case.

Oct. 1 The 60th anniversary of the National Day of the People's Republic of China is celebrated in China mainland.

（主要參考書：英文中華民國年鑑、台灣指南、台灣年鑑、紐約時報要聞版專刊、時代雜誌年鑑及舊金山紀事報等書刊。）

TEXT OF THE JOINT COMMUNIQUÉ ISSUED
BY THE UNITED STATES OF AMERICA AND
THE PEOPLE'S REPUBLIC OF CHINA
FEBRUARY 27 IN SHANGHAI

President Richard Nixon, of the United States of American, visited the People's Republic of China at the invitation of Premier Chou En-lai of the People's Republic of China from February 21 to February 28, 1972. Accompanying the President were Mrs. Nixon, U.S. Secretary of State William Rogers, Assistant to the President Dr. Henry Kissinger, and other American officials.

President Nixon met with Chairman Mao Tse-tung, of the Communist Party of China on February 21. The two leaders had a serious and frank exchange of views on Sino-U.S. relations and world affairs.

During the visit, extensive, earnest and frank discussions were held between President Nixon and Premier Chou En-lai on the normalization of relations between the United States of America and the People's Republic of China, as well as on other matters of interest to both sides. In addition, Secretary of State William Rogers and Foreign Minister Chi Peng-fei held talks in the same spirit.

President Nixon and his party visited Peking and viewed cultural, industrial, and agricultural sites, and they also toured Hangchow and Shanghai where, continuing discussions with Chinese leaders, they viewed similar places of interest.

The leaders of the People's Republic of China and the United States of America found it beneficial to have this opportunity, after so many years without contact, to present candidly to one another their views on a variety of issues. They reviewed the international situation in which important changes and great upheavals are taking place and expounded their respective positions and attitudes.

The U.S. side stated: Peace in Asia and peace in the world requires efforts both to reduce immediate tensions and to eliminate the basic causes of conflict. The United States will work for a just and secure peace: just, because it fulfills the aspirations of peoples and nations for freedom and progress; secure, because it removes the danger of foreign aggression.

The United States supports individual freedom and social progress for all the peoples of the world, free of outside pressure or intervention.

The United States believes that the effort to reduce tensions is served by improving communication between countries that have different ideologies so as to lessen the risks of confrontation through accident, miscalculation or misunderstanding.

Countries should treat each other with mutual respect and be willing to compete peacefully, letting performance be the ultimate judge, No country should claim infallibility and each country should be prepared to re-examine its own attitudes for the common good.

The United States stressed that the peoples of Indochina should be allowed to determine their destiny without outside intervention; its constant primary objective has been a negotiated solution: the eight-point proposal put forward by the Republic of Vietnam and the United States on January 27, 1972, represents a basis for the attainment of that objective; in the absence of a negotiated settlement the United States envisages the ultimate withdrawal of all U.S, forces from the region consistent with the aim of self-determination for each country of Indochina.

The United States will maintain its close ties with and support for the Republic of Korea; the United States will support efforts of the Republic of Korea to seek a relaxation of tension and increased communication in the Korean peninsula.

The United States places the highest value on its friendly relations with Japan; it will continue to develop the existing close bonds.

Consistent with the United Nations Security Council resolution of December 21, 1971, the United States favors the continuation of the ceasefire between India and Pakirstan and the withdrawal of all military forces to within their own territories and to their own sides of the ceasefire line in Jammu and Kashmir; the United States supports the right of the people of South Asia to share their own future in peace, free, of military threat, and without having the area become the subject of great power rivalry.

The Chinese side stated: Wherever there is oppression, there is resistance. Countries want independence, nations want liberation and the people want revolution – this has become the irresistible trend of history. All nations, big or small, should be equal; big nations should not bully the small and strong nations should not bully the weak.

China will never be a superpower and it opposes hegemony and power politics of any kind. The Chinese side stated that it firmly supports the struggles of all the oppressed people and nations for freedom and liberation and that the people of all countries have the right to choose their social system according to their own wishes and the right to safeguard the independence, sovereignty and territorial integrity of their own countries and oppose foreign aggression, interference, control and subversion. All foreign troops should be withdrawn to their own countries.

The Chinese side expressed its firm support to the peoples of Vietnam, Laos and

Cambodia in their efforts for the attainment of their goal and its firm support to the seven-point proposal of the provisional revolutionary government of the Republic of South Vietnam and the elaboration of February this year on the two key problems in the proposal, and to that joint declaration of the summit conference of the Indochinese peoples.

It firmly supports the eight-point program for the peaceful unification of Korea put forward by the Government of the Democratic People's Republic of Korea on April 12, 1971, and the stand for the abolition of the "U.N. Commission for the Unification and Rehabilitation of Korea."

It firmly opposes the revival and outward expansion of Japanese militarism and firmly supports the Japanese people's desire to build an independent, democratic, peaceful and neutral Japan.

It firmly maintains that India and Pakistan should, in accordance with the United Nations resolutions on the India-Pakistan question, immediately withdraw all their forces to their respective territories and to their own sides of the ceasefire line in Jammu and Kashmir and firmly supports the Pakistan government and people in their struggle to preserve their independence and sovereignty and the people of Jammu and Kashmir in their struggle for the right of self-determination.

There are essential differences between China and the United States in their social systems and foreign policies. However, the two sides agreed that countries, regardless of their social systems, should conduct their relations on the principles of respect for the sovereignty and territorial integrity of all states, non-aggression against other states, non-interference in the internal affairs of other states, equality and mutual benefit, and peaceful coexistence. International disputes should be settled on this basis, without resorting to the use or threat of force. The United States and the People's Republic of China are prepared to apply these principles to their mutual relations.

With these Principles of international relations in mind the two sides stated that:

-- Progress toward the normalization of relations between China and the United States is in the interests of all countries; both wish to reduce the danger of international military conflict;

-- Neither should seek hegemony in the Asia-Pacific region and each is opposed to efforts by any other country or group of countries to establish such hegemony; and

-- Neither is prepared to negotiate on behalf of any third party or to enter into agreements or understandings with the other directed at other states.

Both sides are of the view that it would be against the interests of the peoples of the world for any major country to collude with another against other countries, or for major countries to divide up the world into spheres of interest.

The two sides reviewed the long-standing serious disputes between China and the United States. The Chinese side reaffirmed its position: the Taiwan question is the crucial question obstructing the normalization of relations between China and the United States; the Government of the People's Republic of China is the sole Legal government of China; Taiwan is a province of China which has long been returned to the motherland; the liberation of Taiwan is China's internal affair in which no other country has the right to interfere; and all U.S. forces and military installations must be withdrawn from Taiwan. The Chinese government firmly opposes any activities which aim at the creation of "one China, one Taiwan," "one China, two governments," "two Chinas," and "independent Taiwan" or advocate that "the status of Taiwan remains to be determined."

The U.S. side declared: The United States acknowledges that all Chinese on either side of the Taiwan Strait maintain there is but one China and that Taiwan is a part of China. The United States Government does not challenge that position. It reaffirms its interest in a peaceful settlement of the Taiwan question by the Chinese themselves. With this prospect in mind, it affirms the ultimate objective of the withdrawal of all U.S. forces and military installations from Taiwan. In the meantime, it will progressively reduce its forces and military installations on Taiwan as the tension in the area diminishes.

The two sides agreed that it is desirable to broaden the understanding between the two peoples. To this end, they discussed specific areas in such fields as science, technology, culture, sports and journalism, in which people-to-people contacts and exchanges would be mutually beneficial. Each side undertakes to facilitate the further development of such contacts and exchanges.

Both sides view bilateral trade as another area from which mutual benefit can be derived, and agreed that economic relations based on equality and mutual benefit are in the interest of the peoples of the two countries. They agree to facilitate the progressive development of trade between their two countries.

The two sides agreed that they will stay in contact through various channels, including the sending of a senior U.S. representative to Peking from time to time for concrete consultations to further the normalization of relations between the two countries and continue to exchange views on issues of common interest.

The two sides expressed the hope that the gains achieved during this visit would open up new prospects for the relations between the two countries. They believe that the normalization of relations between the two countries is not only in the interest of the Chinese and American peoples but also contributes to the relaxation of tension in Asia and the world.

President Nixon, Mrs. Nixon and the American party expressed their appreciation for the gracious hospitality shown them by the government and people of the People's Republic of China.

(From USIS Taipei Taiwan)

後　記

　　中華民國三十七年（一九四八）二月廿二日，我與同學五人一行，自南京經上海乘輪船抵達基隆，搭火車轉往高雄縣鳳山鎮，進入孫立人將軍總部報到服務，到現在早已滿了六十年。從那時到今天，台灣的一切一切都變了。

　　一九七三年八月廿五日，大兒子留在台北至好党先生家繼續讀書、我帶著兩個幼兒，搭飛機離開台灣來到舊金山，與早一年來美國深造的妻子團聚，到現在快滿四十年了。從那時到今天，美國的一切一切也都變了。

　　應該插一句。抗戰勝利後，我隨母校國立政治大學從重慶復員到南京續學。由於閩籍學友曾君的介紹，在台中市出版的「自由日報」約我充當在學的「首都記者」。這是我與台灣關係的開始。

　　從大陸到台灣，從台灣到美國，委實是一切都變，而不變的卻很少。就我來說，則是新聞工作始終未變，從台北開始，做到在舊金山退休為止，而且一直是與中、英文有關。正是如此，在開始計劃本書時，我就想到了「雙語」——移民家庭的共同問題。因此，在中文之後增編了較簡略的英文紀事。希望本書能對國內外人士與一些外籍人士都適用。

　　本書是編輯的，而非個人的著作，是根據多年來收集的中英文

書籍、專刊、剪報及資料等編寫成的。因此，特別在這裡謹向所有的書刊、報紙、各種資料的原作者和出版者表示衷心的感激，更希望他們的指教。我使用的基本參考書刊，包括台灣、大陸、香港及美國等地的出版品，主要的如：傳記文學社的「民國大事日誌」、「蔣介石總統哀思錄」、「中華民國年鑑」、「台灣年鑑」、「台灣指南」、「中國國民黨大事記」、「新中國大事典」、「中華人民共和國大事日誌」、「美國時代雜誌年鑑」、「紐約時報二十世紀大事集」、英國的「世界大事記」、「韋氏百科全書」、「舊金山新聞紀事報」、舊金山的「世界日報」及「星島日報」等。

二〇〇八年五月，本書初稿完成，偕同妻子、兒子等再度赴歐洲旅行，在「音樂之都」寫下幾句紀念話：

> 維也納多瑙河上：
> 多瑙河藍黃河黃，
> 是我家鄉愛一樣，
> 河水流去人生事，
> 是戲是夢無續場。

馬全忠

美國加利福尼亞州舊金山市

中華民國九十八年（二〇〇九）七月七日

國家圖書館出版品預行編目資料

台灣紀事六十年

馬全忠編. – 初版. – 臺北市：臺灣學生，2010.03
面；公分
中英對照

ISBN 978-957-15-1486-4 (平裝)

1. 台灣史 2. 中華民國史 3. 年表

733.29202   99000048

台灣紀事六十年（全一冊）

編　　　者：馬　　　　全　　　　忠
出　版　者：臺　灣　學　生　書　局　有　限　公　司
發　行　人：孫　　　　善　　　　治
發　行　所：臺　灣　學　生　書　局　有　限　公　司
　　　　　　臺北市和平東路一段七十五巷十一號
　　　　　　郵　政　劃　撥　帳　號：00024668
　　　　　　電　話：（02）23928185
　　　　　　傳　眞：（02）23928105
　　　　　　E-mail : student.book@msa.hinet.net
　　　　　　http : //www.studentbooks.com.tw
本書局登
記證字號：行政院新聞局局版北市業字第玖捌壹號

印　刷　所：長　欣　印　刷　企　業　社
　　　　　　中和市永和路三六三巷四二號
　　　　　　電　話：（02）22268853

定價：平裝新臺幣四六○元

西　元　二　○　一　○　年　三　月　初　版